AI in Diagnostics

AI in Diagnostics

Riley Ross
Colin Hamilton

Kruger Brentt
Publishers
2026

Kruger Brentt Publishers UK. LTD.
Company Number 9728962

Regd. Office: 68 St Margarets Road, Edgware, Middlesex HA8 9UU

ISBN: 978-1-78715-598-5

For information on all our publications visit our website at http://krugerbrentt.com/

Preface

AI in Diagnostics explores one of the most transformative applications of artificial intelligence in modern medicine—its role in detecting, predicting, and interpreting health conditions with remarkable speed and accuracy. With healthcare systems worldwide facing growing demands for precision, efficiency, and accessibility, artificial intelligence has emerged as a powerful ally to physicians, researchers, and patients alike. This book aims to provide a comprehensive understanding of how AI is revolutionizing diagnostics, bridging the gap between cutting-edge technology and clinical practice.

Artificial intelligence in diagnostics encompasses a wide range of tools, from machine learning algorithms that identify subtle patterns in medical imaging to natural language processing systems that analyze clinical notes and electronic health records. These advancements are enabling healthcare professionals to detect diseases earlier, improve accuracy in differential diagnoses, and personalize treatment strategies. This book takes readers through these emerging innovations while critically examining their benefits, challenges, and ethical implications.

The book begins by laying the foundation of AI technologies relevant to healthcare diagnostics. Readers are introduced to machine learning, deep learning, computer vision, and natural language processing, with examples tailored to medical applications. This groundwork helps to demystify the technology and set the stage for exploring its practical applications in diagnostic fields such as radiology, pathology, cardiology, dermatology, and genomics.

One of the central themes of the book is medical imaging. AI-powered imaging systems have demonstrated unprecedented capabilities in interpreting X-rays, CT scans, MRIs, and ultrasounds. The book discusses how these systems not only assist radiologists in identifying abnormalities like tumors, fractures, and cardiovascular conditions but also reduce human error and improve efficiency in high-volume clinical environments. Case studies illustrate how AI algorithms, sometimes surpassing human-level performance, are being integrated into clinical workflows to support early detection and treatment.

Pathology, another cornerstone of diagnostics, is also undergoing a transformation. The book explains how digital pathology and AI algorithms can analyze vast numbers of histopathological slides, recognizing cellular abnormalities that may be invisible to the human eye. By automating routine tasks and augmenting the pathologist's expertise, AI systems are contributing to more accurate diagnoses of cancers, infectious diseases, and genetic disorders.

Beyond imaging and pathology, AI in Diagnostics delves into applications in genomics and precision medicine. By analyzing complex genomic data, AI tools are helping to identify genetic risk factors, predict disease susceptibility, and guide targeted therapies. In cardiology and dermatology, AI-powered apps and devices are enabling non-invasive, real-time monitoring and diagnostics, often extending advanced healthcare to underserved populations.

Equally important are the ethical, legal, and social considerations of AI in healthcare diagnostics. The book critically examines concerns such as data privacy, algorithmic bias, accountability in decision-making, and the role of AI as an assistive rather than autonomous tool. It emphasizes the importance of maintaining human oversight, building trust between patients and AI systems, and ensuring equitable access to AI-driven healthcare.

Another key focus is the integration of AI into clinical practice. While AI tools hold immense potential, their adoption requires collaboration between clinicians, technologists, and policymakers. The book explores challenges related to regulatory approval, standardization, interoperability of systems, and training healthcare professionals to effectively use AI-assisted diagnostic tools.

The discussion is enriched with global perspectives, highlighting how AI in diagnostics is addressing healthcare disparities, especially in low-resource settings. Mobile AI applications, cloud-based diagnostic platforms, and portable devices are bringing diagnostic capabilities to remote regions, thereby democratizing access to quality healthcare.

In conclusion, AI in Diagnostics presents a balanced and insightful examination of how artificial intelligence is reshaping the landscape of medical diagnostics. It highlights both the transformative opportunities and the practical challenges of adopting AI in clinical settings. The book underscores that AI is not here to replace physicians, but to empower them with advanced tools that enhance accuracy, efficiency, and patient outcomes.

For healthcare professionals, researchers, students, and policymakers, this book serves as a valuable guide to understanding the current and future potential of AI in diagnostics. By exploring both technological innovations and ethical responsibilities, it provides readers with the knowledge to navigate and contribute to the evolving field of AI-enabled healthcare.

Riley Ross

Colin Hamilton

Contents

CHAPTER 1

Introduction to AI in Diagnostics

1.1 WHAT IS DIAGNOSTIC AI?

Diagnostic AI represents a transformative force in modern medicine, offering unparalleled accuracy, efficiency, and scalability in disease detection. While challenges related to bias, regulation, and ethics must be addressed, the potential benefits for patients and healthcare systems are immense. As AI technology continues to evolve, its integration into diagnostics will likely become standard practice, ushering in a new era of precision medicine and improved patient outcomes. The collaboration between AI and healthcare professionals will be key to realizing this future, ensuring that technology enhances rather than replaces the human touch in medicine. The future of diagnostic AI is promising, with ongoing advancements poised to further enhance its capabilities. Emerging technologies such as federated learning—where AI models are trained across multiple institutions without sharing raw data—could improve model accuracy while preserving patient privacy. Additionally, the integration of AI with wearable devices and remote monitoring tools will enable real-time diagnostics, allowing for continuous health assessments outside traditional clinical settings.

Personalized medicine will also benefit from AI-driven diagnostics. By analyzing genetic, lifestyle, and environmental data, AI can help tailor treatments to individual patients, improving therapeutic outcomes. Furthermore, as AI systems become more interpretable, clinicians will gain deeper insights into how diagnoses are generated, fostering greater collaboration between humans and machines. In the long term, diagnostic AI could democratize healthcare by making high-quality diagnostics accessible in low-resource regions. Mobile AI applications and portable diagnostic devices could bring expert-level medical analysis to underserved populations, bridging gaps in global healthcare disparities.

1.1.1 How Diagnostic AI Works

Diagnostic AI relies on sophisticated algorithms trained on extensive medical datasets. Machine learning models, particularly deep neural networks, are fed with labeled data—such as X-rays, MRI scans, or pathology slides—to learn the distinguishing features of various diseases. Once trained, these models can analyze new patient data and generate diagnostic predictions with high accuracy. For example, AI systems like Google's DeepMind and IBM's Watson have demonstrated remarkable capabilities in detecting diabetic retinopathy and lung cancer from medical imaging.

Natural language processing (NLP) is another critical component of diagnostic AI, enabling systems to extract meaningful information from unstructured clinical notes, research papers, and patient histories. By combining imaging analysis with NLP, AI can provide a comprehensive diagnostic assessment that considers both visual and textual data. Furthermore, reinforcement learning allows AI systems to continuously improve their performance by learning from new cases and clinician feedback, ensuring that diagnostic accuracy evolves over time.

1.1.2 Applications of Diagnostic AI in Medicine

Diagnostic AI is being applied across various medical specialties, revolutionizing how diseases are detected and managed. In radiology, AI-powered tools assist in interpreting X-rays, CT scans, and mammograms, often identifying early signs of tumors or fractures faster than human radiologists. For instance, AI algorithms have been shown to detect breast cancer with a sensitivity comparable to expert radiologists, reducing false negatives and improving early diagnosis rates.

In pathology, AI enhances the analysis of tissue samples by identifying malignant cells in biopsy specimens. Digital pathology platforms use AI to scan slides at high resolution. This not only speeds up diagnosis but also minimizes human error. Similarly, in cardiology, AI analyzes electrocardiograms (ECGs) and echocardiograms to detect arrhythmias, heart failure, and other cardiac abnormalities with high precision.

Neurological diagnostics also benefit from AI, particularly in the early detection of conditions like Alzheimer's and Parkinson's disease. AI models can assess brain scans and cognitive test results to predict disease progression, enabling timely interventions. Additionally, AI-driven diagnostic tools are being used in primary care to analyze symptoms, recommend tests, and prioritize high-risk patients thereby improving triage efficiency in busy clinical settings.

1.1.3 Advantages

One of the most significant advantages of diagnostic AI is its ability to enhance accuracy and reduce diagnostic errors. Studies suggest that medical errors contribute to thousands of deaths annually, many of which stem from misdiagnosis. AI systems, with their ability to process vast amounts of data without fatigue, can minimize these errors by providing second opinions and highlighting overlooked findings. Another key benefit is efficiency. AI can analyze medical images or lab results in seconds, significantly reducing the time between testing and diagnosis.

This is particularly crucial in emergency situations, such as stroke detection, where rapid intervention is vital. Moreover, AI can handle repetitive tasks, allowing healthcare professionals to focus on complex cases and patient care rather than routine analyses. Cost reduction is another advantage. By automating parts of the diagnostic process, hospitals and clinics can lower operational expenses while maintaining high standards of care. Early and accurate diagnosis also reduces the need for expensive treatments associated with advanced disease stages, ultimately lowering healthcare costs for patients and providers alike.

1.1.4 Challenges and Ethical Considerations

Despite its potential, diagnostic AI faces several challenges. One major concern is data quality and bias. AI models are only as good as the data they are trained on, and if the training datasets lack diversity, the AI may perform poorly for underrepresented populations. For example, an AI trained primarily on data from Caucasian patients may be less accurate in diagnosing skin conditions in individuals with darker skin tones. Ensuring diverse and representative datasets is essential to avoid biased outcomes.

Regulatory and validation hurdles also pose challenges. Before AI diagnostic tools can be widely adopted, they must undergo rigorous testing to meet regulatory standards such as those set by the FDA or EMA. Clinicians must trust these systems, which requires transparent validation studies demonstrating their reliability and safety. Additionally, integrating AI into existing healthcare workflows can be complex, requiring training for medical staff and adjustments to hospital IT infrastructure. Ethical considerations include patient privacy and accountability. AI systems rely on sensitive patient data, raising concerns about data security and consent. Furthermore, if an AI system makes an incorrect diagnosis, determining liability—whether it lies with the developers, healthcare providers, or the AI itself—remains a legal gray area. Establishing clear guidelines for AI accountability and data governance is critical to fostering trust in these technologies.

1.2 HISTORICAL EVOLUTION OF AI IN MEDICAL DIAGNOSTICS

1.2.1 Early Beginnings and Conceptual Foundations (1950s–1970s)

The foundational ideas of AI in medicine emerged during the 1950s and 1960s when computing technology was still in its infancy. Pioneers like Alan Turing posed fundamental questions about whether machines could simulate human intelligence. Although these ideas were largely theoretical at the time, they laid the groundwork for future exploration. In the 1960s, the first wave of AI systems appeared, characterized primarily by rule-based logic and symbolic reasoning. One of the earliest medical expert systems was MYCIN, developed in the 1970s at Stanford University. MYCIN was designed to diagnose bacterial infections and recommend antibiotic treatments based on a set of if-then rules. Despite its success in academic settings, MYCIN was never deployed in clinical practice due to concerns about accountability, data limitations, and user acceptance. Nonetheless it demonstrated the potential of AI to aid in medical decision-making and inspired subsequent developments.

1.2.2 Rise of Expert Systems and Knowledge-Based Models (1980s–1990s)

The 1980s witnessed a growing interest in expert systems and knowledge-based models in medicine. These systems sought to replicate the decision-making processes of experienced clinicians by incorporating structured knowledge bases and inference engines. They were typically developed through close collaboration between medical professionals and computer scientists. Systems like INTERNIST-I and CASNET became prominent examples, focusing on internal medicine and ophthalmology, respectively.

The key strength of these early systems was their ability to reason through complex cases using explicit knowledge representations. However, they also suffered from limitations, including difficulty in scaling, challenges in updating knowledge bases and the inability to handle uncertain or incomplete data effectively. Furthermore these systems often required manual input and were not integrated into existing clinical workflows, reducing their practicality and adoption. Nevertheless, this era established important principles for AI development, such as the need for domain-specific knowledge, interpretability, and collaboration between disciplines.

1.2.3 Integration with Statistical and Probabilistic Models (1990s–2000s)

By the 1990s, the limitations of purely rule-based systems led to a shift toward statistical and probabilistic models. The growing availability of electronic health records (EHRs) and medical databases enabled researchers to apply statistical learning techniques to real-world clinical data. Bayesian networks, decision trees, and logistic regression models began to supplement or replace rule-based systems. These approaches allowed for greater flexibility in handling uncertainty and variability in clinical data.

For example, probabilistic models could estimate disease likelihood based on a range of symptoms, test results, and patient history, providing more nuanced and individualized diagnostic support. The integration of statistical methods also marked a philosophical shift from deterministic to probabilistic thinking in AI diagnostics. Importantly, during this time, the development of natural language processing (NLP) techniques began to enable AI systems to extract and analyze information from unstructured clinical notes, expanding the scope of diagnostic applications. However, while these systems improved predictive accuracy, they were still limited by computational power, data quality, and concerns about transparency.

1.2.4 Advent of Machine Learning and Early Image Analysis (2000s–2010s)

The early 2000s marked the beginning of a new phase in AI diagnostics with the advent of machine learning, particularly supervised learning methods. These algorithms could learn patterns from labeled datasets and make predictions on new, unseen data. The application of machine learning in medical diagnostics expanded to areas such as pathology, radiology, dermatology, and cardiology. Image analysis became a major focus, with algorithms trained to detect abnormalities in medical images like X-rays, CT scans, and MRIs.

These tools demonstrated significant potential for assisting radiologists by highlighting suspicious areas or automating routine tasks. One notable milestone was the development of computer-aided detection (CAD) systems for breast cancer screening through mammography. While these systems initially faced criticism for false positives and limited specificity, they represented a step forward in integrating AI into routine diagnostic workflows. Machine learning also found applications in predictive modeling, identifying patients at risk for diseases like diabetes, heart failure, and sepsis. These models enabled earlier intervention and better resource allocation. Despite progress, the lack of large annotated datasets and concerns about algorithm transparency remained challenges.

1.2.5 Deep Learning and Breakthroughs in Diagnostic Accuracy (2010s–Present)

The past decade has witnessed unprecedented growth in the application of deep learning to medical diagnostics. Deep learning, a subset of machine learning based on artificial neural networks with multiple layers, has demonstrated remarkable capabilities in pattern recognition, particularly in image, speech, and text analysis. The rise of deep learning has been fueled by the convergence of large-scale datasets, powerful computational hardware, and open-source frameworks like TensorFlow and PyTorch.

In the realm of medical diagnostics, convolutional neural networks (CNNs) have achieved human-level or even superhuman performance in tasks such as detecting diabetic retinopathy in retinal images, identifying skin cancer from dermatological photographs, and interpreting chest X-rays. One landmark study published by Google Health in 2019 showed that deep learning algorithms could match expert radiologists in detecting lung cancer from low-dose CT scans. Similar advancements have been made in ophthalmology, pathology, and cardiology, where AI tools assist in interpreting complex data and reducing diagnostic errors. Moreover, natural language processing has advanced to the point where AI can extract clinically relevant information from free-text medical records, aiding in diagnosis and documentation.

1.3 CURRENT LANDSCAPE: ADOPTION ACROSS SPECIALTIES

1.3.1 Radiology: The Vanguard of AI Adoption

Radiology stands at the forefront of AI adoption in diagnostics, serving as a model for other specialties. The digital nature of radiological imaging, coupled with the vast repositories of annotated data, has made this field particularly amenable to AI-driven solutions. Deep learning algorithms, especially convolutional neural networks, have demonstrated exceptional performance in image recognition tasks, often rivaling or surpassing human experts in detecting abnormalities such as tumors, fractures, and hemorrhages.

AI-powered tools are now routinely used to assist radiologists in interpreting X-rays, CT scans, and MRIs, enhancing both speed and accuracy. These systems can flag suspicious findings, prioritize urgent cases, and even automate measurements, thereby reducing workload and minimizing diagnostic errors. The widespread adoption in radiology is further propelled by robust validation studies and regulatory approvals, with several AI-based diagnostic tools receiving clearance from agencies like the FDA and CE.

1.3.2 Pathology: Digital Transformation and AI Synergy

Pathology, traditionally reliant on manual examination of tissue samples under a microscope, is undergoing a digital transformation that paves the way for AI integration. The digitization of pathology slides enables the application of AI algorithms to analyze complex histopathological patterns, identify malignancies, and grade tumors with high precision. AI systems in pathology are particularly valuable in standardizing diagnoses, reducing inter-observer variability, and uncovering subtle features that may be overlooked by the human eye. While adoption is still in its early stages compared to radiology, leading academic centers and large hospital networks are increasingly incorporating AI into their pathology workflows. The synergy between digital pathology and AI not only enhances diagnostic accuracy but also facilitates remote consultations and collaborative research, expanding access to expert opinions in underserved regions.

1.3.3 Ophthalmology: Early Detection and Screening

Ophthalmology has emerged as another specialty where AI is making significant inroads, particularly in the screening and early detection of retinal diseases. AI algorithms trained on large datasets of retinal images can accurately identify conditions such as diabetic retinopathy, age-related macular degeneration, and glaucoma. These tools are especially valuable in primary care and community settings, where access to ophthalmologists may be limited. By enabling automated, point-of-care screening, AI helps in the early identification of sight-threatening diseases, allowing timely intervention and reducing the burden of preventable blindness. The adoption of AI in ophthalmology is supported by strong clinical evidence and successful pilot programs in various countries, demonstrating its potential to improve population health outcomes.

1.3.4 Cardiology: Enhancing Precision and Predictive Power

In cardiology, AI is being leveraged to enhance the precision and predictive power of diagnostic modalities such as electrocardiograms (ECGs), echocardiograms, and cardiac imaging. Machine learning models can detect subtle patterns in ECG signals that may indicate arrhythmias, myocardial infarction, or other cardiac abnormalities, often before they become clinically apparent. AI-driven analysis of echocardiographic images aids in the assessment of cardiac function, valve disorders, and structural anomalies. Furthermore, predictive analytics powered by AI can stratify patients based on their risk of adverse cardiac events, enabling personalized management strategies. While the adoption of AI in cardiology is growing, it is tempered by the need for rigorous validation and integration with existing clinical decision-making processes.

1.3.5 Oncology: Personalized Diagnostics and Prognostics

Oncology represents a rapidly evolving frontier for AI in diagnostics, driven by the complexity and heterogeneity of cancer. AI algorithms are being developed to analyze a wide array of data, including medical images, pathology slides, genomic profiles, and electronic health records, to provide more accurate and personalized diagnoses. In imaging, AI assists in tumor detection, segmentation, and characterization, supporting radiologists and oncologists in treatment planning. In pathology, AI helps in identifying molecular subtypes and predicting response to targeted therapies. The integration of multi-modal data through AI holds promise for advancing precision oncology, enabling clinicians to tailor interventions based on individual patient profiles. However, the adoption of AI in oncology is challenged by the need for large, diverse datasets and the complexity of integrating disparate data sources.

1.3.6 Primary Care and General Practice: Expanding Access and Efficiency

AI adoption in primary care and general practice is gaining momentum, particularly in the context of triage, decision support, and population health management. AI-powered diagnostic tools can assist clinicians in evaluating symptoms, suggesting differential diagnoses, and recommending appropriate investigations. These systems are especially valuable in resource-limited settings, where access to specialists may be constrained. By streamlining the diagnostic process and reducing unnecessary referrals, AI has the potential to improve efficiency and patient outcomes in primary care. However, concerns about over-reliance on algorithms and the need for clinician oversight remain important considerations in this setting.

1.3.7 Laboratory Medicine: Automation and Quality Assurance

In laboratory medicine, AI is being utilized to automate the interpretation of complex test results, identify patterns indicative of disease, and ensure quality assurance. AI-driven systems can analyze large volumes of laboratory data, flagging abnormal results and suggesting potential diagnoses. This not only enhances the accuracy and consistency of laboratory diagnostics but also supports clinicians in making informed decisions. The adoption of AI in laboratory medicine is facilitated by the structured nature of laboratory data and the increasing digitization of laboratory processes.

1.4 AI VS. TRADITIONAL DIAGNOSTIC METHODS: STRENGTHS AND LIMITATIONS

The comparison between AI and traditional diagnostic methods highlights a landscape of complementary strengths and shared challenges. Traditional methods bring clinical wisdom, patient-centric reasoning, and regulatory maturity, while AI offers speed, consistency, and powerful pattern recognition. Each has its own limitations, from human error to algorithmic opacity. The goal is not to choose one over the other but to integrate them in a way that leverages their respective advantages. By fostering collaboration between clinicians and AI systems, and by addressing ethical, technical, and practical concerns, the medical community can unlock the full potential of both approaches to deliver better, faster, and more equitable diagnostic care.

1.4.1 Strengths of Traditional Diagnostic Methods

Traditional diagnostic methods are deeply rooted in decades of clinical practice and scientific validation. One of their primary strengths lies in the role of the physician's clinical experience and judgment. A well-trained doctor combines textbook knowledge with an understanding of individual patient history, lifestyle, and physical examination to arrive at a diagnosis that is both informed and personalized. Human diagnosticians are also capable of applying contextual reasoning, making them well-suited to consider multiple concurrent symptoms, rare conditions, or ambiguous presentations that do not fit a clear diagnostic pattern.

Another major advantage of traditional diagnostics is the regulatory approval and clinical trust they have garnered over time. Laboratory tests, such as blood panels, urine analysis, and biopsies, are standardized and validated for accuracy and reproducibility. Medical imaging techniques such as X-rays, MRIs, and CT scans have been refined to high precision, with radiologists trained extensively to interpret them. These methods form the bedrock of evidence-based medicine, and they have undergone rigorous clinical trials and peer-reviewed research to ensure safety and efficacy.

Traditional diagnostics also offer a degree of explainability that is central to the doctor-patient relationship. Physicians can communicate their reasoning, explain the steps they took to reach a conclusion, and discuss potential differential diagnoses with the patient. This transparency fosters trust and allows patients to engage meaningfully in their own care decisions.

1.4.2 Strengths of AI-Based Diagnostic Methods

Artificial Intelligence brings a transformative set of strengths to the field of diagnostics. One of its most significant advantages is the ability to analyze massive volumes of data at a speed and scale that human diagnosticians cannot match. AI algorithms, particularly deep learning models, can process thousands of images, test results, or patient records in seconds, identifying patterns that may be too subtle or complex for the human eye. This capability is particularly valuable in fields like radiology, dermatology, and ophthalmology, where visual pattern recognition is key. Another important strength of AI lies in its consistency and objectivity. Unlike human diagnosticians, AI systems are not influenced by fatigue, emotional stress, or cognitive biases. Once trained on a validated dataset, an AI model can apply the same analytical standards across all cases, reducing variability in diagnoses. This makes AI especially useful in high-volume settings or underserved areas where access to expert specialists may be limited.

Moreover, AI enables predictive diagnostics, going beyond current symptoms to anticipate future health risks based on patterns in the data. For example, machine learning models can assess the likelihood of a patient developing cardiovascular disease by analyzing lifestyle factors, genetic data, and past medical records. Such predictive capabilities have the potential to shift healthcare from reactive treatment to proactive prevention. AI also supports integration across diverse data types—imaging, genomics, lab reports, and clinical notes—creating a holistic view of the patient's condition. This integrative approach enhances diagnostic precision and enables the personalization of treatment plans. Furthermore, recent advancements in natural language processing allow AI to extract relevant information from unstructured clinical narratives, improving the speed and efficiency of diagnosis.

1.4.3 Limitations of Traditional Diagnostic Methods

Despite their strengths, traditional diagnostic methods are not without limitations. One of the main drawbacks is the dependence on the clinician's subjective interpretation, which can lead to inconsistencies or diagnostic errors. Even experienced doctors are susceptible to cognitive biases such as anchoring, availability heuristic, or confirmation bias, which can skew decision-making. Additionally, time constraints, patient overload, and systemic inefficiencies in healthcare delivery can impair a physician's ability to conduct thorough assessments.

Another limitation lies in the difficulty of managing and synthesizing large volumes of patient data. With the increasing digitization of healthcare records and the growing complexity of medical information, it is challenging for individual practitioners to integrate all relevant data points effectively. This can result in missed diagnoses or delayed treatment, particularly in cases involving multiple comorbidities or rare diseases. Moreover, traditional diagnostics often require time-consuming procedures such as lab work or imaging appointments, which can delay diagnosis and treatment initiation. In resource-limited settings, access to advanced diagnostic equipment and specialist consultations may be restricted, leading to inequities in healthcare delivery.

1.4.4 Limitations of AI-Based Diagnostic Methods

While AI has made impressive strides, it is not without its shortcomings. One of the most critical issues is the "black box" nature of many AI systems, especially deep learning models. These algorithms often provide output without clear explanations of how the decision was reached. This lack of interpretability raises concerns about accountability, particularly in high-stakes medical decisions where patient lives are involved. Data bias is another significant limitation. AI systems are only as good as the data on which they are trained. If training datasets are not diverse or representative of the general population, AI models may underperform or generate biased outcomes for certain demographic groups. For example, an AI trained primarily on data from a specific ethnic group may not diagnose skin conditions accurately in patients with different skin tones.

Additionally, AI systems are highly sensitive to the quality of input data. Inaccurate, incomplete, or poorly labeled data can compromise the performance of the algorithm. In real-world clinical environments, data often come from multiple sources with varying standards, increasing the risk of inconsistency. There are also infrastructural and operational barriers to AI integration in clinical settings. Deploying AI tools requires substantial investment in technology infrastructure, staff training, and workflow redesign. Many healthcare systems, especially in low-income regions, lack the resources to implement and maintain such systems. Furthermore, the regulatory landscape for AI in medicine is still evolving, with questions around liability, data governance, and ethical use remaining unresolved.

1.4.5 Complementarity and the Path Forward

Rather than viewing AI and traditional diagnostic methods as mutually exclusive, it is more productive to consider them as complementary. AI can serve as a powerful decision-support tool, augmenting the capabilities of human diagnosticians rather than replacing them. For instance, AI can pre-screen imaging data, flagging potential areas of concern for the radiologist to review. This not only enhances efficiency but also allows clinicians to focus their expertise on the most complex cases. The future of diagnostics lies in hybrid models that integrate human intuition with algorithmic precision. Clinicians will continue to play a critical role in interpreting AI-generated insights, contextualizing them within the broader clinical picture, and communicating with patients. Meanwhile, AI will take on repetitive tasks, uncover hidden patterns, and provide data-driven recommendations, ultimately improving the accuracy and timeliness of diagnoses.

1.5 AI IN DIAGNOSTICS AND THE FUTURE OF HEALTHCARE DELIVERY

AI is poised to revolutionize diagnostics and healthcare delivery, offering tools that enhance precision, efficiency, and accessibility. From early disease detection to personalized treatment recommendations and remote patient monitoring, AI's applications are vast and transformative. However, realizing this potential requires addressing challenges related to data privacy, algorithmic bias, and regulatory oversight. By fostering collaboration between technology and medicine, healthcare systems can harness AI's power to improve outcomes, reduce costs, and deliver patient-centered care at scale. As AI continues to evolve, its integration into healthcare will redefine what is possible in medicine. The future lies in a harmonious partnership between human expertise and artificial intelligence, where technology amplifies clinicians' abilities rather than replaces them. In this new era, healthcare will become more proactive, predictive, and personalized, ensuring better health for individuals and populations alike. The journey has just begun, and the possibilities are limitless.

1.5.1 How AI is Revolutionizing Medical Diagnostics

AI's impact on diagnostics is most evident in medical imaging, where deep learning algorithms excel at detecting abnormalities in X-rays, MRIs, CT scans, and ultrasounds. These systems are trained on millions of labeled images, allowing them to recognize patterns associated with conditions such as lung cancer, brain tumors, and fractures with remarkable accuracy. For example, AI models have demonstrated the ability to identify early-stage breast cancer in mammograms with sensitivity levels comparable to—and sometimes surpassing—those of experienced radiologists. This capability not only speeds up diagnosis but also reduces the likelihood of human error, particularly in cases where subtle signs of disease may be overlooked.

Beyond imaging, AI is enhancing pathology by digitizing tissue samples and using computer vision to detect cancerous cells in biopsies. Digital pathology platforms equipped with AI can scan entire slides at high resolution. This approach not only improves diagnostic consistency but also allows for faster turnaround times which is crucial in oncology where early detection significantly impacts treatment success. Similarly, in cardiology, AI-driven analysis of electrocardiograms (ECGs) and echocardiograms can detect arrhythmias, heart failure, and other cardiac conditions with high precision, enabling timely interventions.

AI is also making strides in non-imaging diagnostics, such as interpreting laboratory results and genetic data. Machine learning models can analyze blood tests, biomarker levels, and genomic sequences to predict disease risks and recommend personalized treatment plans. For instance, AI algorithms have been used to identify patients at high risk of sepsis or diabetic complications by analyzing trends in their lab results. By integrating these insights into clinical decision support systems, AI empowers healthcare providers to make more informed, data-driven decisions, ultimately improving patient outcomes.

1.5.2 Future of Healthcare Delivery with AI

The widespread adoption of AI in diagnostics is paving the way for a more efficient and patient-centered healthcare system. One of the most significant shifts will be the move toward predictive and preventive medicine. Instead of waiting for symptoms to manifest, AI can analyze patient data—including genetic predispositions, lifestyle factors, and real-time health metrics from wearables—to forecast potential health issues before they become critical. This proactive approach allows for early interventions, reducing hospitalizations and long-term healthcare costs.

Another transformative aspect of AI-driven healthcare is the expansion of telemedicine and remote diagnostics. With AI-powered mobile apps and portable diagnostic devices, patients in rural or underserved areas can receive expert-level medical assessments without needing to visit a specialist in person. For example, AI algorithms can analyze retinal scans for diabetic retinopathy or skin images for melanoma, enabling primary care physicians to deliver specialist-grade diagnostics in community settings. This democratization of healthcare ensures that high-quality medical services are accessible to a broader population, reducing disparities in care. Hospital workflows will also benefit from AI integration, as intelligent systems streamline administrative tasks, prioritize urgent cases, and optimize resource allocation. AI can assist in triaging emergency room patients by analyzing symptoms and vital signs, ensuring that those with life-threatening conditions receive immediate attention. Additionally, AI-driven chatbots and virtual health assistants can handle routine patient inquiries, schedule appointments, and provide medication reminders, freeing up clinicians to focus on complex cases. These efficiencies will be crucial as healthcare systems grapple with growing patient volumes and staffing shortages.

1.5.3 Challenges and Ethical Considerations

Despite its immense potential, the integration of AI into diagnostics and healthcare delivery is not without challenges. One of the primary concerns is data privacy and security. AI systems rely on vast amounts of sensitive patient data, raising questions about how this information is stored, shared, and protected. Ensuring compliance with regulations such as the General Data Protection Regulation (GDPR) and the Health Insurance Portability and Accountability Act (HIPAA) is essential to maintaining patient trust and preventing data breaches.

Another critical issue is algorithmic bias. If AI models are trained on datasets that lack diversity, they may produce inaccurate or unfair results for certain demographic groups. For instance, an AI system trained predominantly on data from white patients may underperform when diagnosing skin conditions in people with darker skin tones. Addressing this bias requires intentional efforts to include diverse populations in training datasets and continuously auditing AI systems for fairness and accuracy.

Regulatory and legal challenges also loom large. As AI takes on a greater role in diagnostics, determining liability in cases of misdiagnosis becomes complex. Should responsibility fall on the AI developers, the healthcare providers using the technology, or the institutions that deploy it? Clear legal frameworks must be established to define accountability and ensure that patients have recourse in the event of errors. Additionally, regulatory bodies like the FDA and EMA must develop robust approval processes for AI-based diagnostic tools, balancing innovation with patient safety.

1.5.4 Path Forward: Collaboration between AI and Healthcare Professionals

The future of AI in diagnostics does not entail replacing physicians but rather augmenting their expertise. The most effective healthcare delivery models will combine AI's analytical power with clinicians' judgment, empathy, and experience. For this collaboration to succeed, medical professionals must be trained to interpret AI-generated insights critically and integrate them into patient care appropriately. Continuing medical education programs should include AI literacy, ensuring that doctors, nurses, and technicians understand how to work alongside these technologies effectively. Interdisciplinary collaboration will also be key. Engineers, data scientists, and healthcare providers must work together to design AI solutions that address real-world clinical needs. Feedback loops between AI developers and end-users will help refine algorithms, making them more intuitive and aligned with medical workflows. Furthermore, partnerships between academic institutions, tech companies, and healthcare organizations can accelerate innovation while ensuring ethical standards are upheld.

CHAPTER 2

Foundations of Diagnostic AI Technologies

2.1 MACHINE LEARNING AND DEEP LEARNING BASICS

2.1.1 Supervised Learning

In machine learning, supervised learning (SL) is a type of machine learning paradigm where an algorithm learns to map input data to a specific output based on example input-output pairs. This process involves training a statistical model using labeled data, meaning each piece of input data is provided with the correct output. For instance, if you want a model to identify cats in images, supervised learning would involve feeding it many images of cats (inputs) that are explicitly labeled "cat" (outputs).

The goal of supervised learning is for the trained model to accurately predict the output for new, unseen data. This requires the algorithm to effectively generalize from the training examples, a quality measured by its generalization error. Supervised learning is commonly used for tasks like classification (predicting a category, e.g., spam or not spam) and regression (predicting a continuous value, e.g., house prices).

Steps to Follow

To solve a given problem of supervised learning, the following steps must be performed:

- Determine the type of training samples. Before doing anything else, the user should decide what kind of data is to be used as a training set. In the case of handwriting analysis, for example, this might be a single handwritten character, an entire handwritten word, an entire sentence of handwriting, or a full paragraph of handwriting.
- Gather a training set. The training set needs to be representative of the real-world use of the function. Thus, a set of input objects is gathered together with corresponding outputs, either from human experts or from measurements.
- Determine the input feature representation of the learned function. The accuracy of the learned function depends strongly on how the input

object is represented. Typically, the input object is transformed into a feature vector, which contains a number of features that are descriptive of the object. The number of features should not be too large, because of the curse of dimensionality; but should contain enough information to accurately predict the output.

- Determine the structure of the learned function and corresponding learning algorithm. For example, one may choose to use support-vector machines or decision trees.
- Complete the design. Run the learning algorithm on the gathered training set. Some supervised learning algorithms require the user to determine certain control parameters. These parameters may be adjusted by optimizing performance on a subset (called a validation set) of the training set, or via cross-validation.
- Evaluate the accuracy of the learned function. After parameter adjustment and learning, the performance of the resulting function should be measured on a test set that is separate from the training set.

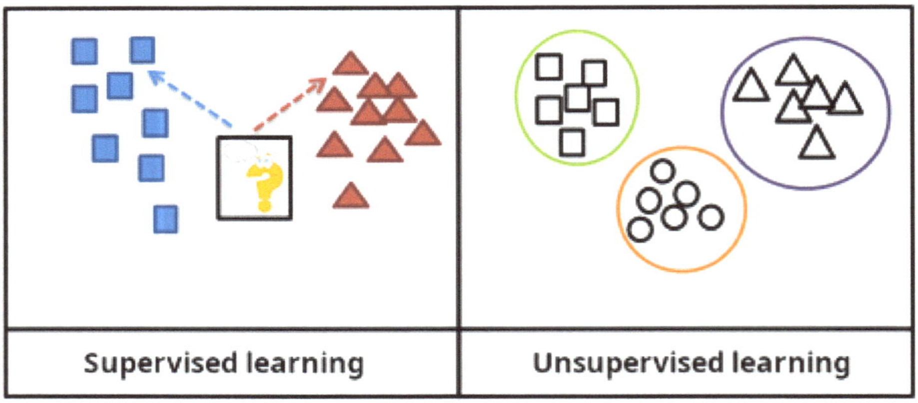

Fig: In Supervised Learning, the Training Data is Labeled with the Expected Answers, while in Unsupervised Learning, the Model Identifies Patterns or Structures in Unlabeled Data

Algorithm Choice

A wide range of supervised learning algorithms are available, each with its strengths and weaknesses. There is no single learning algorithm that works best on all supervised learning problems.

Bias–Variance Tradeoff

A first issue is the tradeoff between bias and variance. Imagine that we have available several different, but equally good, training data sets. A learning algorithm is biased for a particular input x x if, when trained on each of these data sets, it is systematically incorrect when predicting the correct output for x x. A learning algorithm has high variance for a particular input x x if it predicts different output values when trained on different training sets.

The prediction error of a learned classifier is related to the sum of the bias and the variance of the learning algorithm. Generally, there is a tradeoff between bias and variance. A learning algorithm with low bias must be "flexible" so that it can fit the data well. But if the learning algorithm is too flexible, it will fit each training data set differently, and hence have high variance. A key aspect of many supervised learning methods is that they are able to adjust this tradeoff between bias and variance (either automatically or by providing a bias/variance parameter that the user can adjust).

Function Complexity and Amount of Training Data

The second issue is of the amount of training data available relative to the complexity of the "true" function (classifier or regression function). If the true function is simple, then an "inflexible" learning algorithm with high bias and low variance will be able to learn it from a small amount of data. But if the true function is highly complex (e.g., because it involves complex interactions among many different input features and behaves differently in different parts of the input space), then the function will only be able to learn with a large amount of training data paired with a "flexible" learning algorithm with low bias and high variance.

Dimensionality of the Input Space

A third issue is the dimensionality of the input space. If the input feature vectors have large dimensions, learning the function can be difficult even if the true function only depends on a small number of those features. This is because the many "extra" dimensions can confuse the learning algorithm and cause it to have high variance. Hence, input data of large dimensions typically requires tuning the classifier to have low variance and high bias. In practice, if the engineer can manually remove irrelevant features from the input data, it will likely improve the accuracy of the learned function. In addition, there are many algorithms for feature selection that seek to identify the relevant features and discard the irrelevant ones. This is an instance of the more general strategy of dimensionality reduction, which seeks to map the input data into a lower-dimensional space prior to running the supervised learning algorithm.

Noise in the Output Values

A fourth issue is the degree of noise in the desired output values (the supervisory target variables). If the desired output values are often incorrect (because of human error or sensor errors), then the learning algorithm should not attempt to find a function that exactly matches the training examples. Attempting to fit the data too carefully leads to overfitting. You can overfit even when there are no measurement errors (stochastic noise) if the function you are trying to learn is too complex for your learning model. In such a situation, the part of the target function that cannot be modeled "corrupts" your training data – this phenomenon has been called deterministic noise. When either type of noise is present, it is better to go with a higher bias, lower variance estimator.

In practice, there are several approaches to alleviate noise in the output values such as early stopping to prevent overfitting as well as detecting and removing the noisy training examples prior to training the supervised learning algorithm. There are several algorithms that identify noisy training examples and removing the suspected noisy training examples prior to training has decreased generalization error with statistical significance.

Other Factors to Consider

Other factors to consider when choosing and applying a learning algorithm include the following:

- **Heterogeneity of the Data:** If the feature vectors include features of many different kinds (discrete, discrete ordered, counts, continuous values), some algorithms are easier to apply than others. Many algorithms, including support-vector machines, linear regression, logistic regression, neural networks, and nearest neighbor methods, require that the input features be numerical and scaled to similar ranges (e.g., to the [-1,1] interval). Methods that employ a distance function, such as nearest neighbor methods and support-vector machines with Gaussian kernels, are particularly sensitive to this. An advantage of decision trees is that they easily handle heterogeneous data.
- **Redundancy in the Data:** If the input features contain redundant information (e.g., highly correlated features), some learning algorithms (e.g., linear regression, logistic regression, and distance-based methods) will perform poorly because of numerical instabilities. These problems can often be solved by imposing some form of regularization.
- **Presence of Interactions and Non-Linearities:** If each of the features makes an independent contribution to the output, then algorithms based on linear functions (e.g., linear regression, logistic regression, support-vector machines, naive Bayes) and distance functions (e.g., nearest neighbor methods, support-vector machines with Gaussian kernels) generally perform well. However, if there are complex interactions among features, then algorithms such as decision trees and

neural networks work better, because they are specifically designed to discover these interactions. Linear methods can also be applied, but the engineer must manually specify the interactions when using them.

When considering a new application, the engineer can compare multiple learning algorithms and experimentally determine which one works best on the problem at hand. Tuning the performance of a learning algorithm can be very time-consuming. Given fixed resources, it is often better to spend more time collecting additional training data and more informative features than it is to spend extra time tuning the learning algorithms.

Algorithms

The most widely used learning algorithms are:

- Support-vector machines.
- Linear regression.
- Logistic regression.
- Naive Bayes.
- Linear discriminant analysis.
- Decision trees.
- k-nearest neighbors algorithm.
- Neural networks (e.g., Multilayer perceptron).
- Similarity learning.

2.1.2 Unsupervised Learning

Unsupervised learning is a framework in machine learning where, in contrast to supervised learning, algorithms learn patterns exclusively from unlabeled data. Other frameworks in the spectrum of supervisions include weak- or semi-supervision, where a small portion of the data is tagged, and self-supervision. Some researchers consider self-supervised learning a form of unsupervised learning. Conceptually, unsupervised learning divides into the aspects of data, training, algorithm, and downstream applications.

Typically, the dataset is harvested cheaply "in the wild", such as massive text corpus obtained by web crawling, with only minor filtering (such as Common Crawl). This compares favorably to supervised learning, where the dataset (such as the ImageNet1000) is typically constructed manually, which is much more expensive.

There were algorithms designed specifically for unsupervised learning, such as clustering algorithms like k-means, dimensionality reduction techniques like principal component analysis (PCA), Boltzmann machine learning, and autoencoders. After the rise of deep learning, most large-scale unsupervised learning have been done by training general-purpose neural network architectures by gradient descent, adapted to performing unsupervised learning by designing an appropriate training procedure.

Sometimes a trained model can be used as-is, but more often they are modified for downstream applications. For example, the generative pretraining method trains a model to generate a textual dataset, before finetuning it for other applications such as text classification. As another example, autoencoders are trained to good features, which can then be used as a module for other models, such as in a latent diffusion model.

Tasks

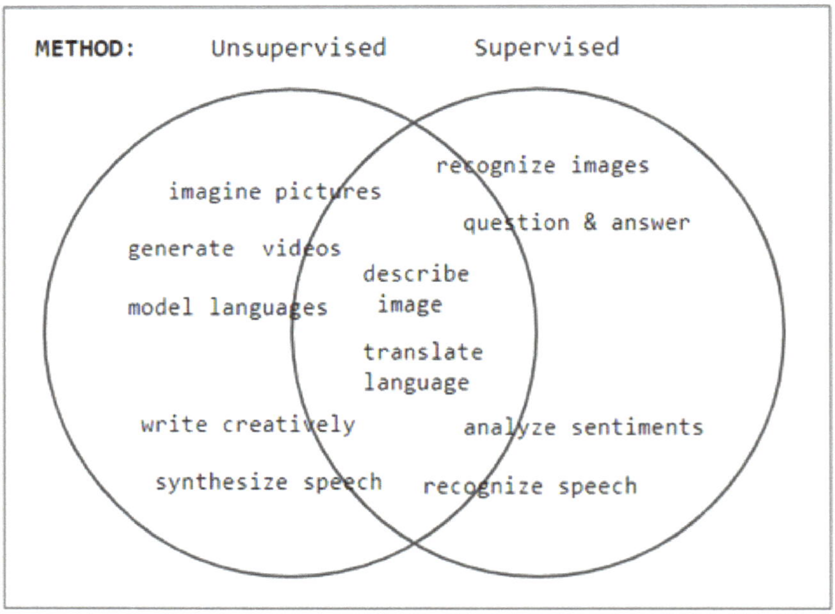

Fig: Tendency for a Task to Employ Supervised vs. Unsupervised Methods. Task Names Straddling Circle Boundaries is Intentional. It Shows that the Classical Division of Imaginative Tasks (left) Employing Unsupervised Methods is Blurred in Today's Learning Schemes

Tasks are often categorized as discriminative (recognition) or generative (imagination). Often but not always, discriminative tasks use supervised methods and generative tasks use unsupervised; however, the separation is very hazy. For example, object recognition favors supervised learning but unsupervised learning can also cluster objects into groups. Furthermore, as progress marches onward, some tasks employ both methods, and some tasks swing from one to another. For example, image recognition started off as heavily supervised, but became hybrid by employing unsupervised pre-training, and then moved towards supervision again with the advent of dropout, ReLU, and adaptive learning rates. A typical generative task is as follows. At each step, a datapoint is sampled from the dataset, and part of the data is removed, and the model must infer the removed part. This is particularly clear for the denoising autoencoders and BERT.

Neural Network Architectures

Training

During the learning phase, an unsupervised network tries to mimic the data it's given and uses the error in its mimicked output to correct itself (i.e. correct its weights and biases). Sometimes the error is expressed as a low probability that the erroneous output occurs, or it might be expressed as an unstable high energy state in the network. In contrast to supervised methods' dominant use of backpropagation, unsupervised learning also employs other methods including: Hopfield learning rule, Boltzmann learning rule, Contrastive Divergence, Wake Sleep, Variational Inference, Maximum Likelihood, Maximum A Posteriori, Gibbs Sampling, and backpropagating reconstruction errors or hidden state reparameterizations.

Networks

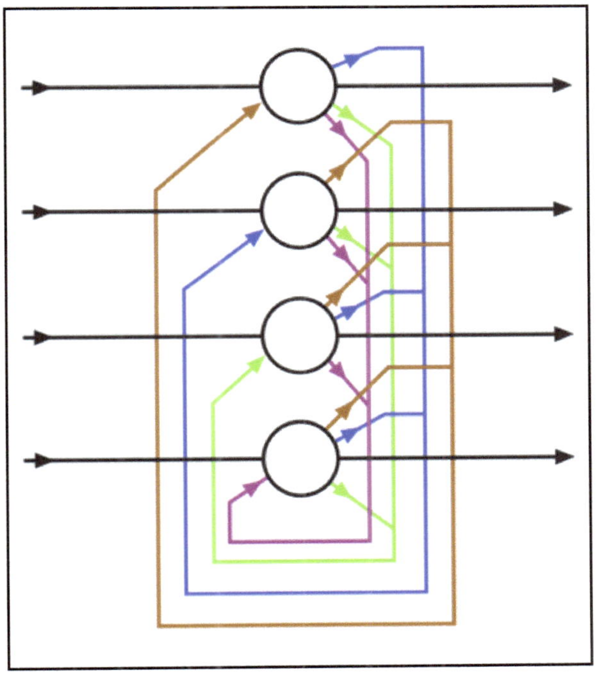

Fig: Hopfield—A Network Based on Magnetic Domains in Iron with a Single Self-Connected Layer. It can be used as a Content Addressable Memory

This connection diagrams of various unsupervised networks, the details of which will be given in the section Comparison of Networks. Circles are neurons and edges between them are connection weights. As network design changes, features are added on to enable new capabilities or removed to make learning faster. For instance, neurons change between deterministic (Hopfield) and stochastic (Boltzmann) to allow robust output, weights are removed within a layer (RBM) to hasten learning, or connections are allowed to become asymmetric (Helmholtz).

Energy

An energy function is a macroscopic measure of a network's activation state. In Boltzmann machines, it plays the role of the Cost function. This analogy with physics is inspired by Ludwig Boltzmann's analysis of a gas' macroscopic energy from the microscopic probabilities of particle motion $p \propto e^{-E/kT}$, where k is the Boltzmann constant and T is temperature.

In the RBM network the relation is $p = e^{-E} / Z$, where p and E vary over every possible activation pattern and $Z = \sum_{\text{All Patterns}} e^{-E(\text{pattern})}$. To be more precise, $p(a) = e^{-E(a)} / Z$, where a is an activation pattern of all neurons (visible and hidden). Hence, some early neural networks bear the name Boltzmann Machine. Paul Smolensky calls $-E$ the Harmony. A network seeks low energy which is high Harmony.

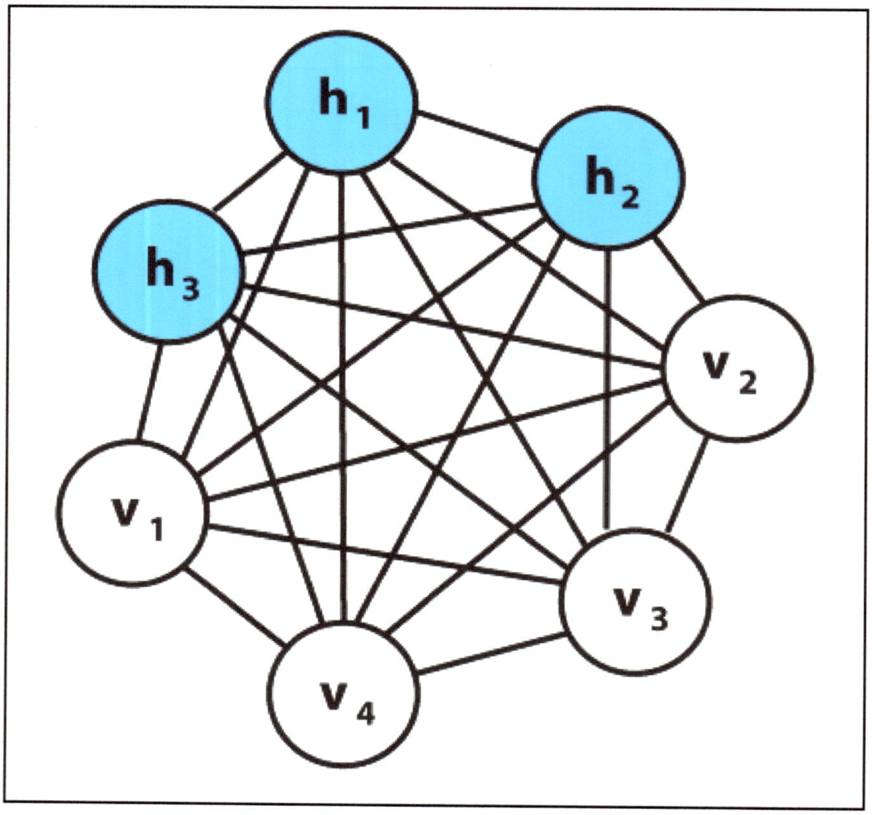

Fig: Boltzmann—Network is Separated into 2 Layers (Hidden vs. Visible), but Still Using Symmetric 2-Way Weights. Following Boltzmann's Thermodynamics, Individual Probabilities Give Rise to Macroscopic Energies

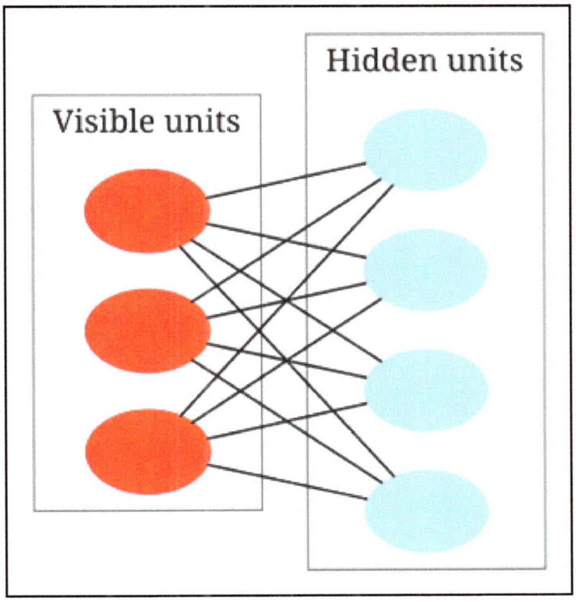

Fig: RBM—Restricted Boltzmann Machine. This is a Boltzmann Machine where Lateral Connections within a Layer are Prohibited to Make Analysis Tractable

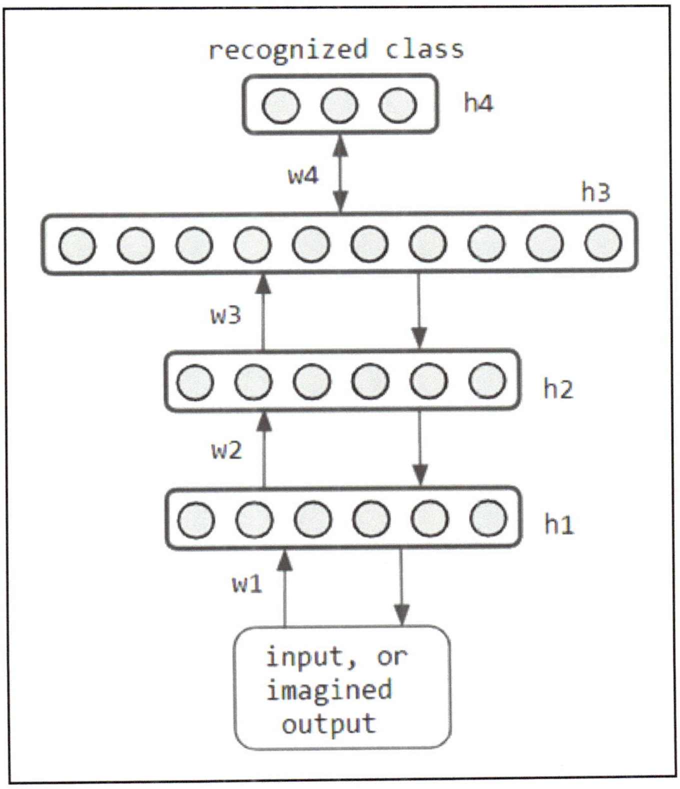

Fig: Stacked Boltzmann—This Network has Multiple RBM's to Encode a Hierarchy of Hidden Features

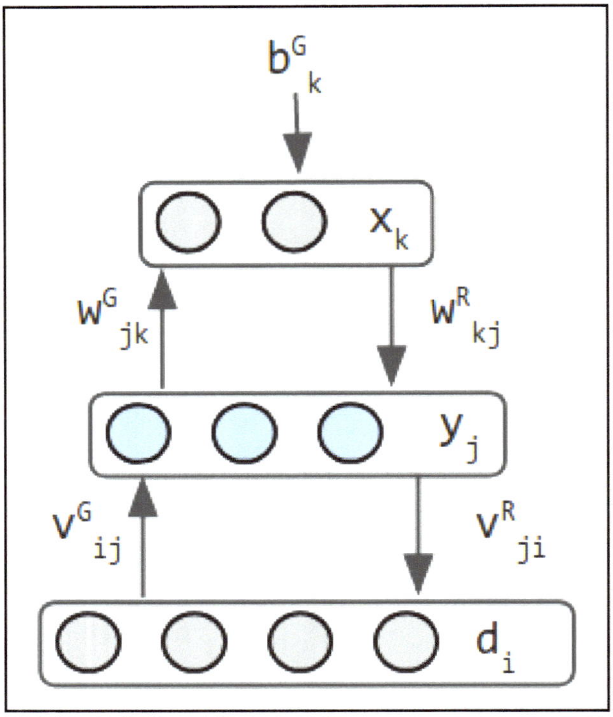

Fig: Helmholtz—Instead of the Bidirectional Symmetric Connection of the Stacked Boltzmann Machines, we have Separate One-Way Connections to Form a Loop. It Does Both Generation and Discrimination

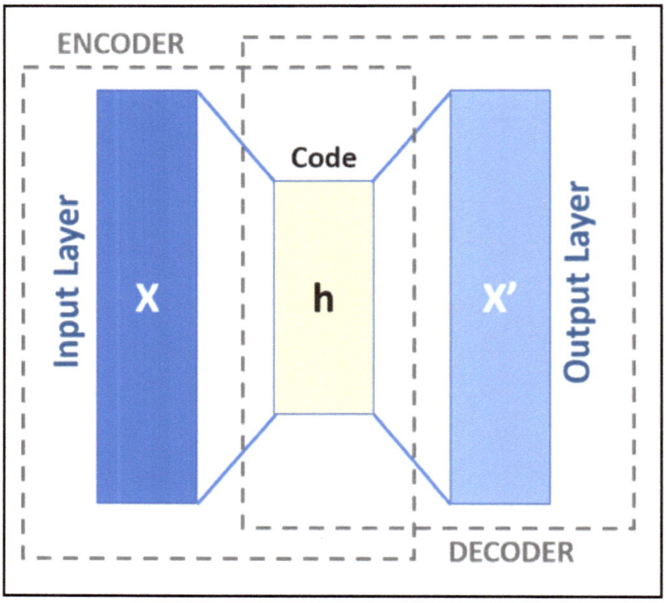

Fig: Autoencoder—A Feed Forward Network that Aims to Find a Good Middle Layer Representation of its Input World. This Network is Deterministic, so it is not as Robust as its Successor the VAE

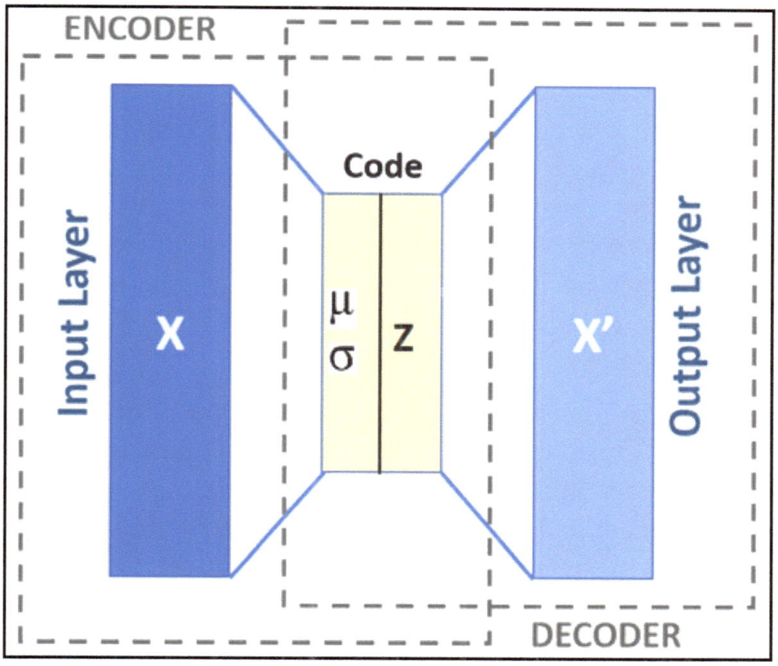

Fig: VAE—Applies Variational Inference to the Autoencoder. The Middle Layer is a Set of Means & Variances for Gaussian Distributions. The Stochastic Nature Allows for More Robust Imagination than the Deterministic Autoencoder

Of the networks bearing people's names, only Hopfield worked directly with neural networks. Boltzmann and Helmholtz came before artificial neural networks, but their work in physics and physiology inspired the analytical methods that were used.

History

1974	Ising magnetic model proposed by WA Little [de] for cognition
1980	Kunihiko Fukushima introduces the neocognitron, which is later called a convolutional neural network. It is mostly used in SL, but deserves a mention here.
1982	Ising variant Hopfield net described as CAMs and classifiers by John Hopfield.
1983	Ising variant Boltzmann machine with probabilistic neurons described by Hinton & Sejnowski following Sherington & Kirkpatrick's 1975 work.
1986	Paul Smolensky publishes Harmony Theory, which is an RBM with practically the same Boltzmann energy function. Smolensky did not give a practical training scheme. Hinton did in mid-2000s.
1995	Schmidthuber introduces the LSTM neuron for languages.
1995	Dayan & Hinton introduces Helmholtz machine
2013	Kingma, Rezende, & co. introduced Variational Autoencoders as Bayesian graphical probability network, with neural nets as components.

Specific Networks

- **Hopfield Network:** Ferromagnetism inspired Hopfield networks. A neuron correspond to an iron domain with binary magnetic moments Up and Down, and neural connections correspond to the domain's influence on each other. Symmetric connections enable a global energy formulation. During inference the network updates each state using the standard activation step function. Symmetric weights and the right energy functions guarantees convergence to a stable activation pattern. Asymmetric weights are difficult to analyze. Hopfield nets are used as Content Addressable Memories (CAM).
- **Boltzmann Machine:** These are stochastic Hopfield nets. Their state value is sampled from this pdf as follows: suppose a binary neuron fires with the Bernoulli probability p(1) = 1/3 and rests with p(0) = 2/3. One samples from it by taking a uniformly distributed random number y and plugging it into the inverted cumulative distribution function which in this case is the step function thresholded at 2/3. The inverse function = { 0 if x <= 2/3, 1 if x > 2/3 }.
- **Sigmoid Belief Net:** Introduced by Radford Neal in 1992, this network applies ideas from probabilistic graphical models to neural networks. A key difference is that nodes in graphical models have pre-assigned meanings whereas Belief Net neurons' features are determined after training. The network is a sparsely connected directed acyclic graph composed of binary stochastic neurons. The learning rule comes from Maximum Likelihood on $p(X)$: $\Delta w_{ij} \propto s_j * (s_i - p_i)$, where $p_i = 1 / \left(1 + e^{\text{weighted inputs into neuron } i}\right)$
  s_j's are activations from an unbiased sample of the posterior distribution and this is problematic due to the Explaining Away problem raised by Judea Perl. Variational Bayesian methods uses a surrogate posterior and blatantly disregard this complexity.
- **Deep Belief Network:** Introduced by Hinton, this network is a hybrid of RBM and Sigmoid Belief Network. The top 2 layers is an RBM and the second layer downwards form a sigmoid belief network. One trains it by the stacked RBM method and then throw away the recognition weights below the top RBM. As of 2009, 3-4 layers seems to be the optimal depth.
- **Helmholtz Machine:** These are early inspirations for the Variational Auto Encoders. Its 2 networks combined into one—forward weights operates recognition and backward weights implements imagination. It is perhaps the first network to do both. Helmholtz did not work in

machine learning but he inspired the view of "statistical inference engine whose function is to infer probable causes of sensory input". the stochastic binary neuron outputs a probability that its state is 0 or 1. The data input is normally not considered a layer, but in the Helmholtz machine generation mode, the data layer receives input from the middle layer and has separate weights for this purpose, so it is considered a layer. Hence this network has 3 layers.

- **Variational Autoencoder**: These are inspired by Helmholtz machines and combines probability network with neural networks. An Autoencoder is a 3-layer CAM network, where the middle layer is supposed to be some internal representation of input patterns. The encoder neural network is a probability distribution q_{φ}(z given x) and the decoder network is p_{θ}(x given z). The weights are named phi & theta rather than W and V as in Helmholtz—a cosmetic difference. These 2 networks here can be fully connected, or use another NN scheme.

Hebbian Learning, ART, SOM

The classical example of unsupervised learning in the study of neural networks is Donald Hebb's principle, that is, neurons that fire together wire together. In Hebbian learning, the connection is reinforced irrespective of an error, but is exclusively a function of the coincidence between action potentials between the two neurons. A similar version that modifies synaptic weights takes into account the time between the action potentials (spike-timing-dependent plasticity or STDP). Hebbian Learning has been hypothesized to underlie a range of cognitive functions, such as pattern recognition and experiential learning. Among neural network models, the self-organizing map (SOM) and adaptive resonance theory (ART) are commonly used in unsupervised learning algorithms. The SOM is a topographic organization in which nearby locations in the map represent inputs with similar properties. The ART model allows the number of clusters to vary with problem size and lets the user control the degree of similarity between members of the same clusters by means of a user-defined constant called the vigilance parameter. ART networks are used for many pattern recognition tasks, such as automatic target recognition and seismic signal processing.

Probabilistic Methods

Two of the main methods used in unsupervised learning are principal component and cluster analysis. Cluster analysis is used in unsupervised learning to group, or segment, datasets with shared attributes in order to extrapolate algorithmic relationships. Cluster analysis is a branch of machine learning that groups the data that has not been labelled, classified or categorized. Instead of responding to feedback, cluster analysis identifies commonalities in the data and reacts based on the presence or absence of such commonalities in each new piece of data. This approach helps detect anomalous data points that do not fit into either group. A central application of unsupervised learning is in the field of density estimation in statistics, though unsupervised learning encompasses many other domains involving summarizing and explaining data features. It can be contrasted with supervised learning by saying that whereas supervised learning intends to infer a conditional probability distribution conditioned on the label of input data unsupervised learning intends to infer an a priori probability distribution.

Approaches

Some of the most common algorithms used in unsupervised learning include: (1) Clustering, (2) Anomaly detection, (3) Approaches for learning latent variable models. Each approach uses several methods as follows:

- Clustering methods include: hierarchical clustering, k-means, mixture models, model-based clustering, DBSCAN, and OPTICS algorithm.
- Anomaly detection methods include: Local Outlier Factor, and Isolation Forest.
- Approaches for learning latent variable models such as Expectation–maximization algorithm (EM), Method of moments, and Blind signal separation techniques (Principal component analysis, Independent component analysis, Non-negative matrix factorization, Singular value decomposition).

Method of Moments

One of the statistical approaches for unsupervised learning is the method of moments. In the method of moments, the unknown parameters (of interest) in the model are related to the moments of one or more random variables, and thus, these unknown parameters can be estimated given the moments. The moments are usually estimated from samples empirically. The basic moments are first and second order moments. For a random vector, the first order moment is the mean vector, and the second order moment is the covariance matrix (when the mean is zero). Higher order moments are usually represented using tensors which are the generalization of matrices to higher orders as multi-dimensional arrays.

In particular, the method of moments is shown to be effective in learning the parameters of latent variable models. Latent variable models are statistical models where in addition to the observed variables, a set of latent variables also exists which is not observed. A highly practical example of latent variable models in machine learning is the topic modeling which is a statistical model for generating the words (observed variables) in the document based on the topic (latent variable) of the document. In the topic modeling, the words in the document are generated according to different statistical parameters when the topic of the document is changed. It is shown that method of moments (tensor decomposition techniques) consistently recover the parameters of a large class of latent variable models under some assumptions. The Expectation–maximization algorithm (EM) is also one of the most practical methods for learning latent variable models. However, it can get stuck in local optima, and it is not guaranteed that the algorithm will converge to the true unknown parameters of the model. In contrast, for the method of moments, the global convergence is guaranteed under some conditions.

2.1.3 Reinforcement Learning

Reinforcement learning (RL) is an interdisciplinary area of machine learning and optimal control concerned with how an intelligent agent should take actions in a dynamic environment in order to maximize a reward signal. Reinforcement learning is one of the three basic machine learning paradigms, alongside supervised learning and unsupervised learning.

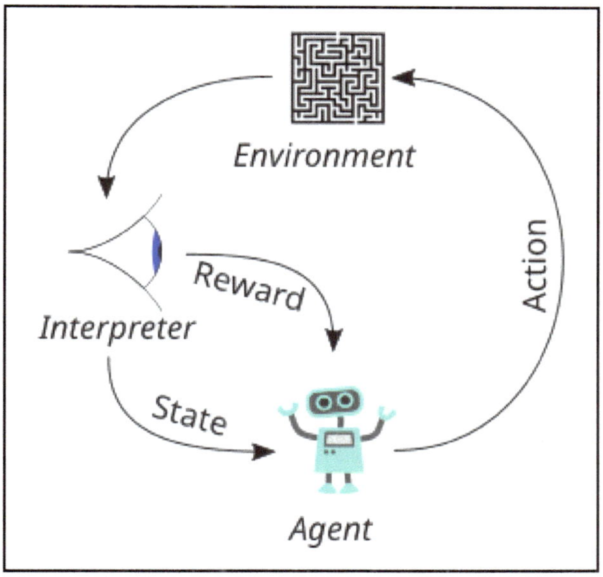

Fig: The Typical Framing of a Reinforcement Learning (RL) Scenario: An Agent takes Actions in an Environment, which is Interpreted into a Reward and a State Representation, which are Fed Back to the Agent

Reinforcement learning differs from supervised learning in not needing labelled input-output pairs to be presented, and in not needing sub-optimal actions to be explicitly corrected. Instead, the focus is on finding a balance between exploration (of uncharted territory) and exploitation (of current knowledge) with the goal of maximizing the cumulative reward (the feedback of which might be incomplete or delayed). The search for this balance is known as the exploration–exploitation dilemma.

The environment is typically stated in the form of a Markov decision process (MDP), as many reinforcement learning algorithms use dynamic programming techniques. The main difference between classical dynamic programming methods and reinforcement learning algorithms is that the latter do not assume knowledge of an exact mathematical model of the Markov decision process, and they target large MDPs where exact methods become infeasible.

Principles

Due to its generality, reinforcement learning is studied in many disciplines, such as game theory, control theory, operations research, information theory, simulation-based optimization, multi-agent systems, swarm intelligence, and statistics. In the operations research and control literature, RL is called approximate dynamic programming, or neuro-dynamic programming. The problems of interest in RL have also been studied in the theory of optimal control, which is concerned mostly with the existence and characterization of optimal solutions, and algorithms for their exact computation, and less with learning or approximation (particularly in the absence of a mathematical model of the environment). Basic reinforcement learning is modeled as a Markov decision process:

- A set of environment and agent states (the state space), $\mathcal{S}$;
- A set of actions (the action space), $\mathcal{A}$, of the agent;
- $P_a(s, s') = \Pr(S_{t+1} = s' \mid S_t = s, A_t = a)$, the transition probability (at time t) from state s to state s' under action a.
- $R_a(s, s')$, the immediate reward after transition from s to s' under action a.

The purpose of reinforcement learning is for the agent to learn an optimal (or near-optimal) policy that maximizes the reward function or other user-provided reinforcement signal that accumulates from immediate rewards. This is similar to processes that appear to occur in animal psychology. For example, biological brains are hardwired to interpret signals such as pain and hunger as negative reinforcements, and interpret pleasure and food intake as positive reinforcements. In some circumstances, animals learn to adopt behaviors that optimize these rewards.

This suggests that animals are capable of reinforcement learning. A basic reinforcement learning agent interacts with its environment in discrete time steps. At each time step t, the agent receives the current state S_t and reward R_t. It then chooses an action A_t from the set of available actions, which is subsequently sent to the environment. The environment moves to a new state S_{t+1} and the reward R_{t+1} associated with the transition (S_t, A_t, S_{t+1}) is determined. The goal of a reinforcement learning agent is to learn a policy:

$$\pi : \mathcal{S} \times \mathcal{A} \rightarrow [0,1]$$
$$\pi(s, a) = \Pr(A_t = a \mid S_t = s)$$

That maximizes the expected cumulative reward. Formulating the problem as a Markov decision process assumes the agent directly observes the current environmental state; in this case, the problem is said to have full observability. If the agent only has access to a subset of states, or if the observed states are corrupted by noise, the agent is said to have partial observability, and formally the problem must be formulated as a partially observable Markov decision process. In both cases, the set of actions available to the agent can be restricted.

For example, the state of an account balance could be restricted to be positive; if the current value of the state is 3 and the state transition attempts to reduce the value by 4, the transition will not be allowed. When the agent's performance is compared to that of an agent that acts optimally, the difference in performance yields the notion of regret. In order to act near optimally, the agent must reason about long-term consequences of its actions (i.e., maximize future rewards), although the immediate reward associated with this might be negative. Thus, reinforcement learning is particularly well-suited to problems that include a long-term versus short-term reward trade-off. It has been applied successfully to various problems, including energy storage, robot control, photovoltaic generators, backgammon, checkers, Go (AlphaGo), and autonomous driving systems. Two elements make reinforcement learning powerful: the use of samples to optimize performance, and the use of function approximation to deal with large environments. Thanks to these two key components, RL can be used in large environments in the following situations:

- A model of the environment is known, but an analytic solution is not available.
- Only a simulation model of the environment is given (the subject of simulation-based optimization).
- The only way to collect information about the environment is to interact with it.

The first two of these problems could be considered planning problems (since some form of model is available), while the last one could be considered to be a genuine learning problem. However, reinforcement learning converts both planning problems to machine learning problems.

Exploration

The exploration vs. exploitation trade-off has been most thoroughly studied through the multi-armed bandit problem and for finite state space Markov decision processes in Burnetas and Katehakis (1997). Reinforcement learning requires clever exploration mechanisms; randomly selecting actions, without reference to an estimated probability distribution, shows poor performance. The case of (small finite Markov decision processes is relatively well understood. However, due to the lack of algorithms that scale well with the number of states (or scale to problems with infinite state spaces), simple exploration methods are the most practical.

One such method is ε-greedy, where $0 < \varepsilon < 1$ is a parameter controlling the amount of exploration vs. exploitation. With probability $1 - \varepsilon$, exploitation is chosen, and the agent chooses the action that it believes has the best long-term effect (ties between actions are broken uniformly at random). Alternatively, with probability ε, exploration is chosen, and the action is chosen uniformly at random. ε is usually a fixed parameter but can be adjusted either according to a schedule (making the agent explore progressively less), or adaptively based on heuristics.

Statistical Comparison of Reinforcement Learning Algorithms

Efficient comparison of RL algorithms is essential for research, deployment and monitoring of RL systems. To compare different algorithms on a given environment an agent can be trained for each algorithm. Since the performance is sensitive to implementation details, all algorithms should be implemented as closely as possible to each other. After the training is finished, the agents can be run on a sample of test episodes, and their scores (returns) can be compared. Since episodes are typically assumed to be i.i.d, standard statistical tools can be used for hypothesis testing, such as T-test and permutation test. This requires to accumulate all the rewards within an episode into a single number—the episodic return. However, this causes a loss of information, as different time-steps are averaged together, possibly with different levels of noise. Whenever the noise level varies across the episode, the statistical power can be improved significantly, by weighting the rewards according to their estimated noise.

Challenges and Limitations

- **Sample Inefficiency:** RL algorithms often require a large number of interactions with the environment to learn effective policies, leading to high computational costs and time-intensive to train the agent. For instance, OpenAI's Dota-playing bot utilized thousands of years of simulated gameplay to achieve human-level performance. Techniques like experience replay and curriculum learning have been proposed to deprive sample inefficiency, but these techniques add more complexity and are not always sufficient for real-world applications.
- **Stability and Convergence Issues:** Training RL models, particularly for deep neural network-based models, can be unstable and prone to divergence. A small change in the policy or environment can lead to

extreme fluctuations in performance, making it difficult to achieve consistent results. This instability is further enhanced in the case of the continuous or high-dimensional action space, where the learning step becomes more complex and less predictable.

- **Generalization and Transferability:** The RL agents trained in specific environments often struggle to generalize their learned policies to new, unseen scenarios. This is the major setback preventing the application of RL to dynamic real-world environments where adaptability is crucial. The challenge is to develop such algorithms that can transfer knowledge across tasks and environments without extensive retraining.
- **Bias and Reward Function Issues:** Designing appropriate reward functions is critical in RL because poorly designed reward functions can lead to unintended behaviors. In addition, RL systems trained on biased data may perpetuate existing biases and lead to discriminatory or unfair outcomes. Both of these issues requires careful consideration of reward structures and data sources to ensure fairness and desired behaviors.

2.2 NATURAL LANGUAGE PROCESSING (NLP) IN CLINICAL TEXT ANALYSIS

Natural Language Processing is reshaping the landscape of clinical text analysis, transforming unstructured narratives into structured insights that drive improved healthcare outcomes. From streamlining documentation and enhancing decision support to enabling large-scale research and monitoring public health, NLP is becoming an indispensable tool in modern medicine.

However, to fully realize its potential, it is essential to overcome challenges related to data quality, model transparency, workflow integration, and ethical use. With continued research, collaboration, and investment, NLP will play a central role in building a more intelligent, responsive, and patient-centered healthcare system.

2.2.1 Importance of Clinical Text in Healthcare

Clinical text represents one of the richest sources of medical information, capturing a clinician's reasoning, observations, impressions, and decisions in natural language. Unlike structured data fields, which are limited to predefined options, free-text documentation allows healthcare providers to describe complex clinical scenarios with nuance and detail.

For example, a physician may write a note about a patient's unusual reaction to a medication or record subtle findings in a physical exam that do not fit into standard data fields. These insights are often critical for comprehensive patient care and clinical decision-making. However, because clinical text is unstructured and varies significantly in format and language style, it is challenging to extract and analyze without specialized tools. This is where NLP comes in, enabling the conversion of unstructured text into usable and analyzable data.

2.2.2 Fundamentals of NLP in Clinical Contexts

NLP in clinical settings involves a variety of techniques designed to handle the specific characteristics of medical language. These techniques include tokenization, part-of-speech tagging, named entity recognition, syntactic parsing, and semantic analysis. Tokenization involves breaking down text into individual words or phrases, while named entity recognition (NER) identifies and classifies key medical terms such as drug names, disease conditions, body parts, and lab values. Semantic analysis further helps in understanding the meaning of sentences, including context and negation. For instance, recognizing the difference between "no evidence of pneumonia" and "evidence of pneumonia" is critical in clinical interpretation.

One unique challenge in clinical NLP is the use of domain-specific terminology, abbreviations, and jargon. Clinicians often use shorthand, acronyms, and telegraphic language in their notes, which makes standard NLP techniques insufficient. To address this, clinical NLP systems are often trained on specialized corpora and use medical ontologies such as SNOMED CT, ICD, LOINC, and UMLS to standardize and map terms. These efforts ensure that the extracted data is both meaningful and compatible with other health information systems.

2.2.3 Applications of NLP in Clinical Text Analysis

NLP is being applied in a wide range of clinical applications, revolutionizing the way healthcare providers interact with and utilize medical information. One of the most prominent uses is in automated coding and documentation. NLP systems can extract diagnostic and procedural codes from physician notes, facilitating billing and compliance with regulatory standards. This reduces administrative burden and ensures accurate reimbursement.

Another significant application is clinical decision support. NLP can extract relevant information from patient histories and combine it with real-time data to generate alerts or recommendations. For example, if a physician notes that a patient has a history of adverse reactions to a drug, an NLP-powered system can flag this information before the drug is prescribed again. Similarly, NLP can help identify patients who meet the criteria for specific clinical trials or who require follow-up for chronic conditions, thereby enhancing care coordination.

NLP is also used in disease surveillance and epidemiological studies. By analyzing large volumes of clinical text, public health organizations can detect outbreaks, monitor disease trends, and evaluate treatment effectiveness. In oncology, for example, NLP can be used to extract cancer staging, biomarker status, and treatment responses from pathology reports, enabling population-level research on cancer outcomes. Patient safety is another domain where NLP has shown promise. Systems can scan clinical notes to detect mentions of adverse drug events, falls, infections, and other complications. These insights can then be used to improve safety protocols and reduce harm. Moreover, NLP has applications in patient sentiment analysis and feedback by processing comments from patient surveys, social media, or online health forums, offering insights into patient experiences and satisfaction.

2.2.4 Challenges in Clinical NLP Implementation

Despite its potential, the implementation of NLP in clinical text analysis faces several challenges. One of the foremost issues is data privacy and security. Clinical text contains highly sensitive information, and any NLP system handling such data must comply with strict regulations such as HIPAA. This limits access to large annotated datasets required for training robust models, especially in multi-institutional or cross-border contexts.

Another challenge is variability in language usage. Clinicians use different styles of writing, and even within the same institution, there can be significant differences in how medical notes are documented. This inconsistency complicates the task of developing generalizable NLP models. Furthermore, the presence of ambiguous terms, misspellings, and context-specific meanings can lead to errors in interpretation. Model transparency and interpretability are additional concerns. Clinicians and healthcare administrators need to understand how NLP systems arrive at their conclusions, especially when used in decision support. Many NLP models, particularly those based on deep learning, operate as “black boxes” with limited interpretability. This can hinder trust and adoption in clinical environments.

Integration into clinical workflows also presents a hurdle. For NLP systems to be effective, they must be seamlessly embedded into electronic health record systems and align with the needs and routines of healthcare professionals. Poorly integrated tools can increase cognitive load or create new documentation tasks, reducing rather than enhancing efficiency.

2.2.5 Recent Advancements and Future Directions

Recent advancements in NLP, particularly through the use of transformer-based models such as BERT, GPT, and BioBERT, have significantly improved performance in clinical text tasks. These models can understand context, handle long-form text, and generate more accurate interpretations of complex medical language. BioBERT and ClinicalBERT, which are pre-trained on biomedical and clinical text respectively, have shown strong performance in tasks such as entity recognition, relation extraction, and question answering. Another promising development is the integration of NLP with other AI technologies, including machine learning, image analysis, and predictive analytics. Multimodal systems that combine clinical text with imaging, lab data, and genomics are being developed to provide a more comprehensive view of the patient and support precision medicine. Looking forward, the adoption of open standards and shared datasets will be crucial for accelerating progress. Initiatives such as MIMIC (Medical Information Mart for Intensive Care) and n2c2 (National NLP Clinical Challenges) provide researchers with access to de-identified clinical text, fostering innovation and collaboration. Efforts to improve explainability, reduce bias, and ensure fairness in NLP systems are also gaining momentum, ensuring that these technologies are equitable and trustworthy.

2.3 COMPUTER VISION IN MEDICAL IMAGING

Computer vision in medical imaging represents not a replacement for human expertise but rather a powerful augmentation of clinical capabilities. The most effective implementations will leverage the strengths of both AI and human practitioners—combining the speed, consistency, and pattern recognition of machine learning with the clinical judgment, experience, and patient-centered focus of healthcare professionals. As the technology matures and overcomes current challenges, it has the potential to significantly improve diagnostic accuracy, reduce healthcare costs, and enhance patient outcomes across numerous medical specialties.

The successful integration of computer vision into routine clinical practice will require continued collaboration between AI developers, radiologists, healthcare administrators, and regulators. Addressing concerns about data privacy, algorithmic bias, and clinical validation will be essential to building trust in these systems. Medical education must also evolve to prepare future physicians for working alongside AI tools, emphasizing both technical understanding and critical evaluation of algorithmic outputs. Ultimately, the goal is not to automate diagnosis but to create synergistic human-AI partnerships that deliver better, faster, and more accessible healthcare for all patients. As computer vision technology continues its rapid advancement, its role in medical imaging will only grow more central, ushering in a new standard of precision medicine and diagnostic excellence. The future of computer vision in medical imaging promises even more sophisticated applications as technology continues to advance.

One exciting development is the emergence of multimodal AI systems that can analyze and correlate findings across different imaging modalities—for example, combining MRI, CT, and PET scans to provide a more comprehensive diagnostic assessment. These integrated approaches may uncover disease patterns that would be invisible when examining single imaging types in isolation. Another promising direction is the incorporation of clinical context into image analysis, where AI systems consider patient history, lab results, and other medical data alongside imaging findings to generate more holistic diagnostic interpretations.

Real-time imaging analysis represents another frontier for computer vision applications. In interventional radiology and image-guided surgery, AI systems could provide instantaneous feedback during procedures, helping clinicians navigate complex anatomy and avoid critical structures. Portable imaging devices equipped with computer vision capabilities are also being developed for point-of-care diagnostics in resource-limited settings, potentially democratizing access to advanced medical imaging. Furthermore, the combination of computer vision with augmented and virtual reality technologies may revolutionize medical education and surgical planning, allowing physicians to interact with three-dimensional reconstructions of patient anatomy.

Perhaps most transformative will be the integration of computer vision with other AI technologies like natural language processing to create comprehensive diagnostic support systems. These platforms could automatically generate structured radiology reports, correlate imaging findings with electronic health records, and even suggest appropriate follow-up tests or treatments. As these systems become more sophisticated, they may evolve into true clinical decision support tools that assist throughout the entire diagnostic and treatment pathway rather than just analyzing individual images.

2.4 MULTIMODAL AI: INTEGRATING IMAGE, TEXT, AND GENOMIC DATA

The field of artificial intelligence (AI) in healthcare is undergoing a profound transformation, driven by the increasing availability of diverse data types and the need for more comprehensive diagnostic and prognostic tools. Multimodal AI, which refers to the integration of multiple data modalities such as medical images, clinical text, and genomic information, is at the forefront of this revolution.

By combining these distinct yet complementary sources of information, multimodal AI systems are poised to deliver a more holistic understanding of patient health, improve diagnostic accuracy, and enable truly personalized medicine. The current landscape of multimodal AI is shaped by advances in machine learning algorithms, the proliferation of digital health records, and the growing recognition that single-modality approaches often fall short in capturing the complexity of human disease.

2.4.1 Rationale for Multimodal Integration

Traditional AI models in healthcare have typically focused on a single data type, such as radiological images or structured laboratory results. While these models have achieved impressive results in specific tasks, they are inherently limited by the scope of the data they analyze. Human health, however, is multifaceted, with disease processes manifesting across various biological, anatomical, and clinical dimensions. For example, a cancer diagnosis may rely on imaging findings, histopathological features, genetic mutations, and patient history. Multimodal AI seeks to bridge these silos by integrating data from different sources, thereby capturing the full spectrum of disease characteristics. This approach not only enhances the richness of the information available for analysis but also mirrors the way clinicians synthesize diverse data points to arrive at a diagnosis or treatment plan.

2.4.2 Integrating Medical Images: Beyond Visual Patterns

Medical imaging remains a cornerstone of diagnosis in many specialties, providing critical insights into anatomical structures and pathological changes. AI models, particularly those based on deep learning, have demonstrated remarkable proficiency in interpreting images such as X-rays, CT scans, and MRIs. However, the true potential of imaging data is realized when it is combined with other modalities. For instance, in oncology, the integration of radiological images with histopathological slides and genomic profiles can reveal correlations between tumor appearance, cellular architecture, and underlying genetic drivers. Multimodal AI systems can analyze these relationships, uncovering patterns that may not be apparent when each data type is considered in isolation. This capability is especially valuable in complex cases where imaging findings are ambiguous or where subtle features may have significant clinical implications.

2.4.3 Harnessing Clinical Text: Unlocking Unstructured Data

A significant portion of healthcare data exists in unstructured text form, including physician notes, discharge summaries, pathology reports, and patient narratives. Natural language processing (NLP) techniques have advanced rapidly, enabling AI systems to extract meaningful information from these textual sources. When integrated with imaging and genomic data, clinical text provides essential context that can refine diagnostic and prognostic models. For example, a radiology report may describe incidental findings or clinical suspicions that are not captured in the image itself. Similarly, patient history documented in electronic health records can inform risk stratification and guide personalized treatment recommendations. Multimodal AI leverages NLP to synthesize this wealth of unstructured data, ensuring that critical clinical nuances are not overlooked in the decision-making process.

2.4.4 Genomic Data: The Blueprint of Disease

The advent of high-throughput sequencing technologies has ushered in a new era of precision medicine, with genomic data playing an increasingly central role in diagnosis and therapy selection. Genetic mutations, gene expression profiles, and other molecular markers provide insights into disease mechanisms, prognosis, and therapeutic response. However, the interpretation of genomic data in isolation can be challenging, as the clinical significance of many variants remains uncertain. Multimodal AI addresses this challenge by integrating genomic information with imaging and clinical data, enabling a more comprehensive assessment of disease. For instance, in oncology, the combination of tumor imaging, pathology, and genomic sequencing can inform the selection of targeted therapies and predict treatment outcomes. This integrated approach not only enhances diagnostic accuracy but also supports the development of novel biomarkers and therapeutic strategies.

2.4.5 Technical Advances Enabling Multimodal AI

The successful integration of image, text, and genomic data requires sophisticated machine learning architectures capable of handling heterogeneous inputs. Recent advances in deep learning, particularly the development of transformer models and attention mechanisms, have facilitated the fusion of multiple data modalities. These models can learn complex relationships between different types of data, allowing for joint representation and analysis. Additionally, the increasing availability of large, annotated multimodal datasets has accelerated the training and validation of these systems. Data harmonization and standardization efforts are also critical, as they ensure that information from disparate sources can be effectively combined. Cloud computing and high-performance hardware further support the computational demands of multimodal AI, enabling real-time analysis and deployment in clinical settings.

2.4.6 Clinical Applications and Impact

Multimodal AI is already demonstrating its value across a range of clinical applications. In cancer care, integrated models are being used to predict tumor behavior, guide biopsy decisions, and personalize treatment plans. For example, a multimodal AI system might combine mammography images, pathology reports, and genetic risk factors to assess the likelihood of breast cancer recurrence. In neurology, the integration of brain imaging, clinical notes, and genetic data is enhancing the diagnosis and management of complex disorders such as epilepsy and neurodegenerative diseases. Cardiovascular medicine is also benefiting from multimodal approaches, with AI models that synthesize echocardiograms, lab results, and patient histories to predict heart failure progression and optimize therapy. These applications underscore the potential of multimodal AI to improve patient outcomes by providing more accurate, timely, and individualized care.

2.4.7 Challenges and Considerations

Despite its promise, the implementation of multimodal AI in healthcare is not without challenges. Data privacy and security are paramount, particularly when integrating sensitive genomic information with clinical records. Ensuring the interoperability of different data systems and formats remains a significant hurdle, as does the need for robust data governance frameworks. The quality and completeness of data are also critical, as missing or inconsistent information can compromise model performance. Moreover, the interpretability of multimodal AI models is an ongoing concern, as clinicians must be able to understand and trust the recommendations generated by these systems. Addressing these challenges requires collaboration among clinicians, data scientists, informaticians, and policymakers, as well as ongoing investment in infrastructure and education.

2.5 DATA REQUIREMENTS AND TRAINING SETS IN DIAGNOSTIC AI

Data is the cornerstone of diagnostic AI, and the quality of training sets determines the ultimate performance, fairness, and safety of AI systems in healthcare. Building effective training datasets requires careful attention to data quantity, diversity, labeling accuracy, and ethical considerations. Challenges such as data access, annotation complexity, and privacy concerns must be addressed through collaborative frameworks, technological innovation, and transparent governance. As diagnostic AI continues to evolve, efforts to standardize data practices, promote data sharing, and invest in inclusive datasets will be key to creating systems that are accurate, equitable, and clinically useful across diverse healthcare environments.

2.5.1 Nature of Training Data

Training data refers to the dataset used to teach an AI model how to recognize patterns and make predictions. In diagnostic AI, this typically includes clinical data such as electronic health records (EHRs), lab results, medical imaging, physician notes, pathology reports, and demographic information. Depending on the diagnostic task, the type of data required can vary significantly. For instance, an AI model built to detect pneumonia in chest X-rays will require thousands of labeled X-ray images, whereas a model aimed at predicting diabetes risk might rely on structured lab values and longitudinal patient histories. The data must be appropriately labeled to be useful for supervised learning, which is the most common training method in diagnostic AI. Labeling involves tagging each piece of data with the correct diagnosis or clinical outcome. In imaging datasets, this may require radiologists to annotate regions of interest or classify the image. In textual data, such as clinical notes, labeling might involve extracting disease mentions, symptoms, or outcomes. High-quality labeling ensures that the AI model learns the correct associations and generalizes well to new, unseen cases.

2.5.2 Data Quantity and Model Performance

One of the most fundamental requirements in diagnostic AI is a large volume of data. AI models, especially deep learning models, perform best when trained on millions of data points. This is particularly true for image-based models, which need a diverse set of examples to learn features such as shape, texture, and anatomical variations. The more data an AI model sees during training, the better it becomes at identifying subtle patterns and distinguishing between similar conditions.

However, more data alone does not automatically result in better performance. The data must be representative of the target population and contain enough examples of both positive and negative cases. For example, in cancer detection, the dataset must include images of both healthy tissue and a range of cancerous lesions. Imbalanced datasets—where one class significantly outweighs another—can lead to biased models that perform poorly in clinical settings. Careful sampling and data augmentation techniques are often used to mitigate such imbalances and improve model robustness.

2.5.3 Data Diversity and Generalization

Beyond quantity, diversity in training data is crucial to ensure that diagnostic AI systems can generalize well across different populations, devices, and clinical settings. Patient data should cover a wide range of demographics, including age, gender, ethnicity, and comorbid conditions. In imaging AI, it is important to include data from different machines, manufacturers, and hospitals to account for variations in image quality and technique.

Lack of diversity in training data can lead to biased AI systems that underperform for underrepresented groups. For example, an AI model trained mostly on light-skinned individuals may not accurately diagnose dermatological conditions in darker-skinned patients. This limitation has serious implications for health equity and patient safety. To address this issue, developers must make concerted efforts to include diverse datasets and conduct fairness audits during model development. Moreover, clinical data often varies in terminology, format, and documentation practices. A diagnosis may be described differently across hospitals or even among individual physicians. NLP-based diagnostic systems must be trained on a linguistically and contextually diverse dataset to interpret clinical notes accurately. Ensuring cross-institutional variability in the training set helps build models that are more adaptable and reliable across different healthcare systems.

2.5.4 Labeling and Annotation Challenges

Accurate labeling of training data is a labor-intensive and expertise-driven process, especially in diagnostic AI. The reliability of model predictions heavily depends on the quality of annotations. In medical imaging, labels must be assigned by trained specialists such as radiologists, pathologists, or dermatologists. These professionals often need to annotate not only the presence or absence of disease but also its severity, location, and progression.

The complexity increases further in text-based data, where annotations might involve identifying medical concepts, relationships, and contextual nuances such as negation and temporality. For example, distinguishing between "history of stroke" and "no evidence of stroke" requires contextual understanding that can be challenging to capture with simple keyword tagging.

To streamline the annotation process, tools such as semi-automated labeling systems and collaborative platforms are often employed. Still, the process remains expensive and time-consuming. Moreover, inter-annotator variability—differences in labeling decisions among experts—can introduce noise and reduce model performance. Strategies such as consensus annotation and adjudication panels are used to maintain consistency and reliability in the labeled data.

2.5.5 Data Privacy and Ethical Considerations

The use of patient data in training diagnostic AI models raises important ethical and legal concerns, especially related to privacy and consent. Health data is among the most sensitive types of information, and its use is tightly regulated under laws such as HIPAA in the United States and GDPR in the European Union. Before using any clinical data for training, developers must ensure it is de-identified to protect patient identities. However, even de-identified data can sometimes be re-identified through sophisticated data linkage methods, posing a risk to patient confidentiality.

Ethical use of data also requires transparency about how the data was collected, what it will be used for, and who will benefit from the AI model. Informed consent is a key principle, although it can be complex to implement in retrospective data collection scenarios. Additionally, AI developers must consider issues of data ownership, access, and sharing. Institutions contributing valuable datasets should be acknowledged, and fair data-sharing agreements should be established to promote collaboration while respecting data sovereignty.

2.5.6 Synthetic Data and Data Augmentation

In cases where real-world data is limited or difficult to obtain, synthetic data and data augmentation techniques are often employed. Synthetic data refers to artificially generated datasets that mimic the properties of real data. For example, generative adversarial networks (GANs) can create synthetic medical images that resemble real X-rays or MRIs. These synthetic examples can be used to supplement training sets, particularly for rare conditions that are underrepresented in clinical datasets.

Data augmentation techniques involve modifying existing data to create new examples. In image analysis, this may include rotating, flipping, or altering the contrast of images. In text-based models, augmentation might involve paraphrasing or inserting synonyms. These methods help increase the effective size and variability of the dataset, improving model generalization and reducing overfitting.

While useful, synthetic and augmented data must be used cautiously. If the synthetic data does not accurately reflect clinical reality, it can introduce artifacts or mislead the model. Therefore, validation by domain experts and careful calibration are essential steps when incorporating such data into training sets.

2.5.7 Validation and Benchmarking

Once a diagnostic AI model is trained, its performance must be rigorously validated using test datasets that were not seen during training. These datasets should be as diverse and representative as possible to assess the model's generalizability. Key performance metrics include accuracy, sensitivity, specificity, precision, recall, and the area under the receiver operating characteristic curve (AUC-ROC). In diagnostic applications, false positives and false negatives carry different clinical consequences, and these must be considered in evaluating model effectiveness.

Benchmarking against existing diagnostic standards, such as human expert performance or clinical guidelines, is also necessary. Many studies now use head-to-head comparisons between AI systems and physicians to assess diagnostic accuracy. External validation on datasets from different hospitals or regions is increasingly regarded as a best practice to confirm robustness and mitigate overfitting to local data idiosyncrasies.

CHAPTER 3

Clinical Applications of AI in Diagnostics

3.1 RADIOLOGY AND IMAGING

3.1.1 Tumor Detection (CT, MRI, PET, X-ray)

CT

A computed tomography scan (CT scan), formerly called computed axial tomography scan (CAT scan), is a medical imaging technique used to obtain detailed internal images of the body. The personnel that perform CT scans are called radiographers or radiology technologists. CT scanners use a rotating X-ray tube and a row of detectors placed in a gantry to measure X-ray attenuations by different tissues inside the body.

The multiple X-ray measurements taken from different angles are then processed on a computer using tomographic reconstruction algorithms to produce tomographic (cross-sectional) images (virtual "slices") of a body. CT scans can be used in patients with metallic implants or pacemakers, for whom magnetic resonance imaging (MRI) is contraindicated.

Since its development in the 1970s, CT scanning has proven to be a versatile imaging technique. While CT is most prominently used in medical diagnosis, it can also be used to form images of non-living objects. The 1979 Nobel Prize in Physiology or Medicine was awarded jointly to South African-American physicist Allan MacLeod Cormack and British electrical engineer Godfrey Hounsfield "for the development of computer-assisted tomography".

Types

On the basis of image acquisition and procedures, various type of scanners are available in the market.

- **Sequential CT:** Sequential CT, also known as step-and-shoot CT, is a type of scanning method in which the CT table moves stepwise. The table increments to a particular location and then stops which is followed by the X-ray tube rotation and acquisition of a slice. The table then increments again, and another slice is taken. The table movement stops while taking slices. This results in an increased time of scanning.

- **Spiral CT:** Spinning tube, commonly called spiral CT, or helical CT, is an imaging technique in which an entire X-ray tube is spun around the central axis of the area being scanned. These are the dominant type of scanners on the market because they have been manufactured longer and offer a lower cost of production and purchase. The main limitation of this type of CT is the bulk and inertia of the equipment (X-ray tube assembly and detector array on the opposite side of the circle) which limits the speed at which the equipment can spin. Some designs use two X-ray sources and detector arrays offset by an angle, as a technique to improve temporal resolution.

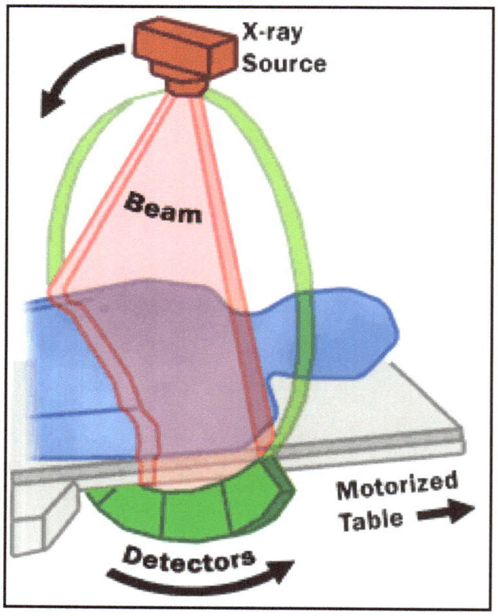

Fig: Drawing of CT Fan Beam and Patient in a CT Imaging System

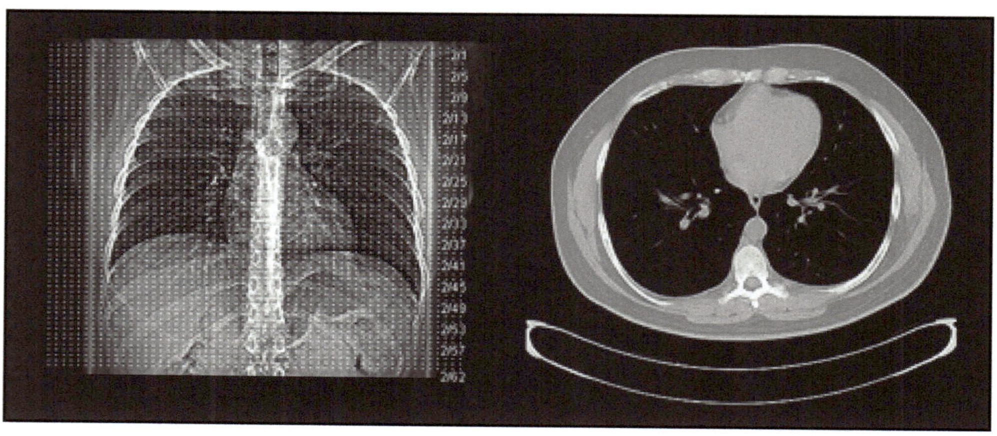

Fig: CT Scan of the Thorax. The Axial Slice (Right) is the Image that Corresponds to Number 2/33 on the Coronal Slice (Left)

- **Electron Beam Tomography:** Electron beam tomography (EBT) is a specific form of CT in which a large enough X-ray tube is constructed so that only the path of the electrons, travelling between the cathode and anode of the X-ray tube, are spun using deflection coils. This type had a major advantage since sweep speeds can be much faster, allowing for less blurry imaging of moving structures, such as the heart and arteries. Fewer scanners of this design have been produced when compared with spinning tube types, mainly due to the higher cost associated with building a much larger X-ray tube and detector array and limited anatomical coverage.

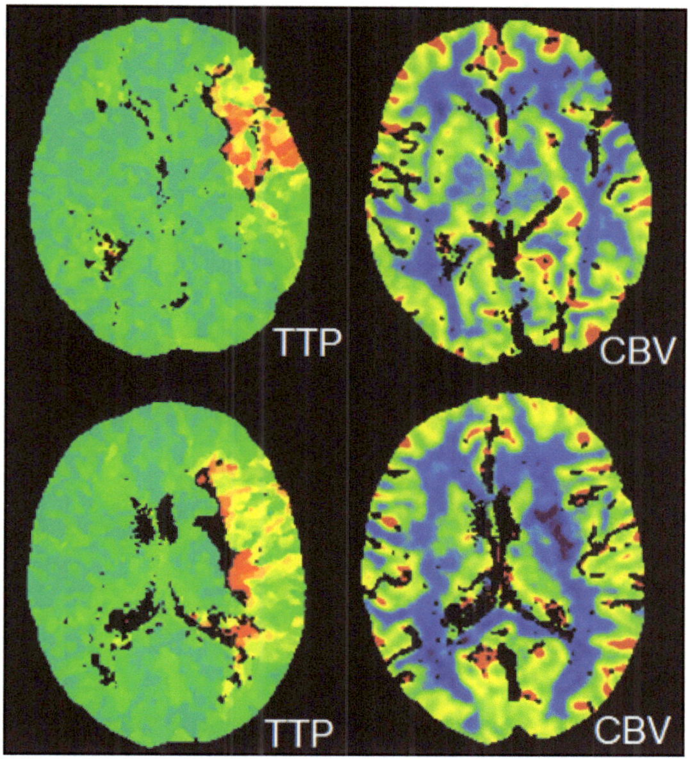

Fig: CT Perfusion Scan of the Brain

- **Dual Energy CT:** Dual energy CT, also known as spectral CT, is an advancement of computed Tomography in which two energies are used to create two sets of data. A dual energy CT may employ dual source, single source with dual detector layer, single source with energy switching methods to get two different sets of data.
  - Dual source CT is an advanced scanner with a two X-ray tube detector system, unlike conventional single tube systems. These two detector systems are mounted on a single gantry at 90° in the same plane. Dual source CT scanners allow fast scanning with higher temporal resolution by acquiring

a full CT slice in only half a rotation. Fast imaging reduces motion blurring at high heart rates and potentially allowing for shorter breath-hold time. This is particularly useful for ill patients having difficulty holding their breath or unable to take heart-rate lowering medication.

- Single source with energy switching is another mode of dual energy CT in which a single tube is operated at two different energies by switching the energies frequently.

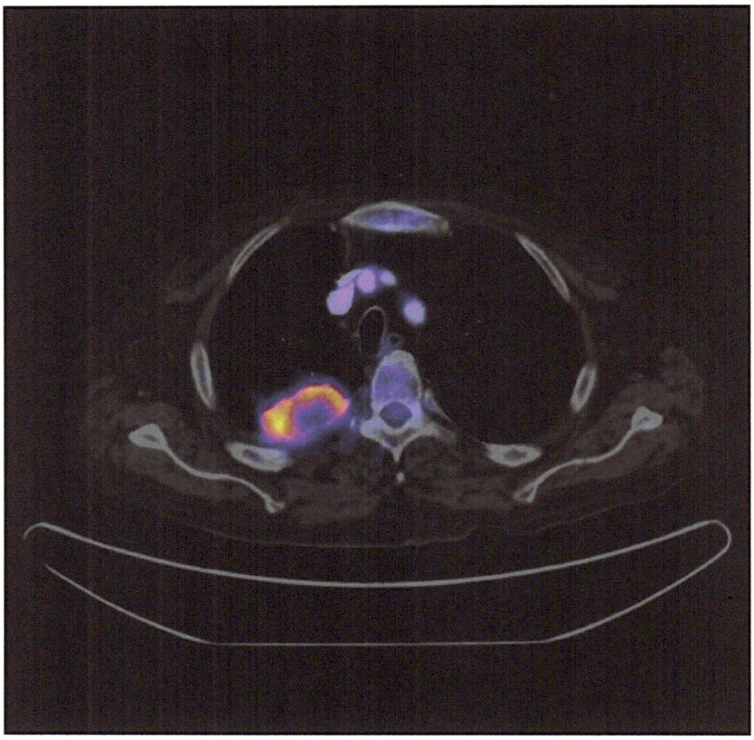

Fig: PET-CT Scan of Chest

- **CT Perfusion Imaging:** CT perfusion imaging is a specific form of CT to assess flow through blood vessels whilst injecting a contrast agent. Blood flow, blood transit time, and organ blood volume, can all be calculated with reasonable sensitivity and specificity. This type of CT may be used on the heart, although sensitivity and specificity for detecting abnormalities are still lower than for other forms of CT. This may also be used on the brain, where CT perfusion imaging can often detect poor brain perfusion well before it is detected using a conventional spiral CT scan. This is better for stroke diagnosis than other CT types.
- **PET CT:** Positron emission tomography–computed tomography is a hybrid CT modality which combines, in a single gantry, a positron emission tomography (PET) scanner and an X-ray computed tomography (CT) scanner, to acquire sequential images from both devices in the same

session, which are combined into a single superposed (co-registered) image. Thus, functional imaging obtained by PET, which depicts the spatial distribution of metabolic or biochemical activity in the body can be more precisely aligned or correlated with anatomic imaging obtained by CT scanning. PET-CT gives both anatomical and functional details of an organ under examination and is helpful in detecting different type of cancers.

Medical Use

Since its introduction in the 1970s, CT has become an important tool in medical imaging to supplement conventional X-ray imaging and medical ultrasonography. It has more recently been used for preventive medicine or screening for disease, for example, CT colonography for people with a high risk of colon cancer, or full-motion heart scans for people with a high risk of heart disease. Several institutions offer full-body scans for the general population although this practice goes against the advice and official position of many professional organizations in the field primarily due to the radiation dose applied. The use of CT scans has increased dramatically over the last two decades in many countries. An estimated 72 million scans were performed in the United States in 2007 and more than 80 million in 2015.

- **Head:** CT scanning of the head is typically used to detect infarction (stroke), tumors, calcifications, haemorrhage, and bone trauma. Hypodense (dark) structures can indicate edema and infarction, hyperdense (bright) structures indicate calcifications and haemorrhage and bone trauma can be seen as disjunction in bone windows. Tumors can be detected by the swelling and anatomical distortion they cause, or by surrounding edema. CT scanning of the head is also used in CT-guided stereotactic surgery and radiosurgery for treatment of intracranial tumors, arteriovenous malformations, and other surgically treatable conditions using a device known as the N-localizer.
- **Neck:** Contrast CT is generally the initial study of choice for neck masses in adults. CT of the thyroid plays an important role in the evaluation of thyroid cancer. CT scans often incidentally find thyroid abnormalities, and so is often the preferred investigation modality for thyroid abnormalities.
- **Lungs:** A CT scan can be used for detecting both acute and chronic changes in the lung parenchyma, the tissue of the lungs. It is particularly helpful because normal two-dimensional X-rays do not show such defects. A variety of techniques are used, depending on the suspected abnormality. For evaluation of chronic interstitial processes such as

emphysema, and fibrosis, thin sections with high spatial frequency reconstructions are used; often scans are performed both on inspiration and expiration. This special technique is called high resolution CT that produces a sampling of the lung, and not continuous images.

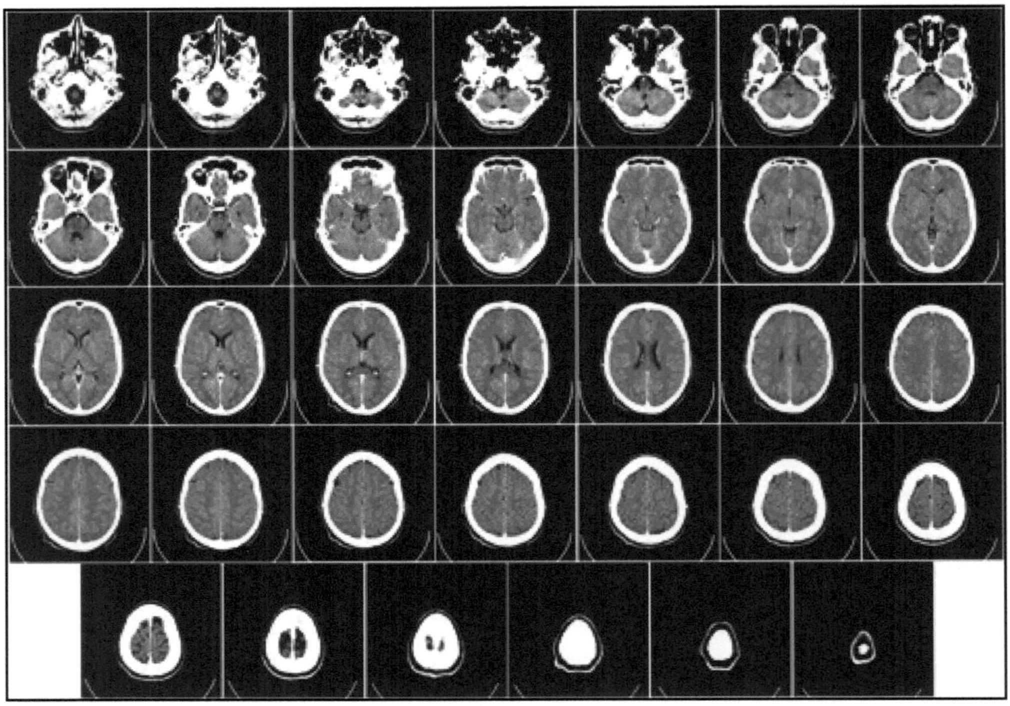

Fig: Computed Tomography of Human Brain, from Base of the Skull to Top. Taken with Intravenous Contrast Medium

- **Bronchial Wall Thickening:** Bronchial wall thickening can be seen on lung CTs and generally (but not always) implies inflammation of the bronchi. An incidentally found nodule in the absence of symptoms (sometimes referred to as an incidentaloma) may raise concerns that it might represent a tumor, either benign or malignant. Perhaps persuaded by fear, patients and doctors sometimes agree to an intensive schedule of CT scans, sometimes up to every three months and beyond the recommended guidelines, in an attempt to do surveillance on the nodules. However, established guidelines advise that patients without a prior history of cancer and whose solid nodules have not grown over a two-year period are unlikely to have any malignant cancer. For this reason, and because no research provides supporting evidence that intensive surveillance gives better outcomes, and because of risks associated with having CT scans, patients should not receive CT screening in excess of those recommended by established guidelines.

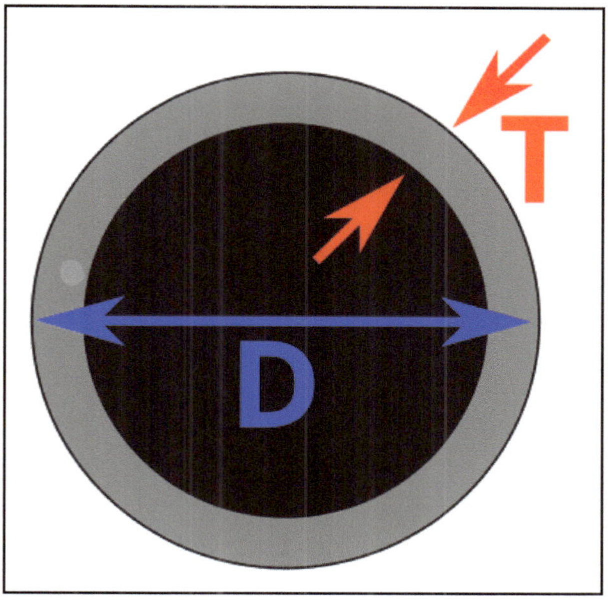

Fig: Bronchial Wall Thickness (T) and Diameter of the Bronchus (D)

- **Angiography:** Computed tomography angiography (CTA) is a type of contrast CT to visualize the arteries and veins throughout the body. This ranges from arteries serving the brain to those bringing blood to the lungs, kidneys, arms and legs. An example of this type of exam is CT pulmonary angiogram (CTPA) used to diagnose pulmonary embolism (PE). It employs computed tomography and an iodine-based contrast agent to obtain an image of the pulmonary arteries. CT scans can reduce the risk of angiography by providing clinicians with more information about the positioning and number of clots prior to the procedure.
- **Cardiac:** A CT scan of the heart is performed to gain knowledge about cardiac or coronary anatomy. Traditionally, cardiac CT scans are used to detect, diagnose, or follow up coronary artery disease. More recently CT has played a key role in the fast-evolving field of transcatheter structural heart interventions, more specifically in the transcatheter repair and replacement of heart valves. The main forms of cardiac CT scanning are:
  - **Coronary CT Angiography (CCTA):** The use of CT to assess the coronary arteries of the heart. The subject receives an intravenous injection of radiocontrast, and then the heart is scanned using a high-speed CT scanner, allowing radiologists to assess the extent of occlusion in the coronary arteries, usually to diagnose coronary artery disease.
  - **Coronary CT Calcium Scan:** Also used for the assessment of severity of coronary artery disease. Specifically, it looks for calcium deposits in the

coronary arteries that can narrow arteries and increase the risk of a heart attack. A typical coronary CT calcium scan is done without the use of radio-contrast, but it can possibly be done from contrast-enhanced images as well.

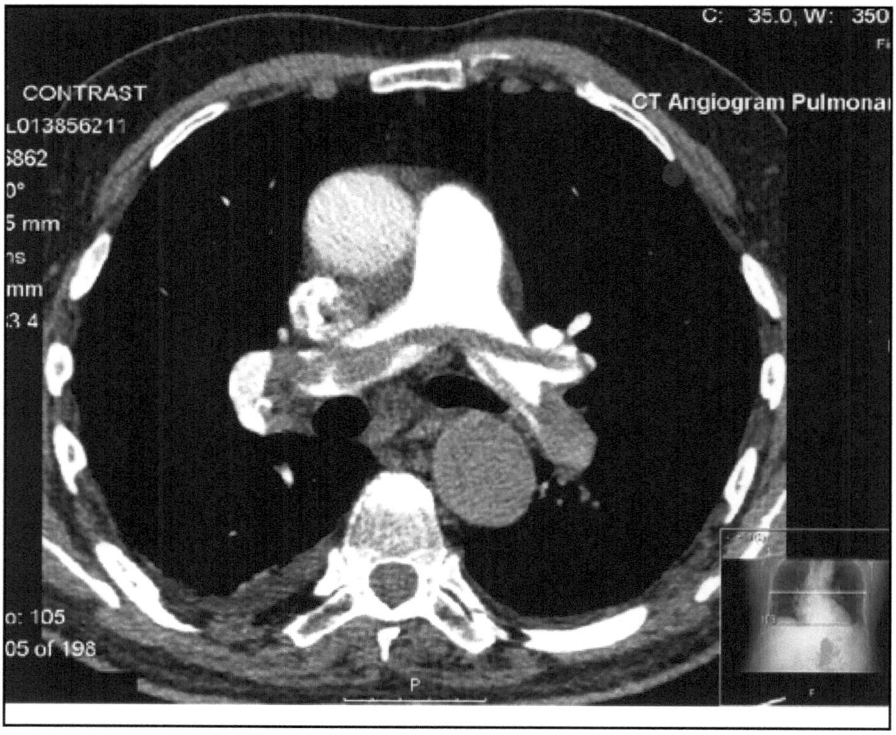

Fig: Example of a CTPA, Demonstrating a Saddle Embolus (Dark Horizontal Line) Occluding the Pulmonary Arteries (Bright White Triangle)

- **Abdomen and Pelvis:** CT is an accurate technique for diagnosis of abdominal diseases such as Crohn's disease, GIT bleeding, and diagnosis and staging of cancer, as well as follow-up after cancer treatment to assess response. It is commonly used to investigate acute abdominal pain. Non-contrast-enhanced CT scans are the gold standard for diagnosing kidney stone disease. They allow clinicians to estimate the size, volume, and density of stones, helping to guide further treatment; with size being especially important in predicting the time to spontaneous passage of a stone.
- **Axial Skeleton and Extremities:** For the axial skeleton and extremities, CT is often used to image complex fractures, especially ones around joints, because of its ability to reconstruct the area of interest in multiple planes. Fractures, ligamentous injuries, and dislocations can easily be recognized with a 0.2 mm resolution. With modern dual-energy CT scanners, new areas of use have been established, such as aiding in the diagnosis of gout.

- **Biomechanical Use:** CT is used in biomechanics to quickly reveal the geometry, anatomy, density and elastic moduli of biological tissues.

MRI

Magnetic resonance imaging (MRI) is a medical imaging technique used in radiology to generate pictures of the anatomy and the physiological processes inside the body. MRI scanners use strong magnetic fields, magnetic field gradients, and radio waves to form images of the organs in the body. MRI does not involve X-rays or the use of ionizing radiation, which distinguishes it from computed tomography (CT) and positron emission tomography (PET) scans. MRI is a medical application of nuclear magnetic resonance (NMR) which can also be used for imaging in other NMR applications, such as NMR spectroscopy.

MRI is widely used in hospitals and clinics for medical diagnosis, staging and follow-up of disease. Compared to CT, MRI provides better contrast in images of soft tissues, e.g. in the brain or abdomen. However, it may be perceived as less comfortable by patients, due to the usually longer and louder measurements with the subject in a long, confining tube, although "open" MRI designs mostly relieve this. Additionally, implants and other non-removable metal in the body can pose a risk and may exclude some patients from undergoing an MRI examination safely.

MRI was originally called NMRI (nuclear magnetic resonance imaging), but "nuclear" was dropped to avoid negative associations. Certain atomic nuclei are able to absorb radio frequency (RF) energy when placed in an external magnetic field; the resultant evolving spin polarization can induce an RF signal in a radio frequency coil and thereby be detected. In other words, the nuclear magnetic spin of protons in the hydrogen nuclei resonates with the RF incident waves and emit coherent radiation with compact direction, energy (frequency) and phase.

This coherent amplified radiation is then detected by RF antennas close to the subject being examined. It is a process similar to masers. In clinical and research MRI, hydrogen atoms are most often used to generate a macroscopic polarized radiation that is detected by the antennas. Hydrogen atoms are naturally abundant in humans and other biological organisms, particularly in water and fat.

For this reason, most MRI scans essentially map the location of water and fat in the body. Pulses of radio waves excite the nuclear spin energy transition, and magnetic field gradients localize the polarization in space. By varying the parameters of the pulse sequence, different contrasts may be generated between tissues based on the relaxation properties of the hydrogen atoms therein. Since its development in the 1970s and 1980s, MRI has proven to be a versatile imaging technique. While MRI is most prominently used in diagnostic medicine and biomedical research, it also may be used to form images of non-living objects, such as mummies. Diffusion MRI and functional MRI extend the utility of MRI to capture neuronal tracts and blood flow respectively in the nervous system, in addition to detailed spatial images. The sustained increase in demand for MRI within health systems has led to concerns about cost effectiveness and overdiagnosis.

Diagnostics

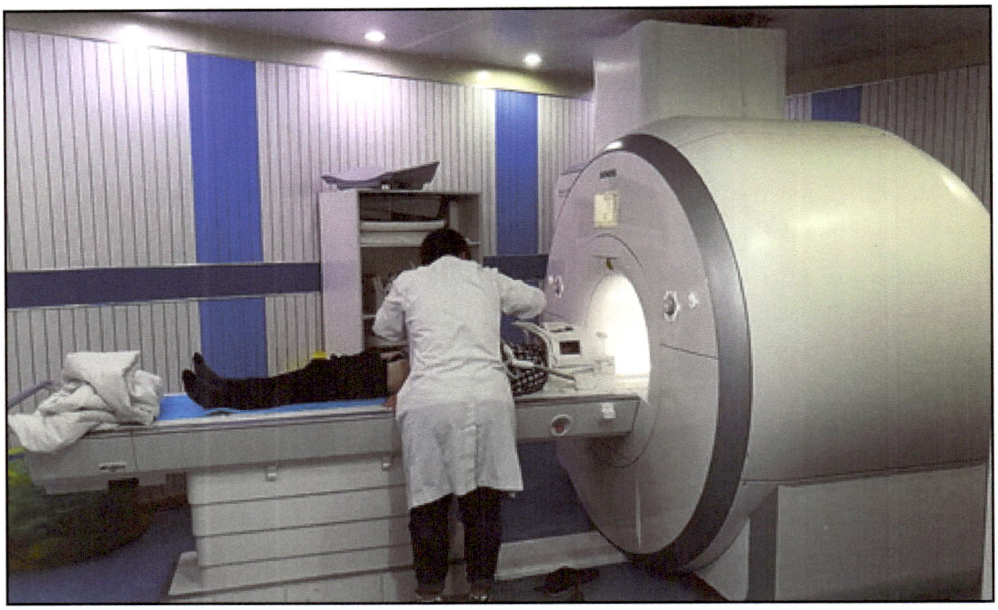

Fig: Patient Being Positioned for MR Study of the Head and Abdomen

MRI has a wide range of applications in medical diagnosis and around 50,000 scanners are estimated to be in use worldwide. MRI affects diagnosis and treatment in many specialties although the effect on improved health outcomes is disputed in certain cases. MRI is the investigation of choice in the preoperative staging of rectal and prostate cancer and has a role in the diagnosis, staging, and follow-up of other tumors, as well as for determining areas of tissue for sampling in biobanking.

- **Neuroimaging:** MRI is the investigative tool of choice for neurological cancers over CT, as it offers better visualization of the posterior cranial fossa, containing the brainstem and the cerebellum. The contrast provided between grey and white matter makes MRI the best choice for many conditions of the central nervous system, including demyelinating diseases, dementia, cerebrovascular disease, infectious diseases, Alzheimer's disease and epilepsy. Since multiple images are taken milliseconds apart, it can show how the brain responds to different stimuli, enabling researchers to study both functional and structural brain abnormalities in psychological disorders. MRI also is used in guided stereotactic surgery and radiosurgery for treatment of intracranial tumors, arteriovenous malformations, and other surgically treatable conditions using a device known as the N-localizer. New tools that implement artificial intelligence in healthcare have demonstrated higher image quality and morphometric analysis in neuroimaging with the application of a denoising system. The record for the highest spatial resolution of a whole intact brain (postmortem) is 100 microns, from Massachusetts General Hospital. The data was published in Nature in October 2019. Though MRI is used widely in research on mental disabilities, based on a 2024 systematic literature review and meta analysis commissioned by the Patient-Centered Outcomes Research Institute (PCORI), available research using MRI scans to diagnose ADHD showed great variability. The authors conclude that MRI cannot be reliably used to assist in making a clinical diagnosis of ADHD.

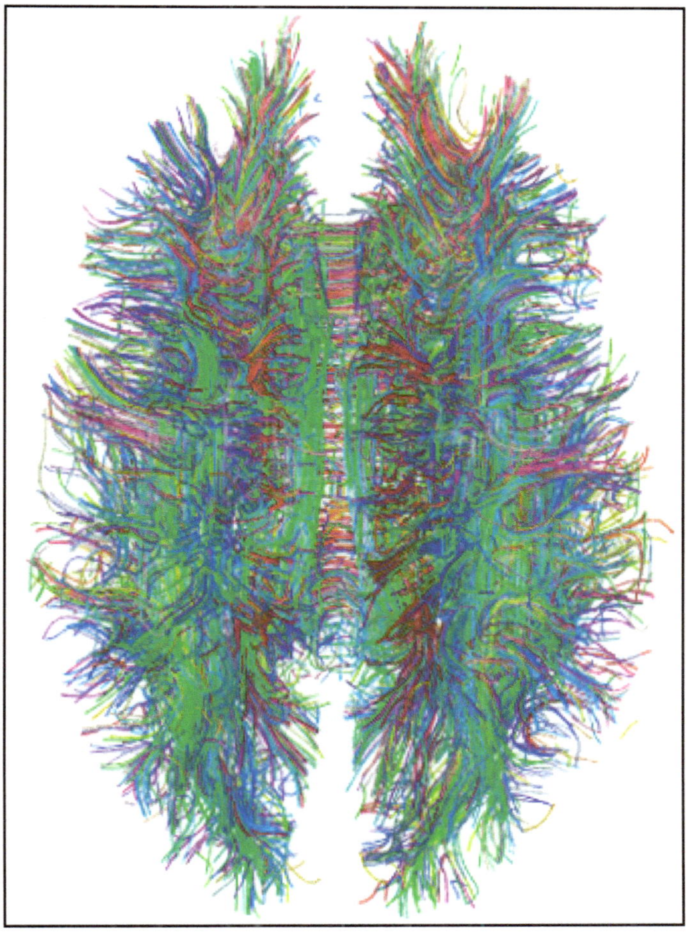

Fig: MRI Diffusion Tensor Imaging of White Matter Tracts

- **Cardiovascular:** Cardiac MRI is complementary to other imaging techniques, such as echocardiography, cardiac CT, and nuclear medicine. It can be used to assess the structure and the function of the heart. Its applications include assessment of myocardial ischemia and viability, cardiomyopathies, myocarditis, iron overload, vascular diseases, and congenital heart disease.
- **Musculoskeletal:** Applications in the musculoskeletal system include spinal imaging, assessment of joint disease, and soft tissue tumors. MRI techniques can also be used for diagnostic imaging of systemic muscle diseases including genetic muscle diseases. Swallowing movements of the throat and esophagus can cause motion artifacts over the imaged spine. Therefore, a saturation pulse applied over this region can help to avoid these artifacts. Motion artifacts arising due to the pumping of the heart can be reduced by timing the MRI pulse according to heart cycles. Blood vessel flow artifacts can be reduced by applying saturation pulses above and below the region of interest.
- **Liver and Gastrointestinal:** Hepatobiliary MRI is used to detect and characterize lesions of the liver, pancreas, and bile ducts. Focal or diffuse disorders of the liver may be evaluated using diffusion-weighted, opposed-phase imaging and dynamic contrast enhancement sequences. Extracellular contrast agents are used widely in liver MRI, and newer hepatobiliary contrast agents also provide the opportunity to perform functional biliary imaging. Anatomical imaging of the bile ducts is achieved by using a heavily T2-weighted sequence in magnetic resonance cholangiopancreatography (MRCP). Functional imaging of the pancreas is performed following administration of secretin. MR enterography provides non-invasive assessment of inflammatory bowel disease and small bowel tumors. MR-colonography may play a role in the detection of large polyps in patients at increased risk of colorectal cancer.
- **Angiography:** Magnetic resonance angiography (MRA) generates pictures of the arteries to evaluate them for stenosis (abnormal narrowing) or aneurysms (vessel wall dilatations, at risk of rupture). MRA is often used to evaluate the arteries of the neck and brain, the thoracic and abdominal aorta, the renal arteries, and the legs (called a "run-off"). A variety of techniques can be used to generate the pictures, such as administration of a paramagnetic contrast agent (gadolinium) or using a technique known as "flow-related enhancement" (e.g., 2D and 3D time-of-flight sequences), where most of the signal on an

image is due to blood that recently moved into that plane. Techniques involving phase accumulation (known as phase contrast angiography) can also be used to generate flow velocity maps easily and accurately. Magnetic resonance venography (MRV) is a similar procedure that is used to image veins. In this method, the tissue is now excited inferiorly, while the signal is gathered in the plane immediately superior to the excitation plane—thus imaging the venous blood that recently moved from the excited plane.

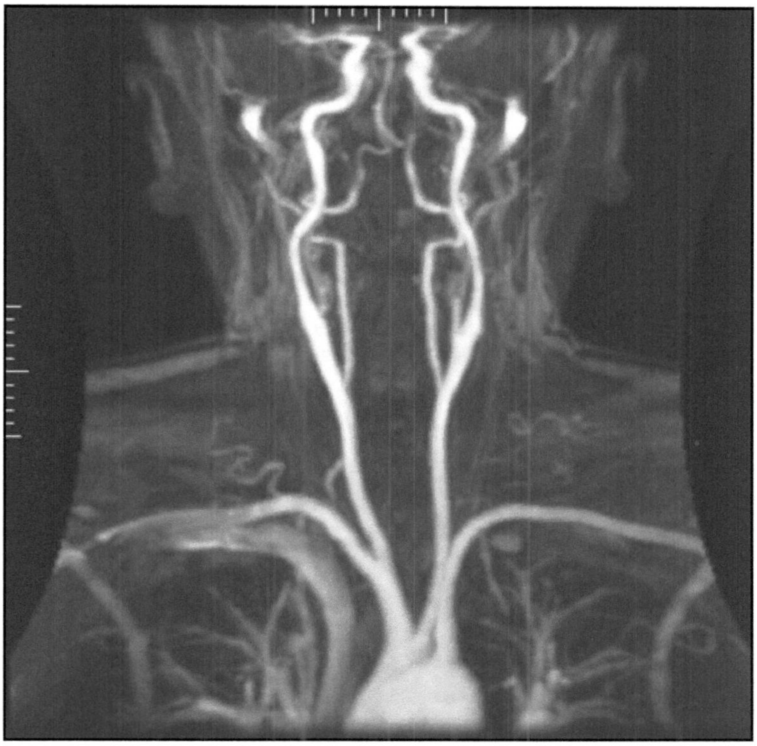

Fig: Magnetic Resonance Angiography

PET

Positron emission tomography (PET) is a functional imaging technique that uses radioactive substances known as radiotracers to visualize and measure changes in metabolic processes, and in other physiological activities including blood flow, regional chemical composition, and absorption. Different tracers are used for various imaging purposes, depending on the target process within the body, such as:

- Fluorodeoxyglucose ([^{18}F]FDG or FDG) is commonly used to detect cancer;
- [^{18}F]Sodium fluoride (Na^{18}F) is widely used for detecting bone formation;
- Oxygen-15 (^{15}O) is sometimes used to measure blood flow.

PET is a common imaging technique, a medical scintillography technique used in nuclear medicine. A radiopharmaceutical—a radioisotope attached to a drug—is injected into the body as a tracer. When the radiopharmaceutical undergoes beta plus decay, a positron is emitted, and when the positron interacts with an ordinary electron, the two particles annihilate and two gamma rays are emitted in opposite directions. These gamma rays are detected by two gamma cameras to form a three-dimensional image.

PET scanners can incorporate a computed tomography scanner (CT) and are known as PET–CT scanners. PET scan images can be reconstructed using a CT scan performed using one scanner during the same session. One of the disadvantages of a PET scanner is its high initial cost and ongoing operating costs.

Uses

PET is both a medical and research tool used in pre-clinical and clinical settings. It is used heavily in the imaging of tumors and the search for metastases within the field of clinical oncology, and for the clinical diagnosis of certain diffuse brain diseases such as those causing various types of dementias. PET is valued as a research tool to learn and enhance knowledge of the normal human brain, heart function, and support drug development. PET is also used in pre-clinical studies using animals. It allows repeated investigations into the same subjects over time, where subjects can act as their own control and substantially reduces the numbers of animals required for a given study. This approach allows research studies to reduce the sample size needed while increasing the statistical quality of its results.

Physiological processes lead to anatomical changes in the body. Since PET is capable of detecting biochemical processes as well as expression of some proteins, PET can provide molecular-level information much before any anatomic changes are visible. PET scanning does this by using radiolabelled molecular probes that have different rates of uptake depending on the type and function of tissue involved. Regional tracer uptake in various anatomic structures can be visualized and relatively quantified in terms of injected positron emitter within a PET scan.

PET imaging is best performed using a dedicated PET scanner. It is also possible to acquire PET images using a conventional dual-head gamma camera fitted with a coincidence detector. The quality of gamma-camera PET imaging is lower, and the scans take longer to acquire. However, this method allows a low-cost on-site solution to institutions with low PET scanning demand.

An alternative would be to refer these patients to another center or relying on a visit by a mobile scanner. Alternative methods of medical imaging include single-photon emission computed tomography (SPECT), computed tomography (CT), magnetic resonance imaging (MRI) and functional magnetic resonance imaging (fMRI), and ultrasound. SPECT is an imaging technique similar to PET that uses radioligands to detect molecules in the body. SPECT is less expensive and provides inferior image quality than PET.

Oncology

PET scanning with the radiotracer [^{18}F]fluorodeoxyglucose (FDG) is widely used in clinical oncology. FDG is a glucose analog that is taken up by glucose-using cells and phosphorylated by hexokinase (whose mitochondrial form is significantly elevated in rapidly growing malignant tumors). Metabolic trapping of the radioactive glucose molecule allows the PET scan to be utilized. The concentrations of imaged FDG tracer indicate tissue metabolic activity as it corresponds to the regional glucose uptake.

FDG is used to explore the possibility of cancer spreading to other body sites (cancer metastasis). These FDG PET scans for detecting cancer metastasis are the most common in standard medical care (representing 90% of current scans). The same tracer may also be used for the diagnosis of types of dementia. Less often, other radioactive tracers, usually but not always labelled with fluorine-18 (^{18}F), are used to image the tissue concentration of different kinds of molecules of interest inside the body.

A typical dose of FDG used in an oncological scan has an effective radiation dose of 7.6 mSv. Because the hydroxy group that is replaced by fluorine-18 to generate FDG is required for the next step in glucose metabolism in all cells, no further reactions occur in FDG. Furthermore, most tissues (with the notable exception of liver and kidneys) cannot remove the phosphate added by hexokinase. This means that FDG is trapped in any cell that takes it up until it decays, since phosphorylated sugars, due to their ionic charge, cannot exit from the cell. This results in intense radiolabeling of tissues with high glucose uptake, such as the normal brain, liver, kidneys, and most cancers, which have a higher glucose uptake than most normal tissue due to the Warburg effect. As a result, FDG-PET can be used for diagnosis, staging, and monitoring treatment of cancers, particularly in Hodgkin lymphoma, non-Hodgkin lymphoma, and lung cancer.

A 2020 review of research on the use of PET for Hodgkin lymphoma found evidence that negative findings in interim PET scans are linked to higher overall survival and progression-free survival; however, the certainty of the available evidence was moderate for survival, and very low for progression-free survival. A few other isotopes and radiotracers are slowly being introduced into oncology for specific purposes. For example, ^{11}C-labelled metomidate (11C-metomidate) has been used to detect tumors of adrenocortical origin. Also, fluorodopa (FDOPA) PET/CT (also called F-18-DOPA PET/CT) has proven to be a more sensitive alternative to finding and also localizing pheochromocytoma than the iobenguane (MIBG) scan.

Neuroimaging

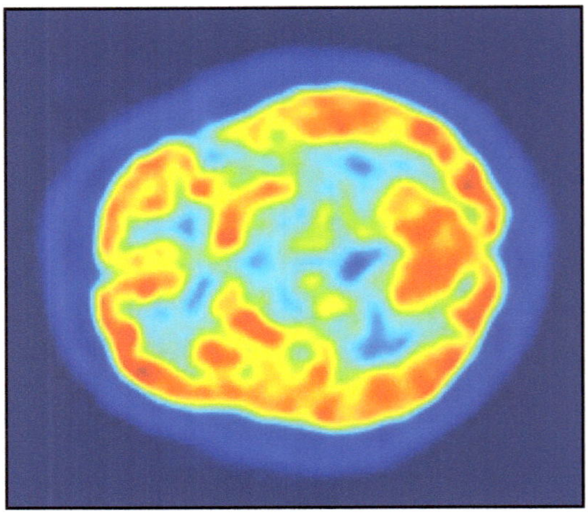

Fig: A PET Scan of the Human Brain

- **Neurology:** PET imaging with oxygen-15 indirectly measures blood flow to the brain. In this method, increased radioactivity signal indicates increased blood flow which is assumed to correlate with increased brain activity. Because of its two-minute half-life, oxygen-15 must be piped directly from a medical cyclotron for such uses, which is difficult. PET imaging with FDG takes advantage of the fact that the brain is normally a rapid user of glucose. Standard FDG PET of the brain measures regional glucose use and can be used in neuropathological diagnosis. Brain pathologies such as Alzheimer's disease (AD) greatly decrease brain metabolism of both glucose and oxygen in tandem. Therefore FDG PET of the brain may also be used to successfully differentiate Alzheimer's disease from other dementing processes, and also to make early diagnoses of Alzheimer's disease. The advantage of FDG PET for these uses is its much wider availability. In addition, some other fluorine-18 based radioactive tracers can be used to detect amyloid-beta plaques, a potential biomarker for Alzheimer's in the brain. These include florbetapir, flutemetamol, Pittsburgh compound B (PiB) and florbetaben. PET imaging with FDG can also be used for localization of "seizure focus". A seizure focus will appear as hypometabolic during an interictal scan. Several radiotracers (i.e. radioligands) have been developed for PET that are ligands for specific neuroreceptor subtypes such as [^{11}C]raclopride, [^{18}F]fallypride and [^{18}F]desmethoxyfallypride for dopamine D_2/D_3 receptors; [^{11}C]McN5652 and [^{11}C]DASB for serotonin transporters; [^{18}F]mefway for serotonin $5HT_{1A}$ receptors; and [^{18}F] nifene for nicotinic acetylcholine receptors or enzyme substrates (e.g. 6-FDOPA for the AADC enzyme). These agents permit the visualization of neuroreceptor pools in the context of a plurality of neuropsychiatric and neurologic illnesses. PET may also be used for the diagnosis of hippocampal sclerosis, which causes epilepsy. FDG, and the less common tracers flumazenil and MPPF have been explored for this purpose. If the sclerosis is unilateral (right hippocampus or left hippocampus), FDG uptake can be compared with the healthy side. Even if the diagnosis is difficult with MRI, it may be diagnosed with PET. The development of a number of novel probes for non-invasive, in-vivo PET imaging of neuroaggregate in human brain has brought amyloid imaging close to clinical use. The earliest amyloid imaging probes included [^{18}F]FDDNP, developed at the University of California, Los Angeles, and Pittsburgh compound B (PiB), developed at the University of Pittsburgh. These probes permit the visualization of amyloid plaques in the brains of Alzheimer's patients and could assist clinicians in making a positive clinical diagnosis of AD pre-mortem and aid in the development of novel anti-amyloid therapies. [^{11}C]polymethylpentene (PMP) is a novel radiopharmaceutical used in PET imaging to determine the activity of the acetylcholinergic neurotransmitter system by acting as a substrate for acetylcholinesterase. Post-mortem examination of AD patients has shown decreased levels of acetylcholinesterase. [^{11}C]PMP is used to map the acetylcholinesterase activity in the brain, which could allow for premortem diagnoses of AD and help to monitor AD treatments. Avid Radiopharmaceuticals has developed and commercialized a compound called florbetapir that uses the longer-lasting radionuclide fluorine-18 to detect amyloid plaques using PET scans.

- **Neuropsychology or Cognitive Neuroscience:** To examine links between specific psychological processes or disorders and brain activity.
- **Psychiatry and Neuropsychopharmacology:** Numerous compounds that bind selectively to neuroreceptors of interest in biological psychiatry have been radiolabeled with C-11 or F-18. Radioligands that bind to dopamine receptors (D_1, D_2, reuptake transporter), serotonin receptors ($5HT_{1A}$, $5HT_{2A}$, reuptake transporter), opioid receptors (mu and kappa), cholinergic receptors (nicotinic and muscarinic) and other sites have been used successfully in studies with human subjects. Studies have been performed examining the state of these receptors in patients compared to healthy controls in schizophrenia, substance abuse, mood disorders and other psychiatric conditions.
- **Stereotactic Surgery and Radiosurgery:** PET can also be used in image guided surgery for the treatment of intracranial tumors, arteriovenous malformations and other surgically treatable conditions.

- **Cardiology:** Cardiology, atherosclerosis and vascular disease study: FDG PET can help in identifying hibernating myocardium. However, the cost-effectiveness of PET for this role versus SPECT is unclear. FDG PET imaging of atherosclerosis to detect patients at risk of stroke is also feasible. Also, it can help test the efficacy of novel anti-atherosclerosis therapies.

- **Infectious Diseases:** Imaging infections with molecular imaging technologies can improve diagnosis and treatment follow-up. Clinically, PET has been widely used to image bacterial infections using FDG to identify the infection-associated inflammatory response. Three different PET contrast agents have been developed to image bacterial infections in vivo are [^{18}F]maltose, [^{18}F]maltohexaose, and [^{18}F]2-fluorodeoxysorbitol (FDS). FDS has the added benefit of being able to target only Enterobacteriaceae.
- **Bio-Distribution Studies:** In pre-clinical trials, a new drug can be radiolabeled and injected into animals. Such scans are referred to as biodistribution studies. The information regarding drug uptake, retention and elimination over time can be obtained quickly and cost effectively compare to the older technique of killing and dissecting the animals. Commonly, drug occupancy at a purported site of action can be inferred indirectly by competition studies between unlabeled drug and radiolabeled compounds to bind with specificity to the site. A single radioligand can be used this way to test many potential drug candidates for the same target. A related technique involves scanning with radioligands that compete with an endogenous (naturally occurring) substance at a given receptor to demonstrate that a drug causes the release of the natural substance.
- **Small Animal Imaging:** A miniature animal PET has been constructed that is small enough for a fully conscious rat to be scanned. This RatCAP (rat conscious animal PET) allows animals to be scanned without the confounding effects of anesthesia. PET scanners designed specifically for imaging rodents, often referred to as microPET, as well as scanners for small primates, are marketed for academic and pharmaceutical research. The scanners are based on microminiature scintillators and amplified avalanche photodiodes (APDs) through a system that uses single-chip silicon photomultipliers. In 2018 the UC Davis School of Veterinary Medicine became the first veterinary center to employ a small clinical PET scanner as a scanner for clinical (rather than research) animal diagnosis. Because of cost as well as the marginal utility of detecting cancer metastases in companion animals (the primary use of this modality), veterinary PET scanning is expected to be rarely available in the immediate future.

- **Musculo-Skeletal Imaging:** PET imaging has been used for imaging muscles and bones. FDG is the most commonly used tracer for imaging muscles, and NaF-F18 is the most widely used tracer for imaging bones.
  - **Muscles:** PET is a feasible technique for studying skeletal muscles during exercise. Also, PET can provide muscle activation data about deep-lying muscles (such as the vastus intermedialis and the gluteus minimus) compared to techniques like electromyography, which can be used only on superficial muscles directly under the skin. However, a disadvantage is that PET provides no timing information about muscle activation because it has to be measured after the exercise is completed. This is due to the time it takes for FDG to accumulate in the activated muscles.
  - **Bones:** Together with [^{18}F]sodium floride, PET for bone imaging has been in use for 60 years for measuring regional bone metabolism and blood flow using static and dynamic scans. Researchers have recently started using [^{18}F]sodium fluoride to study bone metastasis as well.

X-ray

X-ray detectors are devices used to measure the flux, spatial distribution, spectrum, and/or other properties of X-rays. Detectors can be divided into two major categories: imaging detectors (such as photographic plates and X-ray film (photographic film), now mostly replaced by various digitizing devices like image plates or flat panel detectors) and dose measurement devices (such as ionization chambers, Geiger counters, and dosimeters used to measure the local radiation exposure, dose, and/or dose rate, for example, for verifying that radiation protection equipment and procedures are effective on an ongoing basis).

X-ray Imaging

To obtain an image with any type of image detector the part of the patient to be X-rayed is placed between the X-ray source and the image receptor to produce a shadow of the internal structure of that particular part of the body. X-rays are partially blocked ("attenuated") by dense tissues such as bone, and pass more easily through soft tissues. Areas where the X-rays strike darken when developed, causing bones to appear lighter than the surrounding soft tissue.

Contrast compounds containing barium or iodine, which are radiopaque, can be ingested in the gastrointestinal tract (barium) or injected in the artery or veins to highlight these vessels. The contrast compounds have high atomic numbered elements in them that (like bone) essentially block the X-rays and hence the once hollow organ or vessel can be more readily seen. In the pursuit of nontoxic contrast materials, many types of high atomic number elements were evaluated. Some elements chosen proved to be harmful – for example, thorium was once used as a contrast medium (Thorotrast) – which turned out to be toxic, causing a very high incidence of cancer decades after use. Modern contrast material has improved and while there is no way to determine who may have a sensitivity to the contrast, the incidence of serious allergic reactions is low.

X-ray Film

- **Mechanism:** Typical x-ray film contains silver halide crystal "grains", typically primarily silver bromide. Grain size and composition can be adjusted to affect the film properties, for example to improve resolution in the developed image. When the film is exposed to radiation the halide is ionised and free electrons are trapped in crystal defects (forming a latent image). Silver ions are attracted to these defects and reduced, creating clusters of transparent silver atoms. In the developing process these are converted to opaque silver atoms which form the viewable image, darkest where the most radiation was detected. Further developing steps stabilise the sensitised grains and remove unsensitised grains to prevent further exposure (e.g. from visible light).
- **Replacement:** The first radiographs (X-ray images) were made by the action of X-rays on sensitized glass photographic plates. X-ray film (photographic film) soon replaced the glass plates, and film has been used for decades to acquire (and display) medical and industrial images. Gradually, digital computers gained the ability to store and display enough data to make digital imaging possible. Since the 1990s, computerized radiography and digital radiography have been replacing photographic film in medical and dental applications, though film technology remains in widespread use in industrial radiography processes (e.g. to inspect welded seams). The metal silver (formerly necessary to the radiographic & photographic industries) is a non-renewable resource although silver can easily be reclaimed from spent X-ray film. Where X-ray films required wet processing facilities, newer digital technologies do not. Digital archiving of images also saves physical storage space.

Photostimulable Phosphors

Phosphor plate radiography is a method of recording X-rays using photostimulated luminescence (PSL), pioneered by Fuji in the 1980s. A photostimulable phosphor plate (PSP) is used in place of the photographic plate. After the plate is X-rayed, excited electrons in the phosphor material remain 'trapped' in 'colour centres' in the crystal lattice until stimulated by a laser beam passed over the plate surface. The light given off during laser stimulation is collected by a photomultiplier tube, and the resulting signal is converted into a digital image by computer technology.

The PSP plate can be reused, and existing X-ray equipment requires no modification to use them. The technique may also be known as computed radiography (CR).

Fig: A Piece of Photostimulable Phosphor Plate

Image Intensifiers

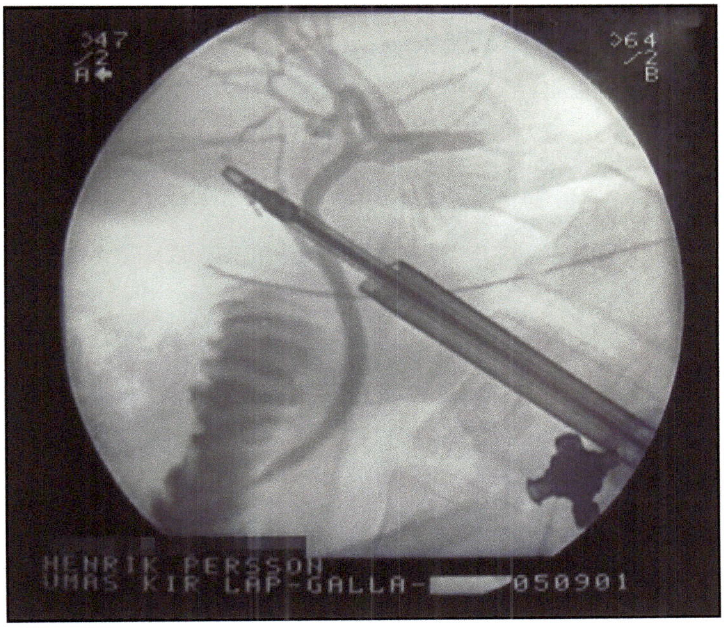

Fig: Radiograph Taken During Cholecystectomy

X-rays are also used in "real-time" procedures such as angiography or contrast studies of the hollow organs (e.g. barium enema of the small or large intestine) using fluoroscopy. Angioplasty, medical interventions of the arterial system, rely heavily on X-ray-sensitive contrast to identify potentially treatable lesions.

Semiconductor Detectors

Solid state detectors use semiconductors to detect x-rays. Direct digital detectors are so-called because they directly convert x-ray photons to electrical charge and thus a digital image. Indirect systems may have intervening steps for example first converting x-ray photons to visible light, and then an electronic signal. Both systems typically use thin film transistors to read out and convert the electronic signal to a digital image. Unlike film or CR no manual scanning or development step is required to obtain a digital image, and so in this sense both systems are "direct". Both types of system have considerably higher quantum efficiency than CR.

Direct detectors:

- Since the 1970s, silicon or germanium doped with lithium (Si(Li) or Ge(Li)) semiconductor detectors have been developed. X-ray photons are converted to electron-hole pairs in the semiconductor and are collected to detect the X-rays. When the temperature is low enough (the detector is cooled by Peltier effect or even cooler liquid nitrogen), it is possible to directly determine the X-ray energy spectrum; this method is called energy-dispersive X-ray spectroscopy (EDX or EDS); it is often used in small X-ray fluorescence spectrometers. Silicon drift detectors (SDDs), produced by conventional semiconductor fabrication, provide a cost-effective and high resolving power radiation measurement. Unlike conventional X-ray detectors, such as Si(Li), they do not need to be cooled with liquid nitrogen. These detectors are rarely used for imaging and are only efficient at low energies.
- Practical application in medical imaging started in the early 2000s. Amorphous selenium is used in commercial large area flat panel X-ray detectors for mammography and general radiography due to its high spatial resolution and x-ray absorbing properties. However Selenium's low atomic number means a thick layer is required to achieve sufficient sensitivity.
- Cadmium telluride (CdTe), and its alloy with zinc, cadmium zinc telluride, is considered one of the most promising semiconductor materials for x-ray detection due to its wide band-gap and high quantum number resulting in room temperature operation with high efficiency. Current applications include bone densitometry and SPECT

but flat panel detectors suitable for radiographic imaging are not yet in production. Current research and development is focused around energy resolving pixel detectors, such as CERN's Medipix detector and Science and Technology Facilities Council's HEXITEC detector.

- Common semiconductor diodes, such as PIN photodiodes or a 1N4007, will produce a small amount of current in photovoltaic mode when placed in an X-ray beam.

Indirect detectors:

- Indirect detectors are made up of a scintillator to convert x-rays to visible light, which is read by a TFT array. This can provide sensitivity advantages over current (amorphous selenium) direct detectors, albeit with a potential trade-off in resolution. Indirect flat panel detectors (FPDs) are in widespread use today in medical, dental, veterinary, and industrial applications.
- The TFT array consists of a sheet of glass covered with a thin layer of silicon that is in an amorphous or disordered state. At a microscopic scale, the silicon has been imprinted with millions of transistors arranged in a highly ordered array, like the grid on a sheet of graph paper. Each of these thin-film transistors (TFTs) is attached to a light-absorbing photodiode making up an individual pixel (picture element). Photons striking the photodiode are converted into two carriers of electrical charge, called electron-hole pairs. Since the number of charge carriers produced will vary with the intensity of incoming light photons, an electrical pattern is created that can be swiftly converted to a voltage and then a digital signal, which is interpreted by a computer to produce a digital image. Although silicon has outstanding electronic properties, it is not a particularly good absorber of X-ray photons. For this reason, X-rays first impinge upon scintillators made from such materials as gadolinium oxysulfide or caesium iodide. The scintillator absorbs the X-rays and converts them into visible light photons that then pass onto the photodiode array.

Dose measurement: Gas Detectors

X-rays going through a gas will ionize it, producing positive ions and free electrons. An incoming photon will create a number of such ion pairs proportional to its energy. If there is an electric field in the gas chamber ions and electrons will move in different directions and thereby cause a detectable current. The behaviour of the gas will depend on the applied voltage and the geometry of the chamber. Ionization chambers use a relatively low electric field of about 100 V/cm to extract all ions and electrons before they recombine. This gives a steady current proportional to the dose rate the gas is exposed to. Ion chambers are widely used as hand held radiation survey meters to check radiation dose levels.

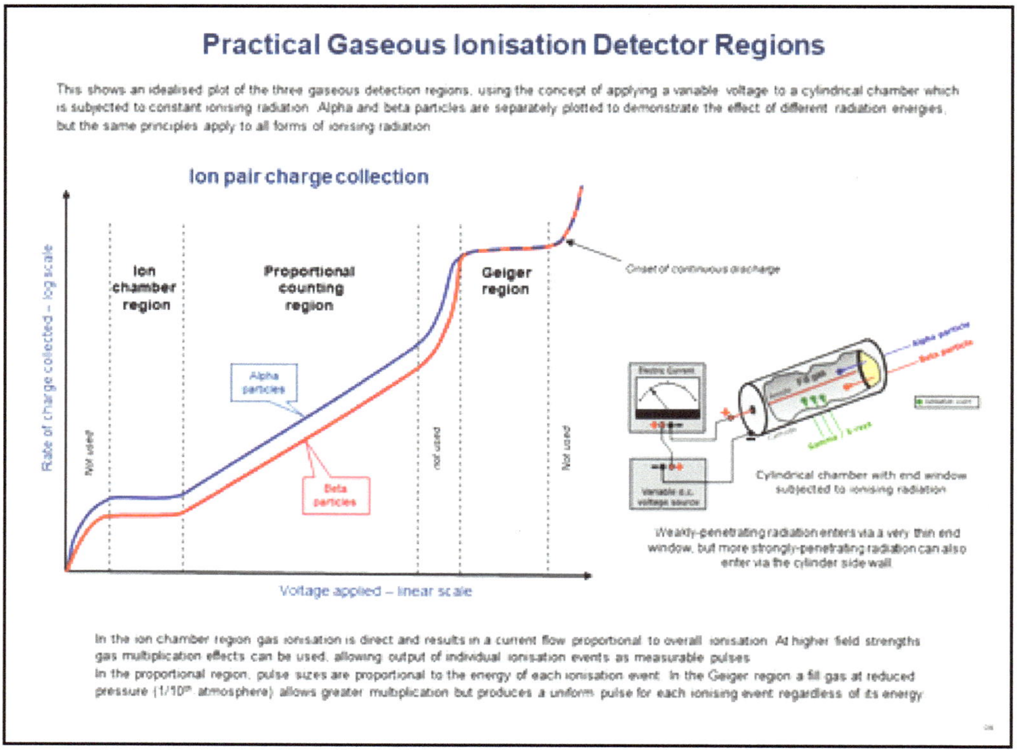

Fig: Plot of Ion Current as Function of Applied Voltage for a Wire Cylinder Gaseous Radiation Detector

Proportional counters use a geometry with a thin positively charged anode wire in the center of a cylindrical chamber. Most of the gas volume will act as an ionization chamber, but in the region closest to the wire the electric field is high enough to make the electrons ionize gas molecules. This will create an avalanche effect greatly increasing the output signal. Since every electron cause an avalanche of approximately the same size the collected charge is proportional to the number of ion pairs created by the absorbed x-ray. This makes it possible to measure the energy of each incoming photon. Geiger–Müller counters use an even higher electric field so that UV-photons are created. These start new avalanches, eventually resulting in a total ionization of the gas around the anode wire. This makes the signal very strong, but causes a dead time after each event and makes it impossible to measure the X-ray energies.

3.1.2 Bone Fracture and Pneumonia Detection

Bone Fracture

A bone fracture (abbreviated FRX or Fx, F_x, or #) is a medical condition in which there is a partial or complete break in the continuity of any bone in the body. In more severe cases, the bone may be broken into several fragments, known as a comminuted fracture. An open fracture (or compound fracture) is a bone fracture where the broken bone breaks through the skin.

A bone fracture may be the result of high force impact or stress, or a minimal trauma injury as a result of certain medical conditions that weaken the bones, such as osteoporosis, osteopenia, bone cancer, or osteogenesis imperfecta, where the fracture is then properly termed a pathologic fracture. Most bone fractures require urgent medical attention to prevent further injury.

Signs and Symptoms

Although bone tissue contains no pain receptors, a bone fracture is painful for several reasons:

- Breaking in the continuity of the periosteum, with or without similar discontinuity in endosteum, as both contain multiple pain receptors.
- Edema and hematoma of nearby soft tissues caused by ruptured bone marrow evokes pressure pain.
- Involuntary muscle spasms trying to hold bone fragments in place.

Damage to adjacent structures such as nerves, muscles or blood vessels, spinal cord, and nerve roots (for spine fractures), or cranial contents (for skull fractures) may cause other specific signs and symptoms.

Complications

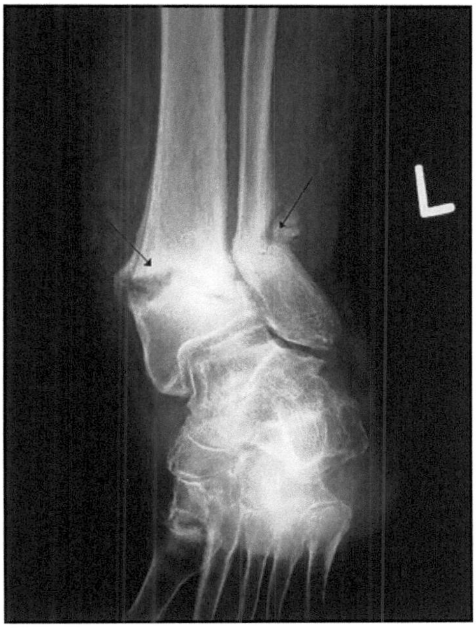

Fig: An Old Fracture with Nonunion of the Fracture Fragments

Some fractures may lead to serious complications, including a condition known as compartment syndrome. If not treated, eventually, compartment syndrome may require amputation of the affected limb.

Other complications may include non-union, where the fractured bone fails to heal, or malunion, where the fractured bone heals in a deformed manner. One form of malunion is the malrotation of a bone, which is especially common after femoral and tibial fractures. Complications of fractures may be classified into three broad groups, depending upon their time of occurrence. These are as follows –

- Immediate complications—occurs at the time of the fracture.
- Early complications—occurring in the initial few days after the fracture.
- Late complications—occurring a long time after the fracture.

Immediate	Early	Late
Systemic Hypovolaemic shock	*Systemic* Hypovolemic shock ARDS – Acute respiratory distress syndrome Fat embolism syndrome Deep vein thrombosis Pulmonary Embolism syndrome Aseptic traumatic fever Sepsis (in open fracture) Crush syndrome	*Imperfect union of the fracture* Delayed union Non-union Malunion Cross union
Local Injury to major vessels Injury to muscles and tendons Injury to joints Injury to viscera	*Local* Infection Compartment syndrome	*Others* Avascular necrosis Shortening Joint stiffness Sudeck's dystrophy Osteomyelitis Ischaemic contracture Myositis ossificans Osteoarthritis

Pathophysiology

The natural process of healing a fracture starts when the injured bone and surrounding tissues bleed, forming a fracture hematoma. The blood coagulates to form a blood clot situated between the broken fragments. Within a few days, blood vessels grow into the jelly-like matrix of the blood clot. The new blood vessels bring phagocytes to the area, which gradually removes the non-viable material. The blood vessels also bring fibroblasts in the walls of the vessels and these multiply and produce collagen fibres. In this way, the blood clot is replaced by a matrix of collagen. Collagen's rubbery consistency allows bone fragments to move only a small amount unless severe or persistent force is applied.

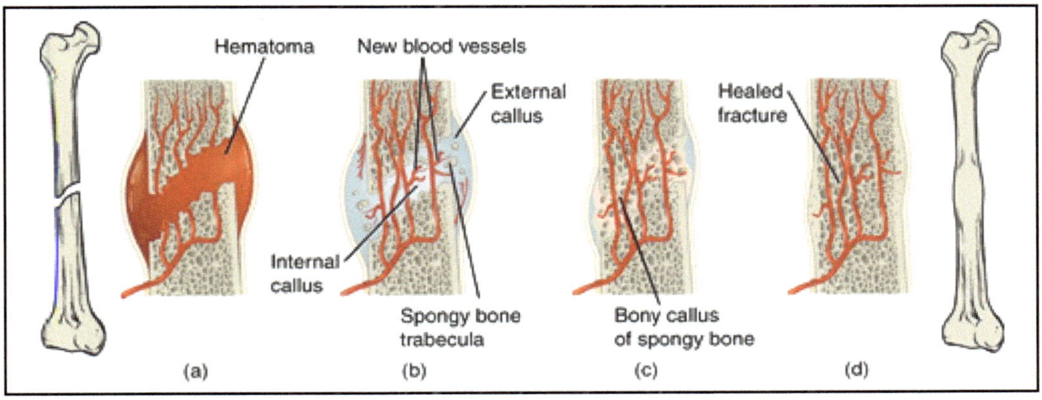

Fig: Stages in Fracture Repair—The Healing of a Bone Fracture follows a Series of Progressive Steps—(a) A Fracture Hematoma Forms (b) Internal and External Calli Form (c) Cartilage of the Calli is Replaced by Trabecular Bone (d) Remodeling Occurs

At this stage, some of the fibroblasts begin to lay down bone matrix in the form of collagen monomers. These monomers spontaneously assemble to form the bone matrix, for which bone crystals (calcium hydroxyapatite) are deposited in amongst, in the form of insoluble crystals. This mineralization of the collagen matrix stiffens it and transforms it into bone.

In fact, bone is a mineralized collagen matrix; if the mineral is dissolved out of bone, it becomes rubbery. Healing bone callus on average is sufficiently mineralized to show up on X-ray within 6 weeks in adults and less in children. This initial "woven" bone does not have the strong mechanical properties of mature bone. By a process of remodelling, the woven bone is replaced by mature "lamellar" bone. The whole process may take up to 18 months, but in adults, the strength of the healing bone is usually 80% of normal by 3 months after the injury.

Several factors may help or hinder the bone healing process. For example, tobacco smoking hinders the process of bone healing, and adequate nutrition (including calcium intake) will help the bone healing process. Weight-bearing stress on bone, after the bone has healed sufficiently to bear the weight, also builds bone strength. Although there are theoretical concerns about NSAIDs slowing the rate of healing, there is not enough evidence to warrant withholding the use of this type analgesic in simple fractures.

Diagnosis

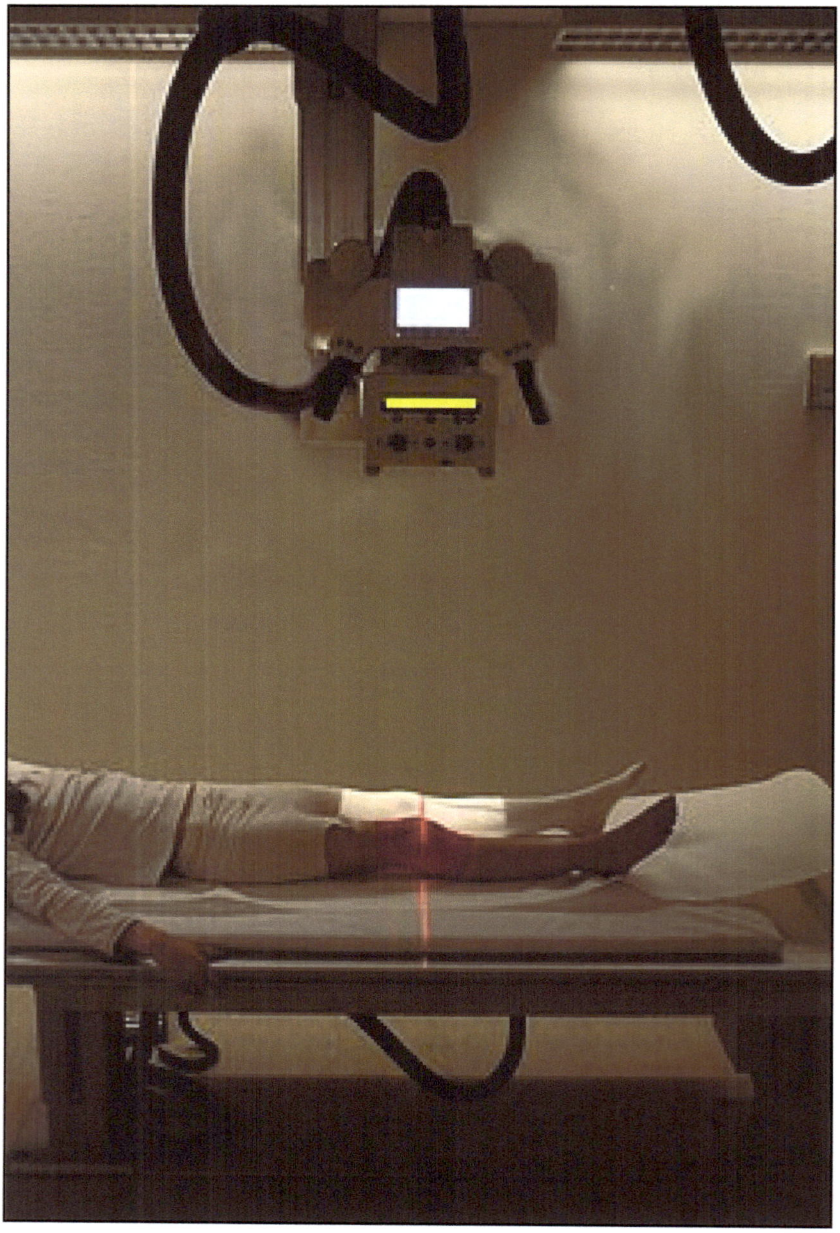

Fig: Radiography to Identify Possible Fractures After a Knee Injury

A bone fracture may be diagnosed based on the history given and the physical examination performed. Radiographic imaging is often performed to confirm the diagnosis. Under certain circumstances, radiographic examination of the nearby joints is indicated to exclude dislocations and fracture-dislocations. In situations where projectional radiography alone is insufficient, Computed Tomography (CT) or Magnetic Resonance Imaging (MRI) may be indicated.

Classification

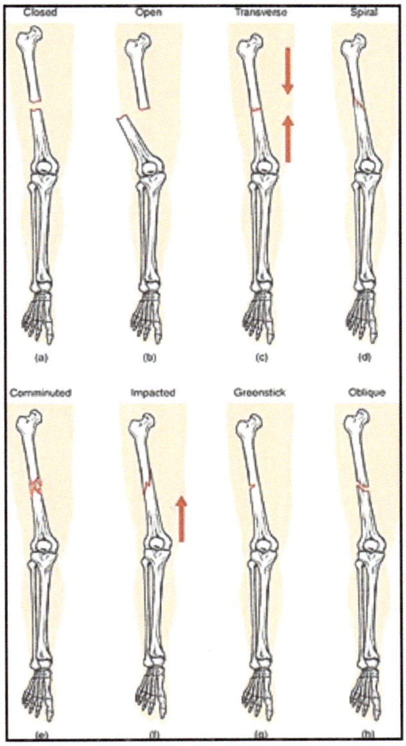

Fig: Compare Healthy Bone with Different Types of Fractures—(a) Closed Fracture (b) Open Fracture (c) Transverse Fracture (d) Spiral Fracture (e) Comminuted Fracture (f) Impacted Fracture (g) Greenstick Fracture (h) Oblique Fracture

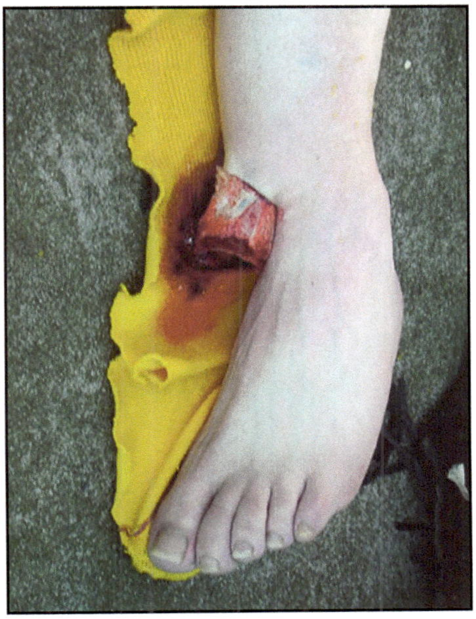

Fig: Open Ankle Fracture with Luxation

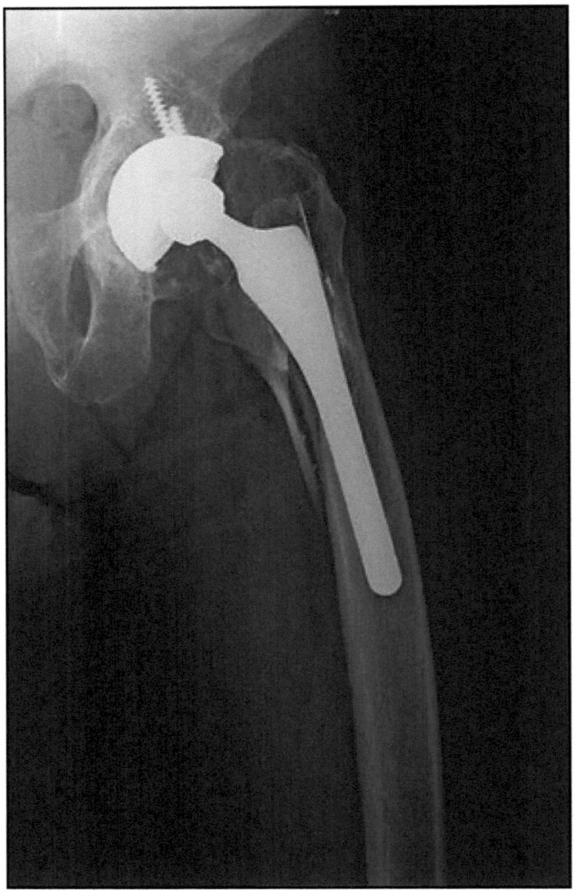

Fig: Periprosthetic Fracture of Left Femur

In orthopedic medicine, fractures are classified in various ways. Historically, they are named after the physician who first described the fracture conditions; however, there are more systematic classifications as well.

They may be divided into stable versus unstable depending on the likelihood that they may shift further.

Mechanism:

- **Traumatic Fracture:** A fracture due to sustained trauma. e.g., fractures caused by a fall, road traffic accident, fight, etc.
- **Pathologic Fracture:** A fracture through a bone that has been made weak by some underlying disease is called a pathological fracture. e.g., a fracture through a bone weakened by metastasis. Osteoporosis is the most common cause of pathological fracture.
- **Periprosthetic Fracture:** A fracture at the point of mechanical weakness at the end of an implant.

Soft-tissue involvement:

- Closed/simple fractures are those in which the overlying skin is intact.
- Open/compound fractures involve wounds that communicate with the fracture, or where fracture hematoma is exposed, and may thus expose bone to contamination. Open injuries carry a higher risk of infection. Reports indicate an incidence of infection after internal fixation of closed fractures of 1-2%, rising to 30% in open fractures.
  - Clean fracture; and
  - Contaminated fracture.

Displacement:

- Non-displaced.
- Displaced:
  - Translated, or ad latus, with sideways displacement.
  - Angulated.
  - Rotated.
  - Shortened, a reduction in overall bone length when displaced fracture fragments overlap.

Fracture pattern:

- **Linear Fracture:** A fracture that is parallel to the bone's long axis.
- **Transverse Fracture:** A fracture that is at a right angle to the bone's long axis.
- **Oblique Fracture:** A fracture that is diagonal to a bone's long axis (more than 30°).
- **Spiral Fracture:** Afracture where at least one part of the bone has been twisted.
- **Compression Fracture/Wedge Fracture:** Usually occurs in the vertebrae, for example when the front portion of a vertebra in the spine collapses due to osteoporosis (a medical condition which causes bones to become brittle and susceptible to fracture, with or without trauma).
- **Impacted Fracture:** A fracture caused when bone fragments are driven into each other.
- **Avulsion Fracture:** A fracture where a fragment of bone is separated from the main mass.

Fragments:

- **Incomplete Fracture:** A fracture in which the bone fragments are still partially joined; in such cases, there is a crack in the osseous tissue that does not completely traverse the width of the bone.

- **Complete Fracture:** A fracture in which bone fragments separate completely.
- **Comminuted Fracture:** A fracture in which the bone has broken into several pieces.

Prevention

Both high- and low-force trauma can cause bone fracture injuries. Preventive efforts to reduce motor vehicle crashes, the most common cause of high-force trauma, include reducing distractions while driving. Common distractions are driving under the influence and texting or calling while driving, both of which lead to an approximate 6-fold increase in crashes. Wearing a seatbelt can also reduce the likelihood of injury in a collision. 30 km/h or 20 mph speed limits (as opposed to the more common intracity 50 km/h / 30 mph) also drastically reduce the risk of accident, serious injury and even death in crashes between motor vehicles and humans. Vision Zero aims to reduce traffic deaths to zero through better traffic design and other measures and to drastically reduce traffic injuries, which would prevent many bone fractures.

A common cause of low-force trauma is an at-home fall. When considering preventative efforts, the National Institute of Health (NIH) examines ways to reduce the likelihood of falling, the force of the fall, and bone fragility. To prevent at-home falls they suggest keeping cords out of high-traffic areas where someone could trip, installing handrails and keeping stairways well-lit, and installing an assistive bar near the bathtub in the washroom for support. To reduce the impact of a fall the NIH recommends to try falling straight down on your buttocks or onto your hands.

Some sports have a relatively high risk of bone fractures as a common sports injury. Preventive measures depend to some extent on the specific sport, but learning proper technique, wearing protective gear and having a realistic estimation of one's own capabilities and limitations can all help reduce the risk of bone fracture. In contact sports, rules have been put in place to protect athlete health, such as the prohibition of unnecessary roughness in American football.

Taking calcium and vitamin D supplements can help strengthen your bones. Vitamin D supplements combined with additional calcium marginally reduces the risk of hip fractures and other types of fracture in older adults; however, vitamin D supplementation alone did not reduce the risk of fractures. Taking vibration therapy can also help strengthening bones and reducing the risk of a fracture.

Treatment

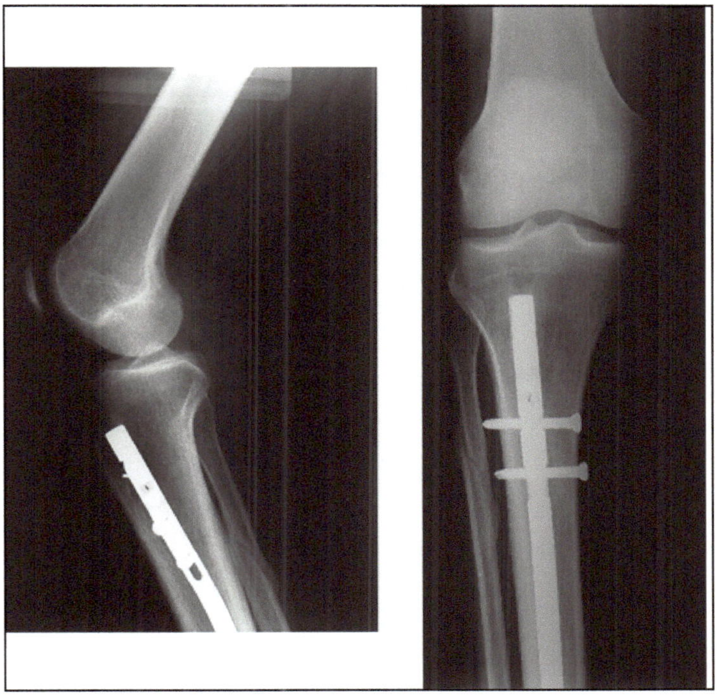

Fig: X-ray Showing the Proximal Portion of a Fractured Tibia with an Intramedullary Nail

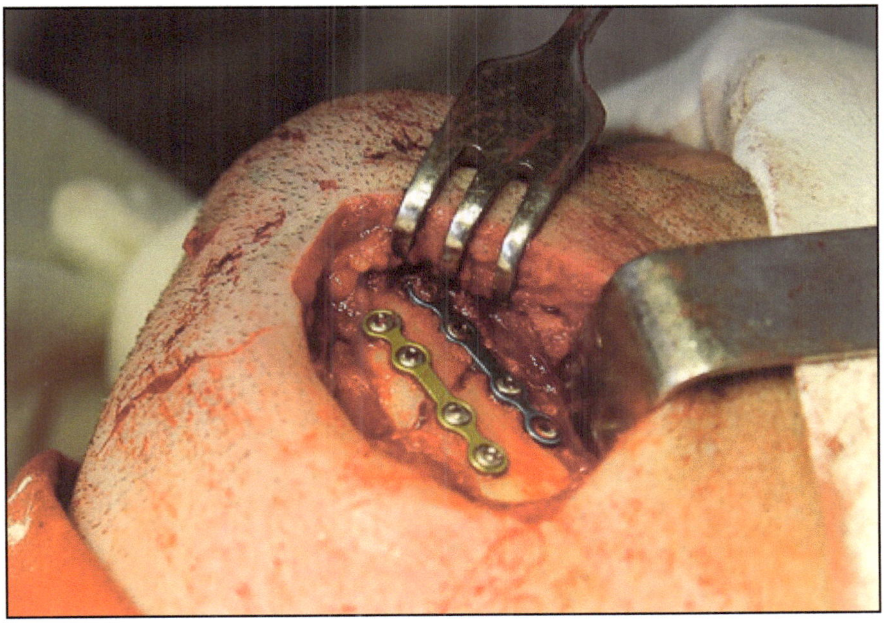

Fig: The Surgical Treatment of Mandibular Angle Fracture; Fixation of the Bone Fragments by the Plates, the Principles of Osteosynthesis are Stability (Immobility of the Fragments that Creates the Conditions for Bones Coalescence) and Functionality

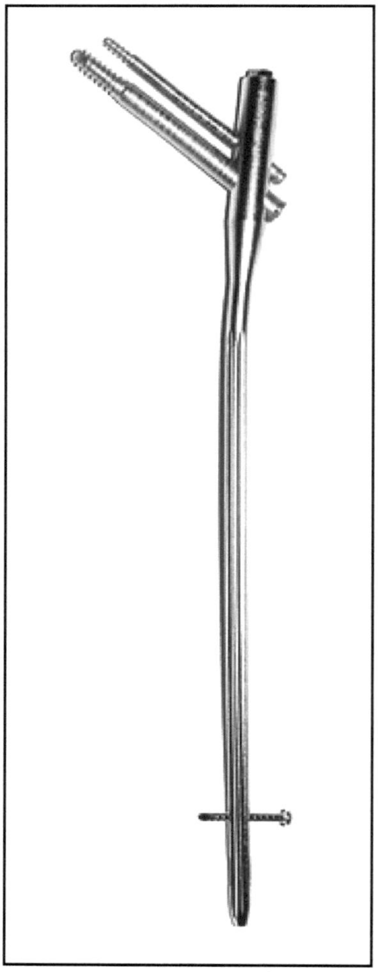

Fig: Proximal Femur Nail with Locking and Stabilisation Screws for Treatment of Femur Fractures of Left Thigh

Treatment of bone fractures are broadly classified as surgical or conservative, the latter basically referring to any non-surgical procedure, such as pain management, immobilization or other non-surgical stabilization. A similar classification is open versus closed treatment, in which open treatment refers to any treatment in which the fracture site is opened surgically, regardless of whether the fracture is an open or closed fracture.

- **Pain Management:** In arm fractures in children, ibuprofen is as effective as a combination of paracetamol and codeine. In the EMS setting it might be applicable to administer 1mg/kg of iv ketamine to achieve a dissociated state.
- **Immobilization:** Since bone healing is a natural process that will occur most often, fracture treatment aims to ensure the best possible function

of the injured part after healing. Bone fractures typically are treated by restoring the fractured pieces of bone to their natural positions (if necessary), and maintaining those positions while the bone heals. Often, aligning the bone, called reduction, in a good position and verifying the improved alignment with an X-ray is all that is needed. This process is extremely painful without anaesthesia, about as painful as breaking the bone itself. To this end, a fractured limb usually is immobilized with a plaster or fibreglass cast or splint that holds the bones in position and immobilizes the joints above and below the fracture. When the initial post-fracture oedema or swelling goes down, the fracture may be placed in a removable brace or orthosis. If being treated with surgery, surgical nails, screws, plates, and wires are used to hold the fractured bone together more directly. Alternatively, fractured bones may be treated by the Ilizarov method, which is a form of an external fixator. Occasionally, smaller bones, such as phalanges of the toes and fingers, may be treated without the cast, by buddy wrapping them, which serves a similar function to making a cast. A device called a Suzuki frame may be used in cases of deep, complex intra-articular digit fractures. By allowing only limited movement, immobilization helps preserve anatomical alignment while enabling callus formation, toward the target of achieving union. Splinting results in the same outcome as casting in children who have a distal radius fracture with little shifting.

- **Surgery:** Surgical methods of treating fractures have their own risks and benefits, but usually, surgery is performed only if conservative treatment has failed, is very likely to fail, or is likely to result in a poor functional outcome. With some fractures such as hip fractures (usually caused by osteoporosis), surgery is offered routinely because non-operative treatment results in prolonged immobilisation, which commonly results in complications including chest infections, pressure sores, deconditioning, deep vein thrombosis (DVT), and pulmonary embolism, which are more dangerous than surgery. When a joint surface is damaged by a fracture, surgery is also commonly recommended to make an accurate anatomical reduction and restore the smoothness of the joint. Infection is especially dangerous in bones, due to the recrudescent nature of bone infections. Bone tissue is predominantly extracellular matrix, rather than living cells, and the few blood vessels needed to support this low metabolism are only able to bring a limited number of immune cells to an injury to fight infection. For this reason, open fractures and osteotomies call for very careful antiseptic procedures and prophylactic use of antibiotics.

Occasionally, bone grafting is used to treat a fracture. Sometimes bones are reinforced with metal. These implants must be designed and installed with care. Stress shielding occurs when plates or screws carry too large of a portion of the bone's load, causing atrophy. This problem is reduced, but not eliminated, by the use of low-modulus materials, including titanium and its alloys. The heat generated by the friction of installing hardware can accumulate easily and damage bone tissue, reducing the strength of the connections. If dissimilar metals are installed in contact with one another (i.e., a titanium plate with cobalt-chromium alloy or stainless steel screws), galvanic corrosion will result. The metal ions produced can damage the bone locally and may cause systemic effects as well.

- **Bone Stimulation:** Bone stimulation with either electromagnetic or ultrasound waves may be suggested as an alternative to surgery to reduce the healing time for non-union fractures. The proposed mechanism of action is by stimulating osteoblasts and other proteins that form bones using these modalities. The evidence supporting the use of ultrasound and shockwave therapy for improving unions is very weak and it is likely that these approaches do not make a clinically significant difference for a delayed union or non-union.
- **Physical Therapy:** Physical therapy exercises (either home-based or physiotherapist-led) to improve functional mobility and strength, gait training for hip fractures, and other physical exercises are also often suggested to help recover physical capacities after a fracture has healed.

Pneumonia Detection

Pneumonia detection is a complex process that relies on a combination of clinical assessment, imaging studies, microbiological analysis, and increasingly, technological innovations like artificial intelligence and molecular diagnostics. Accurate and timely diagnosis is essential for effective treatment and improved patient outcomes. As global health systems continue to face challenges posed by infectious diseases, the integration of advanced diagnostic tools with traditional methods offers a pathway toward better detection, prevention, and management of pneumonia across diverse populations.

Improving pneumonia detection requires a multifaceted approach that combines technological innovation, clinical expertise, and public health strategies. Continued development and validation of AI-based diagnostic tools will play a significant role in enhancing early detection and reducing diagnostic errors. Standardizing imaging protocols and integrating AI into clinical decision support systems will further increase the efficiency of pneumonia diagnosis.

Point-of-care testing, including portable molecular diagnostics and lung ultrasound, offers promise for rapid and bedside evaluation, especially in emergency and rural settings. In addition, the use of integrated health data, such as wearable sensors and remote monitoring systems, may enable early identification of respiratory distress and prompt timely intervention.

Education and training for healthcare providers in both high- and low-resource settings are essential to ensure proper recognition, evaluation, and management of pneumonia. Public health campaigns focusing on vaccination, hygiene, and awareness can help reduce the incidence of pneumonia, particularly in children and the elderly.

Clinical Diagnosis of Pneumonia

The traditional approach to diagnosing pneumonia begins with a thorough clinical examination. Physicians evaluate the patient's medical history, symptoms, and vital signs. Common signs pointing toward pneumonia include persistent cough with or without sputum, shortness of breath, fever, chest pain during breathing, and fatigue. Auscultation with a stethoscope may reveal abnormal lung sounds such as crackles or decreased breath sounds. However, clinical examination alone is not sufficient for a definitive diagnosis because the symptoms of pneumonia can mimic those of other respiratory conditions such as bronchitis, tuberculosis, or chronic obstructive pulmonary disease.

To support clinical findings, laboratory tests such as a complete blood count (CBC) may be ordered to check for elevated white blood cells, indicating infection. Blood cultures can help identify the causative pathogen if the infection has entered the bloodstream. In cases where the patient produces sputum, a sputum culture and Gram stain can provide further insights into the type of bacteria or other pathogens present. Despite these tools, there is still a need for imaging and other diagnostic methods to confirm pneumonia, determine its severity, and guide treatment decisions.

Imaging Techniques in Pneumonia Detection

Radiographic imaging plays a pivotal role in the detection and confirmation of pneumonia. Chest X-ray is the most commonly used imaging method and is often considered the gold standard in pneumonia diagnosis. A chest X-ray can reveal areas of opacity or consolidation in the lungs, indicating the presence of fluid or inflammation. These findings help clinicians determine the location, extent, and pattern of lung involvement. Lobar pneumonia typically presents as a single area of consolidation in one lobe, while bronchopneumonia shows patchy infiltrates in multiple lobes. In some cases, a chest X-ray may be inconclusive, especially during the early stages of infection or in patients with underlying lung diseases.

In such scenarios, computed tomography (CT) scans offer more detailed images of the lung tissues and are used to detect subtle abnormalities that might not be visible on an X-ray. CT scans can differentiate pneumonia from other conditions such as pulmonary edema, lung tumors, or atelectasis. Ultrasound imaging is also being increasingly explored, particularly in critical care settings, to detect pleural effusion or peripheral lung consolidations associated with pneumonia.

Role of Microbiological Testing

Identifying the causative agent of pneumonia is essential for determining the appropriate antimicrobial therapy. Microbiological testing includes blood cultures, sputum analysis, and, in severe cases, bronchoalveolar lavage. These tests help detect pathogens such as Streptococcus pneumoniae, Haemophilus influenzae, or Mycoplasma pneumoniae, which are common bacterial agents of community-acquired pneumonia. Viral agents like influenza viruses, respiratory syncytial virus (RSV), and SARS-CoV-2 are also significant contributors, particularly in seasonal outbreaks or pandemics.

However, microbiological testing has its limitations. The sensitivity of sputum cultures depends on the quality of the sample, and not all patients can produce sputum. Blood cultures often have a low yield and take time to process. Additionally, many cases of pneumonia remain of unknown etiology despite extensive testing, making empirical treatment necessary in a large proportion of cases.

Advancements in Artificial Intelligence for Pneumonia Detection

In recent years, artificial intelligence (AI) has emerged as a promising tool in the detection of pneumonia, especially through the analysis of medical images. AI algorithms, particularly those based on deep learning, can be trained to recognize patterns in chest X-rays and CT scans that are indicative of pneumonia. These systems have shown high accuracy in identifying lung abnormalities and differentiating pneumonia from other pulmonary conditions.

AI models can assist radiologists by providing real-time analysis of imaging studies, highlighting suspicious regions, and even offering probability scores for pneumonia presence. This is particularly beneficial in resource-limited settings where access to radiological expertise may be scarce. In 2017, a Stanford research group developed an AI algorithm called CheXNet that could detect pneumonia in chest X-rays with performance comparable to that of experienced radiologists. Such advancements hold promise for improving diagnostic accuracy and reducing workload in busy clinical environments.

Moreover, AI systems are being integrated into portable X-ray machines and telemedicine platforms, enabling remote diagnosis in rural or underserved areas. The ability of AI to process large volumes of imaging data quickly also supports outbreak monitoring and epidemiological studies, as seen during the COVID-19 pandemic when pneumonia-like lung findings were common in severe cases.

Biomarkers and Molecular Diagnostics

In addition to imaging and microbiological testing, researchers are exploring the use of biomarkers for pneumonia detection. Biomarkers are measurable indicators of biological processes and can help differentiate between bacterial and viral infections. C-reactive protein (CRP) and procalcitonin (PCT) are two such markers that are often elevated in bacterial infections and may aid clinicians in distinguishing pneumonia from other non-infectious causes of lung inflammation.

Molecular diagnostics, including polymerase chain reaction (PCR) tests, have also gained importance, especially in identifying viral pneumonia. PCR can detect the genetic material of viruses with high sensitivity and specificity, allowing for early and accurate identification of pathogens such as influenza viruses, coronaviruses, and adenoviruses. These tests are particularly useful in guiding antiviral therapy and implementing infection control measures in healthcare settings.

Challenges in Pneumonia Detection

Despite the availability of multiple diagnostic tools, pneumonia detection is not without its challenges. One of the major difficulties lies in the non-specific nature of pneumonia symptoms, which can be mistaken for other respiratory or cardiac conditions. Elderly patients and those with weakened immune systems may present with atypical symptoms, making diagnosis more difficult. Furthermore, co-infections and comorbidities can obscure the clinical picture and complicate treatment strategies. Access to advanced diagnostic tools such as CT scans or molecular testing may be limited in low-resource settings, where pneumonia burden is often the highest. This disparity in healthcare infrastructure can lead to delayed or incorrect diagnoses, resulting in poorer outcomes. Over-reliance on antibiotics without confirmed bacterial infection also contributes to the growing problem of antimicrobial resistance, further complicating pneumonia management.

3.1.3 AI in Breast Imaging (Mammography)

Mammography (also called mastography; DICOM modality: MG) is the process of using low-energy X-rays (usually around 30 kVp) to examine the human breast for diagnosis and screening. The goal of mammography is the early detection of breast cancer, typically through detection of characteristic masses, microcalcifications, asymmetries, and distortions. As with all X-rays, mammograms use doses of ionizing radiation to create images. These images are then analyzed for abnormal findings. It is usual to employ lower-energy X-rays, typically Mo (K-shell X-ray energies of 17.5 and 19.6 keV) and Rh (20.2 and 22.7 keV) than those used for radiography of bones. Mammography may be 2D or 3D (tomosynthesis), depending on the available equipment or purpose of the examination. Ultrasound, ductography positron emission mammography (PEM), and magnetic resonance imaging (MRI) are adjuncts to mammography.

Ultrasound is typically used for further evaluation of masses found on mammography or palpable masses that may or may not be seen on mammograms. Ductograms are still used in some institutions for evaluation of bloody nipple discharge when a mammogram is non-diagnostic. MRI can be useful for the screening of high-risk patients, for further evaluation of questionable findings or symptoms, as well as for pre-surgical evaluation of patients with known breast cancer, in order to detect additional lesions that might change the surgical approach (for example, from breast-conserving lumpectomy to mastectomy).

In 2023, the U.S. Preventive Services Task Force issued a draft recommendation statement that all women should receive a screening mammography every two years from age 40 to 74. The American College of Radiology, Society of Breast Imaging, and American Cancer Society recommend yearly screening mammography starting at age 40.

The Canadian Task Force on Preventive Health Care (2012) and the European Cancer Observatory (2011) recommend mammography every 2 to 3 years between ages 50 and 69. These task force reports point out that in addition to unnecessary surgery and anxiety, the risks of more frequent mammograms include a small but significant increase in breast cancer induced by radiation. Additionally, mammograms should not be performed with increased frequency in patients undergoing breast surgery, including breast enlargement, mastopexy, and breast reduction.

Types

Digital

Digital mammography is a specialized form of mammography that uses digital receptors and computers instead of X-ray film to help examine breast tissue for breast cancer. The electrical signals can be read on computer screens, permitting more manipulation of images to allow radiologists to view the results more clearly. The standard digital mammography is "full field" (FFDM), in which the entire breast is imaged in a single view. Digital mammography can also include the use of "spot views", in which a paddle is used to further compress areas of concern.

Digital mammography is also utilized in stereotactic biopsy. Breast biopsy may also be performed using a different modality, such as ultrasound or magnetic resonance imaging (MRI). While radiologists had hoped for more marked improvement, the effectiveness of digital mammography was found comparable to traditional X-ray methods in 2004, though there may be reduced radiation with the technique and it may lead to fewer retests. Specifically, it performs no better than film for postmenopausal women, who represent more than three-quarters of women with breast cancer. The U.S. Preventive Services Task Force concluded that there was insufficient evidence to recommend for or against digital mammography over basic film mammography for breast cancer screening.

Digital mammography is a NASA spin-off, utilizing technology developed for the Hubble Space Telescope. As of 2022, over 99% of certified mammography centers in the United States screening centers use digital mammography. Globally, systems by Fujifilm Corporation are the most widely used. In the United States, GE's digital imaging units typically cost US$300,000 to $500,000, far more than film-based imaging systems. Costs may decline as GE begins to compete with the less expensive Fuji systems.

3D Mammography

Three-dimensional mammography, also known as digital breast tomosynthesis (DBT), tomosynthesis, and 3D breast imaging, is a mammogram technology that creates a 3D view of the breast using X-rays from different angles. Supplementing standard 2D mammography with DBT has been shown to improve cancer detection. Cost effectiveness is unclear as of 2016. Another concern is that it more than doubles the radiation exposure.

Contrast-Enhanced Mammography

Contrast-enhanced mammography is an advanced imaging technique that employs iodinated contrast agents to visualize breast neovascularization, functioning similarly to magnetic resonance imaging. Tumor-associated angiogenesis often results in leaky blood vessels, allowing contrast material to accumulate within the tumor tissue and produce an iodine-enhanced image. This enhances the visibility of malignancies that might otherwise be obscured by dense breast tissue. Contrast-enhanced mammography is also referred to as contrast-enhanced spectral mammography, contrast-enhanced digital mammography, or contrast-enhanced dual-energy mammography.

A large randomized controlled trial published in The Lancet in 2025 found that contrast-enhanced mammography detects significantly more invasive breast cancers in women with dense breast tissue than standard mammography or ultrasound. Conducted across 10 U.K. screening sites with over 9,000 participants, the study reported that contrast-enhanced mammography identified 15.7 invasive cancers per 1,000 exams, compared to 4.2 for ultrasound and 15 for MRI, with no statistically significant difference between Contrast-enhanced mammography and MRI. CEM was also found to be more cost-effective and accessible than MRI. Advocates suggest contrast-enhanced mammography could improve early detection and outcomes for women with dense breasts, but acknowledge risks of overdiagnosis.

Photon Counting

Photon-counting mammography was introduced commercially in 2003 and was shown to reduce the X-ray dose to the patient by approximately 40% compared to conventional methods while maintaining image quality at an equal or higher level. The technology was subsequently developed to enable spectral imaging with the possibility to further improve image quality, to distinguish between different tissue types, and to measure breast density.

Galactography

A galactography (or breast ductography) is a now infrequently used type of mammography used to visualize the milk ducts. Prior to the mammography itself, a radiopaque substance is injected into the duct system. This test is indicated when nipple discharge exists.

Medical Uses

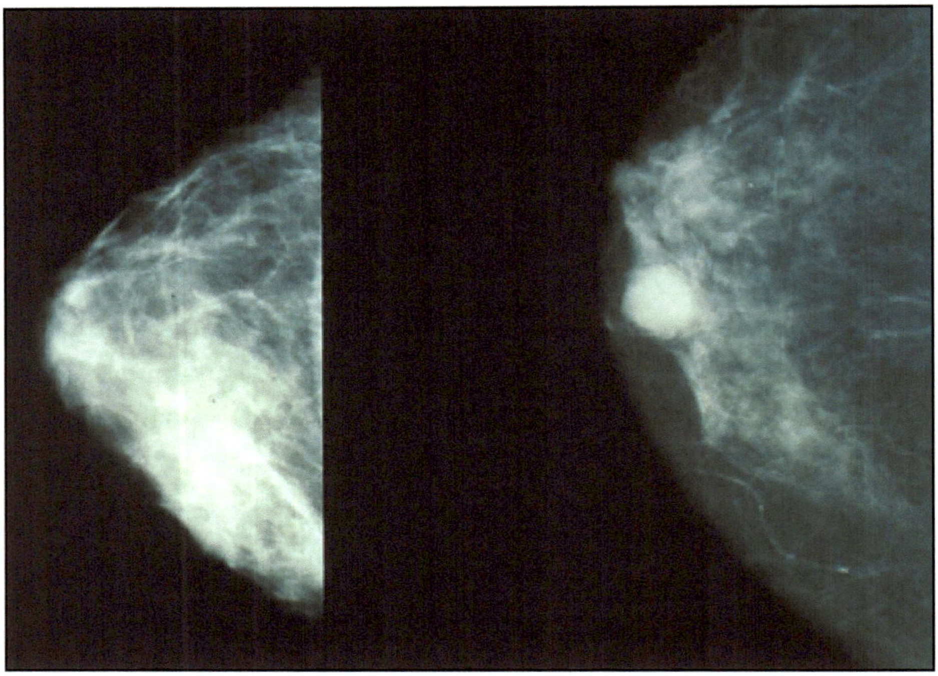

Fig: Normal (Left) versus Cancerous (Right) Mammography Image

Mammography can detect cancer early when it's most treatable and can be treated less invasively (thereby helping to preserve quality of life). According to National Cancer Institute data, since mammography screening became widespread in the mid-1980s, the U.S. breast cancer death rate, unchanged for the previous 50 years, has dropped well over 30 percent. In European countries like Denmark and Sweden, where mammography screening programs are more organized, the breast cancer death rate has been cut almost in half over the last 20 years.

Mammography screening cuts the risk of dying from breast cancer nearly in half. A recent study published in Cancer showed that more than 70 percent of the women who died from breast cancer in their 40s at major Harvard teaching hospitals were among the 20 percent of women who were not being screened. Some scientific studies have shown that the most lives are saved by screening beginning at age 40.

A recent study in the British Medical Journal shows that early detection of breast cancer – as with mammography – significantly improves breast cancer survival. The benefits of mammography screening at decreasing breast cancer mortality in randomized trials are not found in observational studies performed long after implementation of breast cancer screening programs (for instance, Bleyer et al.)

When to Start Screening

In 2014, the Surveillance, Epidemiology, and End Results Program of the National Institutes of Health reported the occurrence rates of breast cancer based on 1000 women in different age groups. In the 40–44 age group, the incidence was 1.5 and in the 45–49 age group, the incidence was 2.3. In the older age groups, the incidence was 2.7 in the 50–54 age group and 3.2 in the 55–59 age group.

While screening between ages 40 and 50 is somewhat controversial, the preponderance of the evidence indicates that there is a benefit in terms of early detection. Currently, the American Cancer Society, the American Congress of Obstetricians and Gynecologists (ACOG), the American College of Radiology, and the Society of Breast Imaging encourage annual mammograms beginning at age 40.

The National Cancer Institute encourages mammograms every one to two years for women ages 40 to 49. In 2023, United States Preventive Services Task Force (USPSTF) revised the recommendation that women and transgender men undergo biennial mammograms starting at the age of 40, rather than the previously suggested age of 50. This adjustment is prompted by the increasing incidence of breast cancer in the 40 to 49 age group over the past decade.

In contrast, the American College of Physicians, a large internal medicine group, has recently encouraged individualized screening plans as opposed to wholesale biannual screening of women aged 40 to 49. The American Cancer Society recommendations for women at average risk for breast cancer is a yearly mammogram from age 45 to 54 with an optional yearly mammogram from age 40 to 44.

Screening for High-Risk Population

Women who are at high risk for early-onset breast cancer have separate recommendations for screening. These include those who:

- Have a known BRCA1 or BRCA2 gene mutation.

- Have a 1st-degree relative (parent, brother, sister, or child), 2nd-degree relative (aunts, uncles, nieces, or grandparents), or 3rd-degree relative with a known BRCA1 or BRCA2 gene mutation.
- Have a lifetime risk of breast cancer >20% according to risk assessment tools.
- History of radiation therapy to chest between 10 and 30 years of age.
- Have or has a 1st-degree relative with a genetic syndrome including Li-Fraumeni syndrome, Cowden syndrome, or Bannayan-Riley-Ruvalcaba syndrome.

The American College of Radiology recommends these individuals to get annual mammography starting at the age of 30. Those with a history of chest radiation therapy before age 30 should start annually at age 25 of 8 years after their latest therapy (whichever is latest). The American Cancer Society also recommends women at high risk should get a mammogram and breast MRI every year beginning at age 30 or an age recommended by their healthcare provider.

The National Comprehensive Cancer Network advocates screening for women who possess a BRCA1 or BRCA2 mutation or have a first-degree relative with such a mutation, even in the absence of the patient being tested for BRCA1/2 mutations. For women at high risk, the network recommends undergoing an annual mammogram and breast MRI between the ages of 25 and 40, considering the specific gene mutation type or the youngest age of breast cancer occurrence in the family. Additionally, the network suggests that high-risk women undergo clinical breast exams every 6 to 12 months starting at age 25. These individuals should also engage in discussions with healthcare providers to assess the advantages and disadvantages of 3D mammography and acquire knowledge on detecting changes in their breasts.

Adverse Effects

- **Radiation:** The radiation exposure associated with mammography is a potential risk of screening, which appears to be greater in younger women. In scans where women receive 0.25–20 Gray (Gy) of radiation, they have more of an elevated risk of developing breast cancer. A study of radiation risk from mammography concluded that for women 40 years of age and older, the risk of radiation-induced breast cancer was minuscule, particularly compared with the potential benefit of mammographic screening, with a benefit-to-risk ratio of 48.5 lives saved for each life lost due to radiation exposure. This also correlates to a decrease in breast cancer mortality rates by 24%.
- **Pain:** The mammography procedure can be painful. Reported pain rates range from 6–76%, with 23–95% experiencing pain or discomfort.

Experiencing pain is a significant predictor in women not re-attending screening. There are few proven interventions to reduce pain in mammography, but evidence suggests that giving women information about the mammography procedure prior to it taking place may reduce the pain and discomfort experienced. Furthermore, research has found that standardised compression levels can help to reduce patients' pain while still allowing for optimal diagnostic images to be produced.

Procedure

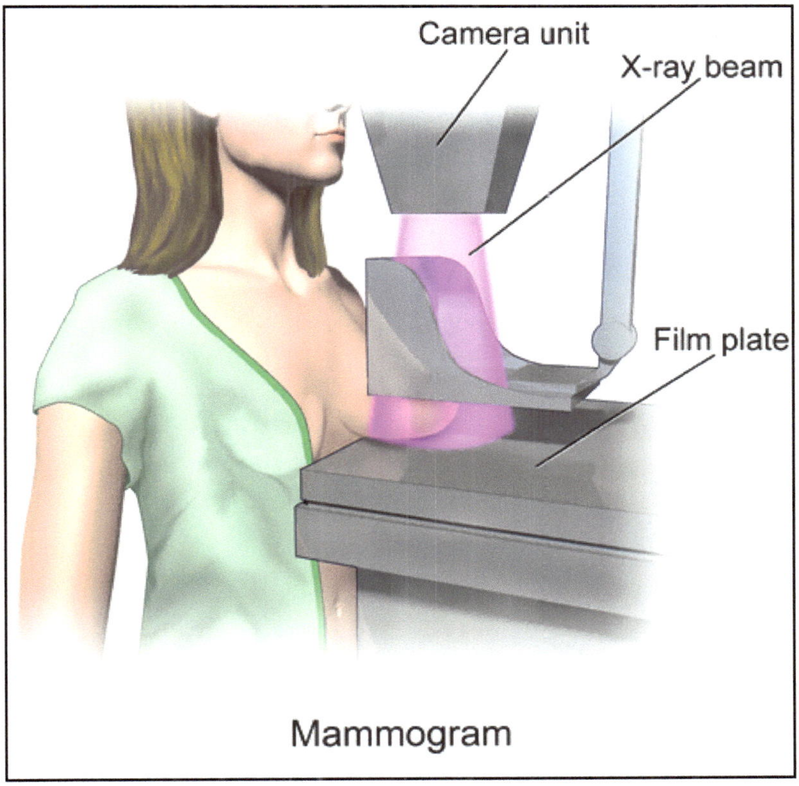

Fig: Illustration of a Mammogram

During the procedure, the breast is compressed using a dedicated mammography unit. Parallel-plate compression evens out the thickness of breast tissue to increase image quality by reducing the thickness of tissue that X-rays must penetrate, decreasing the amount of scattered radiation (scatter degrades image quality), reducing the required radiation dose, and holding the breast still (preventing motion blur). In screening mammography, both head-to-foot (craniocaudal, CC) view and angled side-view (mediolateral oblique, MLO) images of the breast are taken. Diagnostic mammography may include these and other views, including geometrically magnified and spot-compressed views of the particular area of concern. Deodorant, talcum powder or lotion may show up on the X-ray as calcium spots, so women are discouraged from applying them on the day of their exam. There are two types of mammogram studies: screening mammograms and diagnostic mammograms. Screening mammograms, consisting of four standard X-ray images, are performed yearly on patients who present with no symptoms. Diagnostic mammograms are reserved for patients with breast symptoms (such as palpable lumps, breast pain, skin changes, nipple changes, or nipple discharge), as follow-up for probably benign findings (coded BI-RADS 3), or for further evaluation of abnormal findings seen on their screening mammograms. Diagnostic mammograms may also performed on patients with personal or family histories of breast cancer. Patients with breast implants and other stable benign surgical histories generally do not require diagnostic mammograms.

Until some years ago, mammography was typically performed with screen-film cassettes. Today, mammography is undergoing transition to digital detectors, known as digital mammography or Full Field Digital Mammography (FFDM). The first FFDM system was approved by the FDA in the U.S. in 2000. This progress is occurring some years later than in general radiology. This is due to several factors:

- The higher spatial resolution demands of mammography.
- Significantly increased expense of the equipment.
- Concern by the FDA that digital mammography equipment demonstrate that it is at least as good as screen-film mammography at detecting breast cancers without increasing dose or the number of women recalled for further evaluation.

As of March 1, 2010, 62% of facilities in the United States and its territories have at least one FFDM unit. (The FDA includes computed radiography units in this figure.) Tomosynthesis, otherwise known as 3D mammography, was first introduced in clinical trials in 2008 and has been Medicare-approved in the United States since 2015. As of 2023, 3D mammography has become widely available in the US and has been shown to have improved sensitivity and specificity over 2D mammography.

Mammograms are either looked at by one (single reading) or two (double reading) trained professionals: these film readers are generally radiologists, but may also be radiographers, radiotherapists, or breast clinicians (non-radiologist physicians specializing in breast disease). Double reading significantly improves the sensitivity and specificity of the procedure, and is standard practice in the United Kingdom, but not in the United States as it is not reimbursed by Medicare or private health insurance. This is despite multiple trials showing increased accuracy of detection and improved patient outcomes for both morbidity and mortality when double reading is employed. Clinical decision support systems may be used with digital mammography (or digitized images from analogue mammography), but studies suggest these approaches do not significantly improve performance or provide only a small improvement.

Interpretation of Results: BI-RADS

Stratification for breast cancer risk on a mammogram is based on a reporting system known as Breast Imaging-Reporting and Data System (BI-RADS), developed by the American College of Radiology in 1993. It has five general categories of findings: mass, asymmetry, architectural distortion, calcifications, and associated features.

The use of language with BI-RADS is extremely precise, with a limited set of permissible adjectives for lesion margins, shape and internal density, each of which carries a different prognostic significance. Margins of a lesion, for example, can only be described as circumscribed, obscured, micropapillary, indistinct or stellate. Similarly, shape can only be round, oval or irregular. Each of these agreed upon adjectives is referred to as a "descriptor" in the BI-RADS lexicon, with specific positive and negative predictive values for breast cancer with each word. Additionally, each BI-RADS category corresponds with a probability of cancer. This fastiduous attention to semantics with BI-RADS allows for standardization of cancer detection across different treatment centers and imaging modalities.

After describing the findings, the radiologist provides a final assessment ranging from 0 to 6:

- BI-RADS 0 indicates an incomplete assessment which needs additional imaging.
- BI-RADS 1 & 2 indicate a negative and benign screen mammogram respectively.
- BI-RADS 3 indicates probably benign.
- BI-RADS 4 indicates suspicious for malignancy.
- BI-RADS 5 indicates highly suggestive of malignancy.
- BI-RADS 6 is for biopsy-proven breast cancer.

BI-RADS 3, 4 and 5 assessments on screening mammograms require further investigation with a second "diagnostic" study. The latter is a more detailed mammogram that allows dedicated attention to the abnormal finding with additional maneuvers such as magnification, rolling of breast tissue or exaggerated positioning. There may also be imaging with ultrasound at this time, which carries its own parallel BI-RADS lexicon. Suspicious lesions are then biopsied with local anesthesia or proceed straight to surgery depending on their staging. Biopsy can be done with the help of x-rays or ultrasound, depending on which imaging modality shows the lesion best.

In the UK mammograms are scored on a scale from 1–5 (1 = normal, 2 = benign, 3 = indeterminate, 4 = suspicious of malignancy, 5 = malignant). Evidence suggests that accounting for genetic risk, factors improve breast cancer risk prediction.

3.2 PATHOLOGY AND HISTOPATHOLOGY

3.2.1 Digital Slide Analysis and Pattern Recognition

Digital slide analysis and pattern recognition have ushered in a new era in pathology and histopathology, offering unprecedented opportunities for enhancing diagnostic precision, efficiency, and reproducibility. By digitizing tissue samples and leveraging artificial intelligence, pathologists can access powerful tools for analyzing complex patterns and quantifying disease markers. While challenges related to implementation, validation, and data management remain, the benefits of this technological shift are clear. As digital pathology continues to evolve, it will play an increasingly central role in modern medicine, transforming how diseases are diagnosed, studied, and treated.

The future of digital pathology lies in greater integration with other omics data, such as genomics and proteomics, to create comprehensive disease profiles. Multi-modal analysis combining histopathology with genetic and molecular information will enable more precise diagnostics and targeted therapies.

Emerging innovations such as 3D imaging of tissue samples, multiplexed immunofluorescence, and spatial transcriptomics are poised to further expand the capabilities of digital pathology. These technologies provide a deeper understanding of the spatial relationships between cells and their microenvironments, offering new insights into tumor biology and immune responses.

As cloud computing, data sharing frameworks, and federated learning models evolve, collaborative AI development across institutions will become more feasible, enabling the creation of universally applicable diagnostic tools. In addition, educational applications of digital slides will grow, making high-quality histopathology training accessible worldwide through virtual platforms.

From Traditional Microscopy to Digital Pathology

Traditionally, histopathological analysis has relied on optical microscopes to examine glass slides prepared with stained tissue sections. While this approach has been the gold standard for over a century, it has inherent limitations. Slide preservation, physical storage, and the subjectivity associated with manual interpretation can all affect diagnostic consistency. Additionally, collaboration across institutions and remote consultations are hindered by the physical nature of the slides. Digital slide analysis resolves many of these issues by converting physical slides into high-resolution digital images using whole slide imaging (WSI) systems. These digital slides can be stored electronically, shared instantly across geographic boundaries, and revisited indefinitely without degradation. They also facilitate secondary reviews, teaching, quality assurance, and, most importantly, the application of image analysis algorithms and artificial intelligence.

Whole Slide Imaging (WSI) and Its Capabilities

Whole Slide Imaging serves as the foundation for digital pathology. It involves scanning an entire glass slide at high magnification (typically 20x or 40x) to produce a digital replica that retains all morphological details visible under a microscope. These digitized images allow pathologists to examine tissues on a computer screen with the same fidelity as traditional microscopy but with added features like zooming, annotation, and integration with clinical databases.

WSI enables remote diagnostics, often referred to as telepathology, which is particularly valuable in underserved regions or during collaborative research projects. It also facilitates archiving and retrieval of slides, streamlines workflows in pathology departments, and supports training by allowing standardized image access for students and professionals alike.

Pattern Recognition and Artificial Intelligence in Histopathology

One of the most promising areas in digital pathology is the use of pattern recognition algorithms, especially those powered by artificial intelligence and deep learning. These algorithms are trained to recognize patterns in tissue architecture, cellular morphology, and staining characteristics. By analyzing thousands of annotated images, AI systems learn to differentiate between normal and abnormal tissues, identify specific disease entities, and even grade tumors based on histological criteria.

Pattern recognition in pathology leverages convolutional neural networks (CNNs), a type of deep learning model particularly adept at image analysis. These networks can automatically detect features such as mitotic figures, nuclear atypia, glandular formation, and necrosis—all of which are critical for disease diagnosis and prognosis. Once trained, these models can rapidly and consistently analyze large volumes of data, offering substantial time savings and aiding in the reduction of diagnostic errors.

Applications in Cancer Diagnostics

Cancer diagnostics is one of the primary areas where digital slide analysis and pattern recognition are making significant impacts. Algorithms have been developed to detect and classify a variety of cancers, including breast, prostate, lung, and colorectal carcinomas. In breast cancer, for example, AI-based tools can evaluate hormone receptor expression, assess HER2 status, and quantify Ki-67 proliferation indices from immunohistochemically stained slides.

In prostate cancer, AI models can accurately identify cancerous glands within the prostate tissue and assign Gleason scores with high concordance to expert pathologists. This automation helps standardize grading, which has traditionally suffered from interobserver variability. Additionally, the use of AI in tumor quantification aids in identifying tumor margins and lymphovascular invasion, improving surgical planning and treatment decisions.

Improving Accuracy and Reducing Variability

Digital slide analysis offers enhanced accuracy by reducing the subjective variability often associated with traditional microscopy. Interobserver differences in diagnosis and grading are common challenges in histopathology. With AI-assisted pattern recognition, diagnoses can become more reproducible, as algorithms apply consistent criteria across all cases.

Integrating Quantitative Pathology and Biomarker Assessment

Quantitative pathology, made possible through digital slide analysis, involves the numerical measurement of morphological features and biomarker expression levels. This objective data is valuable for both diagnosis and research. For example in immunohistochemistry, digital tools can precisely count the number of positive cells and calculate staining intensities, offering more accurate and reproducible assessments than manual scoring. Biomarker quantification plays a pivotal role in personalized medicine, especially in oncology. Treatment decisions often depend on the presence or absence of certain molecular markers. Digital pathology tools provide a standardized platform for quantifying these markers, supporting the move toward individualized therapeutic strategies.

Challenges in Implementation and Validation

Despite its many benefits, the implementation of digital slide analysis and pattern recognition in pathology faces several challenges. One major hurdle is the requirement for rigorous validation of digital tools to ensure they are as reliable as traditional microscopy. Regulatory agencies such as the FDA require comprehensive studies demonstrating that digital pathology systems are non-inferior to standard diagnostic methods.

Additionally, the development of robust AI algorithms requires access to large, high-quality annotated datasets. These datasets must represent diverse populations, staining protocols, and tissue types to ensure algorithm generalizability. Data privacy and ethical considerations also arise, particularly when dealing with patient information in digital formats. Technical challenges such as large file sizes, storage requirements, and computational infrastructure must also be addressed. Whole slide images can be several gigabytes in size, necessitating significant data management capabilities. Furthermore, integrating digital pathology platforms with existing laboratory information systems and electronic medical records requires careful planning and coordination.

Role of Pathologists in the Digital Era

Far from replacing pathologists, digital slide analysis and AI serve as augmentative tools that enhance the pathologist's role. These technologies handle repetitive and time-consuming tasks, allowing pathologists to focus on complex cases, integrate clinical information, and make informed decisions. The interpretative and contextual knowledge that pathologists bring remains indispensable in diagnostics, especially when correlating morphological findings with clinical history and other laboratory data.

Furthermore, pathologists play a crucial role in training AI models. Their expertise is essential in annotating training datasets, defining diagnostic criteria, and validating algorithm outputs. In this collaborative model, human intelligence and machine learning work together to improve diagnostic outcomes and streamline pathology workflows.

3.2.2 AI in Cancer Grading and Staging

The integration of artificial intelligence into cancer grading and staging represents a paradigm shift in pathology and histopathology, offering solutions to long-standing challenges in diagnostic consistency, efficiency, and precision. While AI will not replace pathologists, it is poised to become an indispensable tool that augments human expertise, enabling more accurate and comprehensive tumor assessments. The technology's ability to analyze vast amounts of histopathological data with consistent attention to detail addresses critical limitations of conventional methods, particularly in the face of increasing case volumes and diagnostic complexity. As AI systems become more sophisticated and better integrated into clinical workflows, they will enhance not only diagnostic accuracy but also the prognostic and predictive value of pathological assessments.

The successful implementation of AI in cancer pathology will require ongoing collaboration between computer scientists, pathologists, clinicians, and regulators to address technical, clinical, and ethical challenges. Standardization of data collection, rigorous validation protocols, and thoughtful workflow integration will be essential to realizing AI's full potential while maintaining patient safety and diagnostic quality. As these efforts progress, AI-assisted grading and staging will likely become standard practice, transforming cancer diagnosis from a subjective, qualitative assessment to a more objective, quantitative science. This evolution promises to improve patient outcomes through earlier detection of high-risk features, more consistent staging, and ultimately, better-informed treatment decisions—ushering in a new era of precision oncology grounded in advanced computational pathology.

How AI is Transforming Histopathological Analysis

Artificial intelligence has made significant strides in analyzing histopathological images, employing convolutional neural networks (CNNs) and other machine learning techniques to interpret tissue samples with remarkable accuracy. These algorithms process digitized whole-slide images (WSIs), identifying key diagnostic features such as nuclear pleomorphism, mitotic activity, and tissue architecture—all critical factors in cancer grading. For instance, in breast cancer, AI models can distinguish between ductal carcinoma in situ (DCIS) and invasive ductal carcinoma while also determining the tumor grade based on the Nottingham grading system. Similarly, in prostate cancer, AI assists in Gleason scoring by detecting glandular patterns and assigning appropriate grades to different tumor regions, a task that traditionally requires substantial pathologist effort and is prone to subjectivity.

The application of AI extends beyond basic grading to more complex aspects of tumor analysis. Advanced algorithms can quantify tumor-infiltrating lymphocytes (TILs), assess stromal reactions, and even predict molecular alterations from histology alone—a concept known as "computational pathology." For example, some AI systems can infer the likelihood of specific genetic mutations in tumors like glioblastoma or colorectal cancer based solely on histopathological features, potentially guiding molecular testing and targeted therapy decisions. This capability is particularly valuable in resource-limited settings where comprehensive genomic profiling may not be readily available. Furthermore, AI-powered image analysis enables precise tumor segmentation and measurement, improving the consistency of staging parameters such as tumor size and invasion depth, which are crucial for accurate TNM classification.

One of the most promising aspects of AI in histopathology is its ability to analyze entire slides rapidly while maintaining consistent attention to detail. Unlike human pathologists who may experience fatigue or oversight when reviewing numerous slides, AI systems can methodically examine every region of a tissue sample, flagging areas of interest for pathologist review. This approach not only reduces diagnostic turnaround times but also minimizes the risk of missing small but clinically significant tumor foci. Additionally, AI can integrate information from multiple tissue sections and stains, correlating findings from hematoxylin and eosin (H&E) slides with immunohistochemical markers to provide a more comprehensive tumor assessment. This multimodal analysis capability is pushing the boundaries of traditional histopathology toward a more quantitative and integrative diagnostic paradigm.

Advancements in AI-Assisted Cancer Staging

Cancer staging has entered a new era with the incorporation of artificial intelligence, which enhances both the accuracy and comprehensiveness of staging assessments.

Traditional staging relies on histopathological evaluation of primary tumors, lymph nodes, and distant metastases, often requiring correlation with radiological findings. AI systems are now capable of automating many aspects of this process, from measuring tumor dimensions and assessing lymphovascular invasion to detecting micrometastases in lymph nodes that might escape human detection. In colorectal cancer, for example, deep learning algorithms can accurately identify tumor budding—a histopathological feature associated with poor prognosis—and quantify its extent more reliably than manual methods. Similarly, in lung cancer, AI assists in distinguishing between invasive adenocarcinoma and pre-invasive lesions, a critical determination that directly impacts staging and treatment decisions.

The integration of AI with digital pathology platforms has enabled more sophisticated staging approaches that incorporate spatial and topological analysis of tumors. Advanced algorithms can map tumor architecture in three dimensions when serial sections are available, providing insights into growth patterns and microenvironment interactions that may influence disease behavior. This capability is particularly valuable for assessing local invasion in cancers like pancreatic or prostate carcinoma, where tumor-stromal interfaces are complex and challenging to evaluate consistently. AI also enhances the detection of perineural invasion and extranodal extension—histopathological features that carry significant staging and prognostic implications but are frequently underreported in conventional pathology practice due to their subtlety or the labor involved in thorough examination.

Beyond primary tumor assessment, AI is revolutionizing lymph node evaluation in cancer staging. Algorithms trained on thousands of lymph node images can rapidly screen for metastatic deposits, significantly reducing the workload associated with sentinel lymph node assessment in cancers like breast cancer and melanoma. Some systems can even detect isolated tumor cells or micrometastases that might be overlooked during routine examination, potentially upstaging patients who would benefit from more aggressive therapy. Furthermore, AI applications are extending staging capabilities to liquid biopsies and circulating tumor cell analysis, creating opportunities for non-invasive monitoring of disease progression and treatment response. These innovations are gradually shifting cancer staging from a static, pathology-report-based system to a more dynamic, multidimensional assessment framework that incorporates real-time histopathological, molecular, and clinical data.

Challenges and Considerations in AI Implementation

Despite its transformative potential, the integration of AI into cancer grading and staging faces several significant challenges that must be addressed for widespread clinical adoption. One of the primary obstacles is the need for large, high-quality and diverse datasets to train robust AI models. Histopathological images vary considerably due to differences in tissue processing, staining protocols, and scanner characteristics across institutions. This variability can lead to performance degradation when AI systems trained on data from one center are applied to slides from another. Developing algorithms that generalize well across different preparation methods and imaging platforms requires extensive multi-institutional collaboration and standardized data collection protocols, efforts that are currently underway but far from complete.

Another critical challenge lies in the validation and regulatory approval of AI systems for clinical use. Unlike many other medical AI applications, cancer grading and staging algorithms must meet exceptionally high accuracy standards because their outputs directly influence life-altering treatment decisions. Regulatory agencies like the FDA and EMA are still establishing appropriate evaluation frameworks for these complex diagnostic tools, balancing the need for rigorous validation with the practicalities of AI's continuous learning nature. The "black box" problem—the difficulty in understanding how some deep learning models arrive at their conclusions—presents additional hurdles for clinical acceptance as pathologists reasonably demand transparency in diagnostic decision-making processes that affect patient care.

Workflow integration poses another significant implementation challenge. Most pathology laboratories still operate primarily with glass slides and microscopes and the transition to fully digital workflows required for seamless AI integration involves substantial infrastructure investments and operational changes. Even in digitized departments, incorporating AI tools into existing laboratory information systems and pathology reporting protocols requires careful planning to avoid disrupting clinical operations. There are also important considerations regarding the changing role of pathologists in an AI-assisted diagnostic environment, including the need for new training paradigms that teach pathology residents how to effectively collaborate with and oversee AI systems while maintaining ultimate diagnostic responsibility.

3.3 CARDIOLOGY

3.3.1 ECG Analysis

Electrocardiogram (ECG or EKG) analysis is one of the most vital diagnostic tools in clinical cardiology. It is a non-invasive procedure used to assess the electrical activity of the heart over time. By placing electrodes on the skin in specific locations, the ECG records the electrical impulses generated by the cardiac muscles during each heartbeat. These signals are graphically represented as waves on

ECG paper or digital monitors. Clinicians and cardiologists analyze these waves to detect a variety of cardiac conditions, ranging from arrhythmias and ischemia to structural abnormalities. The simplicity of the ECG process, combined with its diagnostic potential, makes it an indispensable part of routine and emergency medical practice.

ECG analysis is an indispensable tool in modern medicine for evaluating cardiac function and diagnosing heart disease. Understanding its principles, components, and interpretation techniques allows healthcare providers to identify life-threatening conditions, guide treatment decisions, and monitor therapy effectiveness. While technology has enhanced ECG interpretation through digital tools and artificial intelligence, the foundation of accurate analysis lies in a thorough understanding of cardiac electrophysiology and waveform recognition. As cardiovascular disease continues to be a leading cause of morbidity and mortality worldwide, mastering ECG analysis remains essential for clinicians in all medical disciplines.

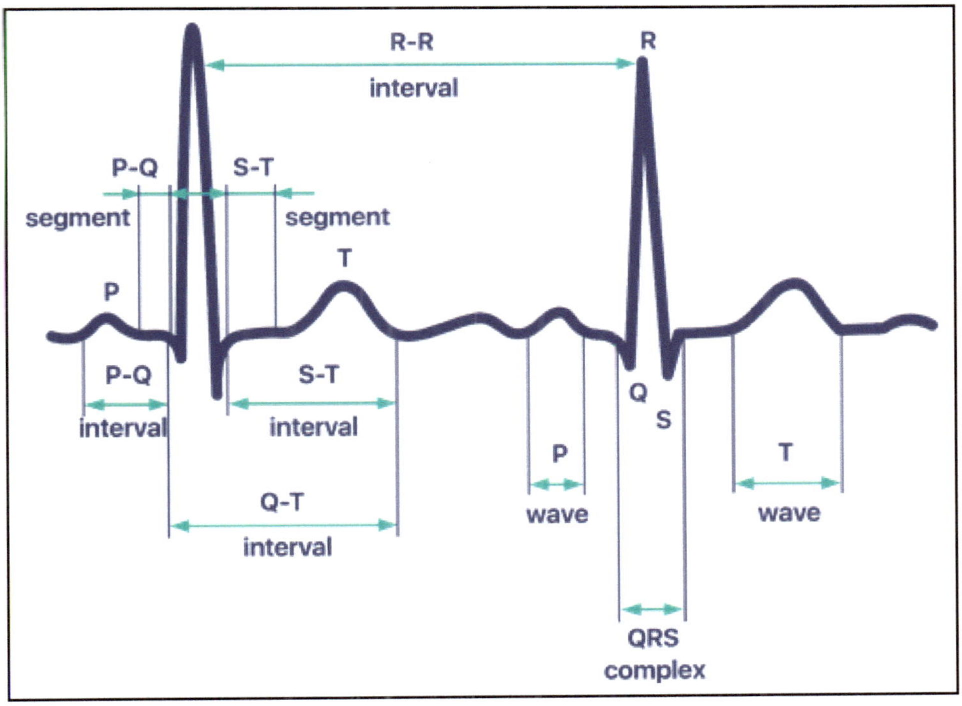

Principles of ECG Functioning

The ECG records the depolarization and repolarization of atrial and ventricular muscles. Depolarization leads to contraction, while repolarization restores the muscles to their resting state. The heart's electrical activity begins in the sinoatrial (SA) node, known as the heart's natural pacemaker. This electrical impulse travels through the atria to the atrioventricular (AV) node, then along the bundle of His, and finally to the Purkinje fibers in the ventricles. Each phase of this conduction pathway is captured as a specific part of the ECG waveform. The recorded output consists of a series of waves identified as the P wave, QRS complex, and T wave each corresponding to a distinct phase of the cardiac cycle.

Components of the ECG Waveform

Understanding the basic components of the ECG is essential for accurate interpretation. The P wave reflects atrial depolarization, which is the electrical activation of the atria. It is usually smooth and rounded. Following this, the PR interval represents the time the impulse takes to travel from the SA node through the AV node and into the ventricles. A prolonged PR interval may indicate a delay or block in the AV node. The QRS complex represents ventricular depolarization, a critical aspect of the ECG since it corresponds to the main pumping action of the heart. It appears as a sharp, tall spike on the ECG and is typically narrower than 120 milliseconds. Finally, the T wave denotes ventricular repolarization. The QT interval, which includes the QRS complex, ST segment, and T wave, measures the total time for ventricular depolarization and repolarization. Anomalies in these waveforms or intervals often point toward underlying cardiac conditions.

ECG Leads and Their Significance

The standard 12-lead ECG provides a comprehensive view of the heart's electrical activity from multiple angles. These leads include three standard limb leads (I, II, III), three augmented limb leads (aVR, aVL, aVF), and six precordial (chest) leads (V1–V6). Limb leads provide information about the frontal plane of the heart, while the precordial leads give insights into the horizontal plane. Each lead captures the heart's activity from a different perspective, helping to localize pathology. For example, abnormalities in leads II, III, and aVF suggest issues in the inferior wall of the heart, often due to right coronary artery blockage. Changes in leads V1–V4 may indicate anterior wall myocardial infarction caused by obstruction in the left anterior descending artery.

Interpreting Normal and Abnormal Rhythms

A fundamental part of ECG analysis is distinguishing between normal and abnormal heart rhythms. A normal sinus rhythm is characterized by a regular rhythm with a P wave before each QRS complex and a consistent PR interval. Arrhythmias occur when there is a deviation from this regular pattern. Bradycardia is a condition where the heart rate is less than 60 beats per minute, while tachycardia exceeds 100 beats per minute. Atrial fibrillation, marked by the absence of distinct P waves and an irregularly irregular rhythm, is a common arrhythmia associated with stroke risk. Ventricular tachycardia and ventricular fibrillation are life-threatening conditions that require immediate medical intervention. ECG analysis helps in the early identification of such disturbances, often enabling timely treatment.

Diagnosing Ischemia and Infarction

One of the most critical uses of ECG analysis is in the diagnosis of myocardial ischemia and infarction. Ischemia occurs when blood flow to the heart muscle is reduced, usually due to a partial blockage of the coronary arteries. This condition can be transient and may not cause permanent damage if treated early. ECG indicators of ischemia include ST-segment depression and T-wave inversion. Myocardial infarction, or heart attack, results from a complete blockage and causes irreversible damage to heart tissue. In such cases, the ECG may show ST-segment elevation, often referred to as ST-elevation myocardial infarction (STEMI). The location of these changes across the leads provides information on the infarcted area. Serial ECGs taken over time also help monitor the progression and recovery following an infarction.

Detecting Electrolyte Imbalances and Drug Effects

Electrolyte disturbances significantly affect cardiac electrophysiology and can manifest on an ECG. Hyperkalemia, or elevated potassium levels, can lead to tall, peaked T waves, widened QRS complexes, and eventually a sine wave pattern before cardiac arrest. Hypokalemia may present with flattened T waves and prominent U waves. Calcium imbalances also influence ECG findings, with hypercalcemia shortening the QT interval and hypocalcemia lengthening it. Certain drugs, such as digitalis, can cause characteristic changes like scooped ST segments. Antiarrhythmic medications may prolong the QT interval, predisposing the patient to a dangerous condition called torsades de pointes. Recognizing these patterns helps in identifying the underlying metabolic or pharmacologic causes and adjusting treatment accordingly.

Artifacts and Technical Considerations

Accurate ECG interpretation also requires attention to technical details and potential artifacts. Artifacts are distortions in the ECG tracing that do not represent true cardiac activity. Common causes include patient movement, poor electrode contact, electrical interference, and muscle tremors. Ensuring proper skin preparation, secure electrode placement, and minimizing external interference are essential to obtaining a high-quality ECG tracing. Misinterpretation of artifacts as genuine arrhythmias can lead to unnecessary interventions or anxiety. Therefore, clinicians must be able to distinguish true abnormalities from technical artifacts during ECG analysis.

Role of Computerized ECG Interpretation

Modern ECG machines are equipped with software that provides preliminary interpretations based on programmed algorithms. These automated readings can highlight potential abnormalities and suggest diagnoses. However, while helpful, computer-generated interpretations are not infallible. They may misclassify rhythms or miss subtle findings. Thus, the clinician's role in manually reviewing and interpreting the ECG remains irreplaceable. A combination of human expertise and machine assistance yields the best results in clinical practice. Continuous training in ECG interpretation is crucial, especially for emergency and critical care physicians who rely on ECGs for rapid decision-making.

Clinical Applications and Limitations

ECG analysis plays a central role in a variety of clinical settings. In emergency rooms, it is used to evaluate patients with chest pain, palpitations, syncope, or dyspnea. In outpatient settings, it helps monitor chronic heart disease, detect silent ischemia, and evaluate drug effects. It is also an essential part of preoperative assessment and sports fitness evaluations. Despite its widespread use, ECG has limitations. Some cardiac conditions, such as intermittent arrhythmias or early-stage structural heart disease, may not be evident on a resting ECG. In such cases further testing with Holter monitoring, echocardiography, or stress testing may be required. Nevertheless, the ECG remains a cornerstone of cardiac diagnostics due to its speed, affordability, and diagnostic value.

3.3.2 Arrhythmia Detection

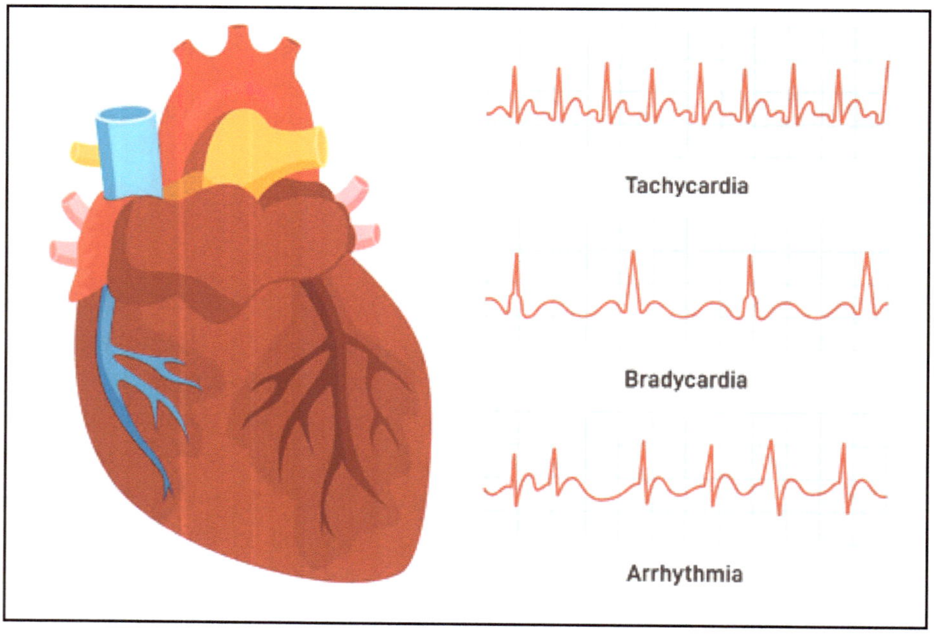

Fig: Fig: Pathological Heart Rhythm

Arrhythmia detection has evolved significantly over the years, from traditional methods such as ECGs and Holter monitors to advanced wearable technology and AI-powered systems. The integration of multi-modal data and the development of personalized treatment plans are further enhancing the accuracy and comprehensiveness of arrhythmia detection. While challenges and limitations persist, ongoing research and innovation hold the promise of overcoming these obstacles and improving patient outcomes.

The future of arrhythmia detection is bright, with the potential to revolutionize the way we manage cardiac health. By fostering collaboration between patients, healthcare providers, and technology developers, we can create more effective and patient-centered solutions for arrhythmia detection and management. Ultimately, the goal is to empower individuals to take control of their heart health, reduce the risk of serious complications, and improve their quality of life. As our understanding of arrhythmias deepens and technology continues to advance, the prospects for early detection and effective management are more promising than ever.

Collaboration between patients, healthcare providers, and technology developers is essential for advancing arrhythmia detection and management. Patients play a crucial role in providing feedback on the usability and effectiveness of monitoring devices, helping to identify areas for improvement. Healthcare providers bring their clinical expertise and experience in interpreting data, ensuring that the information obtained from monitoring devices is accurate and actionable. Technology developers, on the other hand, contribute their innovation and technical skills to create advanced and user-friendly devices. Collaboration between these stakeholders can lead to the development of more effective and patient-centered solutions for arrhythmia detection. This collaborative approach can also help in addressing the challenges and limitations of current technologies, paving the way for more reliable and accessible monitoring tools. Ultimately, the goal of arrhythmia detection is not only to identify abnormal rhythms but also to empower individuals to take control of their heart health and reduce the risk of serious complications.

The future of arrhythmia detection is poised for significant advancements, driven by ongoing research and technological innovation. Advances in sensor technology, miniaturization, and wireless communication are expected to make monitoring devices more comfortable, accessible, and user-friendly.

The development of implantable devices that can continuously monitor heart rhythms and deliver therapy as needed is another area of active research. These devices can provide real-time data and automated interventions, reducing the need for frequent clinical visits and improving patient outcomes. The integration of AI and machine learning algorithms will continue to enhance the accuracy and efficiency of arrhythmia detection, enabling more personalized and proactive management. The use of big data and predictive analytics can help in identifying individuals at high risk of arrhythmias and developing targeted prevention strategies. As technology continues to evolve, the prospects for early detection and effective management of arrhythmias are brighter than ever.

Significance of Early Arrhythmia Detection

Early detection of arrhythmias is paramount in preventing adverse outcomes and improving patient prognosis. Many arrhythmias are asymptomatic, meaning they do not produce noticeable symptoms, making them difficult to detect without specialized monitoring. Even when symptoms such as palpitations, dizziness, or chest pain are present, they may be intermittent and not always indicative of an underlying arrhythmia. Therefore, relying solely on patient-reported symptoms is insufficient for accurate diagnosis. Early detection allows for prompt treatment, which can prevent complications such as blood clots, heart failure, or sudden cardiac arrest. Moreover, early intervention can improve the quality of life for individuals living with arrhythmias, enabling them to manage their condition more effectively and reduce the risk of future episodes.

Traditional Methods

Historically, the electrocardiogram (ECG or EKG) has been the gold standard for arrhythmia detection. This non-invasive test records the electrical activity of the heart, providing a visual representation of the heart's rhythm and rate. ECGs are typically performed in a clinical setting and provide a snapshot of the heart's activity at a specific moment in time. While ECGs are valuable for diagnosing known arrhythmias, they have limitations when it comes to detecting intermittent or sporadic arrhythmias. To address this, extended monitoring techniques have been developed. Holter monitors, for example, record continuous ECG data over 24 to 48 hours, allowing for the detection of arrhythmias that may not be present during a brief clinical ECG. Event recorders, which can be worn for weeks, are another option for capturing intermittent arrhythmias. These devices are activated by the patient when symptoms occur, providing a more targeted approach to monitoring.

Evolution of Wearable Technology

The landscape of arrhythmia detection has been transformed by the advent of wearable technology. Smartwatches, fitness trackers, and other wearable devices equipped with optical sensors and ECG capabilities have made it possible for individuals to monitor their heart rhythms continuously and in real-time. These devices can detect irregularities and alert users to seek medical attention, even in the absence of symptoms. The integration of artificial intelligence (AI) and machine learning algorithms has further enhanced the accuracy of arrhythmia detection by analyzing large volumes of data and identifying subtle patterns that may be missed by traditional methods. Wearable technology not only empowers patients to take a proactive role in their health but also provides clinicians with valuable data for diagnosis and management. The convenience and accessibility of wearable devices make them an attractive option for long-term monitoring, particularly for individuals at high risk of arrhythmias.

Artificial Intelligence and Machine Learning

Artificial intelligence has emerged as a game-changer in the field of arrhythmia detection. Machine learning algorithms can be trained on vast datasets of ECG recordings to recognize various types of arrhythmias with high sensitivity and specificity. These algorithms can process data much faster than human clinicians and are capable of identifying complex patterns that may be indicative of underlying cardiac conditions. AI-powered systems are now being integrated into both hospital-based and consumer-grade devices, enabling continuous and automated monitoring. This has the potential to reduce the burden on healthcare providers, minimize diagnostic errors, and facilitate early intervention for high-risk patients. Furthermore, AI can help in the development of personalized treatment plans by analyzing individual patient data and predicting the likelihood of future arrhythmias. The use of AI in arrhythmia detection is still in its early stages, but its potential to revolutionize the field is immense.

Challenges and Limitations

Despite the advancements in arrhythmia detection, several challenges and limitations persist. One of the primary issues is the occurrence of false positives and false negatives, which can lead to unnecessary anxiety or missed diagnoses. The accuracy of detection depends on the quality of the recorded data, which can be affected by factors such as motion artifacts, poor electrode contact, or interference from other electronic devices. Additionally, not all arrhythmias are clinically significant, and distinguishing between benign and dangerous rhythms remains a complex task. There is also the challenge of ensuring patient compliance with long-term monitoring, as some individuals may find wearable devices uncomfortable or intrusive. The cost of advanced monitoring devices and the need for specialized training to interpret the data are additional barriers to widespread adoption. Addressing these challenges will require ongoing research and innovation to improve the reliability and accessibility of arrhythmia detection technologies.

Role of Multi-Modal Data

The integration of multi-modal data holds promise for enhancing the accuracy and comprehensiveness of arrhythmia detection. Combining ECG data with other physiological signals, such as blood pressure, oxygen saturation, and heart rate variability, can provide a more holistic view of cardiac health. Multi-modal data can help in identifying subtle changes that may not be apparent from a single data source. For example, changes in blood pressure or oxygen saturation levels can indicate underlying arrhythmias that are not captured by ECG alone. The use of wearable devices that can simultaneously monitor multiple physiological parameters is an area of active research. The integration of these data streams can improve the detection of arrhythmias and provide a more comprehensive assessment of a patient's cardiac health. This approach can also help in the development of personalized treatment plans by taking into account the unique physiological characteristics of each individual.

Patient Education and Empowerment

Patient education and empowerment are crucial components of effective arrhythmia detection and management. Educating patients about the signs and symptoms of arrhythmias, as well as the importance of regular monitoring, can help in early detection and timely intervention. Healthcare providers play a key role in guiding patients on the use of monitoring devices, interpreting results, and determining the appropriate course of action.

Empowering patients to take an active role in their health can improve compliance with monitoring and treatment plans, leading to better outcomes. Patient education should also include information on lifestyle modifications, such as diet, exercise and stress management, which can help in reducing the risk of arrhythmias. The use of digital health tools, such as mobile apps and online resources, can further enhance patient education and engagement, providing individuals with the knowledge and support they need to manage their condition effectively.

3.3.3 AI in Coronary Artery Disease Diagnosis

Coronary artery disease (CAD) remains one of the leading causes of morbidity and mortality worldwide. Early and accurate diagnosis is crucial for effective treatment and improved patient outcomes. Traditional diagnostic methods, such as angiography, stress testing, and electrocardiography, have limitations in terms of accuracy, accessibility, and cost. Artificial intelligence (AI) has emerged as a transformative tool in healthcare, offering advanced capabilities in medical imaging, risk prediction, and decision support.

In the context of CAD, AI-driven technologies are revolutionizing diagnosis by enhancing precision, reducing human error, and enabling personalized medicine. The future of AI in CAD diagnosis is promising, with ongoing advancements in multimodal data integration, explainable AI, and real-time decision support systems. Hybrid models combining imaging, genomics, and proteomics data could enable more precise and individualized CAD diagnosis. Collaboration between AI developers, clinicians, and regulatory bodies will be crucial to overcoming current limitations and ensuring safe, effective deployment.

AI in Medical Imaging for CAD Detection

Techniques such as computed tomography angiography (CTA), magnetic resonance imaging (MRI), and echocardiography generate vast amounts of data that require expert analysis. AI algorithms, particularly deep learning models, can process these images with remarkable accuracy.

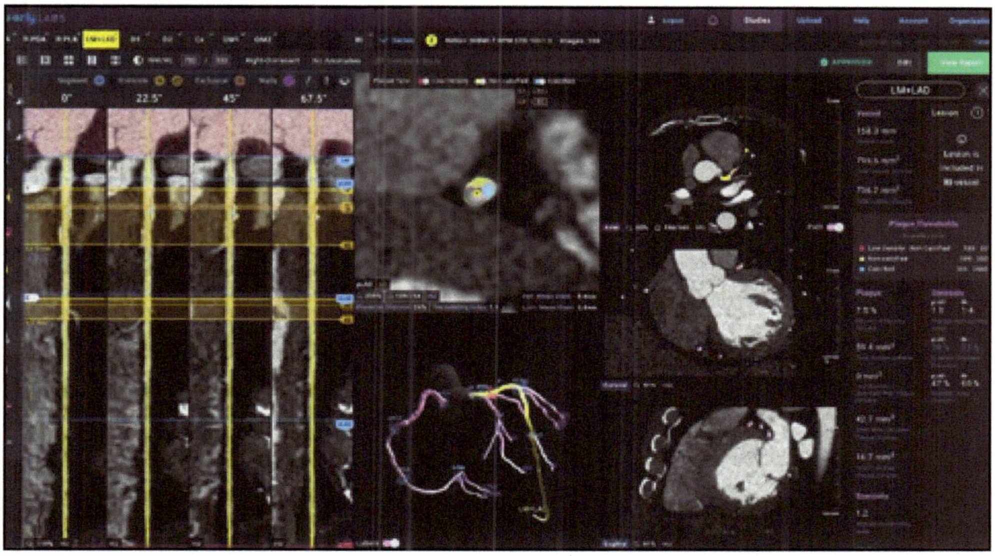

Fig: Medical Imaging Plays a Pivotal Role in Diagnosing CAD and AI has Significantly Improved the Interpretation of Imaging Data

Convolutional neural networks (CNNs) are widely used to detect coronary artery stenosis, plaque composition, and calcification from CTA scans. These models can identify subtle patterns that may be missed by human radiologists, leading to earlier detection of CAD. Similarly, AI-enhanced echocardiography can assess cardiac function, detect wall motion abnormalities, and predict ischemic events. By automating image analysis, AI reduces diagnostic time and improves consistency across different healthcare settings.

AI in Risk Stratification and Predictive Analytics

Beyond imaging, AI excels in risk stratification by integrating clinical, genetic, and lifestyle data to predict CAD likelihood. Machine learning models analyze electronic health records (EHRs) to identify high-risk patients based on factors such as age, cholesterol levels, blood pressure, and smoking history.

Predictive algorithms, such as random forests and support vector machines, outperform traditional risk scores like the Framingham Risk Score by incorporating more variables and detecting non-linear relationships. AI-powered tools also enable dynamic risk assessment by continuously monitoring patient data from wearable devices. For instance, AI can analyze real-time electrocardiogram (ECG) signals to detect early signs of myocardial ischemia, prompting timely intervention. Such predictive capabilities facilitate preventive care, reducing the burden of acute coronary syndromes and hospitalizations.

AI in Enhancing Diagnostic Accuracy and Reducing Errors

Human interpretation of diagnostic tests is subject to variability and bias. AI mitigates these challenges by providing standardized, data-driven assessments. For example, in coronary angiography, AI algorithms can quantify stenosis severity more objectively than visual estimation, reducing inter-observer variability. Additionally, AI can flag discrepancies in diagnostic reports, minimizing oversight and misdiagnosis.

Natural language processing (NLP) techniques further enhance diagnostic accuracy by extracting relevant information from unstructured clinical notes. AI systems can correlate symptoms, lab results, and imaging findings to generate comprehensive diagnostic reports, assisting clinicians in making informed decisions.

Challenges and Limitations of AI in CAD Diagnosis

Despite its potential, AI implementation in CAD diagnosis faces several challenges. Data quality and availability are critical concerns; AI models require large, diverse datasets for training, which may be limited by privacy regulations and data fragmentation across institutions. Algorithmic bias is another issue, as models trained on non-representative populations may perform poorly in different demographic groups.

Regulatory and ethical considerations also arise. The lack of standardized validation protocols for AI-based diagnostic tools raises questions about their reliability in clinical practice. Additionally, the "black box" nature of some AI systems makes it difficult for clinicians to trust and interpret their outputs. Ensuring transparency, explainability, and accountability in AI-driven diagnostics is essential for widespread adoption.

3.4 ONCOLOGY

3.4.1 Precision Diagnostics for Cancer Types

Precision diagnostics represent a paradigm shift in cancer detection, characterization, and treatment. By moving beyond the traditional one-size-fits-all approach, they enable a more nuanced understanding of each patient's unique cancer profile. This facilitates the selection of targeted therapies that are not only more effective but also less harmful. While challenges remain in terms of accessibility, cost, and technological complexity, the potential benefits for patient outcomes and healthcare systems are profound. Continued investment in research, infrastructure, and education will be crucial to ensure that the promise of precision diagnostics becomes a reality for all cancer patients, regardless of their geographic or socioeconomic background.

The future of precision diagnostics in oncology looks promising, with ongoing research focused on identifying new biomarkers, improving sequencing accuracy, and developing point-of-care diagnostic tools. Innovations such as single-cell sequencing, spatial transcriptomics, and multiplex imaging are set to provide deeper insights into tumor heterogeneity and microenvironmental interactions. Integrative omics approaches, combining genomics, proteomics, metabolomics, and epigenomics, are expected to offer a more comprehensive understanding of cancer biology. Additionally, the increasing use of machine learning models for predictive diagnostics and clinical decision support systems will further enhance the precision and personalization of cancer care.

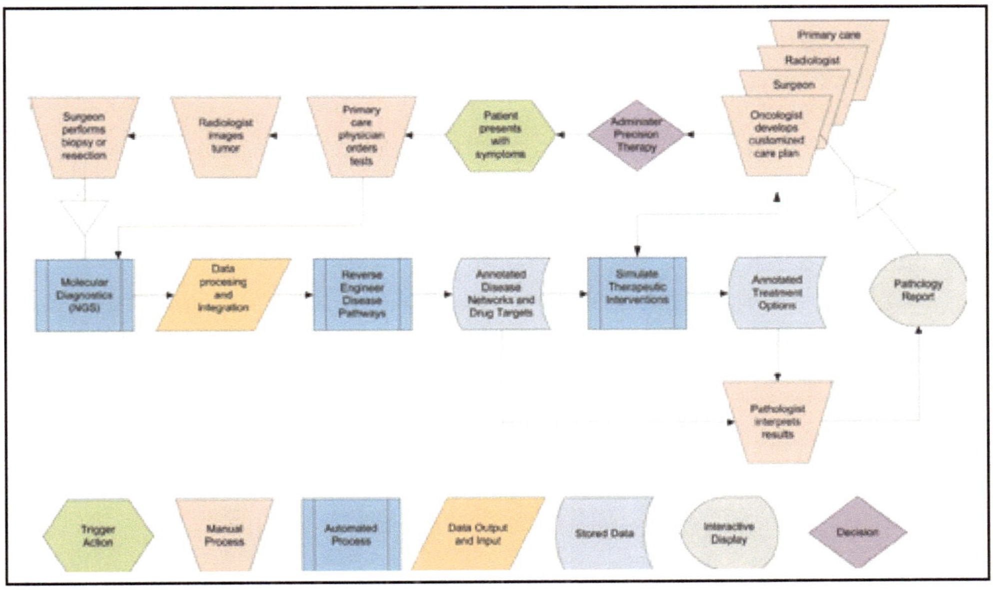

Fig: Workflow for Precision Diagnostics in Personalized Medicine

Despite its numerous advantages, precision diagnostics face several challenges. One of the major limitations is the high cost of advanced molecular testing, which can restrict access in low- and middle-income countries. Technical limitations, such as sample quality, sequencing errors, and data interpretation complexities, also pose hurdles.

Additionally, not all cancers have well-defined molecular targets, and in some cases, the identified mutations may not yet have corresponding targeted therapies. Ethical and privacy concerns related to genomic data handling further complicate the widespread adoption of precision diagnostics. Addressing these challenges requires multidisciplinary collaboration, infrastructure development, and regulatory oversight.

Molecular Profiling and Genetic Biomarkers

At the heart of precision diagnostics lies molecular profiling, which involves analyzing the DNA, RNA, and protein expression of cancer cells. This process identifies specific genetic mutations, gene fusions, copy number variations, and expression profiles that are unique to different cancer types and subtypes. For example, mutations in the EGFR gene are commonly found in non-small cell lung cancer, while BRCA1 and BRCA2 mutations are closely associated with breast and ovarian cancers. These biomarkers not only aid in accurate diagnosis but also serve as predictive tools for targeted therapy response. Molecular profiling has become a standard practice in many oncological settings, and its role continues to expand as new biomarkers are discovered.

Next-Generation Sequencing and Its Role

Next-generation sequencing (NGS) technology has become a cornerstone in precision cancer diagnostics. It allows for the rapid and comprehensive analysis of entire genomes or specific panels of genes associated with cancer. NGS provides high-throughput data, enabling the detection of mutations, insertions, deletions, and gene rearrangements across multiple genes in a single test. This is especially valuable in cases of rare or aggressive cancers where traditional methods might fail to deliver a definitive diagnosis. NGS can be applied to various sample types, including blood, tissue biopsies, and even circulating tumor DNA (ctDNA), making it a versatile tool in both diagnosis and disease monitoring.

Liquid Biopsy and Non-Invasive Techniques

Liquid biopsy is a transformative innovation in the field of precision diagnostics. It involves the analysis of cancer-related components, such as circulating tumor cells (CTCs) and ctDNA, present in the blood or other bodily fluids. This method offers a non-invasive alternative to tissue biopsies, which can be painful and sometimes risky, especially in advanced-stage patients. Liquid biopsy allows for real-time monitoring of tumor evolution, assessment of treatment efficacy, and detection of minimal residual disease or recurrence. Moreover, it facilitates the early detection of cancer by identifying tumor-specific genetic alterations before clinical symptoms arise, thereby significantly improving patient outcomes.

Immunohistochemistry and Companion Diagnostics

Immunohistochemistry (IHC) is a technique that uses antibodies to detect specific antigens in tumor tissues. Although it has been used for decades, its integration into precision diagnostics has become more refined with the development of companion diagnostics. These are tests designed to determine the suitability of a particular therapy based on the presence of a biomarker. For instance, HER2 testing in breast cancer determines whether a patient can benefit from trastuzumab, a targeted therapy. IHC remains a cost-effective and widely accessible method, especially in resource-limited settings, and continues to be a critical component of the precision diagnostic arsenal.

Artificial Intelligence and Digital Pathology

The incorporation of artificial intelligence (AI) into diagnostic pathology has opened new avenues for precision medicine. AI algorithms can analyze digital images of tissue samples with remarkable speed and accuracy, identifying subtle patterns and anomalies that might escape human observation. These tools assist pathologists in diagnosing complex cancer cases and grading tumor aggressiveness. AI also plays a crucial role in integrating and interpreting vast amounts of genomic, clinical, and imaging data, thereby facilitating comprehensive and precise diagnostic conclusions. The synergy between AI and precision diagnostics holds great promise in making cancer diagnosis more efficient, consistent, and scalable.

Cancer Type-Specific Precision Diagnostics

Different types of cancer require distinct diagnostic approaches due to their unique molecular landscapes. In breast cancer, for example, molecular subtyping into luminal A, luminal B, HER2-enriched, and triple-negative categories has a profound impact on treatment decisions. Each subtype exhibits different biological behaviors and responds differently to therapies. In lung cancer, precision diagnostics focus on identifying driver mutations such as EGFR, ALK, and ROS1, which determine eligibility for targeted therapies. Similarly, in colorectal cancer, mutations in KRAS, NRAS, and BRAF genes are critical for selecting appropriate treatment regimens. The ongoing development of cancer-specific diagnostic panels continues to refine the personalization of therapy across a broad spectrum of malignancies.

Impact on Treatment Decisions and Outcomes

Precision diagnostics have dramatically altered the therapeutic landscape by enabling oncologists to match treatments with the individual molecular profiles of tumors. This approach reduces the trial-and-error process of conventional chemotherapy and enhances the likelihood of treatment success. Targeted therapies, immunotherapies, and combination regimens are now selected based on the presence of specific biomarkers, leading to improved survival rates and quality of life for patients. Furthermore, precision diagnostics allow for adaptive treatment strategies, where therapy can be adjusted based on real-time monitoring of tumor response and resistance mechanisms.

3.4.2 AI in Liquid Biopsy and Biomarker Discovery

AI is revolutionizing liquid biopsy and biomarker discovery, paving the way for precision medicine in cancer diagnosis and treatment. By enhancing the sensitivity, specificity, and efficiency of liquid biopsy, AI is enabling earlier detection, real-time monitoring, and personalized treatment of cancer. The integration of multi-omics data, real-time analysis, and point-of-care devices are some of the exciting directions for future research and development.

However, addressing the challenges and ethical considerations associated with AI-driven liquid biopsy will be crucial for its successful implementation. Collaboration and innovation, driven by a multidisciplinary approach, will be key to unlocking the full potential of AI in liquid biopsy. As we continue to advance in this field, the prospects for improving patient outcomes and transforming cancer care are more promising than ever. The synergy between AI and liquid biopsy is not just about detecting cancer but about understanding and treating it at a molecular level, ultimately leading to better health and well-being for patients.

The future of AI in liquid biopsy is promising, with several exciting directions for research and development. One area of focus is the integration of multi-omics data, combining information from genomics, proteomics, metabolomics, and other omics disciplines to provide a more comprehensive view of cancer biology. AI can facilitate this integration by developing algorithms that can analyze and interpret complex, high-dimensional data. Another promising direction is the use of AI for real-time monitoring and dynamic treatment adaptation. AI algorithms can be trained to continuously analyze liquid biopsy data, providing real-time feedback on treatment response and enabling timely adjustments to therapy. This dynamic approach can improve patient outcomes by ensuring that treatments are tailored to the evolving biology of the tumor. Furthermore, the development of point-of-care liquid biopsy devices, powered by AI, can make cancer detection and monitoring more accessible and convenient, particularly in resource-limited settings.

AI-driven liquid biopsy has the potential to revolutionize personalized medicine by enabling the development of tailored treatment strategies for individual patients. By analyzing the unique molecular profile of each patient's cancer, AI can identify specific targets for therapy, predict treatment response, and monitor disease progression in real-time. This personalized approach can improve the efficacy of treatments, reduce side effects, and enhance patient outcomes. Moreover, AI can facilitate the discovery of novel biomarkers and therapeutic targets, expanding the arsenal of tools available for precision medicine. The integration of AI in liquid biopsy is not just about improving cancer detection and monitoring but also about transforming the way we understand and treat cancer at a molecular level.

The advancement of AI in liquid biopsy requires a collaborative and interdisciplinary approach, bringing together experts from various fields, including oncology, genomics, bioinformatics, and AI. Collaboration between academic institutions, industry partners, and healthcare providers is essential for driving innovation and translating research findings into clinical practice. Open data sharing, standardization of protocols, and the development of common platforms for data analysis and interpretation can accelerate progress in this field. Innovation hubs and consortia, focused on AI and liquid biopsy, can foster collaboration, share resources, and catalyze the development of new technologies and approaches. By working together, we can overcome the challenges and harness the full potential of AI in liquid biopsy, ultimately improving patient care and outcomes.

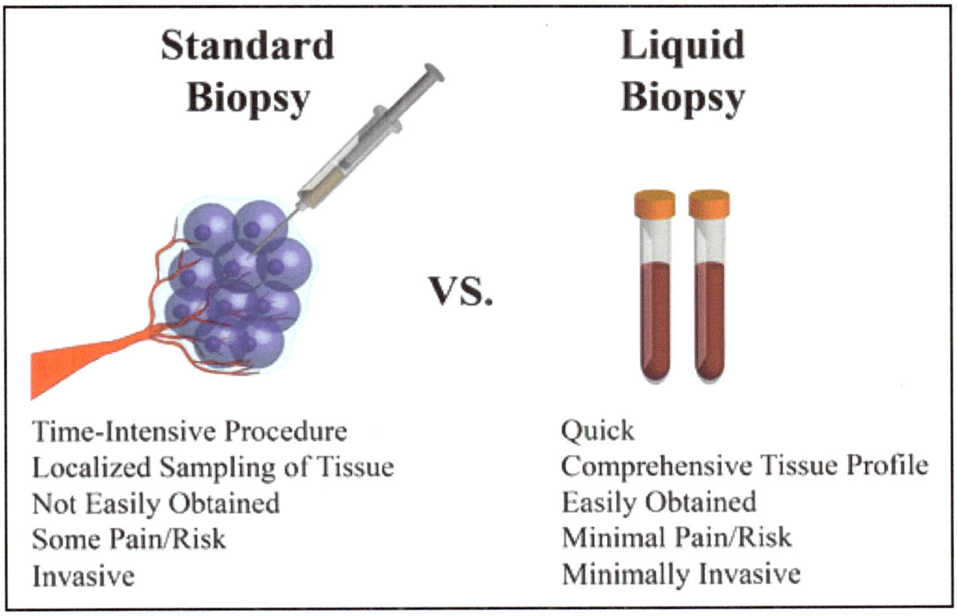

Fig: Liquid Biopsy and its Significance

Liquid biopsy involves the analysis of circulating tumor DNA (ctDNA), circulating tumor cells (CTCs), and other biomarkers present in the bloodstream. These biomarkers are shed by tumors into the blood, providing a real-time snapshot of the cancer's genetic and molecular profile. Unlike traditional tissue biopsies, which are invasive and may not always capture the heterogeneity of the tumor, liquid biopsies offer a more comprehensive and dynamic view of the cancer landscape. This is particularly valuable for monitoring treatment response, detecting recurrence, and identifying mechanisms of drug resistance. The significance of liquid biopsy lies in its potential to revolutionize cancer management by enabling earlier intervention, more precise treatment, and improved patient outcomes.

Role of AI in Enhancing Liquid Biopsy

AI is transforming liquid biopsy by addressing some of its key challenges, such as low abundance of biomarkers, high background noise, and the need for rapid and accurate analysis. Machine learning algorithms can be trained to distinguish between true tumor-derived signals and background noise, enhancing the sensitivity and specificity of biomarker detection. Deep learning techniques, particularly convolutional neural networks (CNNs), can analyze complex imaging data, such as those obtained from digital droplet PCR or next-generation sequencing, to identify subtle patterns indicative of cancer. AI can also integrate multi-omics data, combining information from genomics, proteomics, and metabolomics, to provide a more holistic understanding of the tumor's biology. This multi-modal approach can uncover novel biomarkers and improve the accuracy of cancer diagnosis and prognosis.

AI-Driven Biomarker Discovery

Biomarker discovery is a critical aspect of liquid biopsy, as it involves identifying specific molecules that can serve as indicators of cancer presence, progression, or response to treatment. AI is accelerating biomarker discovery by enabling the analysis of large and complex datasets generated from liquid biopsies. Unsupervised learning algorithms, such as clustering and dimensionality reduction techniques, can identify patterns and subgroups within the data, revealing potential biomarkers that may not be apparent through traditional methods. Supervised learning algorithms can then validate these biomarkers by training on labeled datasets, where the presence or absence of cancer is known. AI can also predict the functional significance of identified biomarkers by integrating them with other biological data, such as gene expression profiles or protein-protein interaction networks. This integrative approach can prioritize biomarkers that are not only detectable but also relevant to cancer biology and treatment.

AI in ctDNA Analysis for Early Cancer Detection

Circulating tumor DNA (ctDNA) is one of the most promising biomarkers for liquid biopsy, as it carries genetic information directly from the tumor. However, the low abundance of ctDNA in the bloodstream, often less than 1% of the total cell-free DNA, poses a significant challenge for detection. AI is addressing this challenge by enhancing the sensitivity of ctDNA analysis. Deep learning algorithms can be trained to distinguish ctDNA from background DNA by recognizing subtle differences in their sequencing patterns. AI can also improve the specificity of ctDNA detection by integrating it with other clinical data, such as patient demographics, medical history, and imaging results. This multi-modal approach can reduce false positives and improve the accuracy of early cancer detection. Furthermore, AI can track the evolution of ctDNA over time, providing valuable insights into tumor dynamics and treatment response.

AI in CTC Analysis for Monitoring Cancer Progression

Circulating tumor cells (CTCs) are another important biomarker for liquid biopsy, as they represent the metastatic potential of the tumor. However, CTCs are extremely rare, with only a few cells present in a milliliter of blood. AI is enhancing CTC detection by improving the sensitivity and specificity of imaging and analysis techniques.

Machine learning algorithms can be trained to recognize the morphological and molecular characteristics of CTCs, distinguishing them from other blood cells. AI can also integrate CTC data with other clinical data, such as ctDNA levels or imaging results, to provide a more comprehensive view of cancer progression. This integrative approach can help in monitoring treatment response, detecting recurrence, and identifying patients at high risk of metastasis. Moreover, AI can analyze the molecular profile of CTCs, revealing potential targets for personalized therapy.

Challenges and Limitations

Despite the significant advancements, AI-driven liquid biopsy faces several challenges and limitations. One of the primary issues is the need for large and well-annotated datasets to train and validate AI algorithms. The rarity of certain cancers and the heterogeneity of tumor biology can make it difficult to obtain sufficient data for robust model training.

Additionally, the quality and pre-processing of liquid biopsy samples can significantly impact the performance of AI algorithms. Factors such as sample storage, handling, and contamination can introduce noise and bias into the data, affecting the accuracy of biomarker detection. Furthermore, the interpretation of AI-driven results requires careful consideration of clinical context and biological relevance. AI algorithms may identify patterns that are statistically significant but not clinically meaningful, leading to false positives or negatives. Addressing these challenges will require ongoing research, standardization of protocols, and collaboration between clinicians, scientists, and AI experts.

Ethical Considerations

The integration of AI in liquid biopsy also raises important ethical considerations. The use of patient data for training and validating AI algorithms must be done with informed consent and adherence to privacy regulations. The potential for AI to uncover incidental findings, such as undiagnosed conditions or genetic predispositions, raises questions about the responsibility of healthcare providers to disclose this information and the potential psychological impact on patients. Moreover, the commercialization of AI-driven liquid biopsy technologies must be balanced with the need for accessibility and affordability, ensuring that these advancements benefit a broad population and not just a privileged few. Ethical guidelines and regulatory frameworks will be crucial in navigating these complexities and ensuring the responsible use of AI in liquid biopsy.

3.5 DERMATOLOGY

3.5.1 AI for Skin Lesion Classification (Melanoma, Psoriasis, etc.)

Skin diseases such as melanoma, psoriasis, basal cell carcinoma, and eczema are among the most common dermatological conditions affecting people worldwide. Accurate and timely diagnosis is critical, particularly in conditions like melanoma, which can become life-threatening if not identified and treated early. Traditional diagnostic methods rely heavily on clinical expertise and dermoscopic examination, which may lead to variability in diagnostic accuracy.

The growing prevalence of skin disorders, along with a global shortage of trained dermatologists, has created an urgent need for advanced diagnostic tools. Artificial intelligence (AI) has emerged as a powerful ally in the field of dermatology, particularly in skin lesion classification, where it can augment diagnostic precision, efficiency, and accessibility.

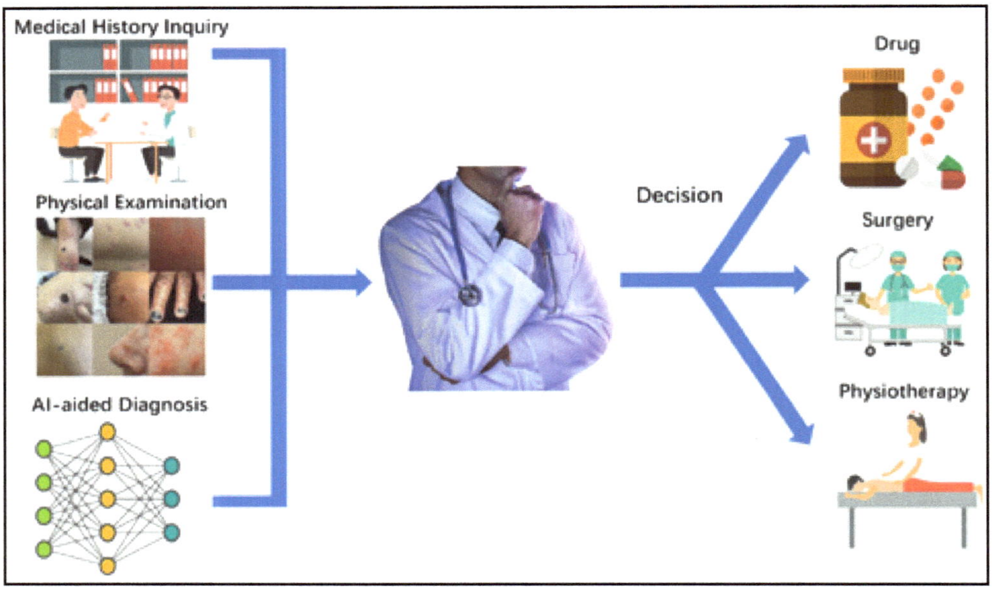

Fig: Artificial Intelligence in Dermatology

AI is transforming the field of dermatology by providing powerful tools for the classification of skin lesions, including life-threatening conditions like melanoma and chronic diseases like psoriasis. Through the application of advanced machine learning algorithms, dermatologists can achieve greater diagnostic accuracy, speed, and consistency. Despite challenges related to data quality, model explainability, and ethical concerns, the integration of AI into clinical practice holds immense promise for improving skin health outcomes. As technology continues to evolve and access becomes more widespread, AI-driven dermatology is poised to become a standard component of modern medical care, benefiting patients and clinicians alike. The future of AI in skin lesion classification is full of exciting possibilities. Ongoing research is exploring the use of generative adversarial networks (GANs) to augment training datasets and improve model robustness. Integration of AI with wearable devices and smartphone apps may facilitate continuous skin monitoring and early detection of changes. Multimodal AI systems combining image data with patient history, genetic information, and environmental factors could offer holistic diagnostic insights. Furthermore, international collaborations and open-source platforms are expected to foster innovation and democratize access to AI-powered dermatology tools globally.

AI and Machine Learning in Dermatology

Artificial intelligence in skin lesion classification primarily utilizes machine learning, particularly deep learning models such as convolutional neural networks (CNNs). These models are capable of processing vast amounts of visual data and learning complex patterns that distinguish between different types of lesions.

By training on large datasets of dermoscopic images annotated by experts, AI systems can learn to recognize subtle features that differentiate melanoma from benign moles or psoriasis from other inflammatory conditions. The ability of AI to continuously improve through training on new data makes it particularly valuable in dermatological diagnostics, where lesion appearances can vary widely based on skin tone, age, and environmental factors.

Melanoma Detection Using AI

Melanoma is one of the most aggressive forms of skin cancer, and early detection significantly improves survival rates. AI has shown remarkable success in classifying melanoma from dermoscopic images. Deep learning algorithms can detect asymmetry, border irregularities, color variations, diameter, and evolving patterns—key indicators traditionally used by dermatologists in the ABCDE rule for melanoma. Several studies have demonstrated that AI models can match or even surpass dermatologists in diagnostic accuracy. For instance, neural networks trained on large datasets from the International Skin Imaging Collaboration (ISIC) have achieved diagnostic performance comparable to expert-level clinicians. By integrating AI tools into clinical practice, the early detection of melanoma can be significantly enhanced, potentially reducing mortality rates.

Classification of Psoriasis and Other Inflammatory Skin Diseases

Unlike melanoma, psoriasis is a chronic autoimmune condition characterized by red, scaly plaques on the skin. Accurate diagnosis of psoriasis is essential for appropriate treatment planning and disease management. AI models trained on image datasets can differentiate psoriasis from other inflammatory skin disorders such as eczema, seborrheic dermatitis, and lichen planus. These conditions often share overlapping visual characteristics, making them difficult to distinguish without biopsy or expert consultation. AI aids in reducing diagnostic uncertainty by analyzing texture, color distribution, and lesion morphology with high precision. Additionally, machine learning algorithms can monitor disease progression and treatment response, helping clinicians adjust therapy regimens effectively.

Technological Foundations and Model Architectures

Convolutional neural networks form the backbone of most AI systems used in skin lesion classification. These networks are designed to process image data in layers, progressively extracting features like edges, shapes, and textures. Common architectures used in dermatology include ResNet, VGGNet, Inception, and DenseNet, each offering unique advantages in terms of depth, speed, and accuracy.

Transfer learning is also widely employed, where models pre-trained on large general datasets like ImageNet are fine-tuned with dermatology-specific images. This approach reduces the need for extremely large labeled medical datasets and accelerates model development. Ensemble methods, which combine predictions from multiple models, further enhance diagnostic performance and reduce errors.

Role of Dermoscopic and Clinical Imaging

AI systems rely on high-quality imaging for optimal performance. Dermoscopic images, captured using specialized magnifying devices, reveal subsurface skin structures and are highly informative for diagnosing pigmented lesions. Clinical images, taken with standard cameras, are also valuable, especially for assessing non-pigmented conditions like psoriasis or eczema.

Multi-modal systems that integrate both dermoscopic and clinical images have demonstrated superior accuracy in classification tasks. Advances in smartphone-based dermoscopy and teledermatology platforms now enable patients and primary care providers to capture and submit images for AI evaluation, thus expanding access to dermatological care in remote and underserved areas.

Data Challenges and Annotation Quality

The success of AI models depends heavily on the quality and diversity of training data. Curated datasets like HAM10000, DermNet, and ISIC have been instrumental in advancing research in AI-based skin lesion classification. However, challenges remain in terms of data imbalance, where certain lesion types are underrepresented, and image variability caused by lighting, skin tone, and image quality. Accurate annotations by experienced dermatologists are essential to train reliable models, and interobserver variability can impact the consistency of labels. To address these issues, collaborative efforts are underway to standardize annotation protocols and diversify datasets to reflect global skin types and conditions.

Explainability and Trust in AI Diagnoses

One of the critical challenges in deploying AI in clinical settings is the need for explainability. Clinicians must be able to understand and trust the decision-making process of AI models, particularly in life-altering diagnoses such as skin cancer. Techniques like saliency maps, Grad-CAM, and layer-wise relevance propagation are used to visualize which parts of an image influenced the model's decision. These tools help validate AI predictions and build confidence among medical professionals. Incorporating explainable AI (XAI) frameworks into dermatology not only enhances trust but also supports educational efforts by highlighting diagnostic features to students and trainees.

Integration into Clinical Workflows

For AI to be effectively used in real-world dermatology practice, it must be seamlessly integrated into clinical workflows. AI tools can serve as decision support systems that provide second opinions or triage capabilities in primary care settings.

For example, AI can help prioritize patients with suspicious lesions for specialist referral, thereby optimizing healthcare resources. Integration with electronic health records (EHRs) and telemedicine platforms ensures that AI outputs are easily accessible and actionable. Pilot programs in hospitals and clinics have demonstrated that AI-assisted dermatology can reduce diagnostic errors, improve efficiency, and enhance patient satisfaction, especially in settings where dermatologists are scarce.

Ethical, Regulatory, and Legal Considerations

The deployment of AI in skin lesion classification raises important ethical and regulatory questions. Issues related to data privacy, informed consent, and algorithmic bias must be carefully addressed. AI models trained predominantly on images of lighter skin tones may underperform in diagnosing conditions in darker-skinned individuals, leading to disparities in care. Regulatory agencies such as the FDA have begun approving AI-based dermatology tools, but rigorous validation, transparency, and post-market surveillance are essential to ensure safety and efficacy. Legal accountability in cases of misdiagnosis also remains a complex area requiring clear guidelines and shared responsibility between clinicians and technology providers.

3.6 OPHTHALMOLOGY

3.6.1 Diabetic Retinopathy

Diabetic retinopathy (also known as diabetic eye disease) is a medical condition in which damage occurs to the retina due to diabetes. It is a leading cause of blindness in developed countries and one of the leading causes of sight loss in the world, even though there are many new therapies and improved treatments for helping people live with diabetes. Diabetic retinopathy affects up to 80 percent of those who have had both type 1 and type 2 diabetes for 20 years or more. In at least 90% of new cases, progression to more aggressive forms of sight-threatening retinopathy and maculopathy could be reduced with proper treatment and monitoring of the eyes. The longer a person has diabetes, the higher their chances of developing diabetic retinopathy. Each year in the United States, diabetic retinopathy accounts for 12% of all new cases of blindness. It is also the leading cause of blindness in people aged 20 to 64.

Signs and Symptoms

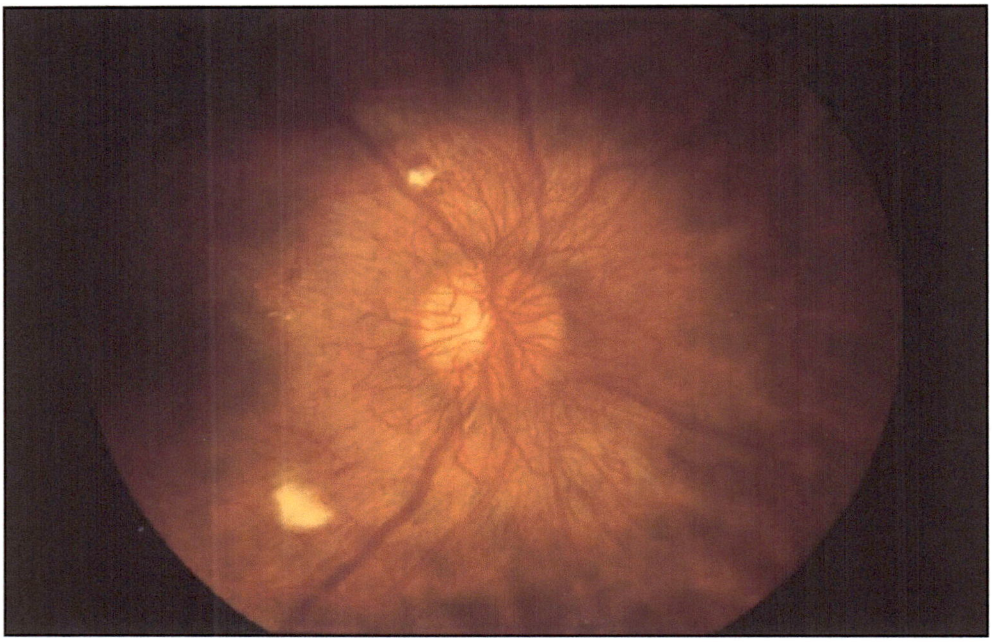

Fig: Proliferative Diabetic Retinopathy

Nearly all people with diabetes develop some degree of retina damage ("retinopathy") over several decades with the disease. For many, that damage can only be detected by a retinal exam, and has no noticeable effect on vision. Over time, progressive retinal damage may appear on a retinal exam, first with small bulges in retinal blood vessels called microaneurysms.

Then larger abnormalities in retinal vessels: cotton wool spots, hemorrhages, lipid deposits called "hard exudates", intraretinal microvascular abnormalities, and abnormal-looking retinal veins. Eventually, many progress to a stage where new blood vessels grow throughout the retina. These new blood vessels often break and bleed. Minor bleeding can cause dark floating spots obstructing vision; major bleeding can completely block vision. Around half of people with diabetic retinopathy develop swelling of the macula, called macular edema, which can begin at any time. If the swelling occurs near the center of the macula, it can cause vision disruptions ranging from mildly blurred vision to severe loss of the center of an affected person's visual field. Left untreated, around 30% of those with such swelling experience vision disruption over the next 3–5 years. Macular edema is the most common cause of vision loss in people with diabetic retinopathy.

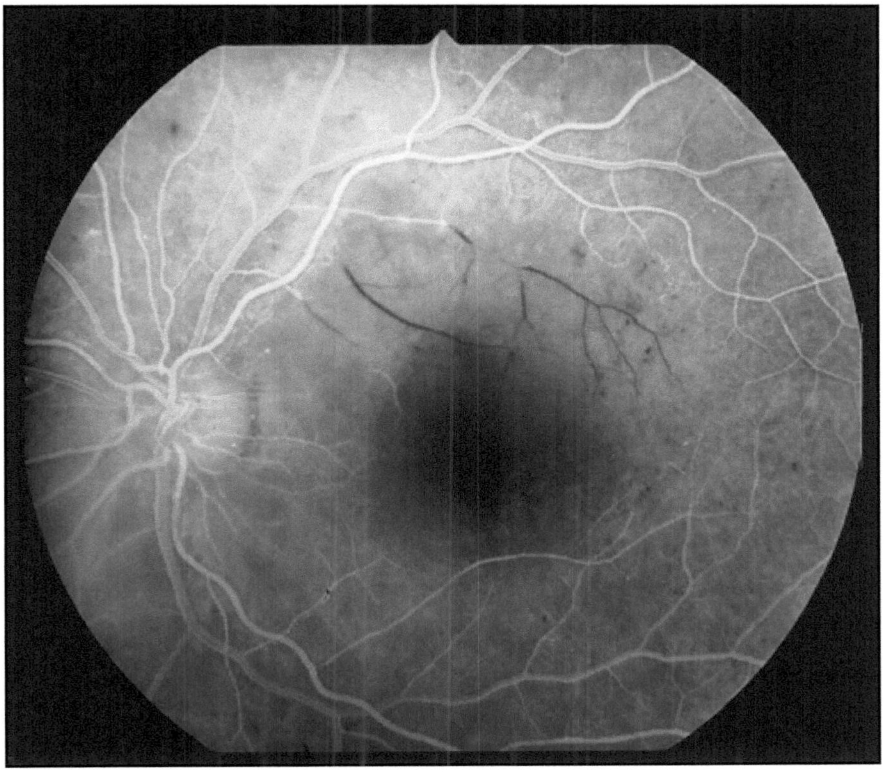

Fig: Emptied Retinal Venules due to Arterial Branch Occlusion in Diabetic Retinopathy (Fluorescein Angiography)

The repeated processes of blood vessel growth, swelling, and scarring can eventually cause retinal detachment, which manifests as the sudden appearance of dark floating spots, flashes of light, or blurred vision.

Diagnosis and Classification

Diabetic retinopathy is typically diagnosed by retinal exam observations using ophthalmoscopy. The American Academy of Ophthalmology divides diabetic retinopathy into five categories of progressive severity. The first category, "no apparent retinopathy", describes those with a healthy retinal exam. The next three categories: mild, moderate, and severe nonproliferative diabetic retinopathy (NPDR), describe increasing levels of damage to the retina. People with mild NPDR have microaneurysms in the retina, but no other damage. Those with severe NPDR have 20+ retinal hemorrhages in each quadrant of the retina, a distinctive pattern of damage on the veins of the retina called "venous beading" in at least two retinal quadrants, and obvious intraretinal microvascular abnormalities anywhere on the retina. Moderate NPDR is defined as more severe than mild NPDR, but not yet meeting the criteria for severe NPDR. The fifth stage, proliferative diabetic retinopathy, is for those with new blood vessels forming throughout the retina ("retinal neovascularization"), or blood leaking into the vitreous humor ("vitreous hemorrhage") or between the vitreous membrane and retina ("preretinal hemorrhage").

The same guidelines separately categorize macular edema into two categories: "macular edema apparently absent" and "macular edema apparently present." The latter is further subdivided into "mild"—retinal thickening or lipid deposits far from the macula's center; "moderate"— thickening or deposits near the center; and "severe"—thickening or deposits on the macula center. Optical coherence tomography is frequently used to assess macular edema. Fluorescein angiography is used by retina specialists to assess diabetic retinopathy severity further and to determine sites of macular damage.

Screening

Due to the lack of symptoms, most people with diabetic retinopathy are unaware that they have the condition until they visit an eye doctor. Both the American Diabetes Association (ADA) and the International Council of Ophthalmology (ICO) recommend regular eye exams for those with diabetes to screen for diabetic retinopathy (except those with gestational diabetes). The ADA recommends a comprehensive eye examination at the time of type 2 diabetes diagnosis, and within five years of the onset of type 1 diabetes. For women with diabetes who become pregnant, the ADA recommends an eye examination before pregnancy, in each trimester, and for a year postpartum. The ICO recommends eye examinations for those with diabetes include a visual acuity examination and a retinal examination via ophthalmoscopy or retinal photography.

Iceland, Ireland, and the United Kingdom are the only countries with national diabetic retinopathy screening programs, while substantial regional screening programs have been implemented in parts of mainland Europe, parts of Asia, and Botswana. In the UK, screening for diabetic retinopathy is part of the standard of care for people with diabetes. After one normal screening in people with diabetes, further screening is recommended every year. Teleophthalmology has been employed in these programs.

Causes

Diabetic retinopathy is caused by prolonged high blood glucose damaging the small blood vessels of the retina, though the mechanism by which this occurs is unknown. Progression of diabetic retinopathy is accompanied by loss of capillary cells, increased blood vessel permeability in the retina, and altered retinal blood flow, all of which can reduce the amount of blood oxygen that gets delivered to the retina.

Poor oxygenation of tissues drives the formation of new blood vessels throughout the retina, resulting in the proliferative stage of disease. These new blood vessels tend to rupture easily, causing bleeding within the eye, scarring, and damage to the retina or macula. Recent evidence has found a strong association between diabetic retinopathy and inflammation.

Risk Factors

The major risk factors for developing diabetic retinopathy are duration of diabetes, poor blood sugar control, and, to a lesser extent, high blood pressure. Five years after diabetes diagnosis, around 25% of those with type 1 diabetes have some degree of diabetic retinopathy, while 2% have proliferative diabetic retinopathy. By 15 years after diagnosis, that increases to 80% with some retinopathy, and 25% with proliferative disease. Children are an exception—regardless of duration of diabetes, children rarely experience sight-threatening retinopathy; however, puberty can accelerate retinopathy progression. Pregnancy can also accelerate the progression of diabetic retinopathy (although women with gestational diabetes are not at risk).

Both chronically high blood sugar (measured by a high HbA1c) and highly variable blood sugar are associated with developing diabetic retinopathy. Several more minor risk factors also exacerbate diabetic retinopathy, namely kidney disease, abnormal blood lipids, high body mass index, and smoking.

Genetic predisposition to diabetic retinopathy in type 2 diabetes consists of many genetic variants across the genome that are collectively associated with diabetic retinopathy (polygenic risk) and overlaps with genetic risk for glucose, low-density lipoprotein cholesterol, and systolic blood pressure. Several variations in the VEGFC gene have also been associated with an increased risk of developing macular edema.

People with Down syndrome, who have extra chromosome 21 material, rarely acquire diabetic retinopathy. This protection appears to be due to the elevated levels of endostatin, an anti-angiogenic protein, derived from collagen XVIII. The collagen XVIII gene is located on chromosome 21. Incidence of Retinitis Pigmentosa is observed to result in fewer and less severe microvascular lesions in both humans and mouse models. Retinitis Pigmentosa results in loss of rod receptors in the mid peripheral field, reducing the oxygen consumption that is linked with release of VEGF and growth of unwanted blood vessels in the retina.

Obstructive sleep apnea (OSA) has been associated with a higher incidence of diabetic eye disease due to blood desaturation caused by intermittent upper airway obstructions. Treatment for OSA can help reduce the risk of diabetic complications.

Pathogenesis

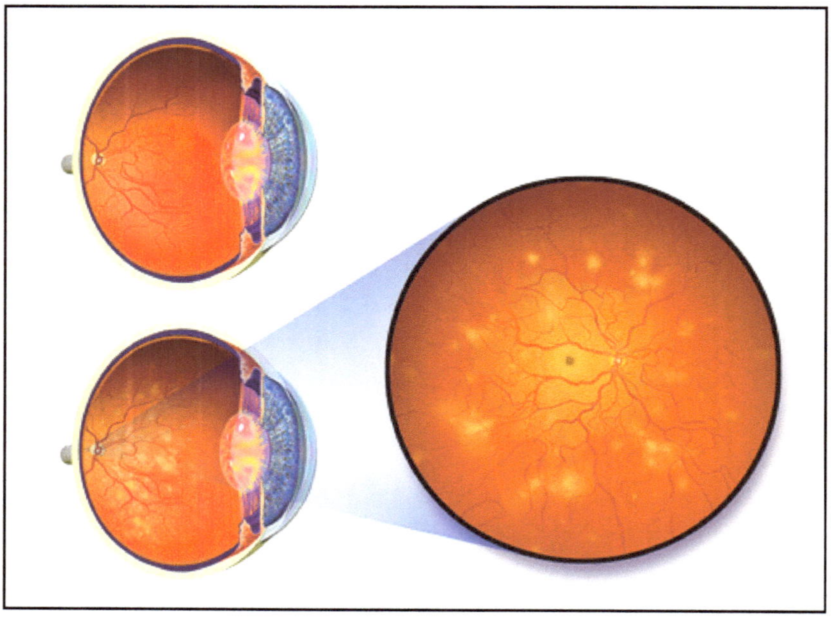

Fig: Illustration Depicting Diabetic Retinopathy

Diabetic retinopathy is the result of damage to the small blood vessels and neurons of the retina. The earliest changes leading to diabetic retinopathy include narrowing of the retinal arteries associated with reduced retinal blood flow; dysfunction of the neurons of the inner retina, followed in later stages by changes in the function of the outer retina, associated with subtle changes in visual function; dysfunction of the blood-retinal barrier, which protects the retina from many substances in the blood (including toxins and immune cells), leading to the leaking of blood constituents into the retinal neuropile. Later, the basement membrane of the retinal blood vessels thickens, capillaries degenerate and lose cells, particularly pericytes and vascular smooth muscle cells. This leads to loss of blood flow and progressive ischemia, and microscopic aneurysms which appear as balloon-like structures jutting out from the capillary walls, which recruit inflammatory cells; and advanced dysfunction and degeneration of the neurons and glial cells of the retina. The condition typically develops about 10–15 years after receiving the diagnosis of diabetes mellitus.

An experimental study suggests that pericyte death is caused by blood glucose persistently activating protein kinase C and mitogen-activated protein kinase (MAPK), which, through a series of intermediates, inhibits signaling through platelet-derived growth factor receptors—signaling that supports cellular survival, proliferation, and growth. The resulting withdrawal of this signaling leads to the programmed cell death (apoptosis) of the cells in this experimental model.

In addition, excessive sorbitol in diabetics is deposited in the retina tissue, and it is also proposed to play a role in diabetic retinopathy. Recent studies have found a strong correlation between retinal inflammation and diabetic retinopathy progression. A genetic study showed that diabetic retinopathy shares a similar genetic predisposition with levels of glucose, low-density lipoprotein cholesterol, and systolic blood pressure, indicating that glycemic control and cardiometabolic factors may be important in the development of diabetic retinopathy. Lipid peroxidation plays a notable role in the progression of diabetic retinopathy. Free radicals such as hydroxyl and hydroperoxyl species with oxygen as functional group oxidize lipids and phospholipids, and at the cellular level bring about membrane lipid peroxidation and in this way can trigger diabetic retinopathy.

Management

There are four common treatments for diabetic retinopathy: anti-VEGF injections, steroid injections, panretinal laser photocoagulation, and vitrectomy. Current treatment regimens can prevent 90% of severe vision loss. Although these treatments are very successful (in slowing or stopping further vision loss), they do not cure diabetic retinopathy. Caution should be exercised in treatment with laser surgery since it causes a loss of retinal tissue. It is often more prudent to inject triamcinolone or anti-VEGF drugs. In some patients, it results in a marked increase in vision, especially if there is an edema of the macula. In addition, standard treatment for diabetic retinopathy includes improving control of blood sugar, blood pressure, and blood cholesterol, all of which can reduce diabetic retinopathy progression.

Mild or Moderate NPDR

For those with mild to moderate non-proliferative diabetic retinopathy, the American Academy of Ophthalmology recommends only more frequent retinal exams—every six to twelve months—as these people are at an increased risk of developing proliferative retinopathy or macular edema. Injection of anti-VEGF drugs or steroids can reduce diabetic retinopathy progression in around half of eyes treated; however, whether this results in improved vision long term is not yet known. The lipid-lowering drug fenofibrate also reduces progression of disease in people with mild to moderate disease.

Diabetic Macular Edema

Those at highest risk of vision loss - that is, with edema near the center of the macula - benefit most from eye injections of anti-VEGF therapies aflibercept, bevacizumab, or ranibizumab. There is no widely accepted dosing schedule though people typically receive more frequent injections during the first year of treatment, with less frequent injections in subsequent years sufficient to maintain remission. Those whose eyes don't improve with anti-VEGF therapy may instead receive laser photocoagulation, typically in the form of short laser pulses.

Those with macular edema but no vision loss do not benefit from treatment; the American Academy of Ophthalmology recommends deferring treatment until visual acuity falls to at least 20/30. The diabetic macular edema manifestation is difficult to predict. Autoantibodies against hexokinase 1 are commonly associated with diabetic macular edema manifestation. Nearly one-third of patients with diabetic macular edema were found to be positive for anti-hexokinase 1 autoantibodies. Importantly, these autoantibodies were rare in patients with diabetic retinopathy only or diabetes mellitus only. However, these autoantibodies fail to predict disease onset. They likely manifest secondary to the tissue-damaging stimulus at diabetic macular edema onset and cannot be used to predict diabetic macular edema before its onset.

Laser Photocoagulation

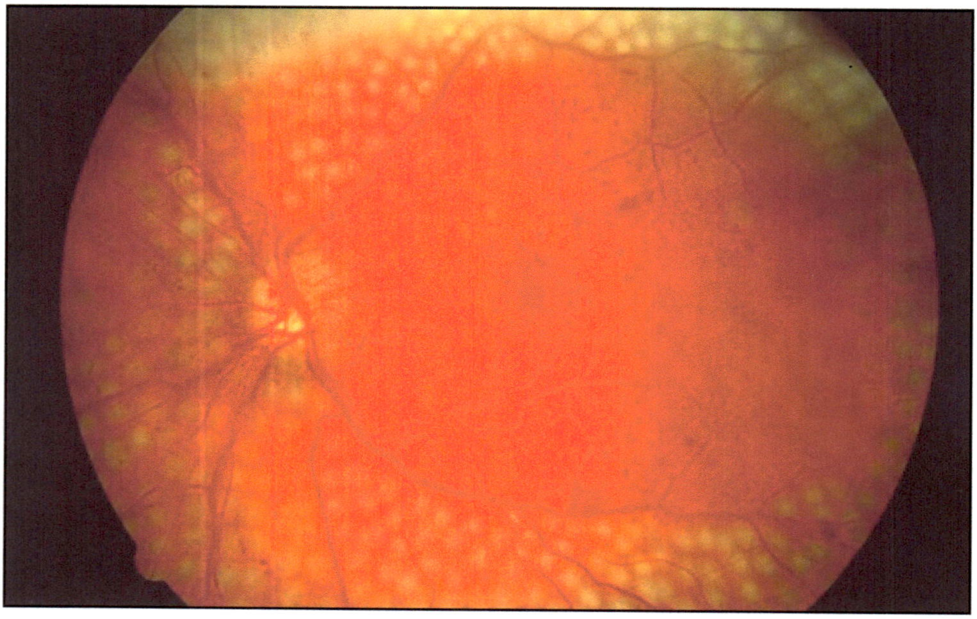

Fig: Image of Fundus Showing Scatter Laser Surgery for Diabetic Retinopathy

Laser photocoagulation can be used in two scenarios for the treatment of diabetic retinopathy. Firstly, to treat macular edema and secondly, for treating the whole retina (panretinal photocoagulation) for controlling neovascularization. It is widely used for the early stages of proliferative retinopathy. There are different types of lasers, and there is evidence available on their benefits to treat proliferative diabetic retinopathy.

Panretinal Laser Photocoagulation

For those with proliferative or severe non-proliferative diabetic retinopathy, vision loss can be prevented by treatment with panretinal laser photocoagulation. The goal is to create 1,600–2,000 burns in the retina with the hope of reducing the retina's oxygen demand, and hence the possibility of ischemia. It is done in multiple sittings. In treating advanced diabetic retinopathy, the burns are used to destroy the abnormal new blood vessels that form in the retina. This has been shown to reduce the risk of severe vision loss for eyes at risk by 50%.

Before using the laser, the ophthalmologist dilates the pupil and applies anaesthetic drops to numb the eye. In some cases, the doctor may also numb the area behind the eye to reduce discomfort. The patient sits facing the laser machine while the doctor holds a special lens on the eye.

The physician can use a single spot laser, a pattern scan laser for two-dimensional patterns such as squares, rings, and arcs, or a navigated laser, which works by tracking retinal eye movements in real time. During the procedure, the patient will see flashes of light. These flashes often create an uncomfortable stinging sensation for the patient. After the laser treatment, patients should be advised not to drive for a few hours while the pupils are still dilated. Vision will most likely remain blurry for the rest of the day. Though there should not be much pain in the eye itself, an ice-cream headache like pain may last for hours afterwards.

Patients will lose some of their peripheral vision after this surgery, although it may be barely noticeable by the patient. The procedure does, however, save the center of the patient's sight. Laser surgery may also slightly reduce colour and night vision. A person with proliferative retinopathy will always be at risk for new bleeding, as well as glaucoma, a complication from the new blood vessels. This means that multiple treatments may be required to protect vision.

Intravitreal Triamcinolone Acetonide

Triamcinolone is a long-acting steroid preparation. Treating people with DME with intravitreal injections of triamcinolone may lead to some degree of improvement in visual acuity when compared to eyes treated with placebo injections. When injected in the vitreous cavity, the steroid decreases the macular edema (thickening of the retina at the macula) caused due to diabetic maculopathy, and that may increase visual acuity.

The effect of triamcinolone is not permanent and may last up to three months, which necessitates repeated injections for maintaining the beneficial effect. Best results of intravitreal Triamcinolone have been found in eyes that have already undergone cataract surgery. Complications of intravitreal injection of triamcinolone may include cataract, steroid-induced glaucoma, and endophthalmitis.

Intravitreal Anti-VEGF

Aflibercept may have advantages in improving visual outcomes over bevacizumab and ranibizumab, after one year, longer term advantages are unclear In cases with vitreous hemorrhage, however, anti-VEGF injections proved to be less effective in restoring visual acuity than vitrectomy combined with panretinal laser-photocoagulation.

Surgery

Instead of laser surgery, some people require a vitrectomy to restore vision. A vitrectomy is performed when there is a lot of blood in the vitreous. It involves removing the cloudy vitreous and replacing it with a saline solution. Studies show that people who have a vitrectomy soon after a large hemorrhage are more likely to protect their vision than someone who waits to have the operation. Early vitrectomy is especially effective in people with insulin-dependent diabetes, who may be at greater risk of blindness from a hemorrhage into the eye.

Vitrectomy may be done under general or local anesthesia. The doctor makes a tiny incision in the sclera, or white of the eye. Next, a small instrument is placed into the eye to remove the vitreous and insert the saline solution into the eye. Patients may be able to return home soon after the vitrectomy, or may be asked to stay in the hospital overnight. After the operation, the eye will be red and sensitive, and patients usually need to wear an eyepatch for a few days or weeks to protect the eye. Medicated eye drops are also prescribed to protect against infection. There is evidence which suggests anti-VEGF drugs given either before or during vitrectomy may reduce the risk of posterior vitreous cavity haemorrhage. Vitrectomy is frequently combined with other modalities of treatment.

3.6.2 Macular Degeneration

Macular degeneration, also known as age-related macular degeneration (AMD or ARMD), is a medical condition which may result in blurred or no vision in the center of the visual field. Early on there are often no symptoms. Some people experience a gradual worsening of vision that may affect one or both eyes. While it does not result in complete blindness, loss of central vision can make it hard to recognize faces, drive, read, or perform other activities of daily life. Visual hallucinations may also occur.

Macular degeneration typically occurs in older people, and is caused by damage to the macula of the retina. Genetic factors and smoking may play a role. The condition is diagnosed through a complete eye exam. Severity is divided into early, intermediate, and late types. The late type is additionally divided into "dry" and "wet" forms, with the dry form making up 90% of cases. The difference between the two forms is categorized by the change in the macula. Those with dry-form

AMD have drusen, cellular debris in their macula that gradually damages light-sensitive cells and leads to vision loss. In wet-form AMD, blood vessels grow under the macula, causing blood and fluid to leak into the retina.

Exercising, eating well, and not smoking may reduce the risk of macular degeneration. No cure or treatment restores the vision already lost. In the wet form, anti–vascular endothelial growth factor injected into the eye or, less commonly, laser coagulation or photodynamic therapy may slow worsening. Dietary antioxidant vitamins, minerals, and carotenoids do not appear to affect the onset; however, dietary supplements may slow the progression in those who already have the disease.

Age-related macular degeneration is a main cause of central blindness among the working-aged population worldwide. As of 2022, it affects more than 200 million people globally with the prevalence expected to increase to 300 million people by 2040 as the proportion of elderly persons in the population increases. It is more common in those of European or North American ancestry, and is about equally common in males and females. In 2013, it was the fourth most common cause of blindness, after cataracts, preterm birth, and glaucoma. It most commonly occurs in people over the age of fifty and in the United States is the most common cause of vision loss in this age group. About 0.4% of people between 50 and 60 have the disease, while it occurs in 0.7% of people 60 to 70, 2.3% of those 70 to 80, and nearly 12% of people over 80 years old.

Signs and Symptoms

Fig: Normal Vision

Fig: The Same View with Age-Related Macular Degeneration

Early or intermediate AMD may be asymptomatic, or it may present with blurred or decreased vision in one or both eyes. This may manifest initially as difficulty with reading or driving (especially in poorly lit areas). Other symptoms of AMD include distortion of vision and blind spots (especially in and around the central visual field). Other signs and symptoms of macular degeneration include:

- Distorted vision in the form of metamorphopsia, in which a grid of straight lines appears wavy and parts of the grid may appear blank. Patients often first notice this when looking at things like miniblinds in their home or telephone poles while driving. There may also be central scotomas, shadows, or missing areas of vision.
- Slow recovery of visual function after exposure to bright light (photostress test).
- Visual acuity drastically decreasing (two levels or more), e.g.: 20/20 to 20/80.
- **Blurred Vision:** Those with nonexudative (dry) macular degeneration may be asymptomatic or notice a gradual loss of central vision, whereas those with exudative (wet) macular degeneration often notice a rapid onset of vision loss (often caused by leakage and bleeding of abnormal blood vessels).
- Trouble discerning colors, specifically dark ones from dark ones and light ones from light ones.
- A loss in contrast sensitivity.

- Formed visual hallucinations and flashing lights have also been associated with severe visual loss secondary to wet AMD.

Macular degeneration by itself will not lead to total blindness. For that matter, only a small number of people with visual impairment are blind. In almost all cases, some vision remains, mainly peripheral. Other complicating conditions may lead to such an acute condition (severe stroke or trauma, untreated glaucoma, etc.), but few macular degeneration patients experience total visual loss.

The area of the macula constitutes only about 2.1% of the retina, and the remaining 97.9% (the peripheral field) remains unaffected by the disease. Even though the macula provides such a small fraction of the visual field, almost half of the visual cortex is devoted to processing macular information. In addition, people with dry macular degeneration often do not experience any symptoms but can experience gradual onset of blurry vision in one or both eyes. People with wet macular degeneration may experience acute onset of visual symptoms.

Risk Factors

The pathogenesis of age-related macular degeneration (AMD) is intricately linked to gene-environment interactions. Key risk factors are age, race/ethnicity, smoking, and family history. Advanced age is the strongest predictor of AMD, particularly over 50.

Race and Ethnicity

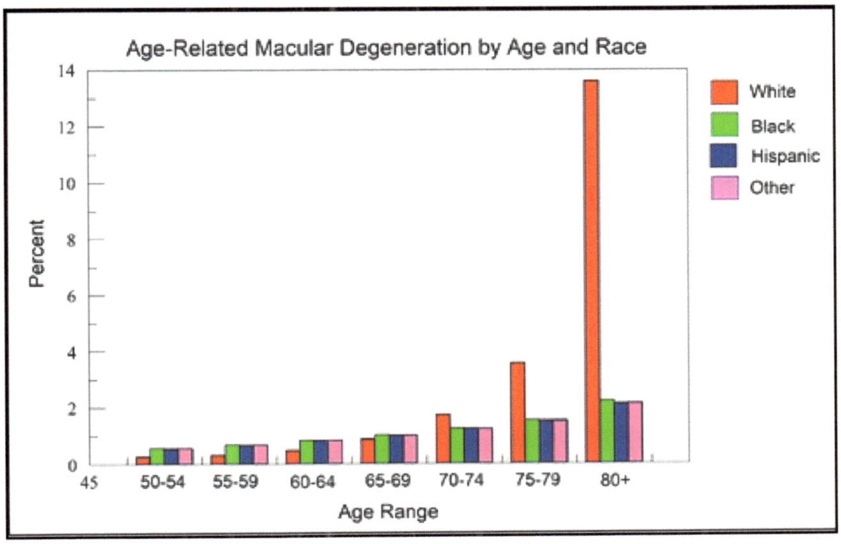

Fig: AMD by Race and Age from National Eye Institute Data

As illustrated by the Figure in this section, derived from data presented by the National Eye Institute of the United States, among those over 80 years of age, White individuals are more than 6-fold more likely to develop AMD than Black or Hispanic individuals. Thus, white background is a major risk factor for AMD. In Caucasian (white) skin, there is a specific group of polymorphic genes (with single nucleotide alterations) that encode for enzymes and transcription factors responsible for the early steps (including the first step, formation of L-DOPA from the amino acid tyrosine) of the melanin synthesis pathway.

Many of these enzymes and transcription factors are reviewed by Markiewicz and Idowu. Also, as reviewed by Sturm et al. "increasing intracellular concentrations of either tyrosine or L-DOPA both increase melanogenesis" or formation of the black pigment melanin. Thus there appears to be an association between reduced L-DOPA production and white skin. As suggested by the Figure and information in this section, reduced L-DOPA, resulting in white skin, appears to be associated with an increased risk of macular degeneration for white individuals over the age of 80.

Environment and Lifestyle

- **Smoking:** Smoking tobacco increases the risk of AMD by two to three times that of someone who has never smoked, and may be the most important modifiable factor in its prevention. A review of previous studies found "a strong association between current smoking and AMD.... Cigarette smoking is likely to have toxic effects on the retina."
- **Hypertension (High Blood Pressure):** In the ALIENOR study 2013, early and late AMD were not significantly associated with systolic or diastolic blood pressure (BP), hypertension, or use of antihypertensive medications, but elevated pulse pressure [(PP) systolic BP minus diastolic BP] was significantly associated with an increased risk of late AMD.
- **High Cholesterol:** Elevated cholesterol may increase the risk of AMD.
- **Obesity:** Abdominal obesity is a risk factor, especially among men.
- **Fat Intake:** Consuming high amounts of certain fats, including saturated fats, trans fats, and omega-6 fatty acids, likely contributes to AMD, while monounsaturated fats are potentially protective. In particular, omega-3 fatty acids may decrease the risk of AMD.

Exposure to UV light from sunlight may be associated with an increased risk of developing AMD, although evidence for this is weaker than for other causes. There is no evidence to support the claim that exposure to digital screens contributes to the risk of macular degeneration.

Genetics

AMD is a highly heritable condition. Recurrence ratios for siblings of an affected individual are three- to six-fold higher than in the general population. Genetic linkage analysis has identified 5 sets of gene variants at three locations on different chromosomes (1, 6 and 10) as explaining at least 50% of the risk. These genes have roles regulating the immune response, inflammatory processes and homeostasis of the retina. Variants of these genes give rise to different kinds of dysfunction in these processes. Over time, this results in the accumulation of intracellular and extracellular metabolic debris. This can cause scarring of the retina or breakdown of its vascularization.

The list of genetic variations associated with AMD includes complement factors, apolipoprotein E, fibroblast growth factor 2, DNA excision repair protein, and age-related maculopathy susceptibility protein 2. Although genetic testing can lead to the identification of genetic variation that can predispose to AMD, the complex pathogenesis of the condition prevents the use of these tests in routine practice. Nevertheless, they can be useful in selecting patients for clinical trials and analyzing their response to treatment. The three loci where identified gene variants are found are designated:

- Complement Factor H (CFH) on chromosome 1 at location 1q31.3.
- HTRA serine peptidase 1/Age Related Maculopathy Susceptibility 2 (HTRA1/ARMS2) on chromosome 10 at location 10q26.
- Complement Factor B/Complement Component 2 (CFB/CC2) on chromosome 6 at 6p21.3.

Specific genes:

- **Polymorphisms in Genes for Complement System Proteins:** Variation in the genes for the complement system proteins factor H (CFH), factor B (CFB) and factor 3 (C3), among others, are strongly associated with a person's risk for developing AMD. CFH is involved in inhibiting the inflammatory response. The mutation in CFH (Y402H) results in reduced ability of the protein to localise to and protect tissues such as the retina from complement overactivation. Absence of the complement factor H-related genes R3 and R1 protects against AMD. Two independent studies in 2007 showed a certain common mutation Arg80Gly in the C3 gene, which is a central protein of the complement system, is strongly associated with the occurrence of AMD. The authors of both papers consider their study to underscore the influence of the complement pathway in the pathogenesis of this disease.
- In two 2006 studies, another gene that has implications for the disease, called HTRA1 (encoding a secreted serine protease), was identified.
- Six mutations of the gene SERPING1 (Serpin Peptidase Inhibitor, Clade G (C1 Inhibitor), Member 1) are associated with AMD. Mutations in this gene can also cause hereditary angioedema.

- **Fibulin-5 Mutation:** Rare forms of the disease are caused by genetic defects in fibulin-5, in an autosomal dominant manner. In 2004, Stone et al. performed a screening on 402 AMD patients and revealed a statistically significant correlation between mutations in fibulin-5 and the incidence of the disease.
- Mitochondrial-related gene polymorphisms such as that in the MT-ND2 molecule, predicts wet AMD.

Pathophysiology

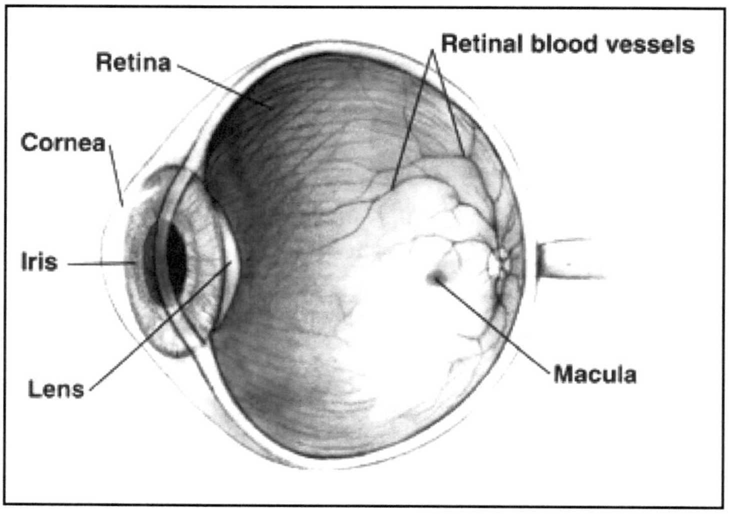

Fig: Human Eye Cross-Sectional View

The pathogenesis of age-related macular degeneration is not fully understood although some theories have been put forward, including oxidative stress mitochondrial dysfunction, and inflammatory processes. The imbalance between the production of damaged cellular components and degradation leads to the accumulation of harmful products, for example, intracellular lipofuscin and extracellular drusen. Incipient atrophy is demarcated by areas of retinal pigment epithelium (RPE) thinning or depigmentation that precedes geographic atrophy in the early stages of AMD. In advanced stages of AMD, atrophy of the RPE (geographic atrophy) and/or development of new blood vessels (neovascularization) result in the death of photoreceptors and central vision loss.

In the dry (nonexudative) form, drusen accumulate between the retina and the choroid, causing atrophy and scarring to the retina. In the wet (exudative) form, which is more severe, blood vessels grow up from the choroid (neovascularization) behind the retina which can leak exudate and fluid and also cause hemorrhaging.

Early work demonstrated a family of immune mediators was plentiful in drusen. Complement factor H (CFH) is an important inhibitor of this inflammatory cascade, and a disease-associated polymorphism in the CFH gene strongly associates with AMD. Thus an AMD pathophysiological model of chronic low grade complement activation and inflammation in the macula has been advanced. Lending credibility to this has been the discovery of disease-associated genetic polymorphisms in other elements of the complement cascade including complement component 3 (C3).

A powerful predictor of AMD is found on chromosome 10q26 at LOC 387715. An insertion/deletion polymorphism at this site reduces expression of the ARMS2 gene through destabilization of its mRNA through deletion of the polyadenylation signal. ARMS2 protein may localize to the mitochondria and participate in energy metabolism, though much remains to be discovered about its function. Other gene markers of progression risk includes tissue inhibitor of metalloproteinase 3 (TIMP3), suggesting a role for extracellular matrix metabolism in AMD progression. Variations in cholesterol metabolising genes such as the hepatic lipase, cholesterol ester transferase, lipoprotein lipase and the ATP-binding cassette A1 correlate with disease progression. The early stigmata of the disease, drusen, are rich in cholesterol, offering face validity to the results of genome-wide association studies.

Stages

In AMD there is a progressive accumulation of characteristic yellow deposits, called drusen (buildup of extracellular proteins and lipids), in the macula (a part of the retina), between the retinal pigment epithelium and the underlying choroid. This accumulation is believed to damage the retina over time. Amyloid beta, which builds up in Alzheimer's disease brains, is one of the proteins that accumulate in AMD, which is a reason why AMD is sometimes called "Alzheimer's of the eye" or "Alzheimer's of the retina". AMD can be divided into 3 stages: early, intermediate, and late, based partially on the extent (size and number) of drusen. AMD-like pathology begins with small yellow deposits (drusen) in the macula, between the retinal pigment epithelium and the underlying choroid. Most people with these early changes (referred to as age-related maculopathy) still have good vision. People with drusen may or may not develop AMD. The majority of people over age 60 have drusen with no adverse effects. The risk of developing symptoms is higher when the drusen are large and numerous, and associated with the disturbance in the pigmented cell layer under the macula. Large and soft drusen are thought to be related to elevated cholesterol deposits.

- **Early AMD:** Early AMD is diagnosed based on the presence of medium-sized drusen, which is about the width of an average human hair. It is usually asymptomatic.
- **Intermediate AMD:** Intermediate AMD is diagnosed by large drusen and/or any retinal pigment abnormalities. Intermediate AMD may

cause some vision loss, but, like early AMD, it is usually asymptomatic. Recently, subgroups of intermediate AMD have been identified, which have a very high risk of progression toward late AMD. This subgroup (depending on the precise definitions) is termed nascent GA and/or iRORA (incomplete retinal pigment epithelium and outer retinal atrophy). These 'high-risk' subgroups of intermediate AMD can be used to inform patients of their prognosis. In addition, these can be applied in clinical trials as endpoints.

- **Late AMD:** In late AMD, enough retinal damage occurs that, in addition to drusen, people will also begin to experience symptomatic central vision loss. The damage can either be the development of atrophy or the onset of neovascular disease. Late AMD is further divided into two subtypes based on the types of damage: Geographic atrophy and Wet AMD (also called Neovascular AMD).
- **Dry AMD:** Dry AMD (also called nonexudative AMD) is a broad designation, encompassing all forms of AMD that are not neovascular (wet AMD). This includes early and intermediate forms of AMD, as well as the advanced form of dry AMD known as geographic atrophy. Dry AMD patients tend to have minimal symptoms in the earlier stages; visual function loss occurs more often if the condition advances to geographic atrophy. Dry AMD accounts for 80–90% of cases and usually progresses slowly. In 10–20% of people, dry AMD progresses to the wet type.
- **Geographic Atrophy:** Geographic atrophy (also called atrophic AMD) is an advanced form of AMD in which progressive and irreversible loss of retinal cells leads to a loss of visual function. Multiple layers make up the retina, and in geographic atrophy, three specific layers undergo atrophy: the choriocapillaris, retinal pigment epithelium, and the overlying photoreceptors. The three layers that undergo atrophy in geographic atrophy are all adjacent to each other. The photoreceptors are the most superficial and they are the cells that are responsible for converting energy from the light from the outside world, into an electrical signal to be sent to the brain. There are several functions of the retinal pigment epithelium. One of the main functions of the retinal pigment epithelium is to minimize oxidative stress. It does so by absorbing light and thus preventing it from getting to the underlying layers. The layers underlying the retinal pigment epithelium are very vascularized so they have very high oxygen tension. Thus, if light were to get to those layers, many free radicals would form and cause damage to nearby tissues. The

deepest layer that undergoes atrophy in geographic atrophy is called the choriocappilaris. It is a capillary network that provides nutrients to the retinal pigment epithelium. The pathophysiology of geographic atrophy is still uncertain. Some studies questioned whether it was due to a deficient retinal pigment epithelium, leading to increased oxidative stress. Other studies have looked for inflammatory causes of damage. Thus far, the medical community is still not certain. Recent studies have begun to look at each layer individually. They found that decreased blood flow in the choriocapillaris precedes atrophy of the retinal pigment epithelium and the overlying photoreceptors. Since the choriocapillaris is a vascular layer, this may be used as an argument for why geographic atrophy could be a disease due to decreased blood flow.

- **Wet AMD:** Neovascular or exudative AMD, the "wet" form of advanced AMD, causes vision loss due to abnormal blood vessel growth (choroidal neovascularization) in the choriocapillaris, through Bruch's membrane. It is usually, but not always, preceded by the dry form of AMD. The proliferation of abnormal blood vessels in the retina is stimulated by vascular endothelial growth factor (VEGF). Because these blood vessels are abnormal, they are also more fragile than typical blood vessels, which ultimately leads to blood and protein leakage below the macula. Bleeding, leaking, and scarring from these blood vessels eventually cause irreversible damage to the photoreceptors and rapid vision loss if left untreated.

Diagnosis

Diagnosis of age-related macular degeneration depends on signs in the macula, not necessarily vision. Early diagnosis of AMD can prevent further visual deterioration and potentially improve vision. Diagnosis of dry (or early stage) AMD may include the following clinical examinations as well as procedures and tests:

- The transition from dry to wet AMD can happen rapidly, and if it is left untreated can lead to legal blindness in as little as six months. To prevent this from occurring and to initiate preventive strategies earlier in the disease process, dark adaptation testing may be performed. A dark adaptometer can detect subclinical AMD at least three years earlier than it is clinically evident.
- There is a loss of contrast sensitivity, so that contours, shadows, and color vision are less vivid. The loss of contrast sensitivity can be quickly and easily measured by a contrast sensitivity test like Pelli Robson performed either at home or by an eye specialist.

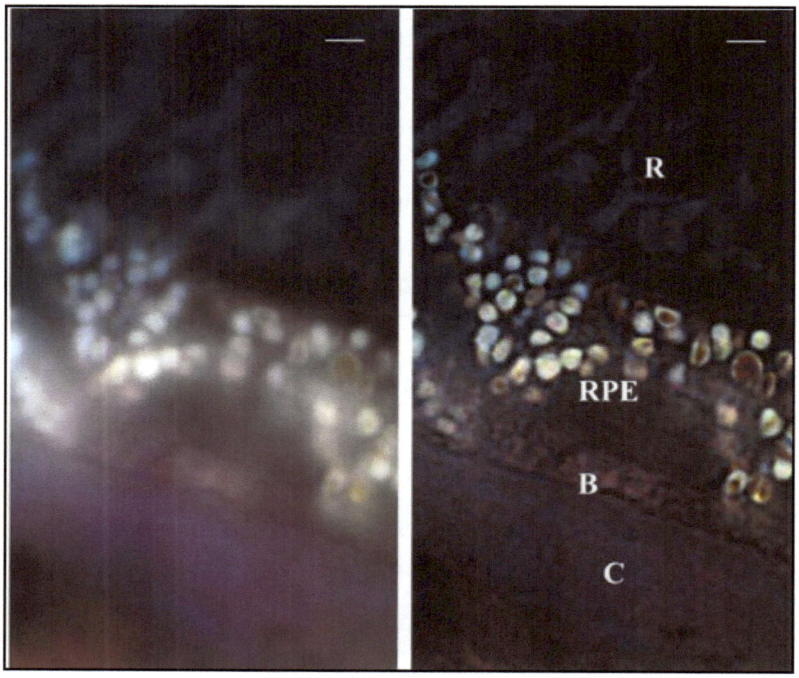

Fig: Super Resolution Microscopic Investigation of Human Eye Tissue Affected by AMD

- When viewing an Amsler grid, some straight lines appear wavy and some patches appear blank.
- When viewing a Snellen chart, at least 2 lines decline.
- In dry macular degeneration, which occurs in 85–90 percent of AMD cases, drusen spots can be seen in Fundus photography.
- Using an electroretinogram, points in the macula with a weak or absent response compared to a normal eye may be found.
- Farnsworth-Munsell 100 hue test and Maximum Color Contrast Sensitivity test (MCCS) for assessing color acuity and color contrast sensitivity.
- Optical coherence tomography is now used by most ophthalmologists in the diagnosis and the follow-up evaluation of the response to treatment with antiangiogenic drugs.

Diagnosis of wet (or late-stage) AMD may include:

- Preferential hyperacuity perimetry changes (for wet AMD). Preferential hyperacuity perimetry is a test that detects drastic changes in vision and involves the macula being stimulated with distorted patterns of dots and the patient identification of where in the visual field this occurs.

- In wet macular degeneration, angiography can visualize the leakage of the bloodstream behind the macula. Fluorescein angiography allows for the identification and localization of abnormal vascular processes.

Histology

Pigmentary Changes in the Retina: In addition to the pigmented cells in the iris (the colored part of the eye), there are pigmented cells beneath the retina. As these cells break down and release their pigment, dark clumps of released pigment and later, areas that are less pigmented may appear.

- **Exudative Changes:** hemorrhages in the eye, hard exudates, subretinal/ sub-RPE/intraretinal fluid.
- **Drusen:** Tiny accumulations of extracellular material that build up on the retina. While there is a tendency for drusen to be blamed for the progressive loss of vision, drusen deposits can be present in the retina without vision loss. Some patients with large deposits of drusen have normal visual acuity. If normal retinal reception and image transmission are sometimes possible in a retina when high concentrations of drusen are present, then, even if drusen can be implicated in the loss of visual function, there must be at least one other factor that accounts for the loss of vision.

Management

Treatment of AMD varies depending on the category of the disease at the time of diagnosis. In general, treatment is aimed at slowing down the progression of AMD. As of 2018, there are no treatments to reverse the effects of AMD. As of 2024, there are two drugs to dissolve the drusen in dry AMD. Early-stage and intermediate-stage AMD is managed by modifying known risk factors such as smoking cessation, management of hypertension and atherosclerosis, and making dietary modifications.

For intermediate-stage AMD, management also includes antioxidant and mineral supplementation. Advanced-stage AMD is managed based on the presence of choroidal neovascularization (CNV): dry AMD (no CNV present) or wet AMD (CNV present). No effective treatments exist for dry AMD. The CNV present in wet AMD is managed with vascular endothelial growth factor (VEGF) inhibitors. Daily use of an Amsler grid or other home visual monitoring tools can be used to monitor for development of distorted vision, which may be a sign of disease progression.

Dietary Supplements

Dietary supplements may be suggested for people with AMD, to reduce damage to the cells in the retina with antioxidants. The formulations commonly suggested are known as AREDS. The specific vitamins and minerals in AREDS-1 are vitamin C (500 mg), zinc (80 mg), vitamin E (400 IU), copper (2 mg) and beta-carotene (15 mg). In the AREDS-2 formulation, lutein (10 mg) and zeaxanthin (2 mg) replaced beta-carotene due to the risk of lung cancer in smokers taking beta-carotene.

There is some evidence to indicate that people with bilateral early or intermediate AMD, or intermediate AMD in one eye and advanced AMD in the other eye may benefit from vitamin and mineral supplementation. AREDS supplementation may help slow the progression to more severe forms of AMD and there is some evidence of improved visual acuity at 5 years. There is no evidence that micronutrient supplementation prevents AMD progression in those with severe disease or prevents disease onset in those without AMD.

With regards to AREDS-1 compared with AREDS-2 formulations, there is only weak evidence comparing the effectiveness of each formulation and the effectiveness of lutein and zeaxanthin as a replacement in the AREDS-2 formulation.

Dry AMD

Pegcetacoplan (Syfovre) and avacincaptad pegol (Izervay) are approved for medical use in the United States. In 2023 it was reported that the aging pigment lipofuscin can be broken down with the help of melanin and drugs through a newly discovered mechanism. The pigment lipofuscin plays a central role in the development of dry AMD and Stargardt's disease. The clinical development of this mechanism, which has the potential to clear Bruch's membrane and reduce the formation of drusen, is in preparation.

Wet AMD

Ranibizumab, aflibercept, brolucizumab, and faricimab are approved VEGF inhibitors for the treatment of CNV in wet AMD. All three drugs are administered via intravitreal injection, meaning they are injected directly into the eye. Bevacizumab is another VEGF inhibitor that has been shown to have similar efficacy and safety as the previous two drugs, however, is not currently indicated for AMD. AMD can also be treated with laser coagulation therapy.

A randomized control trial found that bevacizumab and ranibizumab had similar efficacy, and reported no significant increase in adverse events with bevacizumab. A 2014 Cochrane review found that the systemic safety of bevacizumab and ranibizumab are similar when used to treat neovascular AMD, except for gastrointestinal disorders. Bevacizumab, however, is not FDA-approved for the treatment of macular degeneration. A controversy in the UK involved the off-label use of cheaper bevacizumab over the approved, but expensive, ranibizumab. Ranibizumab is a smaller fragment, Fab fragment, of the parent bevacizumab molecule specifically designed for eye injections. Other approved antiangiogenic drugs for the treatment of neovascular AMD include pegaptanib and aflibercept. These anti-VEGF agents may be administered monthly or adaptively.

For adaptive anti-VEGF treatment, two approaches are conventionally applied. In the case of pro re nata, the patient comes at fixed intervals, but treatment is only administered if an activity is detected (i.e., the presence of fluid). In the case of treat-and-extend, the patients always receive treatment, but the interval to the next visit is extended if the lesion is inactive. Recently, researchers have started to apply AI algorithms to predict the future need for treatment.

The American Academy of Ophthalmology practice guidelines do not recommend laser coagulation therapy for macular degeneration, but state that it may be useful in people with new blood vessels in the choroid outside of the fovea who do not respond to drug treatment. There is strong evidence that laser coagulation will result in the disappearance of drusen but does not affect choroidal neovascularisation. A 2007 Cochrane review found that laser photocoagulation of new blood vessels in the choroid outside of the fovea is an effective and economical method, but that the benefits are limited for vessels next to or below the fovea.

Photodynamic therapy has also been used to treat wet AMD. The drug verteporfin is administered intravenously; light of a certain wavelength is then applied to the abnormal blood vessels. This activates the verteporfin destroying the vessels. Cataract surgery could improve visual outcomes for people with AMD, though there have been concerns about surgery increasing the progression of AMD. A randomized controlled trial found that people who underwent immediate cataract surgery (within two weeks) had improved visual acuity and better quality of life outcomes than those who underwent delayed cataract surgery (6 months).

Radiotherapy has been proposed as a treatment for wet AMD but the evidence to support the use of modern stereotactic radiotherapy combined with anti-VEGF is currently uncertain and is awaiting the results of ongoing studies. Nucleoside reverse transcription inhibitors like they are used in anti-HIV therapy were associated with a reduced risk of developing atrophic macular degeneration. This is because Alu elements undergo L1 (protein)-mediated reverse transcription in the cytoplasm resulting in DNA synthesis. First clinical trials are being prepared as of January 2021.

3.6.3 Fundus Image Analysis with AI

Fundus imaging refers to the capturing of photographs of the interior surface of the eye, including the retina, optic disc, macula, and posterior pole. This technique is vital for the early detection, diagnosis, and monitoring of various ocular and systemic diseases such as diabetic retinopathy, glaucoma, age-related macular degeneration, and hypertensive retinopathy. The widespread use of digital fundus cameras has enabled routine screening and remote diagnosis of these conditions. AI-powered fundus image analysis is revolutionizing ophthalmology by providing efficient, accurate, and scalable diagnostic support for a wide range of ocular diseases.

From diabetic retinopathy and glaucoma to AMD, AI systems offer early detection capabilities that can significantly reduce vision loss and improve patient outcomes. Despite challenges in data quality, interpretability, and regulatory compliance, the momentum behind AI adoption in eye care is strong and growing. With ongoing research and technological refinement, AI is poised to become an integral component of both clinical ophthalmology and public health screening programs, bringing quality eye care to more people than ever before.

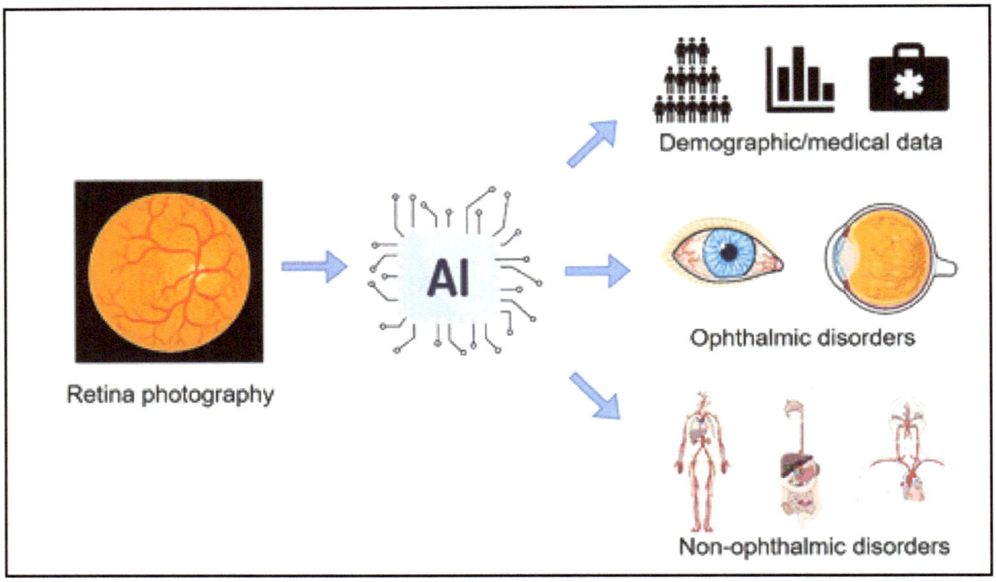

Fig: Retina Fundus Photograph-Based Artificial Intelligence Algorithms in Medicine

The future of AI in fundus image analysis is marked by rapid innovation and growing integration into mainstream clinical practice. Research is ongoing into multimodal AI systems that combine fundus photography with other imaging modalities like OCT and fluorescein angiography for more comprehensive assessments. Personalized AI models that adapt to demographic variables such as age, ethnicity, and systemic health factors are being developed to improve diagnostic equity. Real-time AI analysis embedded in handheld devices and point-of-care systems is expected to revolutionize mass screening and rural healthcare delivery. Continued advancements in computational power, data sharing, and international collaboration will further accelerate progress in this field.

Several AI systems for fundus image analysis have received regulatory approval and are in use commercially. For instance, the IDx-DR system became the first autonomous AI system for diabetic retinopathy to be approved by the US FDA.

Other tools such as EyeArt, Retmarker, and Google's DeepMind system have shown promise in large-scale validation studies. These tools are deployed in various healthcare settings and are being evaluated for cost-effectiveness, scalability, and clinical impact. Regulatory bodies are emphasizing the need for transparency, algorithmic fairness, and ongoing post-market surveillance to ensure the safety and effectiveness of these AI tools.

AI and Machine Learning in Ophthalmology

Artificial intelligence in ophthalmology primarily relies on machine learning, especially deep learning techniques, to process and interpret fundus images. These algorithms can learn complex patterns and features from large annotated datasets, making them highly effective for detecting minute pathological changes in retinal structures. Convolutional neural networks (CNNs), a class of deep learning models, are particularly well-suited for image-based tasks and have become the backbone of AI applications in fundus image analysis. By training CNNs on thousands of labeled images, AI systems can automatically classify retinal diseases, identify abnormalities, and even predict disease progression with remarkable accuracy.

Diabetic Retinopathy Detection Using AI

Diabetic retinopathy is one of the leading causes of blindness globally, especially among working-age populations. Early detection through fundus photography is essential to prevent vision loss. AI-powered systems have shown exceptional performance in detecting diabetic retinopathy by identifying features such as microaneurysms, hemorrhages, and exudates in retinal images. Deep learning models trained on large-scale datasets like the EyePACS and Messidor databases have achieved diagnostic accuracy on par with that of expert ophthalmologists.

Glaucoma Detection and Optic Nerve Head Analysis

Glaucoma is a group of eye conditions characterized by damage to the optic nerve, often associated with increased intraocular pressure. It is typically diagnosed through the analysis of the optic nerve head and retinal nerve fiber layer, features that can be visualized in fundus images. AI algorithms can quantify parameters such as the cup-to-disc ratio and detect signs of optic disc cupping, which are key indicators of glaucoma. By training on labeled datasets, AI models learn to distinguish between glaucomatous and healthy optic nerves with high sensitivity and specificity. These tools are especially valuable in primary care and screening settings, where access to specialized glaucoma diagnostics like optical coherence tomography (OCT) may be limited.

Age-Related Macular Degeneration and AI

Age-related macular degeneration (AMD) affects the central portion of the retina and is a leading cause of vision loss in older adults. It manifests in two forms: dry and wet AMD. Fundus images reveal characteristic changes such as drusen deposits, pigmentary abnormalities, and neovascularization. AI systems trained on high-resolution fundus images can detect and classify AMD at various stages, facilitating timely intervention. Some models can even predict progression from early to advanced stages, enabling proactive treatment planning. The integration of AI in AMD screening programs helps reduce the burden on retina specialists and ensures that patients at risk receive timely care.

Technical Aspects of AI Model Development

The development of AI models for fundus image analysis involves several technical steps, including data preprocessing, model architecture design, training, validation, and deployment. Preprocessing may include contrast enhancement, normalization, and artifact removal to improve image quality. Data augmentation techniques, such as rotation, flipping, and scaling, are used to increase dataset diversity and prevent overfitting. CNN architectures like ResNet, Inception, DenseNet, and EfficientNet are commonly used due to their ability to capture spatial hierarchies in image data. Transfer learning, where models pre-trained on general image datasets are fine-tuned with medical images, is widely adopted to accelerate model development and improve performance.

Challenges in Data Quality and Annotation

One of the main challenges in AI-based fundus image analysis is the availability of high-quality, annotated datasets. Accurate labeling by expert ophthalmologists is time-intensive and may vary across individuals, leading to inconsistencies in ground truth data. Class imbalance, where certain disease stages are underrepresented, can bias model predictions. Image quality issues due to improper focus, lighting conditions, or media opacities can also affect diagnostic accuracy. Efforts are being made to standardize annotation protocols, develop automated labeling tools, and use synthetic data generation techniques such as generative adversarial networks (GANs) to address these limitations and improve model robustness.

Explainability and Clinical Trust in AI Systems

For AI systems to gain acceptance in clinical practice, it is crucial that they are explainable and transparent in their decision-making processes. Techniques like saliency maps and Gradient-weighted Class Activation Mapping (Grad-CAM) allow visualization of the regions in a fundus image that influenced the AI's prediction. This not only aids clinicians in validating the output but also builds trust in AI-assisted diagnoses. Interpretability is particularly important in cases where the AI's assessment may differ from that of a human expert. By providing visual and statistical justifications for predictions, AI systems can become valuable decision support tools rather than opaque black-box solutions.

Integration into Teleophthalmology and Mobile Platforms

AI-powered fundus image analysis is particularly well-suited for integration into teleophthalmology platforms, which are designed to deliver eye care services remotely. Mobile fundus cameras and smartphone-based imaging devices are increasingly being used to capture retinal images in remote or resource-constrained settings. These images can be uploaded to cloud-based AI systems for instant analysis, enabling early detection and timely referral for treatment. Such integration improves accessibility, especially for populations with limited access to ophthalmologists. In many regions, AI-enabled teleophthalmology initiatives have significantly increased screening rates for diabetic retinopathy and other retinal diseases, helping prevent avoidable blindness.

3.7 INFECTIOUS DISEASES

3.7.1 Early Detection of Sepsis

Sepsis is a life-threatening medical emergency that occurs when the body's response to an infection causes widespread inflammation, leading to tissue damage, organ failure, and potentially death. It can be triggered by infections in the lungs, urinary tract, skin, or gastrointestinal system and affects people of all ages, particularly the elderly, newborns, and individuals with compromised immune systems.

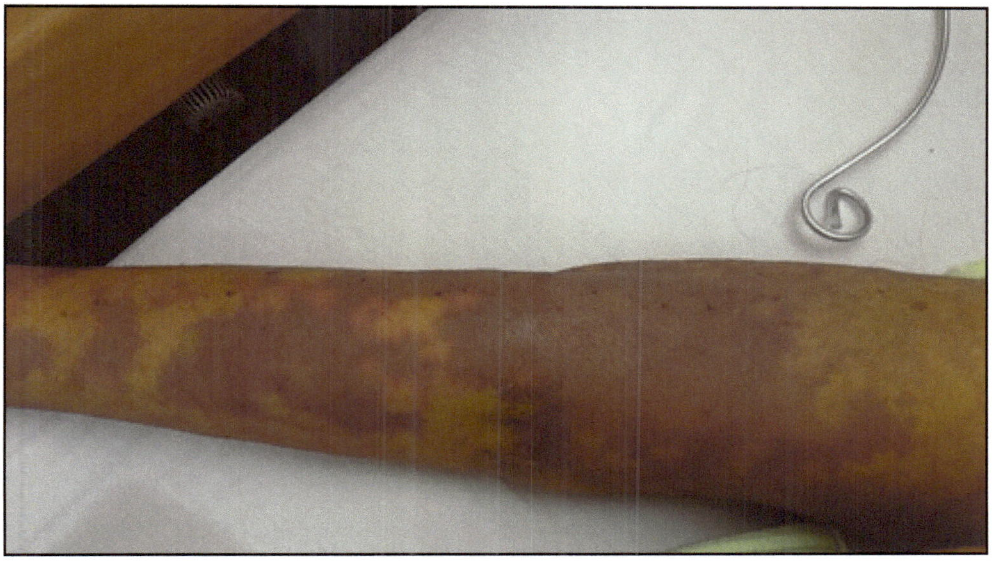

Fig: Symptoms of Sepsis

Globally, sepsis accounts for millions of deaths each year, many of which could be prevented with timely diagnosis and intervention. Early detection is vital because the chances of survival drop significantly with each hour of delayed treatment. Early detection of sepsis is critical for reducing mortality, improving recovery, and optimizing the use of healthcare resources. Despite its complex presentation and diagnostic challenges, significant progress has been made through the use of biomarkers, scoring systems, AI, and rapid diagnostic tools. Recognizing the signs of sepsis promptly and initiating immediate treatment remains a cornerstone of effective care. Continued advancements in technology, combined with education and global collaboration, offer hope for a future where sepsis is identified and treated swiftly in all healthcare settings, ultimately saving countless lives.

Clinical Signs and Diagnostic Challenges

Detecting sepsis in its early stages is challenging because its initial symptoms—such as fever, increased heart rate, shortness of breath, and confusion—are common to many other illnesses. These nonspecific signs often lead to delays in recognizing the onset of sepsis. In many cases, clinicians must rely on a combination of patient history, physical examination, and laboratory results to make a diagnosis. However, early symptoms may be subtle, especially in immunocompromised patients or the elderly, where fever and inflammation may not be pronounced. The overlap with other clinical conditions makes differential diagnosis difficult, highlighting the need for reliable, early diagnostic tools and protocols that can guide swift clinical decision-making.

Importance of Early Diagnosis in Sepsis Management

The window for effective treatment of sepsis is narrow. Research has consistently shown that the early administration of antibiotics and supportive therapy within the first hour of recognition greatly improves patient outcomes. Each hour of delay is associated with a measurable increase in mortality. Early diagnosis enables clinicians to initiate life-saving interventions such as fluid resuscitation, vasopressor support, and infection source control before the condition escalates to severe sepsis or septic shock. Prompt recognition not only reduces the risk of long-term complications such as organ dysfunction and prolonged ICU stays but also decreases the financial burden on healthcare systems through shorter hospitalizations and reduced need for intensive care.

Role of Biomarkers in Early Detection

Biomarkers play a critical role in the early identification and monitoring of sepsis. They provide objective measurements of biological processes, helping differentiate between infectious and non-infectious causes of systemic inflammation. Commonly used biomarkers include C-reactive protein (CRP), procalcitonin (PCT), and lactate. CRP is an acute-phase protein that increases in response to inflammation but lacks specificity for infection. Procalcitonin levels rise significantly in bacterial infections and are useful for distinguishing bacterial sepsis from viral or non-infectious causes of systemic inflammation. Elevated lactate levels indicate tissue hypoperfusion and can serve as an early warning sign of sepsis severity. Emerging biomarkers such as presepsin, interleukin-6 (IL-6), and soluble triggering receptor expressed on myeloid cells-1 (sTREM-1) are being investigated for their potential to provide faster and more accurate detection of sepsis.

Advancements in Artificial Intelligence and Predictive Analytics

The integration of artificial intelligence (AI) and machine learning into clinical care is revolutionizing the early detection of sepsis. Predictive algorithms trained on large datasets of electronic health records can identify subtle patterns and changes in vital signs, laboratory results, and clinical notes that may indicate early sepsis, often before it is apparent to human clinicians. These systems continuously monitor patient data in real time, generating alerts for early intervention. Tools such as the Sepsis Early Warning Score (SEWS) and the Machine Learning for Early Sepsis Alert (MELISA) have demonstrated the ability to improve early detection and reduce mortality. AI-assisted platforms are particularly valuable in emergency departments and intensive care units, where rapid, accurate assessments are essential for initiating timely treatment.

Screening Protocols and Clinical Scoring Systems

Standardized screening protocols and scoring systems are widely used to assist healthcare providers in the early recognition of sepsis. The Sequential Organ Failure Assessment (SOFA) score and its quick version, qSOFA, evaluate organ dysfunction and are useful for assessing the severity of the condition. The Systemic Inflammatory Response Syndrome (SIRS) criteria were previously the standard but have been largely replaced by more accurate tools. The National Early Warning Score (NEWS) and Modified Early Warning Score (MEWS) are other commonly used systems that evaluate physiological parameters such as respiratory rate, oxygen saturation, temperature, blood pressure, and consciousness level. These scores help standardize assessment across healthcare providers, ensuring consistent and objective evaluation of patients at risk of sepsis.

Point-of-Care Testing and Rapid Diagnostics

Point-of-care testing (POCT) technologies have made significant strides in facilitating early sepsis diagnosis, especially in resource-limited settings and emergency situations. These portable devices allow for the rapid analysis of blood samples at the bedside, providing results for key biomarkers like lactate and procalcitonin within minutes. The immediacy of these results enables clinicians to make quicker decisions about initiating antibiotics and other supportive therapies. Furthermore, rapid molecular diagnostic tools such as polymerase chain reaction

(PCR) assays and next-generation sequencing (NGS) can identify specific pathogens in the bloodstream within hours, which is significantly faster than traditional blood cultures. The use of POCT not only accelerates treatment but also improves antibiotic stewardship by minimizing unnecessary broad-spectrum antibiotic use.

Sepsis Detection in Special Populations

Certain populations, such as neonates, elderly individuals, and immunocompromised patients, present unique challenges for the early detection of sepsis. In neonates, the signs of sepsis are often subtle and nonspecific, such as feeding difficulties, irritability and temperature instability. Early-onset neonatal sepsis, in particular, requires high clinical suspicion and prompt empirical treatment. In the elderly, blunted immune responses may mask typical signs of infection, and sepsis may present primarily as confusion or lethargy. Immunosuppressed individuals, including cancer patients and transplant recipients, are at increased risk and may not exhibit typical inflammatory markers. For these populations, tailored screening protocols and heightened clinical vigilance are essential for early diagnosis and management.

Role of Education and Training in Early Detection

Early detection of sepsis depends not only on technological and diagnostic advancements but also on the education and training of healthcare professionals. Regular training programs that focus on sepsis recognition, use of screening tools, and emergency response protocols are essential in improving early diagnosis rates. Clinical staff must be equipped to recognize early warning signs, interpret biomarkers, and respond appropriately to alerts from AI systems or scoring tools. Simulation-based training and case-based learning are effective methods for reinforcing best practices. Empowering nurses, primary care providers, and emergency medical personnel to identify sepsis early ensures that intervention begins at the first point of contact, often before the patient reaches a critical stage.

Global Initiatives and Future Directions

Global initiatives such as the World Health Organization's resolution on sepsis aim to improve prevention, diagnosis, and treatment through increased awareness, standardized protocols, and investment in healthcare infrastructure. Research continues to focus on developing more sensitive and specific biomarkers, refining AI models, and expanding access to point-of-care diagnostics. Personalized medicine approaches, integrating genomics and metabolomics, may further enhance the precision of sepsis detection. Future innovations may include wearable biosensors that monitor physiological data continuously and alert clinicians to early signs of infection and organ dysfunction. Collaborative efforts among researchers, clinicians, policymakers, and technologists will be essential to advance the early detection and management of sepsis worldwide.

3.7.2 Tuberculosis

Tuberculosis (TB) remains one of the most significant infectious diseases worldwide, with a profound impact on public health. Caused by the bacterium Mycobacterium tuberculosis, TB primarily affects the lungs but can also invade other organs, leading to extrapulmonary tuberculosis. Despite advances in medical science, TB continues to be a leading cause of death from a single infectious agent, second only to COVID-19 in recent years. The disease disproportionately affects low- and middle-income countries, where factors such as poverty, malnutrition, and limited healthcare access exacerbate its spread.

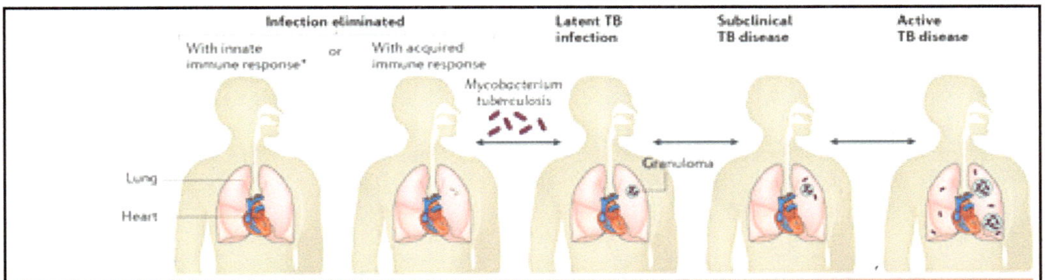

	Infection eliminated (innate)	Infection eliminated (acquired)	Latent TB infection	Subclinical TB disease	Active TB disease
TST	Negative	Positive	Positive	Positive	Usually positive
IGRA	Negative	Positive	Positive	Positive	Usually positive
Culture	Negative	Negative	Negative	Intermittently positive	Positive
Sputum smear	Negative	Negative	Negative	Usually negative	Positive or negative
Infectious	No	No	No	Sporadically	Yes
Symptoms	None	None	None	Mild or none	Mild to severe
Preferred treatment	None	None	Preventive therapy	Multidrug therapy	Multidrug therapy

Fig: Tuberculosis

Tuberculosis remains a formidable global health challenge, demanding sustained efforts in prevention, diagnosis, and treatment. While advancements in diagnostics and therapeutics have improved outcomes, disparities in healthcare access and the threat of drug resistance persist. A multidisciplinary approach, combining scientific innovation, policy reform, and community involvement, is crucial to achieving TB elimination. By addressing these challenges, the global health community can move closer to a world free of tuberculosis, ensuring better health and equity for all.

Tuberculosis is a major global health concern, with an estimated 10 million new cases and 1.5 million deaths reported annually. The World Health Organization (WHO) identifies TB as a top infectious killer, particularly in regions such as sub-Saharan Africa, Southeast Asia, and Eastern Europe. Certain populations, including people living with HIV, migrants, and those in overcrowded settings like prisons, are at higher risk. The emergence of drug-resistant TB strains, such as multidrug-resistant TB (MDR-TB) and extensively drug-resistant TB (XDR-TB), has further complicated control efforts. These resistant forms require longer, more expensive treatment regimens and contribute to higher mortality rates.

Pathogenesis and Transmission

TB spreads through airborne transmission when an infected individual coughs, sneezes, or speaks, releasing M. tuberculosis bacilli into the air. Upon inhalation, the bacteria reach the alveoli of the lungs, where they are engulfed by macrophages. In some cases, the immune system controls the infection, leading to latent TB, where the bacteria remain dormant without causing symptoms. However, in about 5-10% of infected individuals, the bacteria reactivate, leading to active TB disease, especially when the immune system is weakened by conditions such as HIV, diabetes, or malnutrition.

The progression from latent to active TB depends on various factors, including bacterial virulence, host immunity, and environmental conditions. Once active, TB can cause symptoms such as persistent cough, fever, night sweats, and weight loss. If untreated, the disease can lead to severe complications, including lung damage, meningitis, and disseminated TB (miliary TB).

Diagnosis

Early and accurate diagnosis is crucial for effective TB management. Traditional diagnostic methods include sputum smear microscopy, which detects acid-fast bacilli, and culture-based techniques, which remain the gold standard for confirming TB. However, these methods are time-consuming, taking weeks for culture results, and have limited sensitivity, particularly in HIV-positive individuals.

Advances in molecular diagnostics have revolutionized TB detection. The GeneXpert MTB/RIF assay, endorsed by the WHO, provides rapid diagnosis by detecting M. tuberculosis DNA and rifampicin resistance within hours. Other nucleic acid amplification tests (NAATs) and line probe assays further enhance diagnostic accuracy, especially for drug-resistant TB. Imaging techniques, such as chest X-rays and computed tomography (CT), aid in identifying pulmonary and extrapulmonary TB manifestations. Despite these advancements, access to advanced diagnostics remains limited in resource-poor settings, underscoring the need for affordable and portable testing solutions.

Treatment and Management

The standard treatment for drug-susceptible TB involves a six-month regimen of four first-line antibiotics: isoniazid, rifampicin, pyrazinamide, and ethambutol. Adherence to this prolonged treatment is critical to prevent relapse and the development of drug resistance. Directly Observed Therapy (DOT), where healthcare workers supervise medication intake, has been widely implemented to improve compliance. Drug-resistant TB poses a significant challenge, requiring second-line drugs such as fluoroquinolones and injectable agents like amikacin. These treatments are more toxic, last up to 20 months, and have lower success rates. Recently, newer drugs like bedaquiline and delamanid have shown promise in treating MDR-TB, offering shorter and more tolerable regimens. The WHO recommends all-oral treatment protocols to improve patient outcomes and reduce side effects.

Latent TB infection (LTBI) is managed with preventive therapy, typically isoniazid monotherapy or a combination of rifapentine and isoniazid, to reduce the risk of progression to active disease. This approach is particularly important for high-risk groups, including HIV patients and close contacts of TB cases.

Challenges

Despite global efforts, TB elimination faces numerous obstacles. The stigma associated with TB discourages individuals from seeking timely care, leading to delayed diagnosis and increased transmission. Weak healthcare infrastructure in endemic regions hampers effective case detection and treatment adherence. Additionally, the convergence of TB and HIV epidemics complicates management, as co-infected individuals have higher mortality rates.

The rise of drug-resistant TB strains is another major concern, driven by incomplete treatment courses and misuse of antibiotics. Limited access to second-line drugs and diagnostic tools in low-resource settings exacerbates this problem. Furthermore, research and development for new TB vaccines and drugs remain underfunded compared to other infectious diseases. The Bacille Calmette-Guérin (BCG) vaccine, the only licensed TB vaccine, offers partial protection, primarily against severe childhood TB, but is ineffective in preventing pulmonary TB in adults.

Global Efforts

The WHO's End TB Strategy aims to reduce TB deaths by 95% and incidence by 90% by 2035. Key components include scaling up preventive therapy, improving diagnostics, and ensuring universal access to treatment. Innovations such as AI-assisted radiology, point-of-care diagnostics, and shorter drug regimens hold promise for accelerating progress.

Research into novel vaccines, such as the M72/AS01E candidate, and repurposed drugs offers hope for more effective TB control. Strengthening healthcare systems, increasing funding, and fostering international collaboration are essential to overcoming barriers. Public awareness campaigns and community engagement can help reduce stigma and encourage early healthcare-seeking behavior.

3.7.3 COVID-19

The COVID-19 pandemic has been a transformative event in the field of infectious diseases, challenging our understanding and approaches to public health. The rapid spread of SARS-CoV-2, the diverse clinical manifestations, and the global impact have necessitated innovative diagnostic tools, therapeutic interventions, and preventive measures. The unprecedented speed of vaccine development and deployment, the critical role of epidemiology, and the importance of international collaboration have been pivotal in the global response to the pandemic.

The strain on healthcare systems, the economic and social impact, and the need for enhanced preparedness have highlighted the complexities and challenges of managing infectious diseases in a globalized world. As we continue to navigate the COVID-19 pandemic and prepare for future threats, the lessons learned and the advancements made will be instrumental in building a more resilient and adaptive public health system. The future of infectious disease management lies in proactive, collaborative, and evidence-based approaches, ensuring the health and well-being of communities worldwide. The COVID-19 pandemic has not only tested our resilience but also provided an opportunity to reimagine and strengthen our response to infectious diseases, paving the way for a healthier and more secure future.

Fig: The COVID-19 Pandemic

The COVID-19 pandemic has highlighted the need for enhanced preparedness and response to infectious diseases. The development of robust surveillance systems, early warning mechanisms, and rapid response capabilities is essential for detecting and controlling emerging pathogens. The investment in research and development, including vaccine and therapeutic innovation, is crucial for building a resilient and adaptive healthcare system. The strengthening of public health infrastructure, including healthcare workforce, facilities, and technologies, is necessary for responding to future outbreaks and pandemics. The integration of

One Health approaches, recognizing the interconnections between human, animal, and environmental health, is vital for addressing the root causes of infectious diseases. The lessons learned from COVID-19 have underscored the importance of proactive, collaborative, and evidence-based approaches to infectious disease preparedness and response.

Emergence and Spread of SARS-CoV-2

The first cases of COVID-19 were reported in Wuhan, China, in late 2019, with the virus quickly spreading to other parts of the world. SARS-CoV-2, a novel coronavirus, is believed to have originated in bats and possibly passed through an intermediate animal host before infecting humans. The virus's high transmissibility, facilitated by its ability to spread through respiratory droplets and aerosols, has led to rapid and widespread infection. The global spread of SARS-CoV-2 has been exacerbated by international travel, urbanization, and close human-animal interactions. The emergence of COVID-19 has underscored the importance of understanding the zoonotic origins of infectious diseases and the need for robust surveillance systems to detect and respond to emerging pathogens.

Clinical Manifestations and Severity

COVID-19 presents with a wide range of clinical manifestations, from asymptomatic or mild symptoms to severe respiratory distress and multi-organ failure. Common symptoms include fever, cough, shortness of breath, fatigue, and loss of taste or smell. However, the virus can also affect other organ systems, leading to complications such as cardiovascular issues, neurological disorders, and gastrointestinal problems. The severity of COVID-19 varies widely among individuals, with risk factors including age, underlying health conditions, and immune status. Elderly individuals and those with comorbidities such as diabetes, hypertension, and obesity are at higher risk of developing severe disease and experiencing poor outcomes. The clinical spectrum of COVID-19 has challenged healthcare systems, requiring the development of new diagnostic and treatment protocols to manage the diverse presentations of the disease.

Diagnostic Tools and Testing Strategies

The rapid development and deployment of diagnostic tools have been crucial in the fight against COVID-19. Polymerase chain reaction (PCR) tests, which detect the viral RNA in respiratory samples, have been the gold standard for diagnosing active infections. However, the limitations of PCR, including false negatives and the need for specialized equipment, have led to the exploration of alternative diagnostic methods. Antigen tests, which detect viral proteins, offer a quicker and more accessible option, although they may be less sensitive. Serological tests, which detect antibodies against SARS-CoV-2, provide insights into past infections and immune responses. The integration of these diagnostic tools has been essential for tracking the spread of the virus, identifying hotspots, and informing public health decisions. The development of point-of-care testing and home-based testing kits has further expanded access to diagnostic tools, enabling more widespread and timely detection of infections.

Treatment Protocols and Therapeutic Interventions

The treatment of COVID-19 has evolved rapidly, driven by a combination of clinical trials, observational studies, and real-world evidence. Initially, supportive care was the mainstay of treatment, focusing on managing symptoms and preventing complications. However, the identification of effective therapeutic interventions has significantly improved patient outcomes. Antiviral drugs, such as remdesivir and molnupiravir, have shown promise in reducing viral load and shortening the duration of illness. Monoclonal antibodies, which target specific viral proteins, have been used to prevent severe disease in high-risk individuals. Corticosteroids, such as dexamethasone, have been shown to reduce inflammation and improve survival in patients with severe COVID-19. The development of convalescent plasma therapy, which involves transfusing plasma from recovered patients, has also been explored as a potential treatment option. The collaborative efforts of the scientific community have accelerated the discovery and validation of these therapeutic interventions, providing a diverse arsenal of tools to combat the virus.

Vaccine Development and Deployment

The development and deployment of COVID-19 vaccines have been unprecedented in their speed and scale. Traditional vaccine development typically takes years, but the global urgency of the pandemic has driven an accelerated timeline. mRNA vaccines, such as those developed by Pfizer-BioNTech and Moderna, have demonstrated high efficacy and safety profiles. Adenovirus vector vaccines, like those produced by AstraZeneca and Johnson & Johnson, offer an alternative approach, utilizing a modified virus to deliver the genetic instructions for the SARS-CoV-2 spike protein. The rapid development and approval of these vaccines have been facilitated by advanced technologies, international collaboration, and regulatory flexibility. The global rollout of vaccines has been a logistical challenge, requiring the coordination of manufacturing, distribution, and administration across diverse settings. The success of vaccination campaigns has been crucial in reducing the spread of the virus, preventing severe disease, and mitigating the impact of the pandemic.

Public Health Measures and Preventive Strategies

Public health measures have played a pivotal role in controlling the spread of COVID-19 and mitigating its impact. Non-pharmaceutical interventions, such as social distancing, wearing masks, and hand hygiene, have been effective in reducing transmission. Lockdowns and travel restrictions have been implemented to control outbreaks and prevent the overwhelm of healthcare systems.

Contact tracing and quarantine protocols have been essential for identifying and isolating infected individuals, breaking the chain of transmission. The development of digital tools, such as contact tracing apps and health monitoring systems, has enhanced the efficiency and effectiveness of these measures. Public health communication and education have been crucial in promoting adherence to preventive strategies and addressing misinformation. The collective effort of communities, governments, and international organizations has been vital in implementing and sustaining these public health measures.

Role of Epidemiology in Understanding COVID-19

Epidemiology has been at the forefront of understanding the dynamics of COVID-19 and informing public health responses. Epidemiological studies have provided insights into the transmission patterns, incidence, and prevalence of the virus. Modeling and simulation studies have helped predict the spread of the virus and evaluate the impact of interventions.

Surveillance systems, including sentinel surveillance and syndromic surveillance, have been essential for monitoring the epidemic and detecting emerging trends. The analysis of epidemiological data has informed policy decisions, such as the timing and scale of lockdowns, the allocation of resources, and the prioritization of vaccination campaigns. The interdisciplinary nature of epidemiology, integrating data from various sources and disciplines, has been crucial in providing a comprehensive understanding of the pandemic and guiding effective responses.

Impact of COVID-19 on Healthcare Systems

The COVID-19 pandemic has placed an unprecedented strain on healthcare systems worldwide. The surge in cases has led to the overwhelm of hospitals, intensive care units, and healthcare workers. The need for specialized care, such as mechanical ventilation and extracorporeal membrane oxygenation (ECMO), has stretched resources and capacities. The redeployment of healthcare workers, the repurposing of facilities, and the development of field hospitals have been necessary to meet the demand for care. The pandemic has also highlighted the importance of mental health support for healthcare workers, who have faced significant stress, burnout, and trauma. The disruption of routine healthcare services, including elective procedures and preventive care, has had long-term implications for patient health and healthcare systems. The lessons learned from the pandemic have underscored the need for resilient and adaptable healthcare systems, capable of responding to future challenges and emergencies.

Economic and Social Impact of COVID-19

The economic and social impact of COVID-19 has been profound and far-reaching. The pandemic has led to widespread job losses, business closures, and economic downturns. The disruption of supply chains, travel restrictions, and changes in consumer behavior have had global economic repercussions. The social impact of the pandemic has been equally significant, with lockdowns and social distancing measures affecting mental health, social interactions, and community cohesion.

The digital divide, where access to technology and the internet is unequal, has exacerbated disparities in education, employment, and healthcare. The pandemic has also highlighted the vulnerabilities of marginalized communities, including the elderly, low-income individuals, and racial and ethnic minorities, who have been disproportionately affected by the virus and its consequences. The recovery from the pandemic will require comprehensive and inclusive strategies to address these economic and social challenges.

Role of International Collaboration in Combating COVID-19

International collaboration has been crucial in the global response to COVID-19. The sharing of scientific knowledge, data, and resources has accelerated the development of diagnostic tools, therapeutics, and vaccines. International organizations, such as the World Health Organization (WHO), have played a coordinating role in providing guidance, supporting countries, and facilitating global cooperation. The COVAX initiative, aimed at ensuring equitable access to vaccines, has been a significant effort to address global vaccine disparities. The exchange of best practices, lessons learned, and innovative solutions has been essential for improving public health responses and mitigating the impact of the pandemic. The global nature of the pandemic has underscored the importance of solidarity, cooperation, and collective action in addressing shared challenges.

3.7.4 Syndromic Surveillance using AI

Syndromic surveillance refers to the systematic collection, analysis, and interpretation of health-related data to identify patterns indicative of disease outbreaks or public health threats, often before laboratory confirmation. Traditionally, syndromic surveillance systems have relied on clinical data such as emergency department reports, hospital admission records, pharmacy purchases, absenteeism reports, and even news and social media trends.

These systems aim to detect unusual spikes in disease-related symptoms—such as fever, cough, or gastrointestinal distress—enabling earlier responses than conventional diagnostic testing might allow. AI has revolutionized the field of syndromic surveillance, providing powerful tools to detect, monitor, and predict infectious disease outbreaks with unprecedented speed and precision. By leveraging vast and diverse data sources, AI systems can offer early warning signals that inform public health responses before widespread transmission occurs. While challenges related to data quality, ethics, and integration remain, the continued development of responsible and transparent AI technologies promises to strengthen global disease surveillance capabilities. In an increasingly interconnected world where infectious diseases pose ever-evolving threats, AI-driven syndromic surveillance stands as a critical asset for safeguarding public health and enabling timely, informed interventions.

The future of AI in syndromic surveillance holds significant potential. Advances in wearable technologies and smart health devices will provide continuous streams of real-time physiological data, enabling hyper-local detection of illness trends. AI models will likely incorporate genomic and environmental data to improve pathogen tracking and outbreak prediction.

Federated learning and privacy-preserving machine learning methods are being developed to allow sensitive data sharing without compromising individual privacy. Real-time dashboards powered by AI will help health authorities visualize disease trends and respond dynamically. As AI models become more sophisticated, their predictive capabilities will extend beyond outbreak detection to include intervention effectiveness and healthcare resource forecasting.

Need for Early Detection of Infectious Diseases

Infectious diseases pose a constant threat to global health, as evidenced by outbreaks of diseases such as COVID-19, Ebola, Zika, and influenza. Timely detection and response are critical to controlling their spread and mitigating their impact. Traditional surveillance systems often rely on laboratory confirmation and reporting by clinicians, processes that can delay outbreak detection by days or even weeks. By contrast, syndromic surveillance focuses on the early signals that precede formal diagnosis. This approach is particularly valuable in detecting emerging infections, bioterrorism events, or seasonal epidemics. When enhanced with AI, syndromic surveillance can process large, diverse datasets in real-time, recognizing subtle patterns that might otherwise go unnoticed.

Role of Artificial Intelligence

Artificial intelligence enables the automation and enhancement of syndromic surveillance by applying advanced algorithms to detect abnormalities in health data streams. Machine learning models can analyze millions of data points from sources such as electronic health records, insurance claims, social media, news outlets, and search engine queries. Natural language processing allows AI systems to interpret free-text clinical notes or social media posts, extracting relevant information such as symptoms, location, and context. These models can continuously learn from new data, refining their ability to distinguish between normal fluctuations and genuine outbreaks. AI also supports predictive analytics, forecasting the likely trajectory of disease spread based on historical and real-time data.

Data Sources in AI-Powered

Effective AI-driven syndromic surveillance depends on diverse and timely data sources. Electronic health records offer rich clinical data, including patient symptoms, diagnoses, and treatment details. Pharmacy sales and over-the-counter drug purchases provide insight into population-level symptom trends. Data from telemedicine platforms, call centers, and wearable devices also contribute real-time health metrics. In addition to clinical data, AI models utilize non-traditional sources such as social media platforms, internet search trends, and news feeds to detect early public concern or symptom self-reporting. Geographic information system (GIS) data helps map disease spread, and mobility data from smartphones or transportation systems assists in modeling transmission dynamics. The integration of these data types allows AI to form a comprehensive view of public health conditions.

COVID-19 and the Rise of AI-Enhanced Surveillance

The COVID-19 pandemic highlighted both the strengths and limitations of global disease surveillance. Traditional systems were often slow to respond, hindered by bureaucratic delays and fragmented data sharing. AI-powered platforms emerged as critical tools in pandemic response, helping track cases, predict surges, and assess the effectiveness of interventions. Tools like BlueDot, HealthMap, and Google's COVID-19 mobility reports utilized AI to monitor disease progression and inform public health strategies. BlueDot, for instance, was among the first to detect the novel coronavirus outbreak by analyzing global airline ticketing data and news reports. These examples underscore the value of AI in providing early warning signals and guiding timely policy decisions.

Advantages of AI in Infectious Disease Monitoring

AI offers several advantages in syndromic surveillance. One of its most significant strengths is the ability to process and analyze massive datasets in real time, far beyond human capacity. AI can detect weak or hidden patterns in complex data, facilitating the identification of emerging threats even with minimal case counts. Machine learning models can adapt to new pathogens or mutations by retraining with updated data, making them highly flexible. The use of predictive analytics allows for scenario planning, helping authorities allocate resources efficiently and prepare for potential outbreaks. Furthermore, AI reduces reliance on manual reporting, minimizing delays and increasing coverage, especially in regions with limited public health infrastructure.

Challenges

Despite its promise, AI-enhanced syndromic surveillance faces several challenges. Data quality and completeness are critical, and in many settings, health data may be sparse, delayed, or inconsistent. Bias in training data can lead to inaccurate predictions or underreporting in certain populations. For example, reliance on internet search trends or social media posts may disproportionately reflect the behaviors of younger, urban populations, while missing outbreaks in rural or older communities. Privacy and data security concerns also present major obstacles, as surveillance systems often collect sensitive personal health information. Additionally, integrating AI tools into existing public health workflows requires coordination, training, and trust from healthcare providers and policymakers.

3.8 NEUROLOGY

3.8.1 AI in Brain Imaging (MS, Alzheimer's, Stroke)

Artificial intelligence has opened new horizons in the field of brain imaging, offering transformative capabilities in the diagnosis and management of neurological disorders such as multiple sclerosis, Alzheimer's disease, and stroke. By enhancing image interpretation, predicting disease progression, and supporting clinical decision-making, AI is improving both the accuracy and efficiency of neurodiagnostic workflows. While challenges related to data variability, model explainability, and ethical use remain, ongoing research and technological advancement are steadily addressing these barriers. With appropriate integration into clinical practice, AI stands poised to redefine the standards of care in neurology, offering hope for earlier diagnosis, better outcomes, and more personalized patient management in the years ahead.

The future of AI in brain imaging is marked by continuous innovation and interdisciplinary collaboration. Researchers are developing multimodal models that combine imaging data with clinical, genetic, and cognitive metrics for a more comprehensive understanding of neurological diseases. The use of federated learning is gaining traction, allowing models to be trained on decentralized data across multiple institutions while preserving patient privacy.

Real-time, cloud-based AI platforms are being developed to support rapid diagnosis in remote or underserved areas. Predictive modeling is advancing to enable early intervention and personalized treatment strategies. In parallel, explainable AI is evolving to provide transparent decision-making pathways, enhancing clinician trust and facilitating regulatory approval. As computational power increases and datasets become more diverse, AI is expected to become an integral component of routine neuroimaging, enabling faster, more accurate, and more equitable neurological care.

As with any technology that handles personal health information, ethical considerations are central to the deployment of AI in brain imaging. Data used to train AI models must be de-identified and used with informed consent. There is also a risk that AI systems trained on biased or non-representative datasets could produce skewed results, particularly for underrepresented populations. Ensuring equity in diagnosis and treatment recommendations is essential to avoid exacerbating existing health disparities. Legal responsibility in the event of misdiagnosis or errors by AI tools remains a gray area, requiring clear guidelines regarding accountability among developers, healthcare providers, and institutions.

Role of AI in Medical Imaging

Artificial intelligence in medical imaging involves algorithms trained to recognize patterns, detect abnormalities, and even predict disease progression based on imaging data. In brain imaging, AI systems are trained using large datasets of annotated scans, allowing them to learn features associated with normal anatomy as well as disease-specific changes. Deep learning models such as convolutional neural networks (CNNs) are particularly effective at handling the high-dimensional nature of medical images. These models can be applied to various imaging modalities providing valuable support in identifying structural and functional changes that are often imperceptible to the human eye. AI not only accelerates diagnosis but also supports longitudinal tracking, prognostication, and personalized treatment planning.

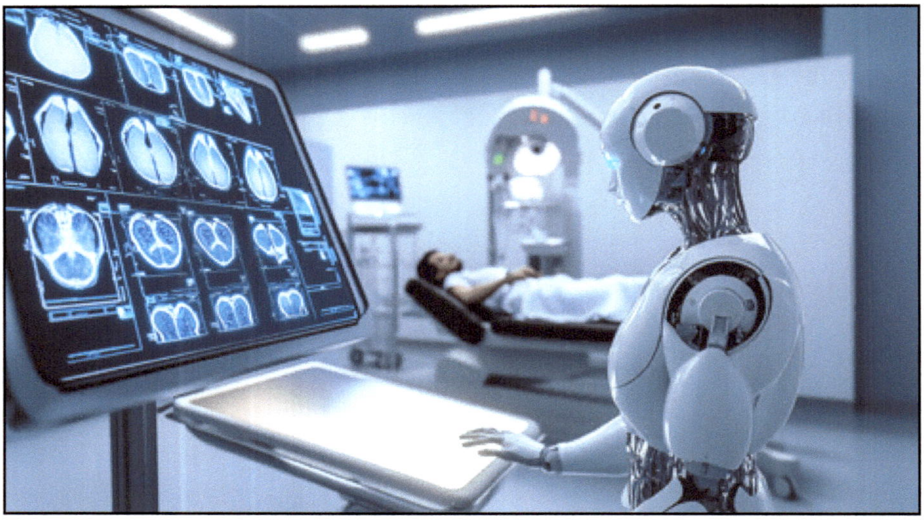

Fig: The State of AI in Medical Diagnostics—Innovations and Insight

AI in Multiple Sclerosis Imaging

Multiple sclerosis is a chronic autoimmune disease that affects the central nervous system, leading to demyelination and neurological disability. MRI is the most important imaging modality for diagnosing and monitoring MS. Traditional MS diagnosis involves detecting white matter lesions, measuring brain volume loss, and identifying new or enhancing lesions over time.

AI algorithms are increasingly being used to automate and improve the accuracy of these tasks. Deep learning models can detect MS lesions with high sensitivity and specificity, often outperforming manual assessments. They can quantify lesion load, segment different brain regions, and monitor subtle changes over time. AI tools help distinguish MS from other neurological conditions with similar radiological appearances, reducing misdiagnosis. In clinical practice, these systems provide objective metrics that support neurologists in evaluating disease progression and treatment efficacy.

AI Applications in Alzheimer's Disease Detection

Alzheimer's disease is the most common form of dementia, characterized by progressive cognitive decline and brain atrophy. Early diagnosis is critical but often challenging due to the slow onset of symptoms and the variability in individual disease progression. Brain imaging techniques such as structural MRI and PET scans are central to the diagnosis of Alzheimer's, providing insights into cortical atrophy, hippocampal volume loss, and amyloid or tau accumulation.

AI plays a transformative role in enhancing early detection and classification of Alzheimer's. Machine learning models can analyze MRI scans to detect early patterns of brain shrinkage associated with mild cognitive impairment (MCI), a precursor to Alzheimer's. AI-based systems have also been trained to analyze PET scans for amyloid deposition, supporting more accurate staging of the disease. Importantly, these models can integrate imaging data with clinical and genetic information to generate personalized risk assessments and progression forecasts.

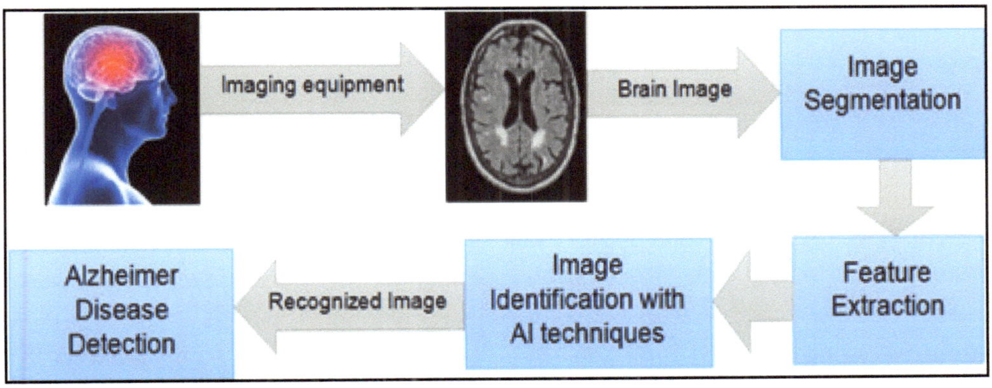

Fig: Alzheimer's Disease Detection Using Artificial Intelligence Techniques

Stroke Imaging and Real-Time AI Decision Support

Stroke is a medical emergency that demands immediate diagnosis and intervention.

Imaging modalities like CT and MRI are used to distinguish between ischemic and hemorrhagic strokes and to determine the extent of brain tissue damage. Time is critical, as rapid decisions must be made regarding thrombolytic therapy or surgical intervention.

AI tools are revolutionizing stroke care by enabling real-time interpretation of imaging data. Algorithms can quickly identify large vessel occlusions, calculate infarct volume, detect hemorrhages, and predict outcomes based on perfusion imaging. AI-driven platforms are now integrated into emergency room workflows, where they provide decision support to radiologists and neurologists, thereby reducing the time from image acquisition to treatment. These tools are particularly valuable in hospitals with limited access to on-site stroke specialists, as they ensure that life-saving treatment decisions are informed by expert-level analysis.

Technical Aspects of AI Model Development

Developing effective AI models for brain imaging involves several technical stages. The first step is assembling high-quality, annotated datasets, often drawn from multi-center studies and public repositories. Data must undergo preprocessing steps such as normalization, registration, and noise reduction to ensure consistency. Deep learning models, particularly CNNs, are then trained using supervised learning techniques to identify and classify disease-relevant features.

Cross-validation and testing on independent datasets are essential to avoid overfitting and to validate model generalizability. Many research efforts now employ transfer learning, where pre-trained models are fine-tuned on brain imaging data to leverage existing knowledge and reduce the need for large training datasets. The complexity of brain anatomy and pathology requires models to be both spatially aware and robust to inter-patient variability, making architecture design a crucial factor in AI performance.

Challenges

Despite the promising results from research studies, integrating AI into clinical neuroimaging practice presents several challenges. One major issue is the variability in imaging protocols, equipment, and patient demographics across different institutions, which can affect AI model performance. Ensuring model generalization and robustness requires extensive validation across diverse populations. Another critical challenge is explainability. Clinicians must be able to understand and trust the outputs of AI systems, especially when used for high-stakes decisions. Black-box models can lead to hesitation or underuse in real-world settings. Additionally, the regulatory landscape for medical AI tools is still evolving. Approvals from authorities such as the FDA and CE mark are essential but require rigorous evidence of clinical benefit and safety. There are also concerns about data privacy and the ethical use of patient data, particularly in AI models trained on sensitive health information.

3.8.2 AI for EEG and Cognitive Function Assessment

AI is transforming EEG and cognitive function assessment, paving the way for precision medicine in neurological diagnosis and treatment. By enhancing the accuracy, efficiency, and accessibility of EEG analysis, AI is enabling earlier detection, real-time monitoring, and personalized management of neurological conditions. The integration of multi-modal data, real-time analysis, and wearable devices are some of the exciting directions for future research and development. However, addressing the challenges and ethical considerations associated with AI-driven neurological assessment will be crucial for its successful implementation.

Collaboration and innovation, driven by a multidisciplinary approach, will be key to unlocking the full potential of AI in neurological assessment. As we continue to advance in this field, the prospects for improving patient outcomes and transforming neurological care are more promising than ever. The synergy between AI and neurological assessment is not just about detecting and diagnosing conditions but about understanding and treating them at a deeper, more personalized level, ultimately leading to better health and well-being for patients. The future of neurological care lies in the integration of AI-driven technologies, enabling more accurate, efficient, and patient-centered approaches to diagnosis and treatment.

EEG and Its Applications

EEG measures the electrical activity of the brain through electrodes placed on the scalp. The resulting waveforms provide insights into brain function, including the detection of abnormal patterns associated with various neurological conditions. EEG is widely used in the diagnosis and monitoring of epilepsy, sleep disorders, and brain tumors. It is also employed in cognitive function assessment, where it can reveal patterns of brain activity associated with attention, memory, and other cognitive processes. Despite its utility, traditional EEG analysis is labor-intensive and subject to human error. The interpretation of EEG data requires extensive training and experience, and the results can be influenced by the interpreter's subjective judgment. These limitations have driven the development of AI-driven approaches to enhance the accuracy and efficiency of EEG analysis.

AI is revolutionizing EEG analysis by automating the detection and interpretation of brain waveforms. Machine learning algorithms can be trained to recognize patterns in EEG data that are indicative of specific neurological conditions or cognitive states. Deep learning techniques, particularly convolutional neural networks (CNNs), are particularly effective in analyzing the complex and high-dimensional data generated by EEG. These algorithms can identify subtle features in the waveforms that may be missed by human observers, improving the sensitivity and specificity of diagnosis. AI-driven EEG analysis can also provide real-time feedback, enabling clinicians to monitor brain activity continuously and make timely interventions. This real-time capability is particularly valuable in critical care settings, where rapid assessment and treatment are essential.

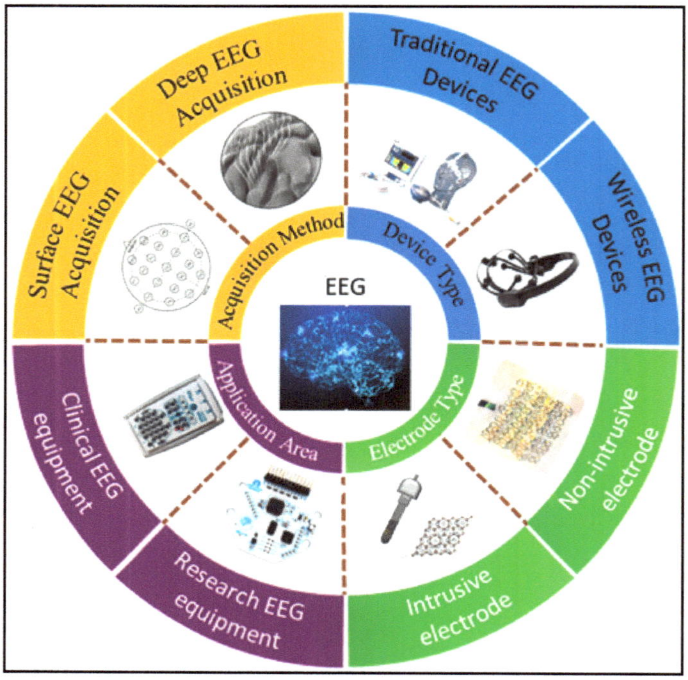

Fig: Application and Development of EEG Acquisition and Feedback Technology

Role of AI in Enhancing EEG Analysis

AI-Driven Cognitive Function Assessment

Cognitive function assessment is a critical component of neurological evaluation, providing insights into an individual's mental abilities and potential impairments. Traditional cognitive assessments rely on standardized tests and clinical observations, which can be time-consuming and subject to variability. AI-driven approaches are enhancing cognitive function assessment by providing objective and quantitative measures of brain activity. Machine learning algorithms can analyze EEG data to identify patterns associated with specific cognitive processes, such as attention, memory, and executive function. These algorithms can also track changes in cognitive function over time, enabling early detection of decline and intervention. AI-driven cognitive function assessment is particularly valuable in the diagnosis and monitoring of conditions such as Alzheimer's disease, traumatic brain injury, and developmental disorders.

Applications in Neurological Disorders

The integration of AI in EEG and cognitive function assessment has wide-ranging applications in the diagnosis and management of neurological disorders. In epilepsy, AI-driven EEG analysis can improve the detection of seizures and interictal activity, enabling more accurate diagnosis and treatment planning. In sleep disorders, AI can analyze EEG data to identify patterns associated with sleep stages and disruptions, providing insights into the underlying causes of sleep disturbances.

In neurodegenerative diseases, such as Alzheimer's and Parkinson's, AI-driven cognitive function assessment can detect early signs of decline, enabling timely intervention and management. In traumatic brain injury, AI can analyze EEG data to assess the extent of damage and monitor recovery, guiding rehabilitation efforts. The versatility of AI-driven approaches makes them valuable tools in the diagnosis and management of a wide range of neurological conditions.

Challenges and Limitations

Despite the significant advancements, AI-driven EEG analysis faces several challenges and limitations. One of the primary issues is the need for large and well-annotated datasets to train and validate AI algorithms. The rarity of certain neurological conditions and the heterogeneity of EEG data can make it difficult to obtain sufficient data for robust model training. Additionally, the quality and pre-processing of EEG data can significantly impact the performance of AI algorithms.

Factors such as electrode placement, signal noise, and artifacts can introduce variability and bias into the data, affecting the accuracy of analysis. Furthermore, the interpretation of AI-driven results requires careful consideration of clinical context and biological relevance. AI algorithms may identify patterns that are statistically significant but not clinically meaningful, leading to false positives or negatives. Addressing these challenges will require ongoing research, standardization of protocols, and collaboration between clinicians, scientists, and AI experts.

Potential of AI in Personalized Neurological Care

AI-driven EEG and cognitive function assessment have the potential to revolutionize personalized neurological care by enabling the development of tailored treatment strategies for individual patients. By analyzing the unique patterns of brain activity and cognitive function, AI can identify specific targets for therapy, predict treatment response, and monitor disease progression in real-time. This personalized approach can improve the efficacy of treatments, reduce side effects, and enhance patient outcomes. Moreover, AI can facilitate the discovery of novel biomarkers and therapeutic targets, expanding the arsenal of tools available for precision medicine. The integration of AI in neurological assessment is not just about improving diagnosis and monitoring but also about transforming the way we understand and treat neurological conditions at a molecular and functional level

Collaboration and Innovation in AI and Neurological Assessment

The advancement of AI in EEG and cognitive function assessment requires a collaborative and interdisciplinary approach, bringing together experts from various fields, including neurology, neuroscience, bioinformatics, and AI. Collaboration between academic institutions, industry partners, and healthcare providers is essential for driving innovation and translating research findings into clinical practice. Open data sharing, standardization of protocols, and the development of common platforms for data analysis and interpretation can accelerate progress in this field. Innovation hubs and consortia, focused on AI and neurological assessment, can foster collaboration, share resources, and catalyze the development of new technologies and approaches. By working together, we can overcome the challenges and harness the full potential of AI in neurological assessment, ultimately improving patient care and outcomes.

CHAPTER

Data Infrastructure and Management

4

4.1 DATA SOURCES: EMRS, PACS, LABORATORY SYSTEMS

The integration of Artificial Intelligence (AI) in the realm of medical diagnostics has fundamentally reshaped the way healthcare professionals approach patient care. Central to this transformative shift are the data sources that feed AI algorithms, enabling them to perform diagnostic assessments with speed and accuracy. Among the most significant sources of clinical data are Electronic Medical Records (EMRs), Picture Archiving and Communication Systems (PACS), and Laboratory Information Systems (LIS). These systems, each harboring a distinct type of medical information, serve as the foundation for training and implementing AI-driven diagnostic tools. The convergence of AI with these structured data sources not only enhances diagnostic precision but also facilitates early disease detection, clinical decision support, and personalized treatment pathways.

4.1.1 Electronic Medical Records (EMRs): The Bedrock of Patient Histories

Electronic Medical Records, often referred to as EMRs, are digital versions of the paper charts traditionally maintained in a clinician's office. These records encompass a wide array of patient information including demographics, clinical notes, medical history, medication lists, immunization status, allergies, and billing information. EMRs are longitudinal in nature, providing a continuous record of patient care over time. The comprehensive data stored in EMRs serve as a rich source of information for AI systems to analyze patterns, predict outcomes, and suggest possible diagnoses.

The power of EMRs in diagnostics through AI lies in their structured and unstructured data. Structured data, such as laboratory test results and vital signs, are quantifiable and easy to integrate into algorithmic models. Unstructured data, such as physician notes and clinical narratives, present a greater challenge but offer deeper insights. Natural Language Processing (NLP) algorithms have emerged as pivotal tools in extracting meaningful content from unstructured EMR data. These algorithms can identify symptoms, disease progression, and clinician observations that may not be captured in coded data, thus enriching the diagnostic process.

Fig: EMR System

AI models trained on EMR datasets can also facilitate risk stratification and early disease detection. For instance, predictive models built using EMR data can identify patients at high risk for chronic conditions such as diabetes, cardiovascular diseases, or cancer. Additionally, AI can automate routine tasks such as appointment scheduling, alert generation for abnormal test results, and reminders for follow-up care, thereby improving workflow efficiency and reducing clinician burden.

4.1.2 Picture Archiving and Communication Systems (PACS): Imaging Data for Visual Diagnosis

PACS, or Picture Archiving and Communication Systems, are integral to the storage, retrieval, and management of medical imaging data. These systems store radiological images such as X-rays, CT scans, MRIs, and ultrasounds, which are vital for diagnosing a myriad of conditions ranging from fractures to tumors and vascular diseases. PACS serve as a repository of visual data that is indispensable for radiologists and increasingly important for AI applications in diagnostic radiology.

AI integration with PACS has revolutionized image analysis by enabling algorithms to detect and classify abnormalities with high levels of accuracy. Deep learning techniques, particularly convolutional neural networks (CNNs), have shown tremendous success in image recognition tasks. These models can be trained on large volumes of annotated images from PACS to identify features indicative of disease, often with performance on par with or exceeding that of human radiologists. For example, AI algorithms have demonstrated proficiency in detecting lung nodules on chest CTs, classifying breast lesions on mammograms, and assessing brain hemorrhages on CT scans.

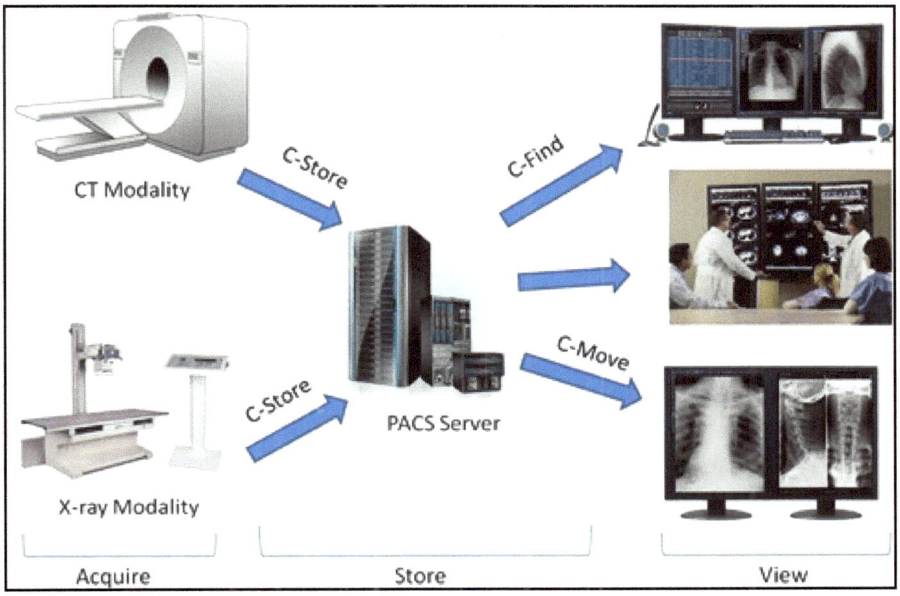

Fig: Picture Archiving and Communication Systems (PACS)

The synergy between PACS and AI not only improves diagnostic accuracy but also reduces turnaround times. Automated image analysis can prioritize critical cases by flagging suspicious findings for immediate review, thereby supporting rapid decision-making in emergency settings. Furthermore, AI can assist in standardizing image interpretation by minimizing inter-observer variability among radiologists. As PACS continue to evolve, integration with AI platforms will further enhance remote diagnostics and telemedicine, allowing for more equitable access to high-quality imaging services.

4.1.3 Laboratory Information Systems (LIS): Quantitative Data for Clinical Interpretation

Laboratory Information Systems manage the workflow and data associated with clinical laboratory tests. These systems are responsible for tracking specimens, managing test results, and ensuring quality control. The data generated by LIS are typically numerical and highly structured, encompassing a wide array of tests such as blood counts, biochemical profiles, microbiological cultures, and molecular diagnostics. These quantitative data form an essential component of clinical decision-making and are increasingly being leveraged by AI to derive diagnostic and prognostic insights.

AI systems can harness laboratory data to detect subtle patterns that may be overlooked by clinicians. For instance, machine learning models can analyze trends in complete blood count results to identify early signs of hematological disorders. Similarly, changes in liver or kidney function tests over time can be used to predict organ dysfunction or adverse drug reactions. In the field of infectious disease diagnostics, AI algorithms can analyze microbiology lab data to monitor antimicrobial resistance patterns and guide empirical therapy decisions.

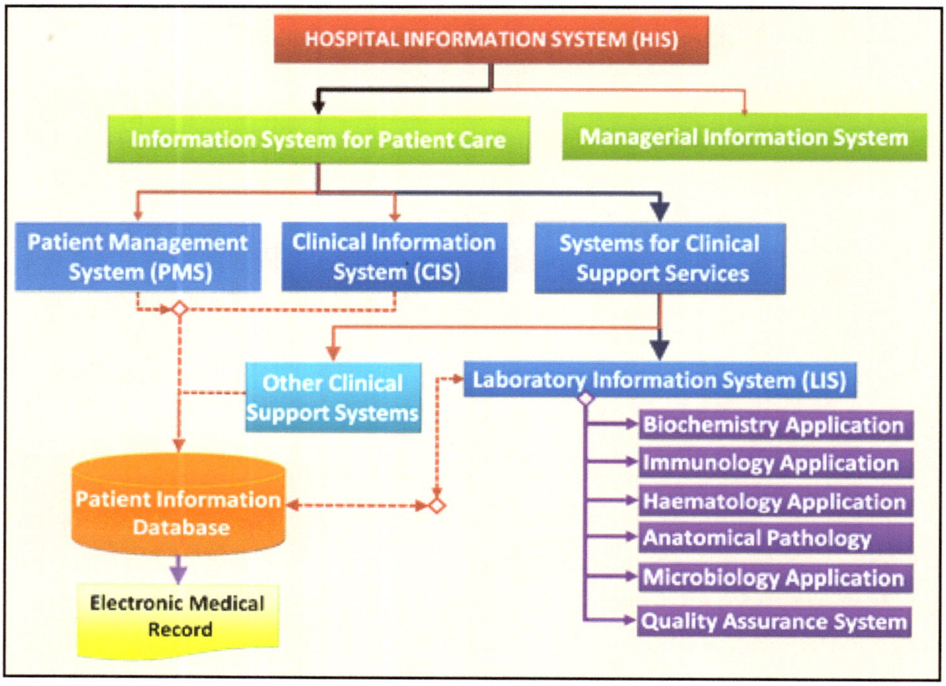

Fig: Laboratory Information Systems (LIS)

Moreover, the integration of laboratory data with EMRs enhances the contextual understanding of test results. For example, an elevated white blood cell count may have different implications depending on the patient's clinical history and presenting symptoms, information typically found in EMRs. AI models that incorporate both LIS and EMR data can provide more accurate and context-sensitive diagnostic recommendations. The real-time availability of lab data also supports AI-driven alert systems that notify clinicians of critical values, contributing to faster intervention and improved patient outcomes.

4.1.4 Interconnected Ecosystem of Diagnostic Data

The true potential of AI in diagnostics is realized when EMRs, PACS, and LIS are integrated into a unified ecosystem. Individually, each system offers valuable insights, but when combined, they provide a comprehensive view of the patient's health. This integration enables AI algorithms to consider multi-modal data inputs—clinical notes, lab values, and imaging findings—thus enhancing diagnostic accuracy and supporting more holistic care.

Such interconnected data ecosystems facilitate the development of sophisticated Clinical Decision Support Systems (CDSS). These AI-powered tools can recommend differential diagnoses, suggest further testing, and even propose treatment options based on a synthesis of the available data. For instance, in a patient with chest pain, AI can correlate ECG findings, cardiac enzyme levels, and imaging results to assess the likelihood of acute coronary syndrome and recommend appropriate interventions.

Additionally, interoperability among data systems is crucial for training robust AI models. Standardization protocols such as HL7, FHIR, and DICOM ensure that data from different sources can be harmonized and analyzed collectively. This standardization also supports the scalability of AI solutions across different healthcare institutions, enhancing their generalizability and clinical utility.

4.1.5 Challenges and Future Directions

Despite the promise of AI in diagnostics, the use of EMRs, PACS, and LIS as data sources is not without challenges. Data quality and completeness remain major concerns, as missing or inaccurate information can compromise the performance of AI models. Furthermore, privacy and security considerations must be addressed to protect patient information, particularly when data are shared across institutions for algorithm training and validation.

Another challenge lies in the interpretability of AI algorithms. Clinicians need to understand how an AI system arrives at its conclusions to trust and act on its recommendations. This has led to the growing emphasis on explainable AI (XAI), which seeks to make algorithmic decision-making more transparent and understandable.

Looking ahead, the continued evolution of AI will depend on the increasing availability of high-quality, annotated data from EMRs, PACS, and LIS. As these systems become more interoperable and enriched with diverse data types—including genomics and wearable sensor data—the scope of AI in diagnostics will expand further. The development of federated learning models, which allow AI to be trained on decentralized data without compromising privacy, is another promising avenue.

4.2 DATA QUALITY AND ANNOTATION STANDARDS

Artificial Intelligence (AI) has emerged as a transformative force in medical diagnostics, promising faster, more accurate, and cost-effective healthcare solutions. However, the effectiveness of AI models is fundamentally dependent on the quality of data used to train and validate them. High-quality data ensures that AI systems can learn patterns, make accurate predictions, and avoid errors that could compromise patient safety. Alongside data quality, the role of annotation standards is equally critical, especially in supervised learning models where labeled data guide the learning process.

4.2.1 Data Quality in Medical Diagnostics

Data quality refers to the condition or characteristics of a dataset that make it suitable for use in analysis, training, and clinical decision-making. In the context of medical diagnostics, data quality is judged based on attributes such as accuracy, completeness, consistency, timeliness, and relevance. Each of these attributes plays a crucial role in shaping the performance of AI systems.

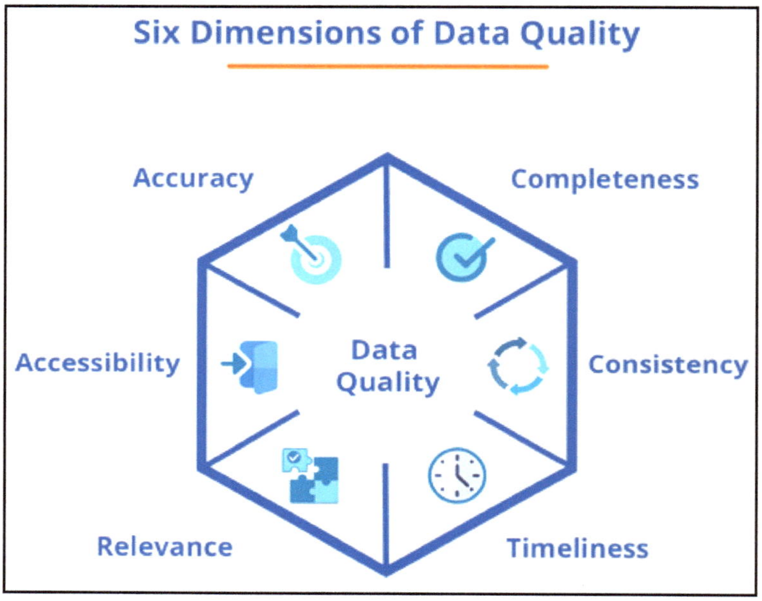

Fig: Managing Data Quality in Healthcare

Accuracy refers to the correctness of the data in reflecting the real-world conditions of the patient. For instance, if a patient's blood pressure is recorded incorrectly in the system, any AI model that uses this data may generate misleading diagnostic outputs. Completeness is another vital dimension, ensuring that all required data elements are present. Missing values in clinical records, such as omitted medication histories or lab results, can severely distort model outcomes. Consistency involves maintaining uniform data entry practices across different departments or institutions. For example, a diagnosis labeled as "myocardial infarction" in one hospital should not be recorded as "heart attack" in another without standardizing the terminology.

Timeliness of data ensures that the information used by AI systems reflects the most current clinical status of the patient. Diagnostic decisions based on outdated data can be not only ineffective but potentially harmful. Relevance is the final pillar of quality, requiring that the data being used is appropriate for the diagnostic question at hand. For example, a model predicting stroke risk should be trained on datasets rich in cardiovascular, neurological, and lifestyle indicators, rather than unrelated variables.

4.2.2 Sources of Poor Data Quality in Diagnostic AI

Several factors contribute to poor data quality in the development of diagnostic AI. These include manual data entry errors, variability in clinical workflows, lack of interoperability between systems, and incomplete documentation. Human error in typing, transcribing, or interpreting clinical information can introduce noise into the dataset.

Inconsistent clinical practices across different settings can lead to heterogeneous data, making it difficult for AI models to generalize well. When Electronic Medical Records (EMRs), Picture Archiving and Communication Systems (PACS), and Laboratory Information Systems (LIS) are not fully interoperable, data integration becomes a significant challenge, often resulting in fragmented or duplicated records. Additionally, time constraints and administrative burdens may lead clinicians to leave out essential details from medical records, compromising the completeness and richness of data.

4.2.3 Importance of Annotation in Diagnostic AI

While high-quality data forms the foundation, annotated data is the cornerstone for training supervised AI models. Annotation refers to the process of labeling data elements with specific information that helps AI systems learn and identify patterns. In diagnostics, annotation typically involves labeling images, text, or clinical records with diagnoses, anatomical markers, symptoms, or other relevant medical concepts. For example, in radiology, annotating chest X-rays with labels such as “pneumonia,” “nodule,” or “normal” allows AI models to distinguish between different disease states.

Proper annotation is essential not only for training AI models but also for evaluating their performance. Without precise labels, it is impossible to assess whether the AI system is making correct predictions. Annotated data also enable the development of explainable AI, where clinicians can understand the rationale behind algorithmic decisions. Moreover, annotations are crucial in multiclass classification problems and segmentation tasks where the AI must identify specific regions of interest within medical images, such as tumors or lesions.

4.2.4 Standardization of Annotation Practices

One of the biggest challenges in data annotation for diagnostics is the lack of standardized guidelines. Inconsistent labeling practices across datasets can result in poor model performance and limited applicability in clinical settings. To mitigate this, several initiatives have been launched to establish annotation standards, particularly in radiology, pathology, and genomics. These standards define how data should be labeled, what terminology should be used, and how inter-observer agreement should be measured.

For example, the Radiological Society of North America (RSNA) has developed annotated imaging datasets that serve as benchmarks for AI training. Similarly, the American College of Radiology (ACR) has promoted the use of standardized lexicons such as BI-RADS for breast imaging and LI-RADS for liver imaging. These frameworks provide structured reporting language and consistent annotation schemes, thereby reducing variability in interpretation.

The use of controlled vocabularies and ontologies such as SNOMED CT, ICD-10, and LOINC also helps in maintaining semantic consistency across different datasets and institutions. By standardizing the way diseases, symptoms, and procedures are labeled, these tools facilitate better interoperability and more effective model training. Inter-annotator agreement metrics like Cohen's kappa are often used to assess the reliability of annotations, ensuring that multiple experts agree on the labeling and reducing the subjectivity in data interpretation.

4.2.5 Human-in-the-Loop and Expert Annotation

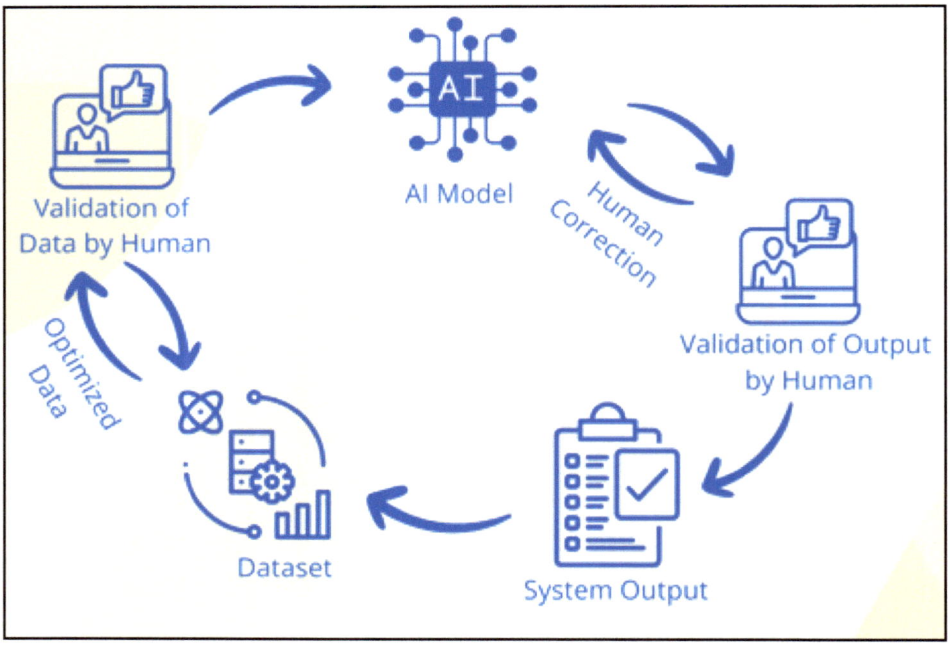

Fig: Responsible AI use with Human-in-the-Loop (HITL)

Given the complexity of medical diagnostics, annotations are often performed by clinical experts such as radiologists, pathologists, and specialists. Human expertise is vital in ensuring that annotations are both clinically accurate and contextually relevant. The concept of human-in-the-loop (HITL) systems has gained prominence, where AI models are trained in conjunction with expert input. In such systems, initial annotations may be generated automatically, but are reviewed and corrected by human experts to improve data quality.

Expert annotation not only enhances model performance but also supports continuous learning. Feedback from clinicians can be used to refine annotations and update AI algorithms accordingly. This iterative process ensures that the AI system remains current with evolving medical knowledge and clinical practices. Additionally, involving domain experts in the annotation process builds trust among end users, which is crucial for the adoption of AI in clinical workflows.

4.2.6 Ethical and Regulatory Considerations

Data quality and annotation practices also intersect with ethical and regulatory domains. Patient consent, data anonymization, and compliance with data protection laws such as the Health Insurance Portability and Accountability Act (HIPAA) or the General Data Protection Regulation (GDPR) are critical considerations. Annotated datasets often contain sensitive information, and maintaining the confidentiality and security of patient data is non-negotiable.

From a regulatory standpoint, annotated data must meet the criteria set by governing bodies such as the U.S. Food and Drug Administration (FDA) or the European Medicines Agency (EMA) for clinical-grade AI tools. Regulatory agencies often require extensive documentation of data sources, annotation protocols, and quality assurance processes before approving AI applications for diagnostic use. Therefore, standardized and transparent annotation practices are essential not just for model development, but also for regulatory compliance and market readiness.

4.3 CLINICAL DATA INTEGRATION AND INTEROPERABILITY

Artificial Intelligence (AI) is transforming the field of medical diagnostics by enabling faster, more precise, and predictive healthcare interventions. However, the full potential of AI in diagnostics can only be realized when it is supported by seamless clinical data integration and robust interoperability.

Healthcare data is often stored in fragmented silos across multiple systems such as Electronic Medical Records (EMRs), Picture Archiving and Communication Systems (PACS), Laboratory Information Systems (LIS), and other ancillary data sources. These systems are frequently developed by different vendors, use varying data standards, and operate in disconnected infrastructures. This fragmentation poses a significant challenge to AI models, which require access to high-quality, comprehensive, and harmonized data to deliver accurate and clinically relevant results. Therefore, integrating clinical data across diverse platforms and ensuring interoperability is foundational to the effective use of AI in medical diagnostics.

4.3.1 Challenge of Fragmented Clinical Data

In modern healthcare environments, data is generated at every point of care, from primary consultations and specialist referrals to imaging studies, laboratory tests, and surgical procedures. This data is stored in multiple systems, each designed for a specific function, often with limited ability to communicate with other systems. As a result, a patient's diagnostic history may be spread across various platforms, creating barriers to data access and interpretation. For example, imaging data stored in a radiology PACS may not be easily linked with laboratory results in an LIS or clinical notes in an EMR. This siloed structure makes it difficult for AI algorithms to analyze data holistically, potentially limiting diagnostic accuracy and clinical decision support.

Another major issue is the variability in data formats and terminologies used by different institutions and vendors. One hospital may record a diagnosis using the ICD-10 coding system, while another may use SNOMED CT or even free-text entries. Similarly, imaging data may be stored in DICOM format in one system but lack standardized annotations in another. This lack of consistency complicates data integration and can significantly reduce the effectiveness of AI models trained on heterogeneous datasets. Without interoperability, valuable clinical information remains trapped in isolated systems, limiting the scope of AI-based diagnostics.

4.3.2 Importance of Clinical Data Integration for AI

Clinical data integration refers to the process of aggregating and harmonizing data from disparate sources into a unified view that can be used for analysis, diagnosis, and treatment planning. For AI in diagnostics, data integration is not merely a technical necessity but a strategic enabler. Integrated data provides a richer context for AI algorithms to learn from and allows models to recognize patterns that span multiple domains of healthcare.

When AI systems are trained on integrated datasets that combine clinical notes, imaging results, pathology reports, and lab values, their diagnostic capabilities are significantly enhanced. For instance, in cancer diagnostics, an AI model that considers radiological images in conjunction with histopathology findings and genetic test results is more likely to produce an accurate diagnosis than a model trained on a single data modality. Integrated data also supports longitudinal analysis, enabling AI to track disease progression over time and predict outcomes based on historical trends. Moreover, data integration facilitates the development of personalized diagnostic tools. By merging patient-specific data across multiple healthcare episodes, AI can tailor its diagnostic recommendations based on an individual's unique clinical profile, leading to more precise and effective care. Integration also supports real-time analytics and decision-making, allowing clinicians to access comprehensive diagnostic insights at the point of care.

4.3.3 Role of Interoperability in Data Sharing

Interoperability is the ability of different information systems, devices, or applications to connect, exchange, and interpret shared data effectively. It is a critical prerequisite for achieving clinical data integration. Interoperability ensures that data captured in one system can be seamlessly accessed and utilized by other systems, regardless of the software or vendor. In the context of AI diagnostics, interoperability is essential for creating the large, diverse datasets needed to train and validate algorithms that are generalizable across different clinical settings.

There are different levels of interoperability, each with its own set of requirements. Technical interoperability refers to the basic exchange of data between systems through standardized protocols. Syntactic interoperability ensures that data exchanged is structured in a format that can be read by different systems, such as XML or HL7 messages. Semantic interoperability goes a step further by ensuring that the meaning of the exchanged data is preserved and understood consistently across systems. Achieving semantic interoperability is particularly important in diagnostics, where the clinical interpretation of data is critical.

To support interoperability, healthcare organizations and technology vendors have adopted various standards and protocols. Health Level Seven (HL7) and Fast Healthcare Interoperability Resources (FHIR) are widely used standards for structuring and exchanging clinical data. FHIR, in particular, has gained traction due to its flexibility, scalability, and ease of integration with modern web technologies. DICOM is the standard for managing medical imaging data and plays a vital role in integrating radiological information into AI systems. Other standards such as LOINC and SNOMED CT are used to ensure consistency in laboratory results and clinical terminologies.

4.3.4 AI-Driven Benefits of Interoperable and Integrated Systems

When clinical data integration and interoperability are achieved, AI systems can unlock a multitude of benefits for diagnostic processes. One of the most significant advantages is improved diagnostic accuracy. AI algorithms that have access to complete patient records can analyze cross-modal data and arrive at more informed conclusions.

For instance, an AI model evaluating a case of suspected pneumonia can cross-reference imaging findings with clinical symptoms, lab results, and historical comorbidities, leading to a more accurate and reliable diagnosis. Interoperable systems also enable the creation of real-world data repositories, which are invaluable for training robust AI models. These repositories, built from diverse patient populations and healthcare settings, help reduce bias in AI algorithms and improve their performance across different demographic and clinical scenarios.

Furthermore, integrated systems support continuous learning in AI by allowing algorithms to update and adapt based on new data and feedback from clinical practice.

Another key benefit is enhanced clinical workflow efficiency. When AI systems operate in an integrated environment, they can automate data retrieval, analysis and reporting processes, thereby reducing the administrative burden on healthcare professionals. For example, AI tools can automatically pull relevant diagnostic information from multiple systems and present it in a unified dashboard, allowing clinicians to make quicker and more informed decisions.

4.3.5 Challenges to Achieving Integration and Interoperability

Despite its importance, achieving seamless clinical data integration and interoperability remains a complex challenge. One of the primary barriers is the existence of proprietary systems that limit data sharing. Vendors may implement closed architectures that hinder the exchange of information with external systems, either due to competitive interests or technical limitations. Overcoming this requires regulatory frameworks and incentives that promote open standards and data sharing.

Data governance and privacy concerns also pose significant challenges. Ensuring patient consent, protecting sensitive health information, and complying with data protection regulations such as HIPAA and GDPR are essential when integrating and sharing clinical data. Institutions must establish robust data governance models that address these concerns while enabling responsible data use for AI applications.

Technical barriers, such as differences in data structures, coding systems, and infrastructure maturity, further complicate integration efforts. Mapping and transforming data from multiple sources into a consistent and analyzable format require significant technical expertise and resources. Additionally, ensuring data quality and resolving inconsistencies across datasets is a time-consuming but necessary step in the integration process.

4.4 FEDERATED LEARNING AND PRIVACY-PRESERVING DATA SHARING

Federated learning and privacy-preserving data sharing represent a paradigm shift in the development and deployment of AI in diagnostics. By enabling collaborative model training without compromising patient privacy, these approaches address one of the most significant barriers to AI adoption in healthcare. The ability to leverage diverse and distributed datasets enhances the accuracy, generalizability, and fairness of AI-driven diagnostics, ultimately improving patient care. While challenges remain, ongoing research, innovation, and collaboration are paving the way for a future where AI can be harnessed to its full potential in a secure and ethical manner. As federated learning becomes more widely adopted, it will not only transform diagnostics but also set new standards for privacy, security, and collaboration in the age of AI-powered healthcare.

The future of federated learning and privacy-preserving data sharing in diagnostics is bright, with ongoing research focused on addressing current challenges and expanding the scope of applications. Advances in communication protocols, optimization algorithms, and privacy-preserving techniques are expected to improve the efficiency and scalability of federated learning. The integration of federated learning with other emerging technologies, such as blockchain, could further enhance data security and transparency. There is also growing interest in applying federated learning to real-time diagnostics, remote monitoring, and personalized medicine. As AI continues to evolve, federated learning will play a critical role in enabling the responsible and ethical use of data in healthcare.

4.4.1 Need for Data in AI-Driven Diagnostics

AI models, particularly those based on deep learning, require vast amounts of data to achieve high accuracy and generalizability. In diagnostics, this data may include medical images, electronic health records, genomic sequences, and other patient information. The diversity and volume of data are crucial for training robust models that can perform well across different populations and clinical settings.

However, healthcare data is highly sensitive, protected by strict regulations such as the Health Insurance Portability and Accountability Act (HIPAA) in the United States and the General Data Protection Regulation (GDPR) in Europe. These regulations are designed to protect patient privacy but can also hinder the sharing of data necessary for AI development. As a result, there is a pressing need for methods that enable collaborative AI research while preserving the privacy and security of patient data.

4.4.2 Federated Learning

Federated learning is a decentralized approach to machine learning that enables multiple institutions to collaboratively train AI models without sharing raw data. In a federated learning setup, the AI model is sent to each participating institution, where it is trained locally on the institution's data. Only the model updates, such as gradients or weights, are shared with a central server, which aggregates the updates to improve the global model. The raw data never leaves the local institution, ensuring that patient information remains private and secure. This approach allows for the development of AI models that benefit from the collective knowledge of multiple datasets while adhering to data privacy regulations. Federated learning has gained significant traction in healthcare, where data privacy is paramount and data is often distributed across various organizations.

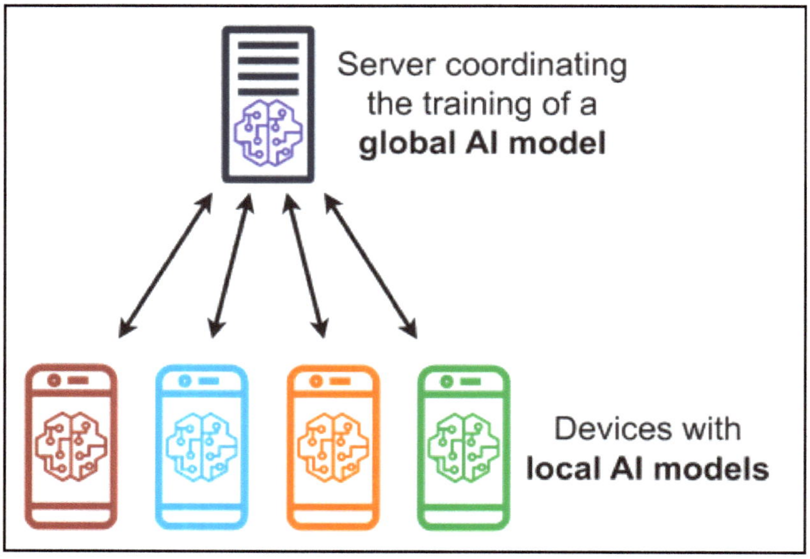

Fig: Federated Learning

4.4.3 Privacy-Preserving Techniques

While federated learning addresses many privacy concerns by keeping data local additional privacy-preserving techniques are often employed to further enhance security. Differential privacy is one such technique, which involves adding noise to the model updates before they are shared with the central server. This makes it difficult to infer any individual's data from the aggregated updates, providing mathematical guarantees of privacy. Homomorphic encryption is another technique that allows computations to be performed on encrypted data, ensuring that sensitive information remains protected even during processing. Secure multi-party computation enables multiple parties to jointly compute a function over their inputs while keeping those inputs private. These privacy-preserving techniques can be combined with federated learning to create a robust framework for secure and collaborative AI model development in diagnostics.

4.4.4 Applications

Federated learning has shown great promise in various diagnostic applications, particularly in medical imaging and predictive analytics. For example, hospitals can collaboratively train AI models to detect diseases such as cancer, pneumonia, or diabetic retinopathy from medical images like X-rays, CT scans, or retinal photographs. By leveraging data from multiple institutions, these models can achieve higher accuracy and generalizability than models trained on data from a single source. Federated learning has also been applied to electronic health records to predict patient outcomes, identify risk factors, and recommend personalized treatments. In genomics, federated learning enables researchers to analyze genetic data from diverse populations without exposing sensitive information. These applications demonstrate the potential of federated learning to accelerate AI-driven diagnostics while maintaining patient privacy.

4.4.5 Challenges and Limitations

Despite its advantages, federated learning faces several challenges that must be addressed to realize its full potential in diagnostics. One major challenge is data heterogeneity, as data collected from different institutions may vary in quality, format, and distribution. This can affect the performance and convergence of federated learning models, requiring sophisticated algorithms to handle non-IID (independent and identically distributed) data. Communication efficiency is another concern, as federated learning involves frequent exchange of model updates between institutions and the central server. Ensuring secure and efficient communication is essential, especially when dealing with large models and limited network bandwidth. Additionally, the implementation of privacy-preserving techniques such as differential privacy and homomorphic encryption can introduce computational overhead and complexity. Addressing these challenges requires ongoing research and collaboration between AI experts, clinicians, and data security professionals.

4.4.6 Ethical and Regulatory Considerations

The adoption of federated learning and privacy-preserving data sharing in diagnostics raises important ethical and regulatory considerations. Ensuring informed consent and transparency is crucial, as patients must understand how their data is being used, even if it never leaves the local institution. Regulatory frameworks must evolve to accommodate new technologies and provide clear guidelines for the use of federated learning in healthcare. There is also a need to address issues of data ownership, accountability, and governance, particularly when multiple institutions are involved in collaborative AI development. Ethical considerations extend to the potential for bias in AI models, as federated learning must ensure that models are fair and equitable across different populations. Ongoing dialogue between stakeholders, including patients, healthcare providers, regulators, and technology developers, is essential to navigate these complex issues.

4.4.7 Role of Collaboration in Advancing AI Diagnostics

Federated learning and privacy-preserving data sharing are fundamentally collaborative approaches, enabling institutions to work together towards common goals without compromising patient privacy. This collaboration is essential for advancing AI diagnostics, as it allows for the pooling of resources, expertise, and data. Multi-institutional collaborations can accelerate the development and validation of AI models, ensuring that they are robust, accurate, and applicable to diverse clinical settings. The success of federated learning initiatives depends on the willingness of institutions to participate, share knowledge, and adopt standardized protocols. Building trust and fostering a culture of collaboration are key to unlocking the full potential of AI in diagnostics.

4.5 SYNTHETIC DATA AND DATA AUGMENTATION FOR RARE CONDITIONS

Synthetic data and data augmentation are transforming the landscape of AI diagnostics for rare conditions, offering innovative solutions to the challenges of data scarcity and diversity. By generating realistic and clinically relevant data, these techniques enable the development of robust AI models that can support the diagnosis and management of rare diseases. While challenges remain, ongoing research, collaboration, and ethical oversight will be essential to ensure that synthetic data is used responsibly and effectively. As the field continues to evolve, the integration of synthetic data and data augmentation will play a pivotal role in advancing AI diagnostics, ultimately benefiting patients, clinicians, and the broader healthcare community.

The integration of synthetic data and data augmentation into AI diagnostics represents a significant step forward in addressing the challenges of rare disease diagnosis. As generative models continue to improve, the quality and realism of synthetic data will increase, enabling the development of more accurate and reliable AI tools. Advances in explainable AI and model interpretability will further enhance the trustworthiness of AI diagnostics, allowing clinicians to understand and validate the reasoning behind model predictions. The combination of synthetic data, data augmentation, and collaborative data sharing frameworks such as federated learning will create a more inclusive and effective ecosystem for AI-driven healthcare innovation. Ultimately, these advances will help ensure that patients with rare conditions receive timely, accurate, and personalized diagnostic support, improving outcomes and quality of life.

4.5.1 Challenge of Rare Conditions

Rare conditions, often defined as diseases affecting fewer than 1 in 2,000 people present unique challenges in the context of AI diagnostics. The limited number of cases means that there is often insufficient data to train machine learning models effectively. This scarcity can lead to overfitting, where models perform well on the limited training data but fail to generalize to new, unseen cases. Furthermore, the lack of data diversity can result in biased models that do not accurately represent the full spectrum of the disease. These issues are compounded by the fact that rare conditions are often heterogeneous, with significant variability in clinical presentation, progression, and response to treatment. As a result, traditional data-driven AI approaches may struggle to deliver reliable diagnostic support for rare diseases, highlighting the need for innovative solutions.

4.5.2 Synthetic Data: Creating New Possibilities

Synthetic data refers to artificially generated data that mimics the statistical properties and patterns of real-world data. In the context of AI diagnostics, synthetic data can be created using a variety of techniques, including generative adversarial networks (GANs), variational autoencoders (VAEs), and other deep learning-based generative models. These methods can produce realistic medical images, electronic health records, and other types of clinical data that closely resemble actual patient data.

The primary advantage of synthetic data is its ability to augment existing datasets, particularly for rare conditions where real data is scarce. By generating additional examples of rare disease cases, synthetic data can help balance datasets, reduce bias, and improve the performance of AI models. Moreover, synthetic data can be used to simulate a wide range of disease presentations, enabling models to learn from a more comprehensive set of examples.

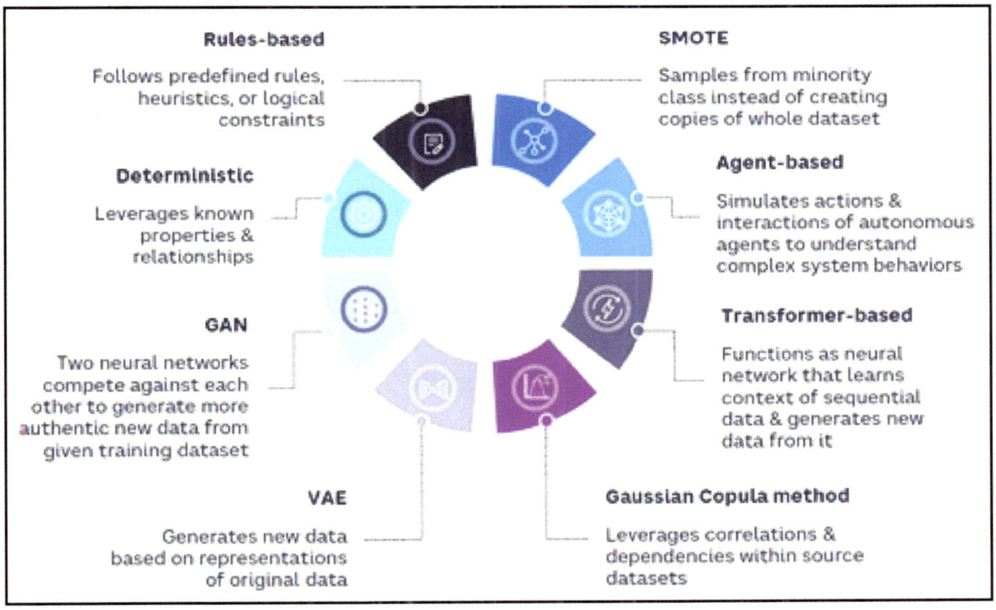

Fig: Synthetic Data

4.5.3 Data Augmentation: Enhancing Diversity and Robustness

Data augmentation is a related technique that involves creating modified versions of existing data to increase the size and diversity of the training dataset. In medical imaging, for example, data augmentation may include transformations such as rotation, scaling, flipping, or adding noise to images. These modifications help

AI models become more robust to variations in data and improve their ability to generalize to new cases. For rare conditions, data augmentation can be particularly valuable, as it allows researchers to make the most of the limited data available. By systematically varying the existing data, augmentation techniques can expose AI models to a broader range of disease manifestations, anatomical differences, and imaging artifacts. This exposure helps reduce overfitting and enhances the model's ability to recognize rare conditions in real-world clinical settings.

4.5.4 Applications of Synthetic Data and Augmentation in Rare Disease Diagnostics

The use of synthetic data and data augmentation has already shown promise in several areas of rare disease diagnostics. In medical imaging, GANs have been used to generate synthetic images of rare tumors, congenital anomalies, and other uncommon pathologies. These synthetic images can be combined with real images to train deep learning models for tasks such as disease detection, segmentation and classification. In genomics, synthetic data can be used to simulate rare genetic variants and their associated phenotypes, enabling the development of AI models that can identify and interpret these variants in patient data. Electronic health records can also be augmented with synthetic patient profiles, allowing for the training of predictive models that can identify rare disease patterns and support early diagnosis. These applications demonstrate the potential of synthetic data and augmentation to bridge the gap between data scarcity and the need for accurate AI diagnostics in rare conditions.

4.5.5 Ensuring Realism and Clinical Relevance

While synthetic data and data augmentation offer significant benefits, it is essential to ensure that the generated data is realistic and clinically relevant. Poorly generated synthetic data can introduce artifacts, unrealistic patterns, or biases that may negatively impact model performance. To address this, researchers employ rigorous validation techniques, including expert review by clinicians, statistical comparison with real data, and performance testing of AI models trained on synthetic data. The goal is to ensure that synthetic data not only mimics the appearance of real data but also captures the underlying clinical and biological variability of rare conditions. Collaboration between data scientists, clinicians, and domain experts is crucial in this process, as it helps ensure that synthetic data generation aligns with clinical realities and supports meaningful diagnostic outcomes.

4.5.6 Privacy and Ethical Considerations

One of the notable advantages of synthetic data is its potential to address privacy concerns associated with sharing real patient data. Since synthetic data does not correspond to actual individuals, it can be shared more freely among researchers, institutions, and AI developers without violating patient confidentiality. This facilitates collaboration and accelerates the development of AI diagnostic tools for rare conditions. However, ethical considerations remain, particularly regarding the use of synthetic data in clinical decision-making. It is important to ensure that synthetic data does not inadvertently encode biases or inaccuracies that could affect patient care. Transparent reporting of synthetic data generation methods, validation processes, and limitations is essential to maintain trust and accountability in AI-driven diagnostics.

4.5.7 Challenges and Limitations

Despite the promise of synthetic data and data augmentation, several challenges must be addressed to fully realize their potential in rare disease diagnostics. Generating high-quality synthetic data that accurately reflects the complexity of rare conditions is a non-trivial task. Some rare diseases may have subtle or highly variable features that are difficult to capture with current generative models. Additionally, the use of synthetic data may not fully compensate for the lack of real-world diversity, particularly in cases where rare conditions intersect with other demographic or clinical factors. There is also a risk that over-reliance on synthetic data could lead to models that perform well in controlled settings but fail to generalize to real-world clinical practice. Ongoing research is needed to improve the fidelity of synthetic data, develop better validation methods, and integrate synthetic and real data in a way that maximizes diagnostic accuracy.

CHAPTER 5

Model Development and Validation

5.1 MODEL TRAINING: FROM RAW DATA TO ALGORITHMS

Model training in AI-based diagnostics is a complex, multi-stage process that transforms raw, heterogeneous clinical data into actionable diagnostic algorithms. It involves data cleaning, annotation, feature extraction, model selection, training, validation, and eventual deployment, all governed by strict clinical and ethical standards. As technology evolves, the integration of AI in diagnostics holds the potential to revolutionize healthcare delivery by enabling earlier, faster, and more accurate disease detection. However, the journey from raw data to a reliable diagnostic tool demands meticulous planning, interdisciplinary collaboration, and a commitment to patient safety and clinical transparency.

Training diagnostic models also involves navigating ethical and regulatory landscapes. It is important to ensure that the data used is representative of the population it is intended to serve, avoiding biases that could lead to disparities in healthcare delivery. Informed consent, data anonymization, and transparency in data usage are foundational to ethical AI development. Regulatory bodies such as the FDA in the United States and the European Medicines Agency (EMA) in Europe are increasingly developing frameworks to evaluate the safety and efficacy of AI-based diagnostic tools. Compliance with these frameworks is essential before any AI model can be used in real-world clinical practice.

5.1.1 Raw Data in Diagnostics

Raw data in diagnostics encompasses a wide range of formats and sources. It includes structured data such as electronic health records (EHRs), laboratory test results, and imaging metadata, as well as unstructured data like medical imaging (X-rays, MRIs, CT scans), clinical notes, pathology slides, and genomic sequences. Each data type presents unique challenges and requires different preprocessing strategies. Raw data often suffers from noise, redundancy, inconsistencies, and missing values, which can significantly hinder the training process if not addressed properly. Before any machine learning algorithm can be trained, the data must be cleansed, transformed, and standardized to ensure uniformity and compatibility with the model architecture.

5.1.2 Data Preprocessing and Annotation

Preprocessing is a vital step in the model training pipeline that aims to transform raw data into a usable format. In the case of medical images, preprocessing may involve resizing, normalization, contrast enhancement, and segmentation. For text data such as clinical notes or patient histories, it involves tokenization, stemming, and removal of irrelevant information.

Beyond technical formatting, data must be labeled accurately to serve as a learning guide for the algorithm. This annotation process is particularly important in supervised learning, where the model learns from examples with known outputs. Expert annotations by radiologists, pathologists, or clinicians are often used to ensure the medical relevance and accuracy of labels. However, this process is time-consuming and resource-intensive, and introduces the possibility of inter-observer variability, which must be minimized to ensure consistent training outcomes.

5.1.3 Feature Extraction and Representation

Once the data is cleaned and annotated, the next phase involves extracting relevant features that the model will use to learn patterns. In traditional machine learning, feature engineering is a manual process where domain experts define which aspects of the data are most informative.

For example, in diagnostic imaging, features might include texture, shape, and intensity of lesions. In more advanced deep learning approaches, particularly convolutional neural networks (CNNs), the model learns to extract hierarchical features automatically during training. This representation learning capability is one of the main reasons deep learning has gained prominence in medical diagnostics, as it reduces the dependence on handcrafted features and often achieves superior performance.

5.1.4 Model Selection and Architecture Design

Choosing the right model architecture is crucial for achieving accurate diagnostic outcomes. The selection depends on the nature of the data and the diagnostic task. For image-based diagnosis, CNNs and variants like ResNet, DenseNet, and U-Net are commonly used.

For text-based data, models such as recurrent neural networks (RNNs), Long Short-Term Memory (LSTM), and transformer-based models like BERT or BioBERT are more appropriate. In genomics or multi-modal diagnostic tasks, hybrid architectures that combine different model types may be used. Model complexity must be balanced with interpretability, especially in clinical contexts where explainability is essential. More complex models tend to provide better accuracy but may behave like black boxes, making it difficult to explain decisions to clinicians.

5.1.5 Training and Optimization

Training a diagnostic AI model involves feeding it the prepared dataset and allowing it to iteratively learn from the patterns in the data. During each training iteration or epoch, the model makes predictions, compares them to the true labels using a loss function, and adjusts its parameters through optimization techniques like stochastic gradient descent.

The objective is to minimize the loss, thereby improving the model's ability to make accurate predictions on unseen data. Regularization techniques, dropout layers, and batch normalization are employed to prevent overfitting, where the model memorizes the training data instead of learning generalizable patterns. It is also essential to monitor training through metrics such as accuracy, sensitivity, specificity, area under the curve (AUC), and F1-score to ensure clinical relevance.

5.1.6 Validation and Testing

To ensure that the model performs reliably in real-world diagnostic settings, it must be validated and tested on data that was not used during training. This is typically done by splitting the dataset into training, validation, and test sets. The validation set is used to fine-tune hyperparameters and monitor model performance during training, while the test set evaluates the final model's accuracy and generalization ability. Cross-validation techniques can further enhance model robustness by ensuring that performance is not dependent on a specific data split. In medical diagnostics, external validation using datasets from different institutions is often necessary to assess the model's adaptability to diverse patient populations and imaging protocols.

5.1.7 Challenges

Despite advancements in AI technologies, several challenges persist in training diagnostic models. One major hurdle is data scarcity, especially in rare diseases where annotated examples are limited. Class imbalance is another common issue where one class, such as 'disease positive,' is underrepresented compared to the 'disease negative' class, leading to biased model predictions.

Addressing this requires techniques like data augmentation, synthetic data generation, or weighted loss functions. Another challenge is ensuring data privacy and compliance with regulations like HIPAA and GDPR, especially when using patient data across institutions. Federated learning is emerging as a solution, allowing models to be trained on decentralized data without compromising patient confidentiality.

5.1.8 Model Interpretability and Clinical Integration

Model interpretability is a critical factor in medical diagnostics. Clinicians need to understand the rationale behind a model's decision before incorporating it into patient care. Techniques such as saliency maps, Grad-CAM, LIME, and SHAP are used to highlight which parts of the input data influenced the model's prediction. Integrating AI models into clinical workflows requires collaboration between AI developers, clinicians, and regulatory authorities. The system must be tested in clinical trials, approved by regulatory bodies, and integrated with existing hospital information systems (HIS) and picture archiving and communication systems (PACS). Continuous monitoring and retraining are also essential to adapt to changes in clinical practices or data characteristics over time.

5.2 CLINICAL VALIDATION AND BENCHMARKING

Clinical validation and benchmarking are indispensable for the successful integration of AI into diagnostic medicine. They ensure that AI tools are safe, reliable, and effective in diverse clinical settings. While challenges such as data bias, regulatory complexities, and standardization remain, ongoing advancements in federated learning, explainable AI, and outcome-based studies offer promising solutions. As AI continues to evolve, robust validation and benchmarking frameworks will be critical in unlocking its full potential to revolutionize healthcare diagnostics.

The future of AI in diagnostics will depend on advancements in validation and benchmarking practices. One promising direction is the use of federated learning, where AI models are trained across multiple institutions without sharing raw patient data. This approach enhances dataset diversity while maintaining privacy.

Another emerging trend is the development of explainable AI (XAI), which provides transparent decision-making processes. Clinicians are more likely to trust AI tools if they can understand how diagnoses are generated. Standardization efforts, such as those led by the International Medical Device Regulators Forum (IMDRF), will also play a crucial role in harmonizing validation protocols globally.

Long-term clinical trials assessing AI's impact on patient outcomes—rather than just diagnostic accuracy—will be essential. For instance, does an AI tool for early cancer detection actually improve survival rates? Such studies will provide deeper insights into AI's real-world benefits.

5.2.1 Importance of Clinical Validation in AI Diagnostics

Clinical validation is a fundamental step in the development and deployment of AI-based diagnostic tools. It involves assessing whether an AI model performs as intended in real-world clinical settings, rather than just in controlled research environments. The primary goal is to ensure that the AI system delivers accurate, consistent, and clinically relevant results. Validation helps identify potential biases, errors, and limitations that may arise when the model is applied to diverse patient populations. Without robust clinical validation, AI tools risk being unreliable, leading to false positives, false negatives, or other diagnostic inaccuracies that could harm patients. The validation process typically involves testing the AI model on independent datasets that were not used during its training phase. These datasets should represent the target patient population, including variations in demographics, disease stages, and imaging modalities. Additionally, validation studies must compare AI performance against established diagnostic standards, such as interpretations by board-certified radiologists, pathologists, or other specialists. Only after thorough validation can AI diagnostic tools gain regulatory approval and be integrated into clinical workflows.

5.2.2 Benchmarking AI against Traditional Diagnostic Methods

Benchmarking is the process of comparing an AI diagnostic tool's performance against existing clinical standards or competing AI models. This step is crucial for determining whether AI offers a measurable improvement over conventional diagnostic approaches. Benchmarking studies often use metrics such as sensitivity, specificity, accuracy, area under the receiver operating characteristic curve (AUC-ROC), and precision-recall curves to evaluate performance.

For example, in radiology, an AI model designed to detect lung nodules in CT scans must be benchmarked against radiologists' interpretations. Studies have shown that some AI systems can match or even surpass human performance in specific tasks, such as identifying breast cancer in mammograms or detecting diabetic retinopathy in retinal images. However, benchmarking must also consider real-world factors, such as variations in imaging equipment, patient positioning, and image quality, which can affect AI performance.

Moreover, benchmarking should extend beyond diagnostic accuracy to include workflow efficiency, cost-effectiveness, and patient outcomes. An AI tool that reduces interpretation time without compromising accuracy could significantly enhance clinical productivity. Conversely, if an AI system increases false positives, leading to unnecessary follow-up tests, its real-world utility may be limited despite high technical performance.

5.2.3 Methodologies for Clinical Validation and Benchmarking

The clinical validation and benchmarking of AI diagnostic tools follow structured methodologies to ensure scientific rigor and reproducibility. Key steps include dataset curation, performance evaluation, and regulatory compliance.

Dataset curation involves collecting high-quality, annotated medical data that represents the intended use case. Datasets must be diverse, encompassing different patient demographics, disease subtypes, and imaging conditions. Publicly available datasets, such as the National Institutes of Health (NIH) ChestX-ray dataset or the Digital Database for Screening Mammography (DDSM), are often used for initial validation. However, proprietary datasets from hospitals may be necessary for more specialized applications. Performance evaluation requires standardized metrics and statistical analyses to assess AI model reliability. Cross-validation techniques, such as k-fold validation, help ensure that performance estimates are robust. External validation, where the model is tested on data from different institutions, is particularly important for assessing generalizability.

Regulatory compliance is another critical aspect, with agencies like the U.S. Food and Drug Administration (FDA) and the European Medicines Agency (EMA) setting guidelines for AI-based medical devices. The FDA's Software as a Medical Device (SaMD) framework, for instance, classifies AI tools based on their risk level and intended use, requiring varying degrees of clinical evidence for approval.

5.2.4 Challenges

Despite the promise of AI in diagnostics, several challenges hinder effective clinical validation and benchmarking. One major issue is data bias, where AI models trained on non-representative datasets may underperform in certain populations. For example, an AI system trained predominantly on data from one ethnic group may not generalize well to others, leading to disparities in diagnostic accuracy.

Another challenge is the lack of standardized evaluation protocols. Different studies may use varying metrics, datasets, and comparison methods, making it difficult to compare AI tools objectively. Additionally, the rapid evolution of AI algorithms means that validation studies may become outdated quickly, necessitating continuous re-evaluation.

Regulatory hurdles also pose challenges, as the fast-paced development of AI often outpaces the slower approval processes of medical authorities. Striking a balance between innovation and patient safety remains a key concern. Furthermore, integrating AI into clinical workflows requires addressing ethical, legal, and logistical issues, such as liability in case of diagnostic errors and ensuring patient data privacy.

5.3 GENERALIZABILITY, ROBUSTNESS, AND TRANSFER LEARNING

Generalizability, robustness, and transfer learning are foundational to the success of AI in diagnostics. These principles ensure that AI models can adapt to the complexities and variability of real-world clinical practice, providing reliable and equitable diagnostic support across diverse settings. By prioritizing these aspects in model development and deployment, the medical community can harness the full potential of AI to improve patient outcomes, reduce diagnostic errors, and advance the future of healthcare. As the field evolves, a continued commitment to these principles will be essential for building trust, ensuring safety, and delivering on the promise of AI-driven diagnostics for all. As AI continues to advance, the focus on generalizability, robustness, and transfer learning will become even more central to the development of diagnostic tools that are safe, effective, and widely applicable. The integration of federated learning, synthetic data generation, and advanced domain adaptation techniques will further enhance the ability of AI models to learn from diverse sources while preserving privacy and security. The ongoing collaboration between researchers, clinicians, and policymakers will be vital in addressing the technical, ethical, and regulatory challenges associated with AI in diagnostics. Ultimately, the goal is to create AI systems that not only match but exceed human performance in diagnostic accuracy, while ensuring that these benefits are accessible to all patients, regardless of where they receive care.

The pursuit of generalizability, robustness, and effective transfer learning in AI diagnostics also raises important ethical and practical considerations. Ensuring that AI models perform equitably across different patient groups is critical for reducing health disparities and promoting fairness in healthcare. Transparent reporting of model development, validation, and limitations is necessary to build trust among clinicians and patients. Collaboration between AI developers, clinicians, and regulatory bodies is essential to establish standards for model evaluation, deployment, and ongoing monitoring. Additionally, the use of transfer learning and data sharing must comply with privacy regulations and respect patient confidentiality.

5.3.1 Importance of Generalizability in Diagnostic AI

Generalizability refers to the ability of an AI model to maintain high performance when applied to new, unseen data that may differ from the data on which it was trained. In the context of diagnostics, this means that an AI system trained on data from one hospital, region, or demographic group should be able to accurately diagnose patients from other hospitals, regions, or groups.

Generalizability is crucial because medical data is inherently heterogeneous, reflecting variations in patient populations, disease prevalence, imaging protocols, and clinical practices. A model that performs well only on its training data but fails on external datasets is of limited clinical utility and may even pose risks to patient safety. Ensuring generalizability requires careful attention to data diversity during model development, as well as rigorous external validation on independent datasets. The use of multi-institutional and multi-national datasets during training can help AI models learn more universal features, reducing the risk of overfitting to local idiosyncrasies.

5.3.2 Challenges to Achieving Generalizability

Despite its importance, achieving generalizability in diagnostic AI is challenging. One major obstacle is the presence of data shifts, where the distribution of data in the training set differs from that in the deployment environment. These shifts can arise from differences in imaging equipment, patient demographics, disease prevalence, or even subtle changes in clinical workflow. For example, an AI model trained to detect lung cancer on chest X-rays from one hospital may underperform when applied to images from another hospital that uses a different X-ray machine or serves a different patient population. Another challenge is the limited availability of large, diverse, and well-annotated datasets, especially for rare diseases or underrepresented populations. Addressing these challenges requires not only technical solutions but also collaborative efforts to share data and standardize protocols across institutions.

5.3.3 Robustness: Ensuring Reliability in Real-World Settings

Robustness in AI diagnostics refers to the model's ability to maintain stable and reliable performance in the face of variability, noise, and unexpected perturbations in the input data. In clinical practice, data is rarely perfect; images may be affected by motion artifacts, incomplete scans, or suboptimal acquisition parameters. Electronic health records may contain missing, inconsistent, or erroneous entries. A robust AI model should be able to handle such imperfections gracefully, providing accurate and trustworthy outputs even when confronted with challenging or atypical cases. Robustness is particularly important in high-stakes medical applications, where diagnostic errors can have serious consequences for patient care.

5.3.4 Strategies for Enhancing Robustness

To enhance robustness, AI researchers employ a variety of strategies during model development and evaluation. Data augmentation techniques, such as adding noise, simulating artifacts, or varying image contrast, can expose models to a wider range of input conditions during training, making them more resilient to real-world variability. Adversarial training, where models are deliberately exposed to challenging or misleading examples, can further improve their ability to withstand unexpected inputs. Rigorous testing on out-of-distribution data, including rare or atypical cases, is essential for identifying and addressing potential weaknesses. Additionally, the use of uncertainty estimation methods can help AI systems communicate their confidence in predictions, allowing clinicians to interpret results with appropriate caution.

5.3.5 Transfer Learning: Leveraging Knowledge across Domains

Transfer learning is a powerful technique in AI that involves leveraging knowledge gained from one task or dataset to improve performance on a related but distinct task or dataset. In diagnostics, transfer learning is particularly valuable when data for a specific condition or population is limited. For example, a deep learning model trained on a large dataset of general medical images can be fine-tuned on a smaller dataset of rare disease images, enabling the model to learn relevant features more efficiently. Transfer learning can also facilitate the adaptation of AI models to new clinical environments, imaging modalities, or patient populations. By reusing and adapting pre-trained models, researchers can accelerate the development of diagnostic tools and reduce the need for extensive data collection and annotation.

5.3.6 Applications of Transfer Learning in Diagnostic AI

Transfer learning has been successfully applied in a variety of diagnostic domains. In medical imaging, pre-trained convolutional neural networks (CNNs) developed for natural image recognition have been adapted for tasks such as tumor detection, organ segmentation, and disease classification. In genomics, models trained on large-scale public datasets can be fine-tuned to identify specific genetic variants associated with rare diseases. Transfer learning is also used in natural language processing for extracting clinical information from electronic health records, where models trained on general text corpora are adapted to the medical domain. These applications demonstrate the versatility and efficiency of transfer learning in overcoming data limitations and accelerating AI innovation in diagnostics.

5.3.7 Balancing Generalizability, Robustness, and Transfer Learning

While generalizability, robustness, and transfer learning each address distinct challenges in AI diagnostics, they are deeply interconnected. A model that is generalizable is more likely to be robust, as it has learned to handle diverse data. Transfer learning can enhance both generalizability and robustness by enabling models to leverage broader knowledge and adapt to new conditions. However, balancing these aspects requires careful design and evaluation. Over-reliance on transfer learning without sufficient adaptation to the target domain can lead to suboptimal performance or unintended biases. Similarly, efforts to improve robustness through data augmentation must ensure that synthetic variations are clinically plausible and do not introduce artifacts that mislead the model. Continuous monitoring and post-deployment evaluation are essential to ensure that AI diagnostic tools maintain high standards of performance as clinical environments evolve.

5.4 EXPLAINABILITY AND INTERPRETABILITY IN DIAGNOSTICS

Explainability and interpretability are indispensable components of AI in diagnostics, underpinning trust, accountability, and effective clinical integration. As AI tools become more prevalent in healthcare, ensuring that these systems provide clear and understandable outputs is not merely a technical challenge but a moral and professional imperative. Through ongoing advancements in explainability techniques, regulatory alignment, and clinician education, the diagnostic use of AI can achieve its full potential while upholding the highest standards of medical care. The goal is not to replace the clinician but to empower them with tools that are both powerful and transparent, enabling better decisions, improved outcomes, and deeper trust in the age of intelligent diagnostics.

Research into explainable AI (XAI) is a rapidly growing field, especially in the context of healthcare. New methods are being explored to integrate explainability directly into the architecture of AI models, making them inherently transparent. Neuro-symbolic AI, interpretable deep learning models, and causal inference techniques are among the emerging approaches that promise to bridge the gap between performance and transparency. As diagnostic tasks become more complex and data-rich, the demand for robust, understandable AI systems will only grow. Future diagnostic systems may incorporate interactive explanation interfaces, where clinicians can question, explore, and adjust model reasoning, leading to more dynamic and personalized care.

5.4.1 Need for Explainable AI in Diagnostics

In the diagnostic landscape, decisions made by clinicians carry significant weight, often determining the course of treatment and patient outcomes. When AI tools are introduced into this domain, their outputs must not only be accurate but also understandable to medical professionals. Unlike many other sectors where black-box models might be acceptable, in healthcare, every diagnosis or recommendation must be justifiable and transparent.

A radiologist using an AI model to detect lung nodules or a pathologist using machine learning to classify tumor grades must be able to interpret the model's suggestions. Without explainability, clinicians may be reluctant to rely on AI systems, regardless of their accuracy, because they cannot verify or understand the reasoning behind the outcomes.

5.4.2 Defining Explainability and Interpretability

Explainability and interpretability are closely related concepts but have nuanced differences. Interpretability generally refers to the extent to which a human can understand the internal mechanics of a system. A model is interpretable if one can trace how inputs are transformed into outputs through understandable mathematical or logical steps. Explainability, on the other hand, involves providing reasons or justifications for a decision, possibly through post hoc analysis. In diagnostics, this may involve visualizing which parts of a medical image led to a certain classification or providing linguistic explanations for why a patient's symptoms matched a certain diagnosis. Both are essential for building trust and ensuring safe integration into clinical environments.

5.4.3 Challenges with Black-Box Models in Healthcare

Black-box models, particularly deep neural networks, are known for their powerful performance but poor interpretability. These models can detect subtle and complex patterns in large datasets, which is especially useful in imaging diagnostics or genomics. However, their internal operations are often opaque, with millions of parameters interacting in non-intuitive ways.

This opacity poses serious challenges in healthcare where explanations are necessary for accountability and decision-making. For instance, if an AI model flags a mammogram as suspicious for cancer but cannot show which region of the image or what features contributed to that assessment, the clinician is left with a dilemma: to trust a result that cannot be explained or to disregard it entirely. In high-stakes environments like oncology or cardiology, such uncertainty is unacceptable.

5.4.4 Techniques for Enhancing Explainability

To address the need for explainability, several techniques have been developed to make AI models more transparent. One common approach is feature importance analysis, where the contribution of each input variable to the model's decision is quantified. In imaging applications, methods like saliency maps and Grad-CAM (Gradient-weighted Class Activation Mapping) highlight the regions in an image that most influenced the model's decision. These visual explanations help clinicians understand and verify AI suggestions. For tabular and text data, techniques like SHAP (Shapley Additive Explanations) and LIME (Local Interpretable Model-agnostic Explanations) provide localized explanations by approximating complex models with simpler, interpretable ones in the vicinity of a specific prediction. These tools allow users to see which features—such as patient age, lab values, or clinical history—were most influential in a diagnosis.

5.4.5 Model Design and Interpretability Trade-offs

In the pursuit of interpretability, there is often a trade-off between model complexity and transparency. Simpler models like decision trees, logistic regression, or rule-based systems are inherently more interpretable but may lack the predictive power of deep learning architectures.

In diagnostic applications, striking the right balance is essential. Some researchers advocate for the use of inherently interpretable models, especially in cases where the diagnostic task is relatively straightforward and the risk of misdiagnosis is high. Others suggest a hybrid approach where a powerful black-box model is accompanied by a secondary explanation model that provides interpretable justifications. In all cases, the key objective is to ensure that the end user, typically a clinician, can make informed decisions based on the AI's output.

5.4.6 Explainability for Regulatory Compliance and Clinical Validation

From a regulatory standpoint, explainability is increasingly being recognized as a necessary criterion for the approval of AI-based diagnostic tools. Regulatory bodies such as the U.S. Food and Drug Administration (FDA), the European Medicines Agency (EMA), and the Medical Device Regulation (MDR) in Europe are evolving their frameworks to include transparency requirements. AI models used in diagnostics must not only demonstrate clinical efficacy and safety but also provide sufficient information to users about how the outputs are generated. Clinical validation studies often require explanation modules to assess the alignment between model predictions and expert opinion. Additionally, liability in the case of incorrect diagnoses or adverse outcomes often rests with the healthcare provider who must be able to justify the basis for using AI-generated insights.

5.4.7 Building Clinician Trust through Interpretability

Clinician trust is essential for the successful adoption of AI in diagnostics. Trust is built not only on performance metrics like accuracy and sensitivity but also on the ability to understand how and why a model arrives at its conclusions. Interpretability helps clinicians integrate AI seamlessly into their workflow by enhancing their own diagnostic process rather than replacing it. When an AI model highlights a suspicious area in a CT scan and explains that it matches known tumor morphology, the radiologist can incorporate that insight into their own judgment. This collaborative model of decision-making strengthens the human-AI partnership and reinforces the role of clinicians as the final arbiters of medical decisions.

5.4.8 Patient-Centered Considerations and Ethical Dimensions

Explainability also plays a crucial role in patient engagement and ethical medical practice. Patients increasingly expect transparency in the tools and processes that influence their care. When AI is used to assist in diagnosis, patients may ask how the system arrived at its conclusions, especially in sensitive areas like cancer screening, rare diseases, or prenatal diagnostics. Being able to provide clear, understandable explanations supports informed consent and shared decision-making. Ethically, explainable AI aligns with the principles of beneficence, non-maleficence, autonomy, and justice. It ensures that the use of AI contributes positively to patient outcomes, avoids harm, respects individual rights, and minimizes biases that can arise from opaque algorithms.

5.5 POST-MARKET SURVEILLANCE AND PERFORMANCE MONITORING

Post-market surveillance and performance monitoring are indispensable for the safe and effective use of AI in diagnostic medicine. As AI systems continue to evolve, continuous oversight ensures that they remain accurate, unbiased, and clinically beneficial. While challenges such as data fragmentation, algorithmic bias, and regulatory complexity persist, emerging technologies like federated learning, explainable AI, and automated monitoring offer promising solutions. Collaborative efforts among developers, healthcare providers, and regulators will be key to establishing robust surveillance frameworks that maximize the potential of AI diagnostics while safeguarding patient care. By prioritizing post-market surveillance, the medical community can harness the full power of AI to revolutionize diagnostics and improve global health outcomes.

The future of post-market surveillance in AI diagnostics will be shaped by technological advancements and regulatory innovations. One promising direction is the use of federated learning, where AI models are trained across multiple institutions without centralizing patient data. This approach enhances privacy while enabling continuous performance monitoring across diverse populations.

Explainable AI (XAI) techniques will also play a crucial role in improving transparency and trust. By providing interpretable insights into AI decision-making, XAI helps clinicians and regulators understand performance variations and identify potential failures. Real-world evidence (RWE) platforms, which aggregate data from EHRs, wearables, and patient registries, will further enhance post-market surveillance by enabling large-scale outcome studies.

Automated monitoring tools powered by AI itself can streamline surveillance processes. For example, anomaly detection algorithms can flag unexpected performance drops or data inconsistencies in real time, allowing for prompt corrective actions. Blockchain technology may also be leveraged to ensure data integrity and traceability in performance reporting.

Regulatory agencies are increasingly adopting agile approaches to keep pace with AI advancements. The FDA's Total Product Lifecycle (TPLC) framework, for instance, emphasizes iterative updates and continuous learning, moving away from static pre-market approvals. Similar adaptive regulatory models are being explored globally to balance innovation with patient safety.

5.5.1 Importance of Post-Market Surveillance for AI Diagnostic Tools

Post-market surveillance is a fundamental component of the AI diagnostic lifecycle, ensuring that these tools perform as intended after deployment in diverse clinical environments. While pre-market clinical trials and validation studies provide initial evidence of safety and efficacy, real-world usage often reveals unforeseen challenges, such as data drift, algorithmic bias, and interoperability issues. Continuous monitoring helps identify these problems early, preventing misdiagnoses, patient harm, or systemic inefficiencies.

Regulatory agencies, including the U.S. Food and Drug Administration (FDA) and the European Medicines Agency (EMA), mandate post-market surveillance for AI-based medical devices. These requirements are designed to track performance, detect adverse events, and ensure that updates or modifications do not compromise patient safety. Additionally, healthcare providers and developers rely on PMS data to refine algorithms, improve usability, and enhance clinical integration. Without robust post-market surveillance, AI diagnostic tools risk becoming obsolete or unreliable as medical practices and patient populations evolve.

5.5.2 Key Components of Performance Monitoring in AI Diagnostics

Performance monitoring is a continuous process that evaluates how AI diagnostic tools function in real-world clinical workflows. Unlike static medical devices, AI models may exhibit performance degradation over time due to changes in patient demographics, imaging techniques, or disease patterns. Effective performance monitoring involves several key components, including data quality assessment, model drift detection, and outcome analysis.

Data quality assessment ensures that input data fed into AI systems meet the required standards. Variations in imaging equipment, acquisition protocols, or labeling practices can affect diagnostic accuracy. Regular audits of input data help maintain consistency and prevent errors caused by poor-quality inputs.

Model drift detection is another critical aspect, referring to the phenomenon where an AI model's performance deteriorates over time due to shifts in underlying data distributions. Statistical techniques, such as monitoring feature distributions or prediction confidence scores, can help detect drift early. When significant drift is identified, retraining the model with updated datasets may be necessary to restore performance.

Outcome analysis evaluates the real-world impact of AI diagnostics on patient care. Metrics such as diagnostic accuracy, time-to-diagnosis, and clinical outcomes (e.g., treatment success rates) provide insights into whether AI tools are delivering tangible benefits. Longitudinal studies tracking patient health over time can further validate the long-term effectiveness of AI-assisted diagnostics.

5.5.3 Regulatory Frameworks Governing Post-Market Surveillance

Regulatory bodies worldwide have established frameworks to ensure rigorous post-market surveillance of AI diagnostic tools. In the United States, the FDA's Digital Health Center of Excellence oversees the regulation of AI-based medical devices, requiring manufacturers to submit post-market surveillance plans as part of the approval process. The FDA's Software as a Medical Device (SaMD) framework emphasizes real-world performance monitoring, especially for adaptive AI systems that learn from new data.

In the European Union, the Medical Device Regulation (MDR) and In Vitro Diagnostic Regulation (IVDR) mandate continuous post-market performance follow-up (PMPF) for high-risk AI diagnostic tools. Manufacturers must collect and analyze real-world data, report adverse events, and implement corrective actions when necessary. Similar regulations exist in other regions, such as Japan's Pharmaceuticals and Medical Devices Agency (PMDA) and China's National Medical Products Administration (NMPA), reflecting a global consensus on the need for stringent AI oversight.

Compliance with these regulations requires collaboration between developers, healthcare providers, and regulatory agencies. Transparent reporting mechanisms, such as adverse event databases and performance dashboards, facilitate timely interventions and ensure accountability. As AI diagnostics continue to evolve, regulatory frameworks must also adapt to address emerging challenges, such as cybersecurity risks and ethical considerations.

5.5.4 Challenges in Post-Market Surveillance of AI Diagnostics

Despite its importance, post-market surveillance of AI diagnostics faces several challenges. One major issue is data fragmentation, where patient data is scattered across multiple electronic health record (EHR) systems, making it difficult to aggregate and analyze performance metrics comprehensively. Interoperability standards, such as Fast Healthcare Interoperability Resources (FHIR), aim to address this challenge, but implementation remains inconsistent.

Another challenge is algorithmic bias, which may become apparent only after widespread deployment. If an AI model was trained on non-representative datasets, it may underperform in certain demographic groups, leading to disparities in diagnostic accuracy. Continuous monitoring is essential to detect and mitigate such biases, ensuring equitable healthcare delivery.

The dynamic nature of AI also complicates post-market surveillance. Unlike traditional medical devices with fixed functionality, AI models may receive frequent updates, requiring real-time performance tracking. Ensuring that updates do not introduce new risks or degrade performance is a complex task that demands automated monitoring tools and robust version control systems.

Additionally, healthcare providers may lack the infrastructure or expertise to implement effective performance monitoring. Many institutions struggle with integrating AI tools into existing workflows, let alone establishing continuous surveillance mechanisms. Collaborative efforts between AI developers, regulatory bodies, and healthcare organizations are necessary to overcome these barriers.

CHAPTER 6

Ethical, Legal, and Regulatory Considerations

6.1 INFORMED CONSENT AND DATA USE IN DIAGNOSTIC AI

Informed consent and ethical data use are foundational to the responsible deployment of AI in diagnostic medicine. As AI systems become increasingly integral to healthcare, safeguarding patient autonomy and privacy must remain a top priority. By addressing challenges related to transparency, consent models, and regulatory compliance, stakeholders can build a framework that balances innovation with ethical responsibility.

The future of AI diagnostics depends not only on technological advancements but also on the trust and cooperation of patients, clinicians, and policymakers. Through collaborative efforts, the medical community can harness the power of AI to improve diagnostic accuracy while upholding the highest standards of ethical practice.

Looking ahead, the field of AI diagnostics must address several key areas to strengthen informed consent and ethical data practices. One promising direction is the development of dynamic consent platforms, where patients can adjust their permissions in real time through user-friendly digital interfaces. Such systems would enable more responsive and personalized control over data usage, aligning with the principles of patient-centered care.

Another emerging trend is the integration of explainable AI (XAI) techniques, which provide interpretable insights into how algorithms arrive at diagnostic conclusions. By enhancing transparency, XAI can help patients and clinicians understand the role of their data in AI decision-making, fostering greater trust and engagement. Additionally, the use of synthetic data—artificially generated datasets that mimic real patient information—could reduce reliance on sensitive personal data while still enabling robust AI training and validation.

Ethical AI certification programs, similar to fair-trade labels in consumer goods, may also gain traction, allowing patients to identify diagnostic tools that adhere to high standards of data privacy and consent. Finally, international collaborations to harmonize regulatory frameworks will be essential in addressing cross-border data flows and ensuring consistent protections for patients worldwide.

6.1.1 Importance of Informed Consent in AI Diagnostics

Informed consent serves as the cornerstone of ethical medical practice, ensuring that patients have autonomy over their personal health information. In the context of AI diagnostics, obtaining informed consent becomes particularly nuanced due to the complexity of data processing and the potential for secondary uses. Patients must be adequately informed about how their data will be collected, stored and utilized—whether for training algorithms, validating models, or improving diagnostic accuracy. Transparency is essential, as patients have the right to know if their anonymized data might contribute to research, commercial applications or third-party collaborations.

A key challenge lies in communicating technical concepts in an accessible manner. Many patients may not fully grasp how AI models analyze medical data or the implications of data sharing. Healthcare providers and AI developers must prioritize clear, jargon-free explanations that outline the benefits and risks of participation. Additionally, consent should be dynamic, allowing patients to withdraw permission at any stage without compromising their care. Regulatory frameworks such as the General Data Protection Regulation (GDPR) in the European Union and the Health Insurance Portability and Accountability Act (HIPAA) in the United States emphasize the necessity of explicit consent, reinforcing the ethical obligation to protect patient rights in an era of data-driven medicine.

6.1.2 Challenges

Despite the recognized importance of informed consent, several challenges complicate its implementation in AI diagnostics. One major issue is the broad and often ambiguous scope of data usage. Traditional consent forms for medical procedures are relatively straightforward, but AI applications may involve multiple, evolving purposes that are difficult to anticipate at the time of data collection. For instance, a dataset initially used to train a cancer detection algorithm might later be repurposed for cardiovascular research or sold to pharmaceutical companies. Patients may not fully comprehend these potential future applications, leading to concerns about exploitation or loss of control over personal data.

Another challenge arises from the anonymization and aggregation of data. While de-identification techniques aim to protect patient privacy, advances in data re-identification methods have demonstrated that anonymized datasets can sometimes be traced back to individuals. This risk raises ethical questions about whether patients should be re-consented if their data is used in ways beyond the original agreement. Furthermore, marginalized populations, including those with limited health literacy or non-native language speakers, may face additional barriers in understanding consent forms, exacerbating disparities in data representation and AI model performance.

The dynamic nature of AI development also poses difficulties. Unlike static medical interventions, AI models continuously improve through iterative learning, often requiring new data inputs. Ensuring that consent remains valid over time—especially when algorithms are updated or applied to new clinical contexts—demands flexible and ongoing communication between healthcare providers, AI developers, and patients. Addressing these challenges requires a combination of robust legal safeguards, technological solutions for enhanced transparency, and patient education initiatives to foster trust and engagement.

6.1.3 Best Practices

To navigate the complexities of informed consent and data use in AI diagnostics, stakeholders must adopt best practices that prioritize patient autonomy, transparency, and accountability. One fundamental approach is the implementation of tiered consent models, where patients can choose how their data is utilized—whether strictly for their own care, for research purposes, or for broader commercial applications. Granular consent options empower individuals to make informed decisions aligned with their comfort levels and values. Another critical practice is the use of blockchain and other secure technologies to enhance data traceability. By creating immutable records of data usage and consent agreements, these technologies can help ensure compliance with ethical standards and regulatory requirements. Patients could, in theory, track how their data is being used in real time and revoke access if desired. Additionally, AI developers should prioritize federated learning techniques, which allow models to be trained across decentralized datasets without transferring raw patient data. This method minimizes privacy risks while still enabling advancements in diagnostic accuracy.

Healthcare institutions must also invest in patient education initiatives to bridge the knowledge gap surrounding AI and data usage. Simplified consent forms, interactive digital platforms, and community engagement programs can help demystify AI diagnostics and encourage informed participation. Furthermore, ethical review boards and oversight committees should play an active role in evaluating AI projects, ensuring that data collection and usage protocols adhere to established ethical guidelines. Finally, fostering collaboration between policymakers, technologists, and patient advocacy groups is essential for developing standardized frameworks that balance innovation with ethical responsibility. By establishing clear guidelines on data ownership, consent revocation, and algorithmic transparency, the medical community can build a foundation of trust that supports the sustainable growth of AI in diagnostics.

6.1.4 Regulatory and Legal Considerations

The legal landscape governing data use in AI diagnostics is evolving rapidly, with regional variations that reflect differing cultural and ethical priorities. In the European Union, the GDPR sets stringent requirements for data protection, including the right to be forgotten, which allows patients to request the deletion of their personal data. Similarly, the proposed EU Artificial Intelligence Act aims to classify AI systems based on risk levels, mandating stricter oversight for high-risk applications like medical diagnostics.

In the United States, HIPAA provides a framework for safeguarding protected health information (PHI), but its provisions were not originally designed to address the complexities of AI-driven data analytics. Emerging legislation, such as state-specific laws on biometric data and algorithmic transparency, seeks to fill these gaps. However, the lack of a unified federal approach creates challenges for nationwide implementation of AI diagnostics.

Other regions, such as Canada and Australia, have introduced guidelines emphasizing accountability and fairness in AI applications. Canada's Directive on Automated Decision-Making, for example, requires government agencies to conduct algorithmic impact assessments before deploying AI systems. These regulatory efforts highlight a global recognition of the need to protect patient rights while fostering innovation.

Compliance with these regulations necessitates robust data governance strategies within healthcare organizations. Data protection officers, ethics committees, and legal teams must work collaboratively to ensure that AI deployments align with both local and international standards. As AI continues to advance, ongoing dialogue between regulators and industry stakeholders will be crucial in shaping policies that promote ethical data use without stifling progress.

6.2 BIAS AND FAIRNESS IN DIAGNOSTIC MODELS

Bias and fairness are critical issues in the development and deployment of AI diagnostic models. Addressing these challenges requires a comprehensive approach that encompasses data diversity, algorithmic transparency, stakeholder engagement, and regulatory oversight. As AI becomes increasingly integrated into healthcare, the commitment to fairness will be essential for ensuring that these powerful tools benefit all patients, regardless of their background or circumstances. By confronting bias head-on and striving for equitable AI, the healthcare community can build diagnostic systems that are not only technologically advanced but also just, trustworthy, and aligned with the core values of medicine.

As AI continues to transform medical diagnostics, ensuring fairness and mitigating bias must remain central priorities. Advances in data collection, algorithm design, and evaluation methods will help address many of the technical challenges associated with bias. However, achieving fairness in diagnostic AI is not solely a technical problem; it also requires ongoing attention to ethical, social, and policy considerations. Building fair and trustworthy AI systems will depend on transparency, accountability, and a commitment to equity at every stage of development and deployment. By prioritizing fairness, the medical community can harness the full potential of AI to improve diagnostic accuracy, reduce health disparities, and deliver better care for all patients.

Bias in AI diagnostic models can arise from various sources, including the data used to train the models, the algorithms themselves, and the broader healthcare context in which they are deployed. Data-driven models are particularly susceptible to bias if the training data is not representative of the diverse populations they are intended to serve.

For example, if a diagnostic model for skin cancer is trained primarily on images of lighter skin tones, it may perform poorly on patients with darker skin, leading to missed or incorrect diagnoses. Similarly, if electronic health records used to train a model reflect historical inequities in healthcare access or treatment, the model may inadvertently perpetuate these disparities. Algorithmic bias can also occur if the model's design or optimization criteria favor certain outcomes or groups over others. These biases can manifest in various ways, such as differences in sensitivity, specificity, or overall accuracy across demographic groups.

6.2.1 Impact of Bias on Patient Care

The presence of bias in diagnostic AI models can have serious consequences for patient care. Unequal model performance can result in some groups receiving less accurate diagnoses, delayed treatment, or inappropriate interventions. For instance, a biased model might underdiagnose heart disease in women or fail to detect diabetic retinopathy in certain ethnic groups. These disparities not only affect individual patients but can also contribute to broader public health inequities. Moreover, the perception or reality of bias in AI systems can erode trust among patients and clinicians, hindering the adoption of potentially beneficial technologies. Addressing bias is therefore essential not only for ethical reasons but also for the practical success and acceptance of AI in healthcare.

6.2.2 Sources of Bias

One of the primary sources of bias in diagnostic models is the data used for training and validation. Medical datasets often reflect the demographics, disease prevalence, and clinical practices of the institutions or regions from which they are collected. If certain populations are underrepresented in these datasets, the resulting models may not generalize well to those groups. Additionally, data quality issues such as missing information, inconsistent labeling, or measurement errors can disproportionately affect certain groups. Historical biases in healthcare delivery, such as differences in access to care or diagnostic testing, can also be encoded in the data, further perpetuating inequities. Addressing these issues requires deliberate efforts to collect diverse, high-quality data and to critically examine the sources and context of the data used in model development.

6.2.3 Algorithmic and Model Design Bias

Beyond data, the design of AI algorithms and models can introduce or amplify bias. Choices about which features to include, how to preprocess data, and what optimization criteria to use can all influence model behavior. For example, if a model is optimized primarily for overall accuracy, it may achieve high performance on the majority group while neglecting minority groups. Similarly, the use of proxy variables that correlate with sensitive attributes such as race, gender, or socioeconomic status can inadvertently introduce bias. Model complexity and interpretability also play a role, as more complex models may be harder to audit for fairness and may obscure the mechanisms by which bias is introduced. Transparent and inclusive model design, along with regular auditing for bias, is essential for developing fair diagnostic AI systems.

6.2.4 Evaluating Fairness in Diagnostic Models

Evaluating fairness in diagnostic models involves assessing model performance across different demographic groups and identifying disparities in outcomes. This can include comparing metrics such as sensitivity, specificity, positive predictive value, and negative predictive value for groups defined by race, gender, age, or other relevant characteristics. Fairness metrics such as demographic parity, equal opportunity, and equalized odds can provide additional insights into model behavior. However, achieving fairness is not always straightforward, as different fairness criteria may conflict with one another or with overall model performance. Moreover, the definition of fairness may vary depending on the clinical context and the specific goals of the diagnostic tool. Engaging stakeholders, including patients, clinicians, and ethicists, in the evaluation process is crucial for ensuring that fairness assessments are meaningful and aligned with clinical and ethical priorities.

6.2.5 Mitigating Bias in Diagnostic AI

Mitigating bias in diagnostic AI requires a multifaceted approach that addresses both data and model-related factors. On the data side, efforts should be made to collect and curate diverse datasets that reflect the populations the model is intended to serve. This may involve targeted data collection, data augmentation, or the use of synthetic data to balance underrepresented groups. Data preprocessing techniques such as reweighting, resampling, or imputation can help address imbalances and missing data. On the model side, fairness-aware algorithms and training procedures can be employed to explicitly account for group differences and to optimize for equitable performance. Regular auditing and monitoring of model performance in real-world settings are essential for detecting and addressing emerging biases. Transparency in model development, including clear documentation of data sources, model design choices, and fairness evaluations, is critical for building trust and accountability.

6.2.6 Role of Regulation and Policy

Regulation and policy play an important role in promoting fairness and mitigating bias in diagnostic AI. Regulatory bodies such as the U.S. Food and Drug Administration (FDA) and the European Medicines Agency (EMA) are increasingly recognizing the need for guidelines and standards that address bias and fairness in AI-based medical devices. These may include requirements for diverse data representation, external validation, and post-market surveillance of model performance. Policies that promote data sharing and collaboration across institutions can also help ensure that AI models are trained on more representative datasets. Ethical frameworks and guidelines developed by professional organizations and advocacy groups provide additional guidance for developers and users of diagnostic AI. Ultimately, a combination of technical, regulatory, and ethical measures is needed to ensure that AI-driven diagnostics are fair, equitable, and beneficial for all patients.

6.2.7 Importance of Stakeholder Engagement

Engaging a broad range of stakeholders is essential for addressing bias and promoting fairness in diagnostic AI. Patients, clinicians, data scientists, ethicists, and policymakers all have valuable perspectives on what constitutes fairness and how it should be achieved. Involving patients and communities in the design, development, and evaluation of AI diagnostic tools can help ensure that their needs and concerns are addressed. Clinicians can provide insights into the practical implications of model performance and fairness in real-world settings. Data scientists and ethicists can contribute technical and ethical expertise to the development of fair algorithms and evaluation frameworks. Policymakers can help create the regulatory and policy environment needed to support fairness in AI. Collaborative, interdisciplinary approaches are key to developing diagnostic AI systems that are both effective and equitable.

6.3 LIABILITY IN AI-DRIVEN DIAGNOSES

Liability in AI-driven diagnostics presents one of the most pressing challenges in the digital transformation of healthcare. The interplay of clinicians, developers, institutions, and regulators requires a reimagined approach to responsibility and accountability. While AI has the potential to improve diagnostic accuracy and efficiency, it also introduces new complexities in assigning blame when things go wrong. Addressing these challenges through clear legal frameworks, shared liability models, and ethical AI design will be essential for ensuring that technological advancements in diagnostics are matched by equally robust protections for patients and practitioners alike. Only through such efforts can AI fulfill its promise in healthcare while maintaining public trust and professional integrity.

As AI becomes more deeply embedded in diagnostic medicine, the question of liability cannot be left unresolved. Legal, clinical, and technical communities must work together to develop frameworks that ensure safety, foster accountability, and protect patient welfare. This involves not only legal reforms but also the design of explainable, trustworthy AI systems, transparent deployment protocols, and clearly defined roles for all stakeholders. Collaborative oversight by interdisciplinary teams can further minimize risks and promote ethical AI integration. Ultimately, building a culture of accountability in AI-driven diagnostics is not about restricting innovation but about enabling its responsible and sustainable growth in ways that benefit both patients and healthcare providers.

6.3.1 Changing Nature of Clinical Responsibility

In conventional diagnostics, responsibility is directly linked to the clinician's expertise, judgment, and actions. If a radiologist misinterprets an image or a physician overlooks a symptom, the liability rests with them. With AI becoming a decision-support tool, or even an autonomous diagnostic agent, the traditional lines of responsibility begin to blur.

Clinicians may rely on AI outputs to inform decisions, but to what extent are they responsible if the AI provides incorrect guidance? Conversely, if a clinician overrides an AI's accurate suggestion and errs, who bears the blame? The tension between human judgment and machine recommendation introduces an unprecedented dilemma. The presence of AI does not automatically absolve clinicians of responsibility, yet holding them fully accountable when acting on trusted AI systems raises ethical and legal complications.

6.3.2 Types of AI Systems and their Liability Implications

Different types of AI applications in diagnostics carry varying implications for liability. Rule-based systems that follow fixed decision trees are generally transparent and interpretable, making it easier to audit their outputs and identify errors. In such cases, liability can often be traced back to flawed logic or programming. However, machine learning and deep learning systems function more like black boxes, learning patterns from data in ways that are difficult to explain. These systems may outperform humans in certain tasks, such as image classification, yet their decision-making pathways are opaque. When such models produce erroneous results, it becomes harder to determine whether the fault lies in the model's design, the data used for training, the way it was deployed, or the actions of the end user. Each of these possibilities entails a different locus of liability.

6.3.3 Manufacturer and Developer Responsibility

Software developers and AI manufacturers are key stakeholders in the liability debate. They design, test, and release diagnostic algorithms into clinical settings. If the AI system is flawed due to defective code, inadequate validation, biased training data, or failure to meet regulatory standards, then the manufacturer may be held liable for resulting harm. This responsibility parallels that of medical device manufacturers, who are accountable for ensuring their products are safe and effective. The challenge arises when AI systems are continuously learning and updating post-deployment, making their behavior dynamic and less predictable. In such cases, ongoing responsibility for the model's performance might shift partially or entirely to the developers. Yet, developers often argue that they merely provide tools, while clinicians are the ones making final decisions, thereby complicating the attribution of liability.

6.3.4 Clinical End-User Accountability

Healthcare professionals remain integral to diagnostic processes even when AI is involved. Most current AI systems function as clinical decision support tools, assisting rather than replacing clinicians. In such settings, the physician's responsibility includes evaluating the AI's output, verifying its validity, and making a final decision based on their professional judgment. If a clinician blindly follows an AI's recommendation without critical analysis and a misdiagnosis occurs, they may still be liable under existing standards of medical negligence. However, expecting clinicians to fully understand the inner workings of complex AI systems is unrealistic. The responsibility must therefore be balanced, requiring clinicians to understand the limitations of AI without burdening them with undue legal risk for machine-generated errors they could not foresee or control.

6.3.5 Institutional and Systemic Liability

Hospitals and healthcare organizations also play a role in liability related to AI-driven diagnostics. They are responsible for implementing, maintaining, and overseeing the use of AI technologies within their institutions. This includes selecting appropriate tools, training staff, and ensuring that AI systems are used in accordance with approved guidelines and protocols. If a hospital deploys an AI system that is poorly integrated or lacks adequate monitoring mechanisms, and a diagnostic error results, the institution may be held accountable. Additionally, hospitals may be liable under the doctrine of vicarious liability, where they are held responsible for the actions of their employees, including clinicians using AI tools. Institutional liability thus serves as an essential layer of protection for patients, while also motivating hospitals to adopt rigorous evaluation processes before integrating AI into clinical practice.

6.3.6 Regulatory Frameworks and Legal Precedents

Regulatory frameworks are evolving to address the unique challenges posed by AI in diagnostics. Agencies such as the U.S. Food and Drug Administration (FDA), the European Medicines Agency (EMA), and others are establishing approval pathways for AI-based diagnostic tools, including requirements for transparency, validation and post-market surveillance. Some jurisdictions are considering new legal constructs, such as AI-specific liability laws or the recognition of AI as a distinct legal entity. However, as of now, most legal systems still operate within traditional tort law principles, focusing on negligence, product liability, and informed consent. Legal precedents involving AI in diagnostics are still limited, which makes litigation outcomes unpredictable and policy formation difficult. There is a growing need for comprehensive legal guidelines that clarify the allocation of responsibility among various actors involved in AI-driven diagnosis.

6.3.7 Informed Consent and Patient Rights

From the patient's perspective, understanding how AI contributes to their care is a matter of rights and informed consent. When AI tools are used in diagnostics, patients must be informed about their role, limitations, and any associated risks. Failure to disclose the use of AI, especially when it plays a significant part in the diagnostic process, could lead to legal claims if adverse outcomes occur. Informed consent documents may need to be revised to reflect AI involvement explicitly. Furthermore, patients may question the reliability of AI-generated diagnoses, particularly in sensitive areas such as oncology, prenatal testing, or mental health. Ensuring transparency and open communication not only protects patient rights but also shields providers from legal vulnerability by demonstrating good faith and ethical practice.

6.3.8 Shared Liability and Collaborative Risk Management

Given the complex interplay of stakeholders in AI-driven diagnostics, a shared liability model is increasingly seen as a practical approach. In this model, liability is distributed among clinicians, developers, institutions, and possibly regulators, depending on the specific circumstances of the diagnostic error. Shared liability encourages collaboration, transparency, and shared responsibility, rather than assigning blame to a single party. It also underscores the need for continuous risk management, including robust validation, clinician training, audit trails, and performance monitoring. Risk-sharing mechanisms such as liability insurance, indemnity clauses, and joint accountability agreements may help mitigate legal uncertainty while fostering innovation in AI diagnostics.

6.4 GLOBAL REGULATORY LANDSCAPE

6.4.1 FDA (USA)

Emergency Approvals (EUA)

Emergency Use Authorization (EUA) is a mechanism that was created to facilitate the availability and use of medical countermeasures, including vaccines and personal protective equipment, during public health emergencies such as the Zika virus epidemic, the Ebola virus epidemic and the COVID-19 pandemic.

Regulations

The programs for safety regulation vary widely by the type of product, its potential risks, and the regulatory powers granted to the agency. For example, the FDA regulates almost every facet of prescription drugs, including testing, manufacturing, labeling, advertising, marketing, efficacy, and safety—yet FDA regulation of cosmetics focuses primarily on labeling and safety. The FDA regulates most products with a set of published standards enforced by a modest number of facility inspections. Inspection observations are documented on Form 483.

In June 2018, the FDA released a statement regarding new guidelines to help food and drug manufacturers "implement protections against potential attacks on the U.S. food supply". One of the guidelines includes the Intentional Adulteration (IA) rule, which requires strategies and procedures by the food industry to reduce the risk of compromise in facilities and processes that are significantly vulnerable.

The FDA also uses tactics of regulatory shaming, mainly through online publication of non-compliance, warning letters, and "shaming lists." Regulation by shaming harnesses firms' sensitivity to reputational damage. For example, in 2018, the agency published an online "black list", in which it named dozens of branded drug companies that are supposedly using unlawful or unethical means to attempt to impede competition from generic drug companies.

The FDA frequently works with other federal agencies, including the Department of Agriculture, the Drug Enforcement Administration, Customs and Border Protection, and the Consumer Product Safety Commission. They also often work with local and state government agencies in performing regulatory inspections and enforcement actions.

Food and Dietary Supplements

The regulation of food and dietary supplements by the Food and Drug Administration is governed by various statutes enacted by the United States Congress and interpreted by the FDA. Pursuant to the Federal Food, Drug, and Cosmetic Act and accompanying legislation, the FDA has authority to oversee the quality of substances sold as food in the United States, and to monitor claims made in the labeling of both the composition and the health benefits of foods. The FDA subdivides substances that it regulates as food into various categories—including foods, food additives, added substances (human-made substances that are not intentionally introduced into food, but nevertheless end up in it), and dietary supplements. Dietary supplements or dietary ingredients include vitamins, minerals, herbs, amino acids, and enzymes. Specific standards the FDA exercises differ from one category to the next. Furthermore, legislation had granted the FDA a variety of means to address violations of standards for a given substance category.

Under the Dietary Supplement Health and Education Act of 1994 (DSHEA), the FDA is responsible for ensuring that manufacturers and distributors of dietary supplements and dietary ingredients meet the current requirements. These manufacturers and distributors are not allowed to advertise their products in an adulterated way, and they are responsible for evaluating the safety and labeling of their product.

The FDA has a "Dietary Supplement Ingredient Advisory List" that includes ingredients that sometimes appear on dietary supplements but need further evaluation. An ingredient is added to this list when it is excluded from use in a dietary supplement, does not appear to be an approved food additive or recognized as safe, and/or is subjected to the requirement for pre-market notification without having a satisfied requirement.

FDA-Approved vs. FDA-Accepted in Food Processing

The FDA does not approve applied coatings used in the food processing industry. There is no review process to approve the composition of nonstick coatings, nor does the FDA inspect or test these materials. Through their governing of processes, however, the FDA does have a set of regulations that cover the formulation, manufacturing, and use of nonstick coatings. Hence, materials like Polytetrafluoroethylene (Teflon) are not and cannot be considered as FDA Approved, but rather, they are a "FDA Compliant" or "FDA Acceptable".

Medical Countermeasures (MCMs)

Medical countermeasures (MCMs) are products such as biologics and pharmaceutical drugs that can protect from or treat the health effects of a chemical, biological, radiological, or nuclear (CBRN) attack. MCMs can also be used for prevention and diagnosis of symptoms associated with CBRN attacks or threats. The FDA runs a program called the "FDA Medical Countermeasures Initiative" (MCMi), with programs funded by the federal government. It helps support "partner" agencies and organisations prepare for public health emergencies that could require MCMs.

Medications

The Center for Drug Evaluation and Research uses different requirements for the three main drug product types: new drugs, generic drugs, and over-the-counter drugs. A drug is considered "new" if it is made by a different manufacturer, uses different excipients or inactive ingredients, is used for a different purpose, or undergoes any substantial change. The most rigorous requirements apply to new molecular entities: drugs that are not based on existing medications.

New Medications

New drugs receive extensive scrutiny before FDA approval in a process called a new drug application (NDA). During the first Donald Trump presidency, the agency worked to make the drug-approval process go faster. Critics, however, argue that FDA standards are not sufficiently rigorous to prevent unsafe or ineffective drugs from getting approval. New drugs are available only by prescription by default. A change to over-the-counter (OTC) status is a separate process, and the drug must be approved through an NDA first. A drug that is approved is said to be "safe and effective when used as directed". Drugs being produced by a new manufacturer can be approved through one of two faster processes: the Abbreviated New Drug Application (ANDA) or the 505(b)(2) regulatory pathway for complex generic or biosimilar medications.

Very rare, limited exceptions to this multi-step process involving animal testing and controlled clinical trials can be granted out of compassionate use protocols. This was the case during the 2015 Ebola epidemic with the use, by prescription and authorization, of ZMapp and other experimental treatments, and for new drugs that can be used to treat debilitating and/or very rare conditions for which no existing remedies or drugs are satisfactory, or where there has not been an advance in a long period of time.

The studies are progressively longer, gradually adding more individuals as they progress from stage I to stage III, normally over a period of years, and normally involve drug companies, the government and its laboratories, and often medical schools and hospitals and clinics. However, any exceptions to the aforementioned process are subject to strict review and scrutiny and conditions, and are only given if a substantial amount of research and at least some preliminary human testing has shown that they are believed to be somewhat safe and possibly effective.

Advertising and Promotion:

- The FDA's Office of Prescription Drug Promotion (OPDP) has responsibilities that revolve around the review and regulation of prescription drug advertising and promotion. This is achieved through surveillance activities and the issuance of enforcement letters to pharmaceutical manufacturers. Advertising and promotion for over-the-counter drugs is regulated by the Federal Trade Commission. The FDA also implements regulatory oversight through engagement with third-party enforcer-firms. It expects pharmaceutical companies to ensure that third-party suppliers and labs comply with the agency's health and safety guidelines.

- The drug advertising regulation contains two broad requirements (1) a company may advertise or promote a drug only for the specific indication or medical use for which it was approved by FDA. Also, an advertisement must contain a "fair balance" between the benefits and the risks (side effects) of a drug. The regulation of drug advertising in the U.S. is divided between the Food and Drug Administration (FDA) and the Federal Trade Commission (FTC), based on whether the drug in question is a prescription drug or an over-the-counter (OTC) drug. The FDA oversees the advertising of prescription drugs, while the FTC regulates the advertising of OTC drugs.
- The term off-label refers to the practice of prescribing a drug for a different purpose than what the FDA approved.
- Due to this approval requirement, manufacturers were prohibited from advertising COVID-19 vaccines during the period in which they had only been approved under Emergency Use Authorization.

Post-Market Safety Surveillance:

- After NDA approval, the sponsor must then review and report to the FDA every single patient adverse drug experience it learns of. They must report unexpected serious and fatal adverse drug events within 15 days, and other events on a quarterly basis. The FDA also receives directly adverse drug event reports through its MedWatch program. These reports are called "spontaneous reports" because reporting by consumers and health professionals is voluntary.
- While this remains the primary tool of post-market safety surveillance, FDA requirements for post-marketing risk management are increasing. As a condition of approval, a sponsor may be required to conduct additional clinical trials, called Phase IV trials. In some cases, the FDA requires risk management plans called Risk Evaluation and Mitigation Strategies (REMS) for some drugs that require actions to be taken to ensure that the drug is used safely. For example, thalidomide can cause birth defects, but has uses that outweigh the risks if men and women taking the drugs do not conceive a child; a REMS program for thalidomide mandates an auditable process to ensure that people taking the drug take action to avoid pregnancy; many opioid drugs have REMS programs to avoid addiction and diversion of drugs. The drug isotretinoin has a REMS program called iPLEDGE.

Generic Drugs

Generic drugs are chemical and therapeutic equivalents of name-brand drugs, normally whose patents have expired. Approved generic drugs should have the same dosage, safety, effectiveness, strength, stability, and quality, as well as route of administration. In general, they are less expensive than their name brand counterparts, are manufactured and marketed by rival companies and, in the 1990s, accounted for about a third of all prescriptions written in the United States. For a pharmaceutical company to gain approval to produce a generic drug, the FDA requires scientific evidence that the generic drug is interchangeable with or therapeutically equivalent to the originally approved drug. This is called an Abbreviated New Drug Application (ANDA). 80% of prescription drugs sold in the United States are generic brands.

Generic Drug Scandal:

- In 1989, a major scandal erupted involving the procedures used by the FDA to approve generic drugs for sale to the public. Charges of corruption in generic drug approval first emerged in 1988 during the course of an extensive congressional investigation into the FDA. The oversight subcommittee of the United States House Energy and Commerce Committee resulted from a complaint brought against the FDA by Mylan Laboratories Inc. of Pittsburgh. When its application to manufacture generics were subjected to repeated delays by the FDA, Mylan, convinced that it was being discriminated against, soon began its own private investigation of the agency in 1987. Mylan eventually filed suit against two former FDA employees and four drug-manufacturing companies, charging that corruption within the federal agency resulted in racketeering and in violations of antitrust law. "The order in which new generic drugs were approved was set by the FDA employees even before drug manufacturers submitted applications" and, according to Mylan, this illegal procedure was followed to give preferential treatment to certain companies. During the summer of 1989, three FDA officials (Charles Y. Chang, David J. Brancato, Walter Kletch) pleaded guilty to criminal charges of accepting bribes from generic drugs makers, and two companies (Par Pharmaceutical and its subsidiary Quad Pharmaceuticals) pleaded guilty to giving bribes.
- Furthermore, it was discovered that several manufacturers had falsified data submitted in seeking FDA authorization to market certain generic drugs. Vitarine Pharmaceuticals of New York, which sought approval of a generic version of the drug Dyazide, a medication for high blood pressure, submitted Dyazide, rather than its generic version, for the

FDA tests. In April 1989, the FDA investigated 11 manufacturers for irregularities; and later brought that number up to 13. Dozens of drugs were eventually suspended or recalled by manufacturers. In the early 1990s, the U.S. Securities and Exchange Commission filed securities fraud charges against the Bolar Pharmaceutical Company, a major generic manufacturer based in Long Island, New York.

Over-the-Counter Drugs

Over-the-counter (OTC) are drugs like aspirin that do not require a doctor's prescription. The FDA has a list of approximately 800 such approved ingredients that are combined in various ways to create more than 100,000 OTC drug products. Many OTC drug ingredients had been previously approved prescription drugs now deemed safe enough for use without a medical practitioner's supervision like ibuprofen.

Ebola Treatment

In 2014, the FDA added an Ebola treatment being developed by Canadian pharmaceutical company Tekmira to the Fast Track program, but halted the phase 1 trials in July pending the receipt of more information about how the drug works. This was widely viewed as increasingly important in the face of a major outbreak of the disease in West Africa that began in late March 2014 and ended in June 2016.

Coronavirus (COVID-19) Testing

During the coronavirus pandemic, FDA granted emergency use authorization for personal protective equipment (PPE), in vitro diagnostic equipment, ventilators and other medical devices.

On March 18, 2020, FDA inspectors postponed most foreign facility inspections and all domestic routine surveillance facility inspections. In contrast, the USDA's Food Safety and Inspection Service (FSIS) continued inspections of meatpacking plants, which resulted in 145 FSIS field employees who tested positive for COVID-19, and three who died.

Vaccines, Blood and Tissue Products and Biotechnology

The Center for Biologics Evaluation and Research is the branch of the FDA responsible for ensuring the safety and efficacy of biological therapeutic agents. These include blood and blood products, vaccines, allergenics, cell and tissue-based products, and gene therapy products. New biologics are required to go through a premarket approval process called a Biologics License Application (BLA), similar to that for drugs.

The original authority for government regulation of biological products was established by the 1902 Biologics Control Act, with additional authority established by the 1944 Public Health Service Act. Along with these Acts, the Federal Food, Drug, and Cosmetic Act applies to all biologic products, as well. Originally, the entity responsible for regulation of biological products resided under the National Institutes of Health; this authority was transferred to the FDA in 1972.

Medical and Radiation-Emitting Devices

The Center for Devices and Radiological Health (CDRH) is the branch of the FDA responsible for the premarket approval of all medical devices, as well as overseeing the manufacturing, performance and safety of these devices. The definition of a medical device is given in the FD&C Act, and it includes products from the simple toothbrush to complex devices such as implantable neurostimulators. CDRH also oversees the safety performance of non-medical devices that emit certain types of electromagnetic radiation. Examples of CDRH-regulated devices include cellular phones, airport baggage screening equipment, television receivers, microwave ovens, tanning booths, and laser products.

CDRH regulatory powers include the authority to require certain technical reports from the manufacturers or importers of regulated products, to require that radiation-emitting products meet mandatory safety performance standards, to declare regulated products defective, and to order the recall of defective or noncompliant products. CDRH also conducts limited amounts of direct product testing.

FDA-Cleared vs. FDA-Approved

Clearance requests are required for medical devices that prove they are "substantially equivalent" to the predicate devices already on the market. Approved requests are for items that are new or substantially different and need to demonstrate "safety and efficacy", for example they may be inspected for safety in case of new toxic hazards. Both aspects need to be proved or provided by the submitter to ensure proper procedures are followed.

Cosmetics

Cosmetics are regulated by the Center for Food Safety and Applied Nutrition, the same branch of the FDA that regulates food. Cosmetic products are not, in general, subject to premarket approval by the FDA unless they make "structure or function claims" that make them into drugs. However, all color additives must be specifically FDA approved before manufacturers can include them in cosmetic products sold in the U.S. The FDA regulates cosmetics labeling, and cosmetics that have not been safety tested must bear a warning to that effect. According to the industry advocacy group, the American Council on Science and Health, though the cosmetic industry is primarily responsible for its own product safety, the FDA can intervene when necessary to protect the public. In general, though, cosmetics do not require pre-market approval or testing. The ACSH says that companies must place a warning note on their products if they have not been tested, and that experts in cosmetic ingredient review also play a role in monitoring safety through influence on ingredients, but they lack legal authority. According to the ACSH, it has reviewed about 1,200 ingredients and has suggested that several hundred be restricted—but there is no standard or systemic method for reviewing chemicals for safety, or a clear definition of what 'safety' even means so that all chemicals get tested on the same basis.

However, on December 29, 2022, President Biden signed the '2023 Consolidated Budget Act', which includes the 'Cosmetics Regulatory Modernization Act of 2022 (MoCRA)', which is a stricter regulation that is different from the previous regulations. MoCRA requires compliance with matters such as serious adverse event reporting, safety substantiation, additional labeling, record keeping, and Good Manufacturing Practices (GMP). MoCRA also calls on the FDA to grant Mandatory Recall Authority and establish regulations for GMP rules, flavor allergen labeling rules, and testing methods for cosmetics containing talc.

Veterinary Products

The Center for Veterinary Medicine (CVM) is a center of the FDA that regulates food additives and drugs that are given to animals. CVM regulates animal drugs, animal food including pet animal, and animal medical devices. The FDA's requirements to prevent the spread of bovine spongiform encephalopathy are also administered by CVM through inspections of feed manufacturers. CVM does not regulate vaccines for animals; these are handled by the United States Department of Agriculture.

Tobacco Products

The FDA regulates tobacco products with authority established by the 2009 Family Smoking Prevention and Tobacco Control Act. This Act requires color warnings on cigarette packages and printed advertising, and text warnings from the U.S. Surgeon General. The nine new graphic warning labels were announced by the FDA in June 2011 and were scheduled to be required to appear on packaging by September 2012. The implementation date is uncertain, due to ongoing proceedings in the case of R.J. Reynolds Tobacco Co. v. U.S. Food and Drug Administration. R.J. Reynolds, Lorillard, Commonwealth Brands, Liggett Group and Santa Fe Natural Tobacco Company have filed suit in Washington, D.C. federal court claiming that the graphic labels are an unconstitutional way of forcing tobacco companies to engage in anti-smoking advocacy on the government's behalf.

A First Amendment lawyer, Floyd Abrams, is representing the tobacco companies in the case, contending requiring graphic warning labels on a lawful product cannot withstand constitutional scrutiny. The Association of National Advertisers and the

American Advertising Federation have also filed a brief in the suit, arguing that the labels infringe on commercial free speech and could lead to further government intrusion if left unchallenged.

In November 2011, Federal judge Richard Leon of the U.S. District Court for the District of Columbia temporarily halted the new labels, likely delaying the requirement that tobacco companies display the labels. The U.S. Supreme Court ultimately could decide the matter. In July 2017, the FDA announced a plan that would reduce the current levels of nicotine permitted in tobacco cigarettes. The proposed regulation, identified as RIN 0910-AI76, titled "Tobacco Product Standard for Nicotine Yield of Cigarettes and Certain Other Combusted Tobacco Products," seeks to reduce the nicotine content in cigarettes to approximately 0.7 milligrams per gram of tobacco.

Regulation of Living Organisms

With acceptance of premarket notification 510(k) k033391 in January 2004, the FDA granted Ronald Sherman permission to produce and market medical maggots for use in humans or other animals as a prescription medical device. Medical maggots represent the first living organism allowed by the Food and Drug Administration for production and marketing as a prescription medical device. In June 2004, the FDA cleared Hirudo medicinalis (medicinal leeches) as the second living organism legal to use as a medical device. The FDA also requires that milk be pasteurized to remove bacteria.

International Cooperation

In February 2011, President Barack Obama and Canadian Prime Minister Stephen Harper issued a "Declaration on a Shared Vision for Perimeter Security and Economic Competitiveness" and announced the creation of the Canada-United States Regulatory Cooperation Council (RCC) "to increase regulatory transparency and coordination between the two countries." Under the RCC mandate, the FDA and Health Canada undertook a "first of its kind" initiative by selecting "as its first area of alignment common cold indications for certain over-the-counter antihistamine ingredients (GC 2013-01-10)."

A more recent example of the FDA's international work is their 2018 cooperation with regulatory and law-enforcement agencies worldwide through Interpol as part of Operation Pangea XI. The FDA targeted 465 websites that illegally sold potentially dangerous, unapproved versions of opioid, oncology, and antiviral prescription drugs to U.S. consumers. The agency focused on transaction laundering schemes in order to uncover the complex online drug network.

6.4.2 CE Marking (EU)

The presence of the CE marking on commercial products indicates that the manufacturer or importer affirms the goods' conformity with European health, safety, and environmental protection standards. It is not a quality indicator or a certification mark. The CE marking is required for goods sold in the European Economic Area (EEA); goods sold elsewhere may also carry the mark.

The CE mark indicates that the product may be traded freely in any part of the European Economic Area, regardless of its country of origin. It consists of the CE letter pair and, if applicable, the four digit identification number of the notified body involved in the conformity assessment procedure.

The CE mark on a product indicates that the manufacturer or importer of that product affirms its compliance with the relevant EU legislation and the product may be sold anywhere in the European Economic Area (EEA). It is a criminal offence to affix a CE mark to a product that is not compliant or offer it for sale.

For example, most electrical products must comply with the Low Voltage Directive and the EMC Directive, among others; toys must comply with the Toy Safety Directive (The Low Voltage Directive is about electrical safety; EMC or Electromagnetic Compatibility means the device will work as intended without interfering with, or being affected by, the use or function of any other device.) The CE mark indicates compliance with as many norms (directives and regulations) as apply at the time of the declaration of compliance. In the case of electrical products, several later norms such as the Restriction of Hazardous Substances Directive (RoHS) and Waste Electrical and Electronic Equipment Directive (WEEE) are relevant in addition to the Low Voltage Directive and EMC Directive. The exact significance of the CE mark therefore depends on when it was applied to a specific unit.

The marking does not indicate EEA manufacture or that the EU or another authority has approved a product as safe or conformant. The EU requirements may include safety, health, and environmental protection. If stipulated in any EU product legislation, assessment by a Notified Body or manufacture according to a certified production quality system may be required. Where relevant, the CE mark is followed by the registration number of the notified body involved in conformity assessment.

Not all products need CE marking to be traded in the EEA; only product categories subject to relevant directives or regulations are required (and allowed) to bear CE marking. Most CE-marked products can be placed on the market subject only to an internal production control by the manufacturer with no independent check of the conformity of the product with EU legislation; ANEC has cautioned that, amongst other things, CE marking cannot be considered a "safety mark" for consumers.

Countries Requiring CE Marking

CE marking is mandatory for certain product groups intended for sale within the European Union, the European Free Trade Association (EFTA), and Turkey.

As Northern Ireland (a region of the UK) remains aligned to the European Single Market under the Northern Ireland Protocol, CE marking remains mandatory for products placed on the market there, and the British UKCA mark is not required.

CE marking was not required by countries of the Central European Free Trade Agreement (CEFTA), but CEFTA members Albania, North Macedonia, Serbia, and Montenegro had applied for membership of the European Union, and were adopting many of its standards within their legislation, as had most Central European former member countries of CEFTA that joined the EU, before joining.

As of 2019, the United Kingdom government "intends to extend recognition of the CE marking for placing most goods on the market in Great Britain, indefinitely, beyond December 2024", with "different rules for medical devices, construction products, cableways, transportable pressure equipment, unmanned aircraft systems, rail products, marine equipment and ecodesign".

Rules Underlying CE Marking

The formal legal status of the CE mark is set out in various EU Directives and Regulations. The underlying principles are explained in the Commission's "Blue Guide".

Responsibility for CE marking lies with whoever puts the product on the market in the EU, i.e. an EU-based manufacturer, the importer or distributor of a product made outside the EU, or an EU-based office of a non-EU manufacturer.

The manufacturer of a product affixes the CE marking to it but has to take certain obligatory steps before the product can bear CE marking. The manufacturer must carry out a conformity assessment, set up a technical file, and sign a Declaration stipulated by the leading legislation for the product. The documentation has to be made available to authorities on request.

Importers of products have to verify that the manufacturer outside the EU has undertaken the necessary steps and that the documentation is available upon request. Importers should also make sure that contact with the manufacturer can always be established.

Distributors must be able to demonstrate to national authorities that they have acted with due care and they must have affirmation from the manufacturer or importer that the necessary measures have been taken.

If importers or distributors market the products under their own name, they take over the manufacturer's responsibilities. In this case they must have sufficient information on the design and production of the product, as they will be assuming the legal responsibility when they affix the CE marking. There are certain rules underlying the procedure to affix the marking:

- Products subject to certain EU directives or EU regulations providing for CE marking have to be affixed with the CE marking before they can be placed on the market.
- Manufacturers have to check, on their sole responsibility, which EU legislation they need to apply for their products.
- The product may be placed on the market only if it complies with the provisions of all applicable directives and regulations and if the conformity assessment procedure has been carried out accordingly.
- The manufacturer draws up an EU declaration of conformity or a declaration of performance (for Construction Products) and affixes the CE marking on the product.
- If stipulated in the directive(s) or regulation(s), an authorized third party (Notified Body) must be involved in the conformity assessment procedure or in setting up a production quality system.
- If the CE marking is affixed on a product, it can bear additional markings only if they are of different significance, do not overlap with the CE marking and are not confusing and do not impair the legibility and visibility of the CE marking.

Since achieving compliance can be very complex, CE-marking conformity assessment, provided by a notified body, is of great importance throughout the entire CE-marking process, from design verification, and set up of the technical file to the EU declaration of conformity. A guide to the implementation of directives and regulations based on the New Approach and the Global Approach (the "Blue Guide") was first published by the European Union in 2000. Updated versions were published on 28 February 2014 and 26 July 2016.

Self-Certification

Depending on the level of risk of the product, the CE marking is affixed to a product by the manufacturer or authorized representative who needs to ensure that the product meets all the CE marking requirements. In some cases, if a product has minimal risk, it can be self-certified by a manufacturer making a declaration of conformity and affixing the CE marking to their own product. Self-certification exists only for products that have a minimal risk for their use, and this is clearly foreseen in the relevant directive and regulation according to the product "category". In order to certify, the manufacturer must do several things:

- Investigate whether the product needs to have a CE marking. The product must conform to all Directives and Regulations that apply to the product.

- Choose the conformity assessment procedure from the modules called out by the directive or the regulation for the product according to each category (level of risk) involved. There are several modules available for the Conformity Assessment Procedures, but only a few of them involve self-certification. The most of these procedure require a "type Approval" and a Production conformity assessment by a Notified Body. All procedures (modules) of certification are as listed below which are derivered from Article 5.1.7 of "Blue Guide". A product normally needs more than one procedure (Module) to be implemented:
  - Module A – Internal production control: Module A1 – Internal production control plus supervised product testing. Module A2 – Internal production control plus supervised product checks at random intervals.
  - Module B – EU type examination.
  - Module C – Conformity to EU type based on internal production control: Module C1 – Conformity to EU type based on internal production control plus supervised product testing. Module C2 – Conformity to EU type based on internal production control plus supervised product testing.
  - Module D – Conformity to EU type based on quality assurance of the production process: Module D1 – Quality assurance of the production process.
  - Module E – Conformity to EU type based on product quality assurance: Module E1 – Quality assurance of final product inspection and testing.
  - Module F – Conformity to EU type based on product verification: Module F1 - Conformity based on product verification.
  - Module G – Unit verification.
  - Module H – Full quality assurance: Module H1 – Full quality assurance and Design Examination.

The level of risk is defined by the "category" of each equipment. The higher the category, the higher the risk. After defining the category, the manufacturer, in order to obtain certification, shall then apply the relevant procedures for the specific category of the product or choose the relevant procedures for a higher-category product.

The manufacturer, after insuring that the relevant modules for the product category have been applied, will affix the CE mark and draw up a Declaration of Conformity. The Declaration of Conformity contains a description of the product, the directive(s) and regulation(s) applied, the product category for each directive or regulation, the module chosen, and the name and registration number of the notified body involved in certification procedures (models).

Notified bodies involved in certification procedures are organizations that have been nominated by a member state (according to an accreditation procedure) and have been notified by the European Commission. These notified bodies act as

Independent Inspection organizations and carry out the procedures as listed in the relevant Modules applied as stated by the relevant directives and regulations. A manufacturer can choose any notified body (notified for the certain directive or regulation and relevant Modules) in any Member State of the European Union.

Stage 1: Identify the Applicable Norm(s)

The first step is to identify whether the product needs to bear CE marking or not. Not all products are required to bear CE marking, only the products that fall within the scope of at least one of the sectoral norms (directives and regulations) requiring CE marking. There are more than 20 sectoral product norms requiring CE marking covering, but not limited to, products such as electrical equipment, machines, medical devices, toys, pressure equipment, PPE, wireless devices and construction products.

Identifying which norm(s) may be applicable, as there may be more than one, involves a simple exercise of reading the scope of each norm to establish which apply to the product (Such as the "Low Voltage Directive," 2014/35/EU). If the product does not fall within the scope of any of the sectoral norm, then the product does not need to bear CE marking (and, indeed, must not bear CE marking).

Stage 2: Identify the Applicable Requirements of the Norm(s)

Each norm has slightly different methods of demonstrating conformity depending on the classification of the product and its intended use. Every Directive or Regulation has a number of 'essential requirements' that the product has to meet before being placed on the market.

The best way to demonstrate that these essential requirements have been met is by meeting the requirements of an applicable 'harmonised standard,' which offer a presumption of conformity to the essential requirements, although the use of standards usually remains voluntary. Harmonised standards can be identified by searching the 'Official Journal' on the European Commission's website, or by visiting the New Approach website established by the European Commission and EFTA with the European Standardisation Organisations.

Stage 3: Identify an Appropriate Route to Conformity

The process is not always a self-declaration process, there are various 'attestation routes' to conformity depending on the Directive or Regulation and classification of the product. Many products (such as invasive medical devices, or fire alarm and extinguisher systems, Pressure Equipment, Lifts etc.) in most cases, have a mandatory requirement for the involvement of an authorised third party e.g. a "notified body". There are various attestation routes which include:

- An assessment of the product by the manufacturer.
- An assessment of the product by the manufacturer, with additional requirement for mandatory factory production control audits to be carried out by a third party.
- An assessment by a third party (e.g. EC type test), with the requirement for mandatory factory production control audits to be carried out by a third party.

Stage 4: Assessment of the Product's Conformity

When all of the requirements have been established, the conformity of the product to the essential requirements of the norm(s) needs to be assessed. This usually involves assessment and/or testing, and may include an evaluation of the conformity of the product to the harmonised standard(s) identified in step 2.

Stage 5: Compile the Technical Documentation

Technical documentation, usually referred to as the technical file, relating to the product or range of products needs to be compiled. This information should cover every aspect relating to conformity and is likely to include details of the design, development and manufacture of the product. Technical documentation will usually include:

- Technical description.
- Drawings, circuit diagrams and photos.
- Bill of materials.
- Specification and, where applicable, EU declaration of conformity for the critical components and materials used.
- Details of any design calculations.
- Test reports and/or assessments.
- Instructions.
- EU declaration of conformity.
- Technical documentation can be made available in any format (i.e. paper or electronic) and must be held for a period of up to 10 years after the manufacture of the last unit, and in most cases reside in the European Economic Area (EEA).

Stage 6: Make a Declaration and Affix the CE Marking

When the manufacturer, importer or authorised representative is satisfied that their product conforms to the applicable norms, an EU declaration of conformity must be completed or, for partly completed machinery under the Machinery Directive, an ECU declaration of incorporation.

EU Declaration of Conformity

Under the General Product Safety Regulation (EU) 2023/988 (GPSR), the EU declaration of conformity is a mandatory legal document in which the manufacturer or authorised representative declares that a product complies with all applicable safety requirements.

The EU declaration of conformity must include:

- Manufacturer's or authorised representative's name and full business address.
- Product identification (type, model, serial or batch number).
- A statement that the signatory accepts full responsibility for compliance with the applicable EU legislation.
- Traceability information (e.g., photograph or drawing of the product).
- Reference to relevant regulations (e.g., GPSR, and if applicable CEdirectives) and harmonised standards used.
- Identification of any notified body involved, with its name and identification number, if applicable.
- Place and date of issue.
- Name and position of the person authorised to sign on behalf of the manufacturer or authorised representative.
- A legally binding signature.

Additional requirements:

- The declaration must be drafted before placing the product on the EU market and retained for at least 10 years thereafter by the manufacturer, importer, or authorised representative.
- It must be translated into the official language(s) of each EU country where the product is sold.

The declaration is part of the product's technical documentation and must be submitted to competent authorities on request.

Product Groups

The norms (directives and regulations) requiring CE marking affect the following product groups:

- Active implantable medical devices (excludes surgical instruments).
- Appliances burning gaseous fuels.
- Cableway installations designed to carry persons.

- Construction products according to Regulation (EU) No. 305/2011 under specific rules.
- Eco-design of energy related products.
- Electrical and electronic equipment, including radio equipment.
- Equipment and protective systems intended for use in potentially explosive atmospheres.
- Explosives for civil uses.
- Fertilizers Regulation (EU) No. 1009/2019.
- Hot-water boilers.
- In vitro diagnostic medical devices.
- Lifts.
- Machinery.
- Measuring instruments.
- Medical devices.
- Noise emission in the environment.
- Non-automatic weighing instruments.
- Personal protective equipment.
- Pressure equipment.
- Pyrotechnics.
- Recreational craft.
- Restriction of the use of certain hazardous substances in electrical and electronic equipment (RoHS).
- Toys.
- Simple pressure vessels.

Mutual Recognition of Conformity Assessment

There are numerous 'Agreements on Mutual Recognition of Conformity Assessment' between the European Union and other countries such as the US, Japan, Canada, Australia, New Zealand and Israel. Consequently, CE marking is now found on many products from these countries. Japan has its own marking known as the Conformity Mark. Switzerland and Turkey (which are not members of the EEA) also require products to bear CE marking as an affirmation of conformity.

Characteristics of CE Marking

- The CE marking has to be affixed by the manufacturer or its authorized representative in the European Union according to its legal format visibly, legibly and indelibly to the product.

- When a manufacturer puts the CE marking on a product it implies that it complies with all the Essential Health and safety requirements from all the directives and regulations that applies to its product.
  - For example, for a machine, generally the Machinery directive applies, but often also:
    - Low voltage directive.
    - EMC directive.
    - Sometimes other directives or regulations, e.g. ATEX directive.
    - Sometimes other legal requirements, e.g. for food contact materials.

When the manufacturer of a machine puts the CE marking, it engages itself and guarantees, that it makes all the tests, assessments and evaluation on the product to conform to all the requirements of all the norms that apply to its product.

- CE marking has been introduced by the COUNCIL DIRECTIVE 93/68/EEC of 22 July 1993 amending Directives 87/404/EEC (simple pressure vessels), 88/378/EEC (safety of toys), 89/106/EEC (construction products), 89/336/EEC (electromagnetic compatibility), 89/392/EEC (machinery), 89/686/EEC (personal protective equipment), 90/384/EEC (non-automatic weighing instruments), 90/385/EEC (active implantable medicinal devices), 90/396/EEC (appliances burning gaseous fuels) 91/263/EEC (telecommunications terminal equipment), 92/42/EEC (new hot-water boilers fired with liquid or gaseous fuels), 93/42/EEC (medical devices) and 73/23/EEC (electrical equipment designed for use within certain voltage limits).
- The size of the CE marking must be at least 5 mm, if enlarged its proportions have to be kept.
- If the appearance and workmanship of a product do not allow for the CE marking to be affixed on the product itself, the marking has to be affixed to its packaging or accompanying documents.
- If a norm requires the involvement of a Notified Body in the conformity assessment procedure, depending on the legislation, an identification number may need to be put behind the CE logo. This is done under the responsibility of the Notified Body.

6.4.3 CDSCO (India)

The Central Drugs Standard Control Organisation (CDSCO) is India's national regulatory body for cosmetics, pharmaceuticals and medical devices. It serves a similar function to the Food and Drug Administration (FDA) of the United States or the European Medicines Agency of the European Union. The Indian government has announced its plan to bring all medical devices, including implants and contraceptives under a review of the Central Drugs and Standard Control Organisation (CDSCO).

Within the CDSCO, the Drug Controller General of India (DCGI) regulates pharmaceutical and medical devices and is positioning within the Ministry of Health and Family Welfare. The DCGI is advised by the Drug Technical Advisory Board (DTAB) and the Drug Consultative Committee (DCC). Divided into zonal offices, each one carries out pre-licensing and post-licensing inspections, post-market surveillance, and drug recalls (where necessary). Manufacturers who deal with the authority required to name an Authorized Indian Representative (AIR) to represent them in all dealings with the CDSCO in India.

Divisions

Central Drugs Standard Control Organization has 8 divisions:

- BA/BE.
- New Drugs.
- Medical Device & Diagnostics.
- DCC-DTAB.
- Import & Registration.
- Biological.
- Cosmetics.
- Clinical Trials.

Criticism

The CDSCO has been criticized for having far lower standards for drug approval than the United States' Food and Drug Administration and European Union's European Medicines Agency. In a 2015 interview, the current Drugs Controller General, G. N. Singh, admitted that if the CDSCO held Indian pharmaceutical manufacturers to American standards, most would fail.

6.5COMPLIANCEWITHMEDICALSTANDARDSANDETHICALCODES

Compliance with medical standards and ethical codes represents both a challenge and an opportunity in the development and deployment of AI diagnostic tools. The complex regulatory landscape requires careful navigation, while the ethical dimensions demand thoughtful consideration of how these powerful technologies should be developed and used in medicine. By adhering to established standards and actively contributing to the evolution of new frameworks, stakeholders can harness the tremendous potential of AI diagnostics while maintaining the trust of patients and practitioners. The future of AI in diagnostics depends not just on technological advancement, but equally on our ability to develop and implement robust, ethical compliance structures that ensure these tools serve the best interests of patients and society as a whole. As the field continues to evolve ongoing dialogue between technologists, clinicians, regulators, and ethicists will be essential to shape standards that keep pace with innovation while upholding the fundamental principles of medical ethics.

As AI diagnostic technology evolves, so too must the frameworks governing it Regulatory agencies are developing more sophisticated approaches to address the unique characteristics of AI, such as the FDA's proposed framework for modifications to AI/ML-based software. This recognizes that unlike traditional medical devices, AI systems improve through continuous learning, requiring a more dynamic regulatory approach. International standards organizations are working towards greater harmonization of AI medical device regulations, reducing barriers to global innovation while maintaining rigorous safety standards.

Ethical frameworks are also evolving to address emerging challenges. The development of AI-specific versions of traditional medical ethics guidelines, such as adaptations of the Hippocratic Oath for AI developers, reflects the growing recognition of AI's unique ethical implications. There is increasing emphasis on participatory design approaches that involve patients and clinicians in AI development, ensuring the technology meets real clinical needs while respecting patient values. The concept of algorithmic accountability is gaining traction, with calls for standardized audit procedures to assess AI systems for biases, fairness, and adherence to ethical principles.

The integration of blockchain technology may offer new solutions for compliance verification, creating immutable records of algorithm training data, validation results, and clinical usage. Similarly, the development of standardized benchmark datasets and testing environments could improve the consistency and reliability of AI diagnostic validation across different systems and settings. As these technological and regulatory innovations progress, maintaining the delicate balance between fostering innovation and ensuring patient safety will remain the central challenge in AI diagnostic compliance.

6.5.1 Global Regulatory Frameworks Governing AI Diagnostics

Different regions have developed distinct regulatory approaches to oversee AI applications in diagnostic medicine, reflecting varying legal traditions and healthcare systems. In the United States, the Food and Drug Administration (FDA) has established a risk-based classification system for AI-driven medical devices, with stricter requirements for high-risk applications such as cancer detection or cardiac diagnosis. The FDA's Digital Health Center of Excellence provides specific guidance on software modifications, ensuring that iterative improvements to AI algorithms do not compromise safety or efficacy. Meanwhile, the European Union's Medical Device Regulation (MDR) and In Vitro Diagnostic Regulation (IVDR) impose rigorous conformity assessments, requiring clinical evidence and post-market surveillance for AI diagnostic tools. These regulations emphasize transparency, requiring manufacturers to document algorithmic decision-making processes in detail.

In Asia, regulatory approaches vary significantly. China's National Medical Products Administration (NMPA) has implemented a fast-track approval process for certain AI diagnostics, particularly those addressing public health priorities, while maintaining stringent validation requirements. Japan's Pharmaceuticals and Medical Devices Agency (PMDA) focuses on real-world performance data, encouraging continuous monitoring after deployment. Despite these regional differences, international collaborations such as the International Medical Device Regulators Forum (IMDRF) work towards harmonizing standards, recognizing that AI diagnostics often transcend national boundaries. This global patchwork of regulations presents challenges for developers seeking market approval across multiple jurisdictions, necessitating careful navigation of diverse compliance landscapes.

6.5.2 Ethical Codes and Principles in AI Diagnostic Development

Beyond legal compliance, ethical considerations form the moral foundation for AI in diagnostics. Leading medical associations and AI ethics boards have established principles to guide responsible development and deployment. The World Health Organization (WHO) emphasizes that AI should prioritize patient welfare, ensuring equitable access and avoiding harm. The Helsinki Declaration, traditionally governing medical research, has been adapted to address AI-specific concerns such as algorithmic bias and data privacy. Professional bodies like the American Medical Association (AMA) and the European Society of Radiology have issued guidelines stressing that AI should augment, not replace, physician judgment, maintaining human oversight in diagnostic decision-making.

Transparency emerges as a recurring ethical imperative across these frameworks. The "black box" nature of some AI systems, where decision-making processes are opaque, conflicts with medical ethics' emphasis on explainability. This has led to growing advocacy for explainable AI (XAI) in diagnostics, ensuring that clinicians and patients can understand how conclusions are reached. Another critical ethical principle is justice, requiring that AI diagnostic tools are trained on diverse datasets to prevent biases against underrepresented populations. The ethical principle of beneficence demands that AI applications demonstrate clear clinical benefit, while non-maleficence necessitates robust safeguards against diagnostic errors or system failures. These ethical codes, while not always legally binding, provide essential guidance for developers and practitioners navigating the complex moral landscape of AI diagnostics.

6.5.3 Clinical Validation and Performance Standards for AI Diagnostics

Meeting medical standards requires rigorous clinical validation demonstrating that AI diagnostic tools perform at least as well as existing methods. Validation protocols must adhere to standards such as the Clinical and Laboratory Standards Institute (CLSI) guidelines or the FDA's Software as a Medical Device (SaMD) framework. These require multi-stage testing beginning with retrospective studies using archived patient data, progressing to prospective trials in clinical settings, and culminating in real-world evidence collection post-deployment. Performance metrics extend beyond simple accuracy rates to include sensitivity, specificity, positive predictive value, and area under the receiver operating characteristic curve (AUC-ROC), providing comprehensive assessment of diagnostic capability.

A critical challenge in validation is ensuring that performance remains consistent across diverse patient populations and clinical environments. An AI system trained primarily on data from urban academic hospitals may underperform in rural community clinics with different patient demographics or imaging equipment. Standards therefore mandate external validation using independent datasets from varied settings.

The Digital Imaging and Communications in Medicine (DICOM) standard ensures interoperability between AI systems and medical imaging equipment, while the Integrating the Healthcare Enterprise (IHE) framework standardizes data exchange protocols. Continuous performance monitoring is equally crucial, as AI models may degrade over time due to data drift—changes in disease prevalence, imaging techniques, or patient characteristics. Compliance thus requires not just initial validation but ongoing quality assurance processes throughout the product lifecycle.

6.5.4 Data Privacy and Security in Compliance Frameworks

The data-intensive nature of AI diagnostics necessitates strict adherence to privacy and security standards. Regulations such as the General Data Protection Regulation (GDPR) in the EU and the Health Insurance Portability and Accountability Act (HIPAA) in the US establish stringent requirements for handling sensitive health data. These include data minimization principles, mandating that only necessary information is collected, and purpose limitation, restricting data use to specified diagnostic functions. Anonymization and pseudonymization techniques must meet defined standards to prevent re-identification of patient data, particularly when used for algorithm training or improvement.

Security standards like ISO 27001 provide frameworks for protecting AI systems against cyber threats, which carry heightened risks in healthcare due to the sensitivity of medical data. Encryption protocols for data both at rest and in transit are typically mandated, along with access controls ensuring only authorized personnel can interact with the systems. Emerging techniques such as federated learning, where AI models are trained across decentralized datasets without transferring raw patient data, offer promising solutions to privacy challenges. However, these innovative approaches must themselves be evaluated against existing and evolving privacy standards. The increasing use of edge computing in AI diagnostics, where data processing occurs locally on medical devices rather than in the cloud, presents both opportunities and challenges for compliance with data protection regulations.

6.5.5 Implementing Compliance in AI Diagnostic Workflows

Achieving and maintaining compliance requires systematic integration into every stage of AI diagnostic development and deployment. For developers, this begins with regulatory strategy planning early in the design process, identifying applicable standards and building corresponding requirements into the product roadmap. Quality management systems (QMS) compliant with ISO 13485 are essential for documenting design controls, risk management processes, and verification/validation activities. Hazard analysis techniques such as Failure Mode and Effects Analysis (FMEA) help anticipate and mitigate potential risks in AI diagnostics, from algorithmic biases to cybersecurity vulnerabilities.

Healthcare institutions implementing AI diagnostics face their own compliance challenges. Clinical governance frameworks must be adapted to incorporate AI tools, ensuring clear accountability for diagnostic decisions made with AI assistance. Staff training programs are necessary to ensure healthcare professionals understand the appropriate use, limitations, and oversight requirements for AI diagnostics. Audit trails documenting every AI-assisted decision, along with mechanisms for human override of algorithmic outputs, are typically required to meet medical and ethical standards. Institutions must also establish processes for reporting adverse events related to AI diagnostics to regulatory bodies, contributing to post-market surveillance efforts that inform ongoing compliance assessments.

CHAPTER 7

Integration into Clinical Workflows

7.1 HUMAN-AI COLLABORATION IN DIAGNOSTIC DECISION-MAKING

Human-AI collaboration in diagnostic decision-making represents a significant step forward in modern medicine. By combining the computational power and analytical capabilities of AI with the judgment, empathy, and contextual awareness of human clinicians, healthcare systems can achieve higher diagnostic accuracy, efficiency, and patient satisfaction. However, realizing the full potential of this collaboration requires careful integration, robust training, ethical safeguards, and continuous feedback. Ultimately, the goal is not to create machines that replace doctors, but to build intelligent systems that empower them, resulting in better care for all patients.

Looking ahead, the future of human-AI collaboration in diagnostics is promising. With advancements in natural language processing, computer vision, and multimodal learning, AI systems will become even more capable of supporting complex diagnostic tasks. At the same time, clinicians will continue to play an indispensable role in interpreting, contextualizing, and acting upon AI-generated insights.

The relationship between human and machine will become increasingly symbiotic, with each enhancing the other's strengths and compensating for limitations. Emerging technologies such as augmented reality, voice-enabled interfaces, and personalized diagnostic dashboards will further enhance collaborative experiences. As this evolution continues, the focus must remain on improving patient care, maintaining clinical integrity, and fostering a culture of trust and shared expertise.

As AI assumes a more significant role in diagnostic decision-making, ethical and legal issues must be carefully addressed. Shared responsibility between human and AI raises questions about accountability when errors occur. If a diagnosis is missed or incorrect, determining whether the fault lies with the clinician, the AI system, or both becomes a complex issue. Legal frameworks must evolve to define responsibility in collaborative environments and to protect patient rights. Ethical considerations also involve ensuring that AI use does not compromise patient autonomy, privacy, or dignity. Transparent communication, informed consent, and respect for patient preferences are essential components of ethical human-AI collaboration. Furthermore, AI tools must be designed to mitigate bias and promote equity, ensuring that all patient groups benefit equally from advancements in diagnostic technology.

7.2 USER INTERFACES AND PHYSICIAN TRUST

The relationship between user interfaces and physician trust represents a critical frontier in the successful implementation of diagnostic AI. As artificial intelligence assumes an increasingly prominent role in medical diagnosis, the quality of interface design will largely determine whether these powerful tools are embraced or resisted by clinician users. Effective interfaces serve as translators between algorithmic reasoning and clinical cognition, as integrators of AI into established workflows, and as mediators of the complex trust relationship between physicians and intelligent systems. Future advancements in diagnostic AI must parallel advancements in interface design - not just in terms of technological sophistication but in psychological and clinical sophistication. The most impactful diagnostic AI systems may not be those with the highest algorithmic performance in isolation but those that most effectively combine technical excellence with interface designs that physicians find genuinely trustworthy and useful in their daily practice. By prioritizing physician trust as a core design requirement from the outset, developers can create AI diagnostic tools that fulfill their transformative potential in healthcare.

Emerging interface paradigms promise to further strengthen the physician-AI trust relationship in diagnostic medicine. Mixed reality interfaces that spatially co-locate AI insights with the physical patient or medical imaging equipment could create more intuitive diagnostic environments. Voice-enabled interfaces that allow natural language dialogue with AI systems may lower interaction barriers for physicians less comfortable with traditional software controls. Explainable AI techniques are evolving toward more sophisticated causal reasoning displays that help physicians understand not just what the AI concluded but why those conclusions make clinical sense.

Personalized trust calibration interfaces might learn individual physicians' tendencies to over-rely or under-rely on AI suggestions and adjust presentation styles accordingly. Collaborative filtering interfaces could highlight cases where a physician's peers found particular AI outputs valuable, providing social proof to complement algorithmic evidence. As AI systems increasingly operate across the continuum of care, longitudinal patient journey interfaces will help physicians track how AI-assisted diagnostic decisions unfold over time, reinforcing the connection between interface interactions and patient outcomes. The common thread across all these developments is recognizing that physician trust cannot be assumed as a byproduct of algorithmic accuracy alone, but must be consciously designed for through thoughtful, clinically grounded interface solutions.

7.3 AI-DRIVEN CLINICAL DECISION SUPPORT SYSTEMS (CDSS)

AI-driven Clinical Decision Support Systems are transforming the landscape of diagnostic medicine, offering powerful tools to enhance accuracy, personalize care, and streamline clinical workflows. By harnessing the power of AI to analyze complex medical data, these systems support clinicians in making more informed and timely decisions, ultimately improving patient outcomes.

While challenges related to data quality, interpretability, and ethical considerations remain, ongoing research and collaboration are paving the way for the safe and effective integration of AI-driven CDSS into clinical practice. As the field continues to evolve, AI-driven CDSS will play an increasingly central role in the delivery of high-quality, patient-centered care, marking a new era in the practice of diagnostic medicine.

The deployment of AI-driven CDSS in diagnostics raises important ethical and legal considerations. Issues such as patient consent, data privacy, and accountability for AI-driven decisions must be carefully navigated. Clinicians remain ultimately responsible for patient care, but the use of AI introduces new questions about liability in cases of diagnostic errors or adverse outcomes.

Clear guidelines and regulatory frameworks are needed to define the roles and responsibilities of clinicians, developers, and healthcare organizations in the use of AI-driven CDSS. Ethical considerations also extend to ensuring fairness and equity in AI-driven diagnostics, avoiding biases that could disadvantage certain patient groups. Ongoing dialogue among stakeholders, including patients, clinicians, ethicists, and regulators, is essential for addressing these complex issues and ensuring that AI-driven CDSS are deployed in a manner that upholds the highest standards of medical ethics.

The future of AI-driven CDSS in diagnostics is bright, with ongoing advancements in AI algorithms, data integration, and user interface design poised to further enhance their capabilities. As these systems become more sophisticated, they will increasingly support not only diagnosis but also prognosis, treatment planning, and patient monitoring. The integration of real-time data from wearable devices and remote monitoring tools will enable more proactive and preventive care, shifting the focus from reactive treatment to health maintenance and disease prevention. Collaborative efforts among healthcare providers, technology developers, and policymakers will be essential for realizing the full potential of AI-driven CDSS, ensuring that these tools are accessible, equitable, and aligned with the needs of patients and clinicians.

7.4 WORKFLOW OPTIMIZATION IN IMAGING AND LAB DIAGNOSTICS

AI is redefining workflow optimization in imaging and laboratory diagnostics by enhancing speed, accuracy, and resource efficiency. From triaging images and automating reports to managing lab samples and predicting demand, AI offers a wide array of tools that streamline diagnostic workflows. These innovations not only reduce clinician workload and operational costs but also improve patient outcomes by ensuring timely and precise diagnoses. The successful integration of AI requires thoughtful implementation, seamless system integration, ongoing clinician engagement, and strict adherence to ethical and security standards. As AI continues to evolve, it will play an increasingly central role in building intelligent agile, and patient-centric diagnostic ecosystems that meet the growing demands of modern healthcare.

Imaging and laboratory diagnostics are central to the diagnostic process in modern medicine. However, they are often hampered by workflow bottlenecks. In imaging departments, radiologists face the challenge of reading hundreds of images daily, leading to fatigue, delayed reporting, and potential diagnostic oversights. In laboratories, the process of handling samples, running tests, and interpreting results can be labor-intensive and subject to variations in quality and turnaround time. Additionally, communication gaps between departments and lack of data interoperability can further slow down the diagnostic process. These inefficiencies not only affect the quality of care but also increase operational costs and strain healthcare systems, especially during peak periods or pandemics.

7.5 TRAINING CLINICIANS FOR AI-AUGMENTED DIAGNOSIS

The integration of AI into diagnostic medicine represents not merely a technological shift but a fundamental transformation in the nature of clinical practice. Training clinicians for this AI-augmented future requires more than superficial familiarization with new software - it demands a comprehensive reimagining of medical education that cultivates sophisticated human-machine collaboration skills. By developing structured training pathways that address technical competencies, cognitive integration, psychological barriers, and ethical considerations, the medical community can ensure clinicians are prepared to harness AI's diagnostic potential while preserving the essential human elements of medical practice. The ultimate goal is not to create clinicians who depend on AI, but clinicians who know how to thoughtfully partner with AI to achieve diagnostic excellence. As AI systems become increasingly sophisticated, the value of well-trained clinicians who can artfully combine algorithmic insights with human judgment will only grow - making investment in AI training not just beneficial but essential for the future of diagnostic medicine.

As AI diagnostic capabilities advance, clinician training approaches must evolve in parallel. Adaptive learning systems that themselves use AI to personalize training content based on individual clinician performance will enable more efficient competency development. Virtual reality simulations offering immersive diagnostic experiences with AI collaborators could provide richer training environments than current screen-based tools. The emergence of generative AI capable of engaging in diagnostic dialogue will require new training modules on effective human-AI communication techniques.

Longitudinal training ecosystems that support clinicians throughout their careers will become essential as AI systems continuously learn and change. Micro-credentialing systems may emerge to certify clinicians' proficiency in specific AI diagnostic tools, similar to current credentialing for medical devices or procedures. International collaborations will be necessary to establish standardized training frameworks that ensure consistent AI competency development across health systems. Perhaps most importantly, the medical education community must maintain flexibility to adapt training approaches as the roles of clinicians and AI in diagnosis co-evolve, ensuring that human expertise remains optimally augmented rather than inadvertently diminished by technological advancement.

CHAPTER 8

Economic and Policy Perspectives

8.1 COST-EFFECTIVENESS AND ROI OF DIAGNOSTIC AI

The cost-effectiveness and return on investment of diagnostic AI are increasingly evident across multiple domains of healthcare. From enhancing diagnostic accuracy and reducing labor costs to preventing errors and enabling early intervention, AI offers substantial financial and clinical benefits. However, achieving a positive ROI depends on thoughtful implementation, integration, and ongoing evaluation. While initial investments may be significant, the long-term gains—in efficiency, scalability, and patient outcomes—can be transformative. As AI continues to mature, its role as a cost-effective pillar of diagnostic medicine will become more prominent, offering healthcare systems a sustainable path to deliver high-quality, data-driven, and economically viable care.

- **Cost-Effectiveness in Diagnostic AI:** Cost-effectiveness in healthcare refers to achieving improved health outcomes at a lower or justifiable additional cost. For AI in diagnostics, this means that the technology should not only deliver more accurate or faster diagnoses but do so in a way that either saves money or yields significant value relative to its cost. Evaluating cost-effectiveness requires an analysis of both direct and indirect costs. Direct costs include the price of acquiring, implementing, and maintaining AI tools, while indirect costs involve labor, patient throughput, reduced complications, and time saved. A diagnostic AI solution is considered cost-effective if it leads to better patient outcomes, reduced healthcare utilization, or operational efficiencies that outweigh the initial and recurring investments.
- **Initial Investment and Implementation Costs:** One of the primary concerns regarding the adoption of diagnostic AI is the upfront cost of acquisition and integration. AI solutions often require sophisticated hardware, software licenses, cloud infrastructure, and training for end users. Hospitals may need to upgrade imaging equipment or laboratory systems to ensure compatibility with AI platforms. Additionally, implementation involves technical integration with electronic health

records (EHR), radiology information systems (RIS), and laboratory information systems (LIS), which can incur significant costs. While these investments are substantial, they are often one-time expenses or amortized over several years. Institutions evaluating AI must therefore assess whether these initial expenditures will lead to tangible operational savings and clinical value over time.

- **Operational Savings and Workflow Efficiency:** One of the most immediate financial benefits of diagnostic AI is the improvement in workflow efficiency. In radiology, for example, AI algorithms can pre-screen images, detect abnormalities, and prioritize urgent cases, allowing radiologists to focus on high-value tasks and reduce reporting backlogs. This optimization can lead to faster turnaround times, improved patient satisfaction, and increased imaging department throughput without hiring additional staff. In laboratory diagnostics, AI can automate result interpretation, quality control, and anomaly detection, significantly reducing manual labor and human error. These time and labor savings translate into reduced personnel costs, fewer repeat tests, and better resource utilization, all of which contribute to a more cost-effective operation.
- **Reducing Diagnostic Errors and Avoidable Costs:** Diagnostic errors are a leading cause of medical malpractice claims and result in substantial financial losses for healthcare systems. AI tools, by virtue of their high sensitivity and ability to analyze vast datasets, can assist clinicians in reducing missed or incorrect diagnoses. This is particularly relevant in fields such as radiology, pathology, and cardiology, where complex patterns and minute abnormalities must be accurately interpreted. By reducing errors, AI decreases the likelihood of unnecessary procedures, hospital readmissions, and delayed treatments. These outcomes not only improve patient care but also prevent costly litigation, compensation, and the use of hospital resources for avoidable complications. The financial savings from error reduction alone can significantly impact the ROI of diagnostic AI.
- **Enhancing Early Detection and Preventive Care:** AI-enabled diagnostics excel in early disease detection by identifying subtle markers that may be overlooked by human observers. For chronic conditions like cancer, diabetes, or cardiovascular diseases, early detection is directly linked to lower treatment costs and better outcomes. Treating a condition in its early stages is far less expensive than managing complications of advanced disease. For example, detecting breast cancer at Stage I costs

significantly less than treatment at Stage IV, both in financial terms and patient quality of life. AI tools that facilitate early diagnosis not only reduce the clinical burden but also contribute to long-term healthcare savings. The cumulative impact of early interventions supported by AI directly enhances its cost-effectiveness and long-term ROI.

- **Scalability and Long-Term Financial Gains:** A key strength of AI in diagnostics lies in its scalability. Once deployed and integrated into clinical systems, AI tools can be used across thousands of diagnostic instances with little additional cost. Unlike human labor, which scales linearly with workload, AI can process increasing volumes of data without proportional increases in expense. This scalability is particularly advantageous for large hospitals, diagnostic chains, and public health programs. The more a system uses AI, the more cost-effective it becomes. Additionally, many AI vendors offer subscription-based pricing models, spreading costs over time and allowing healthcare institutions to match investment with usage. These models support sustained ROI by ensuring financial predictability and reducing upfront financial barriers.
- **Data Reusability and Continuous Improvement:** Diagnostic AI systems generate and rely on vast datasets, which can be used for continuous improvement and further innovation. Once data infrastructure is in place, AI tools can be retrained and updated using local data to enhance performance and contextual relevance. This reusability of data eliminates the need for repetitive data collection and supports the development of new diagnostic capabilities without starting from scratch. For instance, a hospital using AI for chest X-ray analysis can repurpose the same data for training a system to detect tuberculosis, lung cancer, or COVID-19. This layered value creation improves the long-term ROI of AI investments, making them more than just single-purpose tools.
- **Comparative Studies and Real-World Evidence:** Several studies have evaluated the cost-effectiveness of diagnostic AI in real-world settings. For example, research has shown that AI systems in radiology can reduce reporting time by up to 40%, enabling radiologists to handle more cases per shift. In diabetic retinopathy screening, AI tools have been found to provide comparable accuracy to ophthalmologists at a fraction of the cost, especially in underserved regions. Similarly, AI-driven lab test optimization has led to reductions in redundant testing and improved test utilization. These real-world outcomes provide empirical

support for the financial viability of AI in diagnostics. However, it is important to note that outcomes can vary based on the clinical setting, infrastructure, and user acceptance.

- **Barriers to Realizing Financial Benefits:** Despite the promising economic advantages, several barriers can hinder the realization of full financial benefits from diagnostic AI. Resistance to change among healthcare providers, lack of technical infrastructure, and insufficient training can delay adoption and reduce utilization. Additionally, regulatory hurdles and concerns around data privacy and algorithm transparency can increase the time and cost required for deployment. Some AI systems may require customization or localization, adding to implementation complexity. Furthermore, financial metrics like ROI may not capture intangible benefits such as improved staff morale, patient confidence, or institutional reputation. Addressing these barriers through stakeholder engagement, training, and clear policy frameworks is essential for maximizing AI's cost-effectiveness.
- **Strategic Planning and Investment Decisions:** For healthcare organizations, realizing ROI from diagnostic AI requires strategic planning. This involves selecting the right use cases, aligning AI deployment with clinical priorities, and setting measurable performance indicators. Cost-benefit analyses, pilot testing, and phased rollouts help manage financial risks and ensure the technology delivers value in specific contexts. Institutions must also consider long-term maintenance, updates, and support costs when calculating ROI. Investing in AI should not be viewed as a one-time expenditure but as an evolving partnership that grows with technological advancement and organizational maturity. Effective vendor collaboration, regulatory compliance, and clinical leadership play pivotal roles in sustaining financial and clinical returns.

8.2 REIMBURSEMENT MODELS AND HEALTH ECONOMICS

The development of appropriate reimbursement models for diagnostic AI represents one of the most pressing challenges in healthcare economics today. Current systems, designed for traditional medical technologies, struggle to accommodate the unique characteristics of AI - its rapid evolution, scalability, and role as both a product and a process enhancer. The solution lies in reimbursement frameworks that recognize AI's multifaceted value proposition while maintaining financial sustainability for healthcare systems. Future models will likely blend elements of fee-for-service, value-based, and alternative payment approaches, tailored to specific clinical applications and healthcare contexts. Success will depend on collaboration among clinicians, health economists, payers, and technology developers to establish fair valuation methodologies and robust outcome measurement systems. As evidence grows about AI's impact on diagnostic accuracy, workflow efficiency, and patient outcomes, reimbursement models must remain flexible enough to incorporate new understanding while providing sufficient predictability to support investment.

The ultimate goal should be reimbursement systems that incentivize adoption of clinically beneficial AI diagnostics without encouraging overutilization or displacing essential human judgment. By aligning financial incentives with patient outcomes and system efficiency, well-designed reimbursement models can accelerate appropriate AI integration while safeguarding healthcare quality and affordability. In this rapidly evolving landscape, continuous dialogue and iterative policy development will be essential to keep pace with technological advancements and ensure that AI's diagnostic potential translates into real-world clinical and economic benefits.

The reimbursement landscape for diagnostic AI will likely evolve significantly in coming years as technologies mature and evidence accumulates. Several trends suggest possible future directions. Value-based reimbursement will probably gain prominence, with payment models increasingly tied to measurable improvements in diagnostic quality and patient outcomes. This shift will require development of standardized performance metrics and robust data infrastructure to support real-world evidence generation.

We may see the emergence of diagnosis-related group (DRG) modifiers that adjust payments based on AI utilization and demonstrated benefits. Such an approach would maintain existing payment structures while recognizing AI's value-add. Similarly, professional fee schedules might incorporate AI augmentation factors that adjust physician reimbursement when AI tools are used appropriately to enhance diagnostic accuracy or efficiency.

Regulatory harmonization efforts could lead to more consistent reimbursement pathways across jurisdictions, reducing barriers to market entry for AI developers. International standards for evidence requirements and performance assessment would facilitate health technology appraisal processes and enable cross-border learning about effective reimbursement strategies. At the same time, personalized medicine approaches enabled by AI may drive demand for more flexible reimbursement models that can accommodate patient-specific diagnostic strategies.

The growing role of real-world data and real-world evidence in healthcare decision-making will likely influence AI reimbursement, with payers increasingly considering observational data alongside clinical trial results. This could accelerate reimbursement for promising AI diagnostics while maintaining safeguards through post-market surveillance requirements. The development of AI-specific health economic evaluation methodologies will provide more nuanced tools for assessing long-term value across complex care pathways.

8.2.1 Value Assessment Frameworks for Diagnostic AI

Health economics principles provide essential tools for evaluating how diagnostic AI creates value in healthcare systems. Comprehensive assessment requires analysis across multiple dimensions, including diagnostic accuracy improvements, workflow efficiencies, and downstream clinical outcomes. AI's ability to detect diseases earlier or with greater precision than conventional methods may lead to reduced treatment costs and improved patient outcomes, creating substantial economic value. However, capturing this value in reimbursement models proves challenging when savings accrue to different parts of the healthcare system than where the initial investment occurs. For example, a hospital's radiology department may bear the cost of an AI diagnostic tool while the financial benefits manifest as reduced oncology treatment expenses months or years later.

Cost-effectiveness analyses for diagnostic AI must account for both direct and indirect economic impacts. Direct costs include software acquisition, implementation, and maintenance expenses, while indirect costs encompass training requirements and potential workflow disruptions. On the benefit side, analysts must consider not only improved patient outcomes but also productivity gains for healthcare professionals and potential reductions in unnecessary testing. The unique challenge with AI diagnostics lies in their scalability - once developed, the marginal cost of applying an algorithm to additional patients approaches zero, suggesting that traditional cost-based reimbursement approaches may be inappropriate. Alternative frameworks that assess value based on performance metrics or health outcomes gained traction as more appropriate models for AI reimbursement, though they require robust measurement systems to implement effectively.

8.2.2 Current Reimbursement Models for AI Diagnostics

Existing reimbursement approaches for diagnostic AI fall into several broad categories, each with distinct advantages and limitations. Fee-for-service models with specific AI billing codes provide transparency but risk incentivizing volume over value. The American Medical Association's Current Procedural Terminology (CPT) system has introduced several AI-specific codes, such as those for autonomous AI analysis of retinal images or cardiac monitoring. However, this approach struggles to accommodate AI tools that augment rather than replace physician work, as the value creation occurs through human-machine collaboration rather than standalone algorithmic analysis.

Bundled payment models that incorporate AI diagnostics into episode-based payments offer an alternative approach. These models recognize AI as a component of comprehensive diagnostic services rather than a separate billable item. While this avoids fragmentation of care, it may undervalue AI's specific contributions and reduce incentives for adoption. Some health systems employ hybrid models where AI tools receive separate reimbursement only when they demonstrably reduce overall episode costs or improve outcomes. The Centers for Medicare & Medicaid Services (CMS) has experimented with alternative payment models through its New Technology Add-on Payment program, which provides additional reimbursement for technologies that substantially improve care.

Global budget systems, common in single-payer healthcare systems, approach AI reimbursement differently by funding hospitals or health networks to deliver care within fixed budgets, allowing local decision-makers to determine how best to incorporate cost-saving technologies. This approach provides flexibility but may slow AI adoption if competing priorities dominate limited budgets. Emerging models explore performance-based reimbursement where payments correlate with measurable improvements in diagnostic accuracy, time-to-diagnosis, or patient outcomes, aligning financial incentives with AI's value proposition.

8.2.3 Barriers to Appropriate AI Diagnostic Reimbursement

Several significant barriers hinder the development of optimal reimbursement models for diagnostic AI. The lack of standardized outcome measures makes comparative effectiveness analyses challenging, as different health systems track different metrics. Regulatory uncertainty compounds this problem, as approval pathways for AI diagnostics continue to evolve, creating reimbursement ambiguities. The rapid iteration cycle of AI algorithms presents another challenge, as traditional reimbursement processes struggle to keep pace with software updates that may significantly alter performance characteristics.

Evidence requirements pose another substantial barrier. Payers typically demand rigorous clinical trials demonstrating improved outcomes, but the validation methodologies for AI diagnostics differ from those used for drugs or medical devices. Many AI systems improve through continuous learning, making static validation studies potentially obsolete shortly after completion. This creates tension between payers' need for evidence and developers' need for reimbursement to fund evidence generation - a classic "catch-22" situation. The misalignment of financial incentives across the healthcare system creates further complications. Diagnostic AI often produces cost savings that benefit payers or other care sectors rather than the organizations that must purchase and implement the technology. Without mechanisms to share these savings, adoption incentives remain weak. Intellectual property protections and data ownership issues add additional layers of complexity, as the value of AI diagnostics depends heavily on access to high-quality training data that may be controlled by various stakeholders with competing interests.

8.2.4 International Perspectives on AI Diagnostic Reimbursement

Comparative analysis of international approaches to AI diagnostic reimbursement reveals diverse strategies reflecting different healthcare system structures. In Germany, the Institute for the Hospital Remuneration System has established specific reimbursement categories for certain AI applications in hospital settings, creating predictable payment pathways. The United Kingdom's National Health Service employs a technology appraisal process through the National Institute for Health and Care Excellence (NICE), which evaluates diagnostic AI alongside other health technologies using standardized cost-effectiveness metrics.

Japan's universal health insurance system has taken a proactive approach, creating special reimbursement categories for AI-assisted diagnosis in specific clinical areas like endoscopy and radiology. These categories often include requirements for physician oversight, reflecting cultural values about the role of human clinicians. In contrast, some Scandinavian countries incorporate AI diagnostics into broader digital health initiatives funded through municipal budgets, emphasizing population health outcomes over specific technology reimbursement.

Developing nations face distinct challenges, often lacking infrastructure for sophisticated reimbursement systems but potentially benefiting more dramatically from AI diagnostics that can compensate for specialist shortages. Some African nations are experimenting with mobile payment systems that allow per-use billing for AI diagnostic services delivered via smartphone applications. These international differences highlight how reimbursement models must adapt to local healthcare system architectures, economic conditions, and cultural values regarding technology's role in medicine.

8.2.5 Innovative Payment Models for AI Diagnostics

Forward-thinking reimbursement approaches are emerging to address the unique characteristics of diagnostic AI. Subscription-based models, where healthcare organizations pay ongoing fees for AI services rather than per-use charges, provide predictable costs while allowing continuous software updates. These models often include performance guarantees or tiered pricing based on utilization levels, sharing risk between developers and healthcare providers.

Outcome-based contracting represents another innovative approach, where reimbursement amounts depend on measured improvements in diagnostic accuracy, time savings, or patient outcomes. These arrangements require robust data infrastructure to track performance metrics reliably and may include clawback provisions if expected benefits fail to materialize. Some contracts incorporate stop-loss protections to prevent excessive payments when AI performance varies across patient populations.

Risk-sharing models distribute the financial burden of AI adoption across stakeholders. In some arrangements, technology developers accept partial payment in the form of a percentage of demonstrated cost savings, aligning their incentives with healthcare providers. Other models create consortiums where multiple organizations jointly fund AI implementation, sharing both costs and benefits. Blockchain-based smart contracts are being explored as mechanisms to automate complex reimbursement calculations based on verifiable performance data.

Capital expenditure models treat AI diagnostics as infrastructure investments rather than recurring expenses, with reimbursement occurring through depreciation accounting or special technology funds. These approaches recognize that some AI tools function more like medical equipment than consumable supplies, though they may struggle to accommodate software-as-a-service delivery models. Hybrid approaches that combine elements of these various models are becoming increasingly common as stakeholders seek flexible solutions tailored to specific clinical applications and organizational circumstances.

8.3 NATIONAL AI HEALTH STRATEGIES AND FUNDING INITIATIVES

National AI health strategies and funding initiatives are foundational to the responsible and effective integration of AI in diagnostics. By providing a coordinated vision, regulatory clarity, and targeted investment, these efforts are enabling the development and deployment of AI-driven diagnostic tools that have the potential to transform healthcare. While challenges remain, the commitment of governments, health authorities, and international partners to advancing AI in diagnostics signals a new era of innovation, collaboration, and improved patient care. As these strategies continue to evolve, they will shape not only the future of diagnostics but also the broader landscape of healthcare in the age of artificial intelligence.

As AI continues to advance, national AI health strategies and funding initiatives will play an increasingly central role in shaping the future of diagnostics. The next generation of strategies is likely to focus on integrating AI across the entire continuum of care, from prevention and early detection to treatment and long-term management. Emphasis will be placed on real-world implementation, continuous monitoring, and iterative improvement of AI tools. The development of adaptive regulatory frameworks, investment in digital health infrastructure, and ongoing public engagement will be essential for sustaining progress. Ultimately, the success of national AI health strategies will be measured by their ability to deliver tangible improvements in health outcomes, reduce disparities, and build resilient, patient-centered healthcare systems.

8.3.1 Rationale for National AI Health Strategies

The integration of AI into healthcare diagnostics is not merely a technological upgrade; it represents a fundamental change in how health systems operate, make decisions, and deliver care. National AI health strategies are essential for providing a coordinated vision and framework for the adoption, regulation, and scaling of AI technologies. These strategies are typically developed in response to several key drivers. First, there is the promise of improved diagnostic accuracy and early disease detection, which can lead to better patient outcomes and reduced healthcare costs. Second, AI can help address workforce shortages and alleviate the burden on clinicians by automating routine tasks and supporting complex decision-making. Third, national strategies are needed to ensure that AI adoption is guided by ethical principles, data privacy standards, and a commitment to health equity. Without a coordinated approach, the deployment of AI in diagnostics risks becoming fragmented, inconsistent, and potentially inequitable.

8.3.2 Key Components of National AI Health Strategies

A comprehensive national AI health strategy typically encompasses several core components. One of the foundational elements is the establishment of clear regulatory frameworks that define the standards for safety, efficacy, and transparency in AI-driven diagnostics. These frameworks are designed to protect patients, foster innovation, and provide clarity for technology developers and healthcare providers. Another critical component is the development of national data infrastructure, including secure, interoperable health data repositories that enable the training and validation of AI models on diverse and representative datasets. National strategies also emphasize workforce development, supporting the education and training of clinicians, data scientists, and health informaticians in AI literacy and application. Additionally, these strategies often include mechanisms for public engagement and stakeholder consultation, ensuring that the perspectives of patients, clinicians, and the broader community are incorporated into AI policy and practice.

8.3.3 Global Examples of National AI Health Strategies

Several countries have emerged as leaders in the development and implementation of national AI health strategies, each with its own approach and priorities. In the United States, the National Artificial Intelligence Initiative Act of 2020 established a coordinated program to accelerate AI research and application across sectors, including healthcare. The National Institutes of Health (NIH) has launched initiatives such as the Bridge2AI program, which funds the creation of high-quality, ethically sourced datasets for AI research in health. In the United Kingdom, the National Health Service (NHS) has developed the NHS AI Lab, a dedicated unit to support the safe and effective adoption of AI technologies in healthcare, with a particular focus on diagnostics and imaging. The European Union has adopted a coordinated plan on AI, emphasizing cross-border collaboration, data sharing, and the development of ethical guidelines for AI in health. In Asia, countries like China and Singapore have invested heavily in AI research, infrastructure, and pilot projects, aiming to position themselves as global leaders in AI-driven healthcare innovation.

8.3.4 Funding Initiatives and Investment in AI Diagnostics

National AI health strategies are underpinned by significant funding initiatives, which provide the resources needed to drive research, development, and implementation of AI in diagnostics. These investments take various forms, including direct government grants, public-private partnerships, and competitive funding programs for startups and academic institutions. Funding is often targeted at key areas such as the development of AI algorithms for disease detection, the creation of annotated medical datasets, and the deployment of AI tools in clinical settings. For example, the US NIH has allocated substantial funding to support AI research in medical imaging, genomics, and electronic health records. The UK government has invested in the AI in Health and Care Award, which supports the testing and scaling of promising AI technologies within the NHS. In Canada, the Pan-Canadian Artificial Intelligence Strategy funds research institutes and collaborative projects focused on AI applications in health. These funding initiatives are critical for bridging the gap between research and real-world impact, enabling the translation of AI innovations from the lab to the clinic.

8.3.5 Challenges in Implementing National AI Health Strategies

Despite the momentum behind national AI health strategies and funding initiatives, several challenges must be addressed to ensure their success. One of the primary challenges is the fragmentation of health data, which is often stored in disparate systems and formats across different institutions and regions.

Achieving interoperability and data sharing while maintaining patient privacy and security is a complex task that requires technical, legal, and organizational solutions. Another challenge is the need for robust evaluation and validation of AI diagnostic tools, ensuring that they perform reliably across diverse populations and clinical settings. Regulatory frameworks must strike a balance between fostering innovation and safeguarding patient safety, which can be difficult in a rapidly evolving technological landscape. Additionally, there is a risk that AI adoption could exacerbate existing health disparities if not carefully managed, particularly if certain populations are underrepresented in training data or lack access to AI-enabled care.

8.3.6 Ethical and Societal Considerations

National AI health strategies must also grapple with a range of ethical and societal considerations. Ensuring fairness and equity in AI diagnostics is paramount, as biased algorithms can perpetuate or even amplify health disparities. Strategies must include measures to promote diversity in data collection, algorithm development and clinical validation. Transparency and explainability are also critical, as clinicians and patients need to understand how AI-driven diagnostic decisions are made. Public trust in AI technologies depends on clear communication, robust oversight, and mechanisms for accountability. National strategies should also address issues related to consent, data ownership, and the right to opt out of AI-driven care. Engaging patients and the public in the development and governance of AI health initiatives is essential for aligning technological innovation with societal values and expectations.

8.3.7 Role of Collaboration and International Partnerships

Given the global nature of AI research and the shared challenges faced by health systems worldwide, international collaboration is a key feature of many national AI health strategies. Cross-border partnerships enable the pooling of data, expertise, and resources, accelerating the development and validation of AI diagnostic tools. Initiatives such as the Global Partnership on Artificial Intelligence (GPAI) and the World Health Organization's efforts to develop global standards for AI in health exemplify the importance of international cooperation. Collaborative research projects, data-sharing agreements, and harmonized regulatory approaches can help ensure that AI-driven diagnostics are safe, effective, and accessible to all, regardless of geographic location.

8.4 ROLE OF AI IN UNIVERSAL HEALTH COVERAGE AND RURAL DIAGNOSTICS

The pursuit of universal health coverage faces its greatest challenges in rural and underserved regions where healthcare infrastructure remains inadequate and specialist providers are scarce. Artificial intelligence emerges as a transformative force in addressing these disparities by bringing advanced diagnostic capabilities to resource-constrained settings. Traditional diagnostic models relying on centralized facilities and highly trained specialists create insurmountable barriers for rural populations, resulting in delayed diagnoses and preventable disease progression. AI-powered diagnostic tools deployed at the point of care can analyze medical images, interpret laboratory results, and assess clinical symptoms with accuracy approaching that of human experts. This technological leap enables community health workers with basic training to deliver specialist-level diagnostics in remote clinics, effectively democratizing access to early and accurate disease detection. The implications for universal health coverage are profound, as AI helps overcome the twin challenges of geographic isolation and workforce shortages that have historically excluded rural populations from quality healthcare services.

The evolving landscape of AI diagnostics promises increasingly sophisticated solutions tailored to rural universal health coverage challenges. Emerging technologies like federated learning will enable AI models to improve continuously by learning from diverse rural populations without requiring centralized data collection, addressing both privacy concerns and infrastructure limitations. Advances in low-power AI chips will make diagnostic capabilities available on ever more affordable devices, while voice interfaces in local languages will reduce literacy barriers to technology adoption.

The integration of AI diagnostics with other technological innovations creates powerful synergies for rural healthcare. Drone-delivered diagnostic kits with built-in AI analysis, blockchain-secured health records accessible across dispersed care points, and AI-optimized supply chain management for rural clinics all show promise in pilot implementations. These combinations demonstrate how AI serves as an enabling layer rather than a standalone solution within broader health system strengthening efforts.

Policy innovations will be equally critical to fully realize AI's potential for rural universal health coverage. National digital health strategies increasingly recognize diagnostic AI as essential infrastructure rather than optional technology, with corresponding budget allocations. Regulatory sandboxes allow testing of innovative AI solutions in controlled rural environments, accelerating safe deployment. International collaborations like the WHO's AI for Health initiative foster knowledge sharing between countries facing similar rural health challenges, preventing duplication of effort and promoting best practice adoption.

As these technical and policy advancements converge, the vision of quality diagnostics reaching every rural community becomes increasingly attainable. The ultimate measure of success will be when place of residence no longer determines diagnostic accuracy or timeliness, marking true progress toward health equity. AI's role in this transformation continues to evolve from novel tool to integral component of sustainable rural health systems, proving that technology can indeed bridge the last mile in universal health coverage when thoughtfully designed and implemented.

8.4.1 AI-Enabled Diagnostic Networks for Rural Healthcare Systems

Effective implementation of AI diagnostics in rural environments requires carefully designed healthcare networks that leverage technology while accommodating local constraints. Portable diagnostic devices equipped with AI interpretation capabilities form the foundation of these networks, allowing frontline health workers to perform ultrasounds, retinal scans, or electrocardiograms with real-time algorithmic analysis. These devices connect through hub-and-spoke models where rural clinics transmit complex cases to centralized specialist teams, with AI serving as both first-line screener and decision-support tool during teleconsultations.

The Indian state of Maharashtra exemplifies this approach, where AI-assisted portable retinal cameras deployed in village health centers have dramatically increased diabetic retinopathy screening coverage. Similar networks in rural China use AI-powered ultrasound systems operated by primary care providers, reducing unnecessary referrals to distant hospitals by 40 percent. These systems demonstrate how AI can optimize limited healthcare resources by stratifying patient risk and directing specialist attention to cases where human expertise is most needed.

The sustainability of rural AI diagnostic networks depends on thoughtful integration with existing healthcare workflows rather than technology imposition. Successful implementations train local health workers as technology stewards, creating community ownership and trust in AI-assisted diagnostics. Maintenance protocols account for intermittent electricity and internet connectivity, with some systems employing edge computing that allows offline AI analysis synchronized when connections resume.

Cost-recovery models often combine public health funding with microinsurance schemes, ensuring financial accessibility for low-income populations. As these networks mature, they generate valuable data that helps health authorities identify disease patterns and allocate resources more effectively across regions, creating a virtuous cycle of improved health intelligence and targeted interventions.

8.4.2 Overcoming Infrastructure Challenges with Adaptive AI Solutions

Rural healthcare environments present unique infrastructure limitations that demand specially adapted AI diagnostic solutions. Conventional medical AI systems designed for well-equipped urban hospitals often prove impractical in settings lacking consistent power, stable internet, or advanced imaging equipment. Innovators have responded by developing lightweight AI algorithms that maintain diagnostic accuracy while requiring minimal computing power, enabling operation on low-cost smartphones or portable devices. Solar-powered diagnostic kits with built-in AI capabilities now support tuberculosis screening in remote African communities, while offline-capable AI models assist in prenatal ultrasound interpretation across Southeast Asia's island communities.

The maintenance and updating of AI systems in rural areas requires equally innovative approaches. Rather than relying on continuous internet connectivity for software updates, some programs use SMS-based model refinements or scheduled synchronization during monthly supply deliveries. Equipment durability becomes paramount, leading to the development of ruggedized AI diagnostic devices resistant to dust, humidity, and rough transportation. Training programs for rural health workers emphasize basic troubleshooting alongside clinical skills, creating local capacity to maintain technological solutions. These adaptations demonstrate how AI diagnostics must evolve beyond technical performance to meet the practical realities of healthcare delivery in resource-limited settings, where robustness and simplicity often outweigh algorithmic sophistication.

Data collection and privacy present additional infrastructure-related challenges in rural AI implementations. While comprehensive health records enhance AI performance, paper-based systems still dominate many rural clinics. Hybrid solutions that combine optical character recognition for paper forms with voice-based data entry through local language interfaces help bridge this digital divide. Privacy protections must account for communal living situations and cultural norms around health information, leading to context-appropriate consent processes and data sharing policies. These adaptations ensure that AI diagnostics respect local contexts while delivering global-standard healthcare quality, proving that technological advancement need not come at the expense of cultural sensitivity.

8.4.3 Economic Models for Sustainable Rural AI Diagnostics

The financial sustainability of AI diagnostic programs in rural areas requires innovative economic models that align with universal health coverage principles. Traditional fee-for-service approaches often fail in low-income rural communities where patients cannot afford even modest out-of-pocket payments. Alternative financing strategies have emerged, including cross-subsidization where urban healthcare facilities help fund rural AI deployments through bundled service payments.

Some national health insurance schemes now include specific reimbursement categories for AI-assisted primary diagnostics, recognizing their role in preventing costly advanced disease complications. Public-private partnerships have proven particularly effective in scaling rural AI diagnostics. In Brazil, partnerships between municipal health departments and AI developers have created screening networks for cervical cancer that combine low-cost HPV testing with algorithmic analysis of cellphone-captured microscopy images. Rwanda's drone-delivered blood sample network coupled with AI diagnostic support demonstrates how multiple technologies can converge to serve remote populations economically. Microinsurance products specifically designed for AI-enabled preventive care are gaining traction in several African and Asian markets, with premiums as low as a few dollars annually covering essential screenings.

The economic case for rural AI diagnostics extends beyond direct healthcare savings. Early disease detection through AI-powered community screening reduces agricultural productivity losses from worker illness and prevents catastrophic health expenditures that drive families into poverty. Health economists in Kenya have documented how AI-assisted malaria diagnostics in rural areas generate a sevenfold economic return when accounting for preserved workforce participation and reduced school absenteeism. These broader socioeconomic benefits justify increased government investment in diagnostic AI as a tool for rural development rather than merely a healthcare expenditure, aligning with the sustainable development goals underpinning universal health coverage aspirations.

8.4.4 Training and Capacity Building for AI-Augmented Rural Healthcare

Successful integration of AI diagnostics into rural healthcare systems demands comprehensive training approaches that empower rather than displace local health workers. Training programs must address both technical competencies in operating AI tools and the cognitive skills required to interpret AI outputs within clinical contexts. In rural India, modified versions of the WHO's Basic Emergency Care course now include modules on using AI decision-support tools for trauma and acute illness assessment, enabling frontline workers to leverage technology while maintaining independent clinical judgment. Similar initiatives in sub-Saharan Africa combine AI diagnostic training with smartphone literacy programs, recognizing that device familiarity precedes effective technology utilization in health contexts.

The psychological aspects of AI adoption among rural health workers require careful attention. Many community health workers initially fear that diagnostic AI might diminish their professional role or expose knowledge gaps. Effective training programs position AI as a collaborative tool that enhances rather than replaces human expertise, using case examples where AI assists with specific tasks while health workers retain overall patient management responsibility. Peer learning networks have proven valuable, where early adopters share positive experiences and practical tips for integrating AI into daily workflows. Mozambique's AI-assisted malaria diagnosis program attributes its success partly to "digital champion" health workers who model confident yet critical use of technology for their colleagues. Training must extend beyond technical skills to encompass ethical considerations and communication strategies. Rural health workers using AI diagnostics need guidance on explaining algorithmic recommendations to patients with varying levels of technology familiarity, often employing metaphors rooted in local experiences.

Privacy training emphasizes securing devices and data in communal living environments where personal boundaries differ from urban norms. Continuous learning mechanisms account for the rapid evolution of AI tools, with some programs using voice message updates or radio broadcasts to reinforce new skills in areas with limited internet access. This holistic approach to capacity building ensures that rural healthcare systems can sustainably harness AI's diagnostic potential while maintaining human-centered care values.

8.4.5 Measuring Impact and Outcomes of Rural AI Diagnostics

Robust impact assessment frameworks are essential to demonstrate the value of AI diagnostics in advancing universal health coverage goals for rural populations. Traditional healthcare metrics require adaptation to capture both the direct and systemic effects of AI implementation.

Coverage indicators must account not just for physical access to facilities but for quality-adjusted diagnostic availability, measuring how AI bridges the gap between rural point-of-care services and specialist-level diagnosis. Quality metrics evolve beyond simple accuracy rates to include appropriateness of AI-guided referrals and timeliness of diagnosis compared to conventional pathways.

Longitudinal studies in several countries reveal compelling patterns emerging from rural AI diagnostic programs. Nepal's AI-assisted ultrasound network for antenatal care has demonstrated a 30 percent reduction in maternal mortality in participating districts, attributed to earlier detection of high-risk pregnancies. Similar programs in Ghana tracking hypertension management show improved medication adherence when community health workers use AI risk prediction tools during home visits. Crucially, these outcomes are achieved while maintaining patient satisfaction levels comparable to traditional specialist consultations, countering concerns that technological solutions might depersonalize rural healthcare.

Health equity metrics form a critical component of impact assessment, ensuring AI diagnostics reduce rather than exacerbate existing disparities. Geographic penetration analyses track whether AI reaches the most remote communities, while socioeconomic stratification examines accessibility across wealth quintiles. Gender-disaggregated data reveals whether AI diagnostics improve care for women who often face additional barriers to seeking traditional healthcare in rural contexts. Such comprehensive measurement not only demonstrates program effectiveness but guides continuous improvement, identifying populations that remain underserved and aspects of implementation requiring refinement. This data-driven approach ensures that AI serves as a genuine tool for health equity rather than another source of technological stratification.

CHAPTER 9

Future Directions in Diagnostic AI

9.1 PERSONALIZED AND PREDICTIVE DIAGNOSTICS

AI is redefining the landscape of diagnostics through its capabilities in personalization and prediction. By utilizing patient-specific data and advanced analytical models, AI enables clinicians to move beyond generic protocols to deliver more targeted, effective, and proactive healthcare. Personalized diagnostics enhance the accuracy of disease identification, while predictive tools forecast risks and allow for timely intervention. The integration of AI into diagnostics fosters a more comprehensive understanding of each patient's health trajectory, facilitating better outcomes and more efficient care. While challenges around data quality, ethical use, and system integration remain, the benefits of personalized and predictive diagnostics—amplified by AI—hold immense promise for the future of medicine. As the technology continues to mature, its role in empowering clinicians and patients alike will become increasingly indispensable in modern healthcare.

The field of personalized and predictive diagnostics is evolving rapidly, driven by advances in machine learning, computational biology, and sensor technology. Future innovations may include AI systems capable of interpreting polygenic risk scores in real time, diagnostic bots that conduct initial patient interviews, or AI platforms that simulate disease progression under various lifestyle scenarios. Integration with digital twins—virtual representations of patients that model physiological responses—may further enhance personalized care planning. As federated learning and privacy-preserving AI models develop, the ability to use large-scale patient data while maintaining confidentiality will unlock even more powerful diagnostic capabilities. Ultimately, the future of diagnostics lies in an ecosystem where AI continuously learns from individual and population data to offer ever more precise, personalized, and predictive insights.

9.1.1 Personalization in Diagnostics

Personalized diagnostics aim to understand and respond to the unique biological and physiological makeup of each patient. AI plays a critical role in this domain by aggregating and analyzing vast amounts of diverse health data, including genomic sequences, electronic health records, medical imaging, lab results, and environmental exposures. AI algorithms can uncover subtle patterns and correlations that would be impossible for humans to detect unaided. This capability enables clinicians to differentiate between similar symptoms caused by vastly different underlying conditions, thereby improving diagnostic accuracy. For example, two patients presenting with chest pain may have entirely different cardiac risks based on their genetic predisposition, biomarkers, and history. AI can integrate all of this information to produce a diagnosis and treatment plan tailored specifically to each individual.

9.1.2 Genomic Data and Molecular Profiling

One of the most promising areas of personalized diagnostics is in the field of genomics. AI algorithms can analyze large-scale genetic data to identify mutations, inherited risks, and potential therapeutic responses. In oncology, for instance, AI tools are being used to interpret next-generation sequencing data to classify tumors based on genetic drivers rather than just anatomical location. This approach allows for more accurate disease subtyping and more effective targeted therapies. The ability to detect actionable mutations enables earlier and more precise intervention, which can significantly improve survival rates. In rare genetic disorders, AI can match phenotypic presentations with genomic variants, expediting diagnosis and reducing the diagnostic odyssey that many patients face. This integration of AI and genomics underscores the shift from symptom-based to data-driven precision diagnostics.

9.1.3 Predictive Modeling for Disease Risk and Onset

Beyond personalizing current diagnoses, AI also facilitates predictive diagnostics by estimating future health risks before symptoms even arise. Predictive models use longitudinal data—including past medical history, lifestyle factors, wearable device inputs, and environmental exposures—to generate individualized risk scores for conditions such as diabetes, cardiovascular disease, and various cancers. These models allow clinicians to identify at-risk individuals early and implement preventive strategies such as lifestyle modifications, early screening, or prophylactic interventions. AI-driven risk prediction models can be continuously updated with new data, ensuring that assessments evolve as the patient's health status changes over time. For instance, a patient showing subtle changes in blood sugar levels, combined with activity and dietary data from wearable devices, may be flagged by an AI system for early diabetic intervention long before clinical symptoms manifest.

9.1.4 Integration of Multimodal Data for Holistic Insights

A major strength of AI in personalized and predictive diagnostics lies in its ability to integrate and synthesize data from multiple sources. Medical data is inherently heterogeneous, coming in the form of images, text, structured numbers, and signals. AI systems, particularly those built using deep learning and ensemble methods, can handle this complexity by combining radiology images, pathology slides, lab values, physician notes, and even patient-reported outcomes. This multimodal approach allows for a more holistic view of the patient's health. For example, in neurology, AI can analyze brain MRI scans in conjunction with genetic markers and cognitive assessments to provide a more accurate prediction of Alzheimer's disease progression. Such comprehensive analyses enable nuanced diagnostics that account for a wide array of contributing factors rather than relying on isolated test results.

9.1.5 Dynamic Monitoring and Real-Time Feedback

AI-powered diagnostics are not confined to static assessments. Instead, they can support continuous monitoring and real-time feedback through wearable devices and remote sensing technologies. These systems allow for the detection of deviations from baseline health parameters, triggering alerts for potential issues before they become severe. In patients with chronic conditions such as heart failure, AI can analyze data from smart devices to detect early signs of deterioration, prompting timely clinical intervention. This real-time predictive capability reduces hospital readmissions, improves quality of life, and reduces the financial burden on healthcare systems. Personalized diagnostic platforms that integrate continuous data inputs represent a shift from episodic care to ongoing health management, fundamentally altering the patient-clinician dynamic.

9.1.6 Clinical Decision Support and Patient Engagement

AI-powered personalized and predictive diagnostics also serve as essential tools for clinical decision support. By presenting clinicians with risk stratifications, potential diagnoses, and suggested tests or treatments based on individual profiles, these systems assist in more informed and confident decision-making. Additionally, they can be used to enhance patient engagement by providing personalized health insights, explanations of risks, and tailored recommendations. Empowered patients are more likely to adhere to preventive measures and treatment regimens, ultimately improving outcomes. For example, a patient informed about their elevated genetic risk for colon cancer and the availability of enhanced surveillance programs is more likely to participate in regular screenings. By fostering transparency and collaboration, AI in personalized diagnostics strengthens the doctor-patient relationship.

9.1.7 Challenges in Implementation and Equity

Despite the promise of personalized and predictive diagnostics, significant challenges remain. One of the foremost issues is data availability and quality. AI algorithms are only as good as the data they are trained on. Incomplete, biased, or unrepresentative datasets can lead to skewed predictions and misdiagnoses, particularly in underrepresented populations. Ensuring data diversity and fairness in AI models is crucial to avoid exacerbating health disparities. Additionally, integrating AI into clinical workflows requires overcoming interoperability issues, securing data privacy, and training healthcare providers to trust and interpret AI outputs appropriately. Regulatory and ethical considerations also loom large, especially when AI is used to make life-altering predictions about disease risk. Transparency, explainability, and accountability must be built into AI systems to ensure patient safety and trust.

9.1.8 Economic Implications and Long-Term Value

Personalized and predictive diagnostics, when effectively implemented, can offer significant cost savings to healthcare systems. Early diagnosis and prevention are inherently more cost-effective than treating advanced disease. AI tools that enable these early interventions reduce the need for extensive hospital stays, expensive procedures, and long-term medications.

However, the economic benefits must be balanced against the costs of deploying AI infrastructure, maintaining data systems, and training clinicians. Long-term ROI is best realized when AI is seamlessly integrated into value-based care models that reward preventive measures and quality outcomes. As the healthcare industry shifts toward more accountable and patient-centered care, personalized diagnostics supported by AI will become central to achieving both economic and clinical goals

9.2 AI FOR POINT-OF-CARE AND HOME-BASED TESTING

The frontier of AI-powered point-of-care and home testing continues to advance rapidly, with several promising directions poised to further transform diagnostic medicine. Next-generation devices are incorporating multi-analyte detection capabilities, allowing a single home test to screen for multiple conditions simultaneously - a particularly valuable approach for pandemic preparedness and chronic disease comorbidity management. Advances in non-invasive sensing technologies, from AI-analysis of breath compounds to hyperspectral imaging of skin, promise to reduce or eliminate the need for blood samples in home testing.

The integration of generative AI into diagnostic interfaces will create more natural and informative interactions for home users, capable of explaining results in contextually appropriate terms and guiding appropriate next steps. Augmented reality applications are being developed to assist users in performing complex self-testing procedures like capillary blood sampling or urine specimen collection. Perhaps most transformative will be the increasing personalization of AI diagnostics, where algorithms adapt to individual users' unique physiological baselines and testing behaviors to improve accuracy and reduce false alarms.These advancements will occur alongside continued improvements in affordability and accessibility, driven by economies of scale and innovative financing models.

Subscription-based home health monitoring services that bundle AI diagnostics with telehealth support are emerging as comprehensive alternatives to traditional disease management approaches. As these technologies mature, they promise to fundamentally redefine the diagnostic landscape, shifting care from reactive interventions in clinical settings to continuous health monitoring and early detection in daily life. The ultimate vision is a healthcare system where advanced diagnostics are ubiquitously available precisely when and where they're needed, with AI serving as both analytical engine and guide to ensure appropriate clinical follow-up when required.

9.2.1 Technological Foundations of AI-Enabled Portable Diagnostics

The remarkable capabilities of AI-driven point-of-care and home testing devices stem from several synergistic technological advancements. Miniaturized biosensors and microfluidic chips now enable complex laboratory assays to be performed in palm-sized devices, while computer vision algorithms can interpret everything from lateral flow test lines to microscopic images captured by smartphone attachments. Advanced signal processing techniques allow AI systems to extract diagnostic signals from noisy environmental data, compensating for the less controlled testing conditions outside clinical laboratories. Machine learning models trained on vast datasets of clinical samples can identify subtle patterns in test results that might escape human observation, such as early biomarkers of disease progression in diabetes or cardiovascular risk.

These systems increasingly incorporate multimodal data analysis, combining inputs from various sensors to enhance diagnostic accuracy. A home-based AI diagnostic platform might analyze voice patterns for neurological screening while simultaneously processing data from a wearable biosensor and a fingerstick blood test, creating a comprehensive health assessment without specialist involvement. Edge computing implementations allow sophisticated AI analysis to occur directly on testing devices without requiring cloud connectivity, addressing privacy concerns and enabling use in areas with limited internet access. The integration of these technologies creates diagnostic tools that are simultaneously more accessible and more analytically powerful than traditional laboratory testing for many applications, representing a true paradigm shift in medical diagnostics.

9.2.2 Clinical Applications Transforming Patient Care

AI-enhanced point-of-care and home testing is making significant impacts across numerous medical specialties, each with unique benefits and implementation challenges. In infectious disease management, smartphone-connected AI systems can now diagnose streptococcal pharyngitis with greater than 95% accuracy using throat swab analysis in community pharmacies, reducing unnecessary antibiotic prescriptions. Home-based sexually transmitted infection testing kits equipped with AI interpretation have dramatically increased screening rates among high-risk populations who avoid clinical settings due to stigma concerns. Chronic disease monitoring has been particularly transformed, with AI algorithms analyzing data from home glucose tests, spirometry measurements, and blood pressure monitors to provide real-time treatment adjustment suggestions for diabetes, asthma, and hypertension patients.

The field of women's health has seen remarkable innovations, with AI-interpreted home hormone tests enabling precise fertility tracking and early menopause detection. Similarly, portable ultrasound devices with AI guidance allow expectant mothers to perform basic fetal monitoring between clinical visits in high-risk pregnancies. Mental health applications are emerging where AI analyzes speech patterns and facial expressions during smartphone-administered cognitive tests to screen for depression and dementia risk. Perhaps most impactful are the cardiovascular risk assessment systems combining AI analysis of home blood tests with wearable device data to predict heart attack risk with accuracy rivaling hospital-based stress tests.

These applications share common benefits: reduced healthcare system burdens, earlier detection of deteriorating conditions, and improved patient engagement in personal health management. However, they also require careful validation to ensure safety when used without direct clinician supervision, and thoughtful design to maintain usability across diverse patient populations with varying levels of health and technological literacy. The most successful implementations combine medical rigor with consumer-friendly design principles to create tools that are both clinically valid and practically usable outside traditional healthcare settings

9.2.3 Regulatory and Quality Assurance Considerations

The rapid proliferation of AI-powered point-of-care and home diagnostic devices presents complex regulatory challenges that balance innovation acceleration with patient safety. Regulatory agencies worldwide have developed varying approaches to oversee these technologies, with the U.S. Food and Drug Administration establishing a digital health precertification program for lower-risk AI diagnostics while maintaining rigorous review for higher-risk applications. The European Union's in vitro diagnostic regulation classifies AI software based on intended use and potential patient impact, with corresponding conformity assessment requirements. These frameworks must continually adapt to address unique aspects of decentralized testing, such as environmental variability in test performance and non-professional operator factors. Quality assurance for AI diagnostics outside controlled clinical environments requires novel approaches beyond traditional laboratory proficiency testing.

Many manufacturers now implement continuous remote monitoring of device performance, with AI systems detecting and flagging potential calibration drifts or abnormal result patterns across deployed units. Some systems incorporate built-in quality control checks that run automatically with each test, using AI to verify proper sample collection and assay performance before reporting patient results. External quality assessment programs are evolving to include simulated home testing scenarios that evaluate both the device's analytical performance and the AI's ability to guide untrained users through proper testing procedures.

The regulatory landscape must also address the dynamic nature of AI algorithms that may update frequently based on new data. Current approaches range from requiring premarket review of all significant algorithm changes to allowing continuous improvement within predefined performance boundaries.

Post-market surveillance is particularly crucial for home-based AI diagnostics, requiring systems to automatically report adverse events and performance metrics while maintaining patient privacy. These regulatory and quality assurance challenges, while substantial, are being addressed through collaborative efforts between developers, clinicians, and policymakers to create frameworks that protect patients without stifling innovation in this rapidly advancing field.

9.2.4 User Experience Design for Non-Clinical Settings

The success of AI-powered diagnostic tools in point-of-care and home settings depends heavily on user experience design tailored for non-professional operators. Unlike clinical laboratory equipment designed for trained technicians, these systems must guide patients or community health workers through testing procedures with minimal prior knowledge.

Leading devices employ multimodal guidance combining visual, auditory, and sometimes haptic feedback to ensure proper sample collection and testing protocol adherence. AI-powered computer vision can now detect common user errors in real-time, such as insufficient blood droplet size on test strips or improper swab technique, providing immediate corrective guidance.

Interface design for home diagnostics requires particular attention to health literacy levels and potential language barriers. Successful implementations use progressive disclosure of information, providing simple initial instructions with optional deeper explanations, and employ culturally adapted visual metaphors rather than medical jargon. Many systems incorporate conversational AI that allows users to ask questions in natural language about testing procedures or result interpretation. The emotional aspect of home testing is equally important, with design elements that reduce anxiety during waiting periods and provide compassionate yet clear communication of potentially concerning results.

Accessibility features are critical for ensuring equitable use across diverse populations. Voice guidance for visually impaired users, high-contrast interfaces for elderly patients, and one-handed operation designs for mobility-limited individuals represent just a few considerations in inclusive design.

The most effective systems undergo extensive usability testing with representative patient populations, iteratively refining designs based on observed challenges in real-world use. This user-centered approach transforms complex diagnostic technologies into tools that genuinely empower patients to take active roles in their healthcare outside traditional clinical environments.

9.2.5 Data Integration and Clinical Workflow Implications

The proliferation of AI-enabled point-of-care and home testing generates vast amounts of decentralized diagnostic data that must be effectively integrated into clinical workflows to realize its full potential. Modern systems connect to electronic health records through secure application programming interfaces, allowing physician oversight of home testing results while maintaining patient privacy.

AI plays a dual role in these ecosystems, first analyzing individual test results and then synthesizing longitudinal data across multiple tests to identify trends that might indicate developing health issues. This creates new paradigms for preventive care, where algorithms flag at-risk patients for clinical intervention based on subtle patterns in home testing data before symptoms emerge.

The integration of these decentralized diagnostics into clinical practice requires rethinking traditional care pathways. Some healthcare systems now implement "virtual diagnostic monitoring" services where clinicians review AI-flagged abnormal results from home tests, determining which require urgent intervention versus continued monitoring. Automated escalation protocols built into AI systems can route concerning results to appropriate care teams based on severity and specialty needs. These approaches help manage the increased data flow from decentralized testing while ensuring patient safety and appropriate clinician workload.

Challenges remain in creating seamless data integration across different manufacturer platforms and healthcare IT systems. Standardization efforts like FHIR (Fast Healthcare Interoperability Resources) for diagnostic data exchange are helping address this, as are collaborative initiatives between industry and healthcare providers to develop shared data models. The ultimate goal is creating connected diagnostic ecosystems where AI analyzes data from both professional and patient-generated tests to provide comprehensive, real-time health assessments that inform personalized care plans while maintaining clear clinician oversight and decision-making authority.

9.3 DIGITAL TWINS AND VIRTUAL DIAGNOSTICS

Digital twins and virtual diagnostics represent a transformative leap forward in the application of AI to healthcare diagnostics. By creating dynamic, personalized models of individual patients, these technologies enable more accurate, proactive, and patient-centered care. While challenges related to data integration, model complexity, and ethical considerations remain, ongoing innovation and collaboration are paving the way for the widespread adoption of digital twins and virtual diagnostics. As these tools become increasingly integrated into clinical practice, they hold the promise of not only improving diagnostic accuracy and efficiency but also fundamentally reshaping the way healthcare is delivered in the digital age.

As AI, data science, and computational modeling continue to advance, the capabilities of digital twins and virtual diagnostics will expand. The integration of real-time data from wearable devices, remote monitoring tools, and even environmental sensors will enable even more dynamic and responsive digital twins. Advances in explainable AI will enhance the interpretability and trustworthiness of virtual diagnostics, supporting their adoption in routine clinical practice. The convergence of digital twins with other emerging technologies, such as genomics, telemedicine, and personalized therapeutics, will create new opportunities for precision health. Collaborative efforts among healthcare providers, technology developers, regulators, and patients will be essential for realizing the full potential of digital twins and virtual diagnostics.

The widespread adoption of digital twins and virtual diagnostics raises important ethical and societal questions. Ensuring equitable access to these advanced technologies is essential to prevent the widening of health disparities. Strategies must be developed to include underrepresented populations in the data used to build and validate digital twins, ensuring that the benefits of AI-driven diagnostics are shared broadly. Transparency in how digital twins are constructed, maintained, and used is necessary to build trust among patients and clinicians. Clear guidelines for data ownership, consent, and the right to opt out of digital twin-based care are also needed. Ongoing public engagement and dialogue will be crucial for aligning technological innovation with societal values and expectations.

9.3.1 Digital Twins in Healthcare

A digital twin in healthcare is a virtual replica of a patient, constructed using a combination of real-time data, historical health records, genetic information, imaging, and other relevant clinical parameters. This digital representation is continuously updated as new data becomes available, allowing it to mirror the patient's current health status and predict future changes.

The concept draws inspiration from its origins in engineering, where digital twins are used to monitor, simulate, and optimize the performance of physical assets such as aircraft engines or manufacturing plants. In medicine, the digital twin serves as a living model of the patient, enabling clinicians to test hypotheses, simulate interventions, and anticipate outcomes without exposing the patient to risk. The creation and maintenance of a digital twin require sophisticated AI algorithms capable of integrating and interpreting vast amounts of heterogeneous data, as well as advanced modeling techniques to accurately represent complex biological systems.

9.3.2 Virtual Diagnostics: A New Paradigm in Disease Detection

Virtual diagnostics refers to the use of AI-driven models and simulations to assess a patient's health status, identify potential diseases, and recommend diagnostic or therapeutic actions. Unlike traditional diagnostics, which rely on physical tests and direct measurements, virtual diagnostics harness the predictive power of digital twins and computational models.

By analyzing the digital twin's data and simulating various scenarios, virtual diagnostics can identify early signs of disease, assess risk factors, and suggest personalized screening or monitoring strategies. This approach is particularly valuable in the context of chronic diseases, where early detection and proactive management can significantly improve outcomes. Virtual diagnostics also hold promise for rare or complex conditions, where conventional diagnostic pathways may be lengthy, invasive, or inconclusive. By providing a non-invasive, data-driven alternative, virtual diagnostics can enhance the accuracy, efficiency, and accessibility of healthcare.

9.3.3 Building and Maintaining Digital Twins

The creation of a digital twin begins with the aggregation of comprehensive patient data, including demographic information, medical history, laboratory results, imaging studies, genetic profiles, and data from wearable devices. AI algorithms are then employed to process and harmonize this data, extracting relevant features and identifying patterns that characterize the patient's health status. Advanced modeling techniques, such as machine learning, systems biology, and computational physiology, are used to construct a dynamic, multi-scale model of the patient. This model is continuously refined and updated as new data is collected, ensuring that the digital twin remains an accurate reflection of the patient's evolving health. The maintenance of digital twins requires robust data infrastructure, interoperability, standards, and secure data sharing protocols to protect patient privacy and ensure data integrity. Collaboration between clinicians, data scientists, and engineers is essential to ensure that digital twins are clinically relevant, interpretable, and actionable.

9.3.4 Applications of Digital Twins and Virtual Diagnostics in Clinical Practice

Digital twins and virtual diagnostics are already finding applications across a range of medical specialties. In cardiology, digital twins can simulate the electrical and mechanical behavior of the heart, enabling personalized risk assessment for arrhythmias, heart failure, or coronary artery disease.

By integrating data from electrocardiograms, imaging, and wearable sensors, these models can predict the likelihood of adverse events and guide the selection of preventive therapies. In oncology, digital twins can model tumor growth and response to treatment, supporting the design of individualized treatment plans and monitoring for recurrence. In diabetes management, digital twins can simulate glucose-insulin dynamics, helping patients and clinicians optimize medication, diet, and lifestyle interventions.

Virtual diagnostics are also being used in infectious disease management, where AI models can predict disease spread, assess individual susceptibility, and recommend targeted testing or vaccination strategies. These applications demonstrate the versatility and potential of digital twins and virtual diagnostics to enhance clinical decision-making and improve patient outcomes.

9.3.5 Advantages of Digital Twins and Virtual Diagnostics

The adoption of digital twins and virtual diagnostics offers several key advantages over traditional diagnostic approaches. First, they enable a shift from reactive to proactive healthcare, allowing clinicians to anticipate and prevent adverse events before they occur. By continuously monitoring and simulating patient health, digital twins can detect subtle changes that may signal the onset of disease, enabling earlier intervention and better outcomes.

Second, digital twins support personalized medicine by tailoring diagnostic and therapeutic strategies to the unique characteristics of each patient. This individualized approach can improve the effectiveness of care, reduce unnecessary testing, and minimize the risk of adverse effects. Third, virtual diagnostics can enhance the efficiency of healthcare delivery by reducing the need for invasive procedures, streamlining diagnostic workflows, and optimizing resource allocation. Finally, digital twins provide a valuable platform for research and innovation, enabling the testing of new hypotheses, the evaluation of novel therapies, and the generation of real-world evidence in silico.

9.3.6 Challenges and Limitations

Despite their promise, the implementation of digital twins and virtual diagnostics in clinical practice faces several challenges. One of the primary obstacles is the integration of diverse and often fragmented health data from multiple sources. Ensuring data quality, interoperability, and standardization is essential for building accurate and reliable digital twins. Another challenge is the computational complexity of modeling human physiology, which requires sophisticated algorithms and significant computing power.

The interpretability and transparency of AI-driven models are also critical, as clinicians must be able to understand and trust the recommendations generated by digital twins and virtual diagnostics. Ethical and legal considerations, including patient consent, data privacy, and accountability for AI-driven decisions, must be carefully addressed. Additionally, the clinical validation and regulatory approval of digital twin-based diagnostics require rigorous testing to demonstrate safety, efficacy, and generalizability across diverse patient populations.

9.4 INTEGRATION WITH GENOMICS AND MULTI-OMICS DATA

The integration of AI with genomics and multi-omics data marks a transformative development in the field of diagnostics. By enabling the analysis of complex and multi-layered biological information, AI facilitates deeper insights into disease mechanisms, earlier and more accurate diagnoses, and personalized treatment plans.

This integrative approach empowers clinicians to move beyond surface-level symptoms to uncover the molecular underpinnings of health and disease. Despite challenges related to data complexity, privacy, and clinical implementation, the future of AI in diagnostics is increasingly centered on the rich tapestry of omics data. As technologies mature and interdisciplinary collaborations grow stronger, AI-driven multi-omics diagnostics will become a cornerstone of precision medicine, ushering in a new era of intelligent, data-driven healthcare.

The future of diagnostics lies in the continued convergence of AI, genomics, and multi-omics. With the advent of single-cell sequencing, spatial transcriptomics, and other emerging technologies, the resolution of omics data is rapidly improving. AI will play a critical role in managing and interpreting these increasingly granular datasets.

Future AI models may incorporate real-time patient data from wearable sensors or mobile health apps alongside multi-omics profiles to provide continuously updated diagnostic insights. The development of federated learning and privacy-preserving AI techniques will enable collaborative analysis across institutions without compromising data privacy. Ultimately, the integration of AI and multi-omics will drive the creation of comprehensive diagnostic ecosystems that are proactive, precise, and personalized.

9.4.1 Role of Genomics in Diagnostics

Genomics focuses on the complete set of DNA within an organism, including all of its genes. In the context of diagnostics, genomics allows the identification of genetic mutations, single nucleotide polymorphisms, and chromosomal abnormalities that are associated with a wide range of diseases. AI plays a pivotal role in interpreting this complex and voluminous data.

Traditional bioinformatics tools are often limited in their ability to handle the scale and intricacy of genomic datasets. AI algorithms, particularly machine learning and deep learning models, can process vast amounts of genomic data, uncover hidden patterns, and associate specific genetic variations with disease phenotypes. This is particularly significant in areas like oncology, where tumor genomics can guide the classification of cancer types and suggest the most effective treatment based on the genetic profile of the tumor.

9.4.2 Expanding beyond Genomics with Multi-omics

While genomics provides critical insights, it only tells part of the biological story. Multi-omics expands this view by incorporating data from other biological layers, including transcriptomics (gene expression), proteomics (protein abundance and modifications), metabolomics (metabolic profiles), and epigenomics (DNA modifications influencing gene expression).

Each omics layer captures a different aspect of cellular function and health status. AI enables the integration of these diverse data types into cohesive diagnostic models. By analyzing correlations across multiple omics layers, AI can reveal mechanisms of disease progression, identify biomarkers, and refine diagnostic criteria. This systems biology approach allows for a more nuanced understanding of disease that surpasses the insights offered by any single omics platform.

9.4.3 Data Integration and Computational Complexity

One of the most significant challenges in integrating genomics and multi-omics data is the heterogeneity and high dimensionality of the datasets. Each omics type has its own structure, noise levels, and data scales. For instance, while genomic data may be relatively static, transcriptomic and proteomic data are dynamic and vary over time or under different physiological conditions.

AI excels in this context by employing models that can learn complex, non-linear relationships and accommodate missing or noisy data. Techniques such as ensemble learning, neural networks, and multi-view learning allow for the fusion of disparate omics layers. These models synthesize insights from each dataset and produce integrative outputs that improve the precision and reliability of diagnostics. As AI models are trained on increasingly rich and diverse multi-omics datasets, their predictive performance and clinical utility continue to improve.

9.4.4 Applications in Precision Medicine

The integration of AI with genomics and multi-omics data has major implications for precision medicine, which seeks to tailor diagnosis and treatment to individual patient profiles. In oncology, for example, multi-omics approaches powered by AI can distinguish between tumor subtypes that appear histologically similar but have different molecular characteristics. This allows for personalized treatment strategies that target specific pathways altered in the patient's cancer. Similarly, in rare diseases, AI models trained on multi-omics data can identify previously unknown disease-associated genes or suggest a genetic diagnosis when conventional approaches fail. In infectious diseases, analyzing host and pathogen omics data together can enhance the accuracy of diagnosis and inform decisions about vaccine efficacy or antimicrobial resistance. These applications highlight the power of integrative diagnostics in delivering more effective and personalized healthcare.

9.4.5 Biomarker Discovery and Disease Stratification

A key benefit of integrating AI with multi-omics data is the identification of novel biomarkers for early detection and disease monitoring. AI algorithms can mine omics datasets to find molecular signatures that correlate with disease onset, progression, or response to therapy. These biomarkers may be single genes or proteins, or more often, composite signatures involving patterns across multiple data types. For instance, in neurodegenerative diseases such as Alzheimer's, AI can combine genomic risk variants with transcriptomic changes and metabolic shifts to identify early diagnostic markers long before clinical symptoms appear. Disease stratification, which involves classifying patients into subgroups based on molecular characteristics, also benefits greatly from AI-driven multi-omics integration. Such stratification is crucial for targeted interventions and for understanding disease heterogeneity, especially in complex conditions like autoimmune disorders or metabolic syndromes.

9.4.6 Enhancing Diagnostic Accuracy and Speed

Another advantage of AI-based multi-omics diagnostics is the potential to enhance diagnostic accuracy and reduce the time to diagnosis. By leveraging multi-layered biological information, AI can differentiate between diseases with overlapping symptoms and provide more specific diagnoses. This is particularly valuable in areas such as hematologic disorders, where morphological assessments may be inconclusive. AI can process omics profiles to arrive at a definitive diagnosis reducing the need for invasive procedures or repeated testing. Moreover, AI systems can automate and accelerate the interpretation of omics data, enabling clinicians to receive actionable results more quickly. This increased efficiency is critical in acute care settings and for conditions where early intervention is vital for favorable outcomes.

9.4.7 Ethical, Regulatory, and Data Governance Considerations

While the integration of AI with genomics and multi-omics data holds great promise, it also raises important ethical and regulatory concerns. Genomic data is highly personal and sensitive, and its misuse could have significant privacy implications. Ensuring secure data storage, robust encryption, and clear patient consent are essential for responsible data governance. Additionally, regulatory frameworks must keep pace with technological advancements to ensure that AI-driven diagnostic tools meet safety and efficacy standards. Transparency in AI models is also a concern. Clinicians and patients need to understand how diagnostic decisions are made, especially when they are based on complex, black-box algorithms. Efforts to improve model explainability and to validate AI tools through rigorous clinical trials are essential to build trust and ensure widespread adoption.

9.4.8 Challenges in Clinical Translation

Despite significant advances, translating AI-integrated multi-omics diagnostics into routine clinical practice faces several obstacles. Standardization of data formats, harmonization of analytical pipelines, and the development of user-friendly interfaces are crucial for successful implementation. Clinicians must be trained to interpret and act on multi-omics results, which often involve a steep learning curve. Moreover, integrating these tools into existing electronic health record systems and clinical workflows remains a technical challenge. Addressing these barriers requires interdisciplinary collaboration among data scientists, clinicians, molecular biologists, and healthcare administrators. Investment in infrastructure, education, and translational research is necessary to bridge the gap between the laboratory and the clinic.

9.5 GENERATIVE AI AND AUTONOMOUS DIAGNOSTIC AGENTS

The future development of generative AI and autonomous diagnostic agents promises to fundamentally reshape the diagnostic landscape across several dimensions. Next-generation systems will likely move beyond passive analysis to active diagnostic partners that engage in iterative hypothesis testing, suggesting targeted follow-up questions and investigations to refine diagnostic certainty. The integration of multimodal data analysis will enable agents to synthesize findings across imaging, laboratory results, wearable device outputs, and even patient-reported symptom dynamics into unified diagnostic frameworks. A particularly transformative frontier involves the identification of novel disease patterns and subtypes.

By analyzing vast clinical datasets free from preconceived diagnostic categories, generative AI may uncover previously unrecognized disease entities or phenotypic variations with therapeutic implications. Early examples include AI-identified subtypes of diabetes and neurological conditions that demonstrate distinct progression patterns and treatment responses. This capability could usher in a new era of data-driven diagnostic nosology, complementing traditional mechanism-based disease classification.

The democratization of diagnostic expertise represents another profound potential impact. As autonomous agents encapsulate specialized diagnostic knowledge, they can make this expertise broadly available beyond academic medical centers, reducing geographic and socioeconomic disparities in diagnostic accuracy. Combined with telemedicine platforms, these systems could provide virtual specialist consultation to underserved areas worldwide, with the AI adapting explanations to match local resource availability and clinical contexts.

Perhaps most significantly, these technologies may transform the very nature of diagnosis from episodic determination to continuous process. Integrated with longitudinal patient monitoring, autonomous diagnostic agents could maintain running assessments of health status, identifying subtle shifts suggestive of emerging conditions long before traditional diagnostic thresholds are crossed. This shift toward anticipatory medicine, where diagnoses are refined continuously rather than determined at discrete moments, could fundamentally alter disease prevention and early intervention paradigms across medical practice.

9.5.1 Architectural Foundations of Autonomous Diagnostic Agents

Autonomous diagnostic agents represent the most advanced implementation of generative AI in medicine, combining multiple artificial intelligence modalities into cohesive clinical decision-support systems. These sophisticated architectures typically integrate several core components: knowledge retrieval systems that access current medical literature and guidelines, patient data interpretation modules that structure electronic health record information, differential diagnosis generators that weigh competing explanations, and evidence evaluation systems that assess hypothesis plausibility.

The most advanced agents incorporate continuous learning mechanisms that update diagnostic frameworks based on new clinical evidence and outcomes data while maintaining rigorous version control for safety and reproducibility. The operational paradigm of these systems follows an iterative reasoning process that closely resembles clinical cognition. Presented with a patient case, the agent first structures available clinical data, identifies relevant patterns and anomalies, then generates and ranks potential diagnostic explanations. Unlike static decision trees, generative agents can articulate the reasoning behind each hypothesis, cite supporting evidence, and identify crucial missing information that could refine diagnostic certainty.

Some experimental systems now engage in dialogic diagnosis, conducting natural language exchanges with clinicians to explore diagnostic possibilities much like specialist consultations. This dynamic interaction capability, powered by advances in few-shot learning and reinforcement learning from human feedback, allows the systems to adapt their communication style and information presentation based on clinician responses and preferences.

9.5.2 Clinical Validation and Performance Benchmarks

The transition of generative AI diagnostic agents from research curiosities to clinical tools demands rigorous validation against established medical standards. Performance evaluation presents unique challenges compared to conventional diagnostic AI, as generative systems excel in unstructured reasoning tasks that resist simple binary assessment. Current validation frameworks employ several complementary approaches: case-based evaluations where systems analyze standardized patient vignettes compared to specialist panels, real-world clinical trials measuring impact on diagnostic accuracy and time-to-diagnosis, and prospective studies assessing patient outcomes following AI-assisted versus conventional diagnosis. Early results from controlled studies reveal both promise and limitations. In complex diagnostic challenges presented to multidisciplinary teams, generative AI agents have demonstrated capability to identify rare diagnoses that eluded initial clinician consideration, particularly in cases with atypical presentations or multiple comorbidities.

The systems show particular strength in synthesizing information across specialty boundaries, potentially reducing diagnostic silos in medicine. However, performance varies substantially by clinical domain, with higher accuracy in pattern-rich specialties like dermatology and radiology compared to more subjective domains like psychiatry. Current benchmarks suggest top generative diagnostic systems achieve diagnostic accuracy comparable to mid-career specialists in controlled environments, though real-world performance typically trails these ideal conditions. An emerging focus in validation involves assessing reasoning quality rather than just diagnostic conclusions. The FDA and other regulatory bodies are developing frameworks to evaluate whether AI-generated diagnostic rationales demonstrate appropriate clinical logic, evidence weighting, and uncertainty calibration. This represents a significant evolution from traditional diagnostic AI validation that focused primarily on output accuracy, recognizing that for generative systems to earn clinician trust, their reasoning processes must be transparent and clinically plausible even when final diagnoses prove incorrect.

9.5.3 Integration Challenges in Clinical Workflows

The potential of autonomous diagnostic agents to transform medical practice faces substantial practical barriers in clinical integration. Unlike narrowly focused diagnostic AI that targets specific tasks like image interpretation, generative systems require comprehensive access to patient data across the medical record while producing outputs that must be reconciled with clinician judgment. Successful integration models are evolving through iterative experimentation, with several emerging patterns demonstrating promise. Embedded consultation models position the AI as a virtual specialist available for case review, operating parallel to but not replacing primary diagnostic workflows. Integrated co-pilot implementations weave AI suggestions directly into clinical documentation systems, presenting diagnostic considerations at relevant decision points without workflow disruption.

The human-computer interaction challenges are substantial, as clinicians require interfaces that present AI-generated diagnostic reasoning without information overload. Effective systems employ progressive disclosure designs, initially summarizing key diagnostic possibilities with options to explore supporting evidence and alternative explanations. Visualization techniques that map the AI's diagnostic reasoning pathways help clinicians quickly assess hypothesis plausibility, while confidence indicators and evidence quality assessments prevent overreliance on speculative suggestions. Some institutions are experimenting with "diagnostic rounding" workflows where AI-generated differentials are reviewed by clinician teams alongside traditional case presentations, fostering mutual learning between human and artificial diagnosticians.

Perhaps the most significant integration challenge lies in liability and accountability frameworks. Current medical malpractice models are unprepared for shared human-AI diagnostic decision-making, raising complex questions about responsibility when diagnostic errors occur. Institutional policies are evolving to define appropriate levels of clinician verification for AI-generated diagnoses, ranging from mandatory confirmation for high-risk conditions to allowance of autonomous AI diagnosis for routine cases with clear diagnostic criteria. These evolving standards aim to balance the efficiency benefits of AI autonomy with necessary safeguards for patient safety and professional accountability.

9.5.4 Emerging Applications and Specialized Implementations

Beyond general diagnostic support, generative AI agents are demonstrating remarkable potential in specialized clinical applications that leverage their unique capabilities.

In genomic medicine, autonomous agents analyze complex variant patterns across entire exomes, integrating clinical phenotypes with rapidly evolving literature to diagnose rare genetic disorders that routinely defy conventional analysis. These systems can generate patient-specific reports explaining genetic findings in context, bridging the gap between raw sequencing data and clinical actionability. Similarly, in oncology, generative models synthesize imaging findings, pathology reports, and molecular profiling to suggest personalized diagnostic classifications and therapeutic implications.

The field of infectious disease has seen particularly innovative applications, where autonomous agents monitor global disease surveillance data, local epidemiology, and individual patient presentations to suggest both common and emerging pathogen considerations. During recent public health crises, experimental systems demonstrated capability to identify novel symptom patterns and generate early warning hypotheses ahead of official pathogen identification. In chronic disease management, generative diagnostic agents track subtle changes across longitudinal patient data, identifying progression patterns that suggest diagnostic re-evaluation or therapeutic adjustment needs.

Perhaps most transformative are applications in resource-limited settings, where autonomous diagnostic agents compensate for specialist shortages. Deployed on mobile platforms with adapted interfaces for community health workers, these systems can guide comprehensive diagnostic evaluations with minimal clinician oversight. Early implementations in sub-Saharan Africa and Southeast Asia have shown particular promise in differentiating clinically similar tropical diseases and identifying rare presentations of common conditions that might otherwise be missed. These specialized applications demonstrate how generative AI can both augment conventional diagnostic practice and enable entirely new models of care delivery where human expertise is scarce.

9.5.5 Ethical Considerations and Risk Mitigation

The deployment of autonomous diagnostic agents raises profound ethical questions that the medical community is only beginning to address. The opacity of some generative AI decision-making processes conflicts with medicine's ethical mandate for transparent reasoning, necessitating ongoing advances in explainable AI techniques. Bias mitigation requires particular attention, as generative models may inadvertently amplify existing disparities in medical knowledge or patient representation within training data. Leading development teams now implement rigorous bias testing protocols that evaluate diagnostic suggestions across demographic groups and adjust model behaviors accordingly.

Patient privacy concerns multiply with systems that require broad data access to function optimally. While traditional diagnostic AI often operates on limited datasets, generative agents typically need comprehensive health records to formulate complete diagnostic pictures. Emerging privacy-preserving techniques like federated learning and homomorphic encryption are being adapted for diagnostic agents, allowing broad data analysis without centralized data pooling. Consent frameworks are evolving to address patient rights regarding AI-assisted diagnosis, including options to opt-out of autonomous analysis or request human-only diagnostic evaluation.

The psychological impact on both patients and clinicians presents another ethical consideration. Patients may experience discomfort with diagnoses generated by algorithms rather than human clinicians, particularly for serious conditions, while practitioners may face erosion of diagnostic skills through overreliance on AI assistance. Thoughtful implementation strategies that maintain appropriate human oversight and emphasize AI's augmentative rather than replacement role can mitigate these concerns. Professional societies are beginning to issue guidelines on ethical AI diagnostic use, emphasizing that autonomous agents should enhance rather than displace the clinician-patient relationship and that ultimate diagnostic responsibility remains with licensed practitioners.

CHAPTER 10

Case Studies and Real-World Implementations

10.1 AI DIAGNOSTIC SYSTEMS IN HOSPITALS (E.G., MAYO CLINIC, NHS)

AI diagnostic systems in hospitals like the Mayo Clinic and NHS illustrate the transformative potential of artificial intelligence in modern medicine. From radiology to pathology, from patient triage to clinical decision support, AI is enhancing the speed, accuracy, and accessibility of diagnostics. These institutions serve as pioneers in demonstrating how to integrate AI responsibly, ethically, and effectively into complex healthcare ecosystems. As the technology matures and evidence accumulates, AI will not only augment human clinicians but also reshape hospital operations and redefine the standards of diagnostic excellence worldwide.

Looking ahead, AI diagnostic systems are poised to become foundational to global healthcare delivery. Hospitals like the Mayo Clinic and NHS institutions are not only refining their internal AI capabilities but also setting benchmarks for others around the world. Through research collaborations, open data initiatives, and international standards development, these hospitals are contributing to a global framework for safe and effective AI diagnostics. In the future, hospitals will increasingly use federated learning models to train AI on decentralized data without compromising patient privacy. Wearable devices, mobile diagnostics, and home testing kits integrated with AI will further expand diagnostic capabilities beyond hospital walls. The hospital of the future will be a smart, connected environment where AI drives both precision and accessibility in diagnostics.

10.1.1 AI at the Mayo Clinic: Innovation and Implementation

The Mayo Clinic has been a global leader in leveraging AI for clinical excellence. This institution has strategically integrated AI into its diagnostic processes across several departments. One of the significant areas of advancement has been in radiology, where deep learning algorithms are used to interpret imaging studies such as CT scans, MRIs, and X-rays. These AI systems assist radiologists by identifying abnormalities such as tumors, aneurysms, and fractures more accurately and at earlier stages than traditional methods. In cardiology, the Mayo Clinic has developed AI-enabled ECG (electrocardiogram) tools that can detect conditions like atrial fibrillation even when the patient is asymptomatic. These innovations demonstrate the potential of AI to identify hidden or pre-symptomatic disease states, contributing to early intervention and better patient outcomes. Moreover, the Mayo Clinic's Center for Digital Health has invested in AI to integrate patient electronic health records with diagnostic imaging and lab results, enabling holistic and timely diagnoses across clinical specialties.

10.1.2 AI Integration in the NHS: Population-Level Diagnostics

The NHS has taken a structured and policy-driven approach to integrating AI in diagnostics, particularly focusing on public health and system-wide efficiency. Given the NHS's scale and responsibility for millions of patients, AI tools have been deployed to manage vast datasets, predict disease outbreaks, and support early diagnosis in primary and secondary care settings. One notable implementation is the use of AI in mammography screening for breast cancer. Pilot programs within the NHS have tested AI algorithms that read mammograms and flag potential cases for radiologist review, reducing diagnostic errors and easing the workload on clinicians. In another instance, AI-powered chatbots and decision-support systems have been introduced in NHS clinics to assist in triaging patients, ensuring that those with potentially serious conditions receive faster appointments and diagnostics. The NHS AI Lab, a dedicated government initiative, supports the research, validation, and safe deployment of AI tools in healthcare, ensuring that technology meets rigorous clinical and ethical standards before full-scale implementation.

10.1.3 Clinical Decision Support and Real-Time Diagnostics

One of the most impactful contributions of AI diagnostic systems in hospitals like Mayo Clinic and the NHS is the development of clinical decision support systems (CDSS). These AI-based platforms are capable of analyzing patient data in real time, generating diagnostic hypotheses, and recommending further tests or treatments. For instance, when a patient presents with chest pain, the AI system can cross-reference symptoms with imaging results, laboratory values, and patient history to determine the likelihood of cardiac issues. In emergency departments, such systems can significantly reduce the time to diagnosis for conditions like stroke or sepsis, where every minute is critical. Hospitals have begun to embed these AI tools directly into electronic medical record systems so that clinicians can access decision support without leaving the workflow. This tight integration boosts adoption and ensures that AI recommendations are contextual and timely, thus improving patient safety and diagnostic precision.

10.1.4 Enhancing Radiology and Pathology through AI

Radiology and pathology are two disciplines that have witnessed profound transformation due to AI in hospitals. These specialties rely heavily on visual data, which is particularly suited to image recognition algorithms and machine learning models. In the Mayo Clinic, AI has been utilized to reduce diagnostic variability among radiologists by standardizing interpretations of complex scans.

These tools can detect subtle anomalies that might be missed by the human eye, such as minute lung nodules or microcalcifications in breast tissue. Similarly, in pathology, AI systems are used to analyze digital slides and histological samples. AI tools can grade tumors, count cells, and identify mitotic activity with speed and consistency, allowing pathologists to focus on more nuanced clinical judgments. The NHS has also experimented with AI tools for automated slide analysis, especially in large pathology labs handling high case volumes. The result is an increase in diagnostic throughput and a reduction in backlogs, which is critical for timely cancer diagnoses.

10.1.5 Patient-Centric AI Diagnostics

AI diagnostic systems in hospitals are not limited to backend processes or specialist domains; they also play an increasingly visible role in patient-facing applications. Hospitals like the Mayo Clinic have started integrating AI into patient portals where symptom checkers, predictive tools, and chatbots guide patients through self-assessment and encourage timely medical consultations. These tools are particularly valuable for patients in remote or underserved areas who may delay seeking care due to accessibility issues. The NHS has adopted similar tools through NHS 111 online services and mobile applications where AI helps patients understand symptoms and directs them to the appropriate level of care. By empowering patients with preliminary diagnostic insights, these AI systems promote proactive health management and reduce the strain on hospital resources.

10.1.6 Training, Collaboration, and Ethical Oversight

The successful implementation of AI diagnostics in hospitals hinges not only on technological capability but also on interdisciplinary collaboration and training. At institutions like the Mayo Clinic, clinicians, data scientists, engineers, and ethicists work together to develop and validate AI tools. Medical staff are trained to interpret AI outputs, understand their limitations, and use them as adjuncts rather than replacements for clinical judgment.

The NHS, being a public entity, places a strong emphasis on transparency and accountability. It has implemented strict regulatory protocols to evaluate AI tools for bias, fairness, and safety before their use in clinical environments. Hospitals participating in AI pilot programs must also report outcomes and participate in audits to ensure the systems are achieving the intended benefits. Such comprehensive oversight builds trust among clinicians and patients and ensures that AI technologies uphold the highest standards of care.

10.1.7 Operational Benefits and Efficiency Gains

In addition to clinical applications, AI diagnostic systems provide significant operational benefits for hospitals. Automating parts of the diagnostic workflow, such as image labeling, triaging lab results, or predicting patient deterioration, frees up clinical staff to focus on complex decision-making and direct patient care. At the Mayo Clinic, AI systems have been used to optimize patient scheduling and reduce diagnostic delays by predicting bottlenecks in imaging departments.

The NHS has employed AI tools for predictive maintenance of diagnostic equipment and for supply chain optimization in pathology labs. These systemic improvements contribute to better resource utilization, cost savings, and improved patient satisfaction. As diagnostic demands continue to grow, especially with aging populations and rising chronic disease burdens, AI-driven operational efficiencies will be indispensable.

10.1.8 Challenges in Implementation and Scaling

Despite their benefits, AI diagnostic systems in hospitals face numerous implementation challenges. Data quality and interoperability remain significant hurdles, especially when integrating AI tools into heterogeneous health IT ecosystems. Hospitals often operate legacy systems that are not compatible with modern AI platforms, making integration costly and time-consuming. Furthermore the generalizability of AI models across different populations and institutions is a concern. An AI tool trained on data from the Mayo Clinic may not perform equally well in a community hospital or within the NHS due to differences in demographics disease prevalence, and care protocols. This necessitates rigorous validation and continuous monitoring to ensure AI performance remains robust across varied clinical settings.

10.2 STARTUPS AND INNOVATIONS IN DIAGNOSTIC AI

The diagnostic AI startup ecosystem continues to evolve rapidly, with several emerging trends shaping its future trajectory. Next-generation startups are moving beyond single-modality analysis to develop integrated diagnostic platforms that synthesize information across imaging, genomics, proteomics, and digital biomarkers. The convergence of diagnostic and therapeutic AI is giving rise to "closed-loop" systems that not only identify diseases but recommend and monitor personalized treatment regimens. Startups at the forefront of this trend are positioning themselves as comprehensive disease management partners rather than just diagnostic providers.

Another significant frontier involves the decentralization of diagnostics through portable and wearable technologies. Startups are developing AI-powered diagnostic wearables that continuously monitor for disease markers, enabling truly proactive medicine. Similarly, breakthroughs in low-cost, portable imaging devices combined with onboard AI interpretation promise to bring advanced diagnostics to primary care clinics and underserved regions worldwide. These innovations align with growing emphasis on preventive and precision medicine, where early detection and individualized risk assessment create the most clinical value.

The startup landscape is also seeing specialization in particular technological approaches. Some companies focus exclusively on transformer-based architectures for medical language understanding, while others pioneer novel neural network designs optimized for specific diagnostic tasks. A growing number of startups are exploring quantum machine learning for diagnostics, anticipating future hardware advances. Perhaps most transformative are the ventures developing generalist medical AI systems that can adapt to multiple diagnostic challenges through few-shot learning—potentially reducing the need for numerous single-purpose diagnostic tools.

As the field matures, successful startups will increasingly differentiate through clinical integration and outcomes rather than just technological novelty. The next wave of diagnostic AI innovation will likely emphasize human-AI collaboration frameworks, decision support interfaces, and measurable improvements in healthcare delivery efficiency. Startups that can demonstrate not just diagnostic accuracy but tangible improvements in patient outcomes and healthcare system performance will lead the transformation of medicine in the AI era.

10.2.1 Emerging Technologies in Diagnostic AI Startups

Innovative startups are pioneering novel technological approaches that expand the boundaries of diagnostic medicine. Computer vision companies have developed deep learning algorithms capable of detecting subtle pathological patterns in medical images that escape human perception, with applications ranging from early cancer detection in radiology to rare disease identification in ophthalmology.

Other ventures specialize in temporal pattern recognition, analyzing longitudinal patient data from electronic health records to predict disease progression and recommend optimal diagnostic pathways. Startups focusing on voice and speech analysis have created diagnostic tools that detect neurological conditions, respiratory diseases, and mental health disorders through vocal biomarkers. The most ambitious companies are developing multimodal diagnostic systems that integrate diverse data streams—genomic, imaging, clinical, and lifestyle—to generate comprehensive diagnostic assessments with minimal human intervention.

Several technical breakthroughs distinguish these startup innovations from conventional diagnostic software. Few-shot learning techniques allow some companies to develop accurate diagnostic models with limited training data, crucial for rare disease applications. Explainable AI architectures enable startups to provide interpretable diagnostic reasoning that builds clinician trust. Edge computing implementations permit sophisticated analysis on low-power devices, bringing AI diagnostics to resource-limited settings. Perhaps most significantly, the best startups recognize that diagnostic AI cannot operate in isolation—their technologies integrate seamlessly with existing clinical workflows through interoperable platforms and intuitive interfaces designed for busy healthcare environments. These technical innovations collectively represent a fundamental shift in how diagnostic information is generated, analyzed, and acted upon in medical practice.

10.2.2 Clinical Applications Disrupting Traditional Diagnostics

Startup-driven AI innovations are making significant clinical impacts across the diagnostic spectrum. In oncology, numerous ventures have developed AI systems that detect early-stage cancers in medical images with superhuman accuracy—one notable example being mammography analysis tools that reduce both false negatives and unnecessary biopsies. Cardiovascular diagnostics have been transformed by startups offering AI-powered analysis of echocardiograms and ECGs that identify subtle abnormalities predictive of future cardiac events. Infectious disease startups created during the COVID-19 pandemic continue to evolve, with platforms that differentiate viral from bacterial infections and predict disease severity trajectories based on initial presentations.

Neurology-focused startups have pioneered AI tools that analyze speech patterns, eye movements, and fine motor control to detect early signs of Parkinson's disease, Alzheimer's, and other neurodegenerative conditions months or years before conventional diagnosis. Gastroenterology ventures employ computer vision to enhance endoscopic detection of precancerous lesions, while dermatology startups enable primary care providers to accurately assess skin lesions through smartphone applications.

Perhaps most groundbreaking are the startups developing "digital biopsy" technologies—non-invasive diagnostic methods using AI analysis of medical imaging or liquid biomarkers to replace traditional tissue sampling in certain clinical scenarios. These applications demonstrate how startup innovations are not merely incrementally improving existing diagnostics but creating entirely new paradigms for disease detection and characterization.

10.2.3 Business Models and Market Strategies

Diagnostic AI startups employ diverse business models tailored to their technologies and target markets. Software-as-a-Service (SaaS) models dominate among imaging analysis companies, offering subscription-based access to cloud-hosted diagnostic algorithms integrated with hospital PACS systems. Other startups adopt a "diagnostics-as-a-service" approach, charging per analysis while handling all technical infrastructure and regulatory compliance. Device-integrated models combine proprietary hardware with AI software, particularly prevalent in point-of-care diagnostic tools for primary care and low-resource settings. A growing number of startups pursue value-based pricing models where reimbursement is tied to measurable improvements in diagnostic accuracy, time-to-diagnosis, or patient outcomes.

Market entry strategies vary based on regulatory pathways and healthcare system structures. Many startups initially target less-regulated markets to generate real-world evidence before pursuing FDA clearance or CE marking. Others partner with established medical technology companies for distribution while maintaining focus on innovation. Direct-to-provider sales work for narrowly focused diagnostic tools, while broader platforms often require health system-level adoption. The most successful startups recognize that commercial success requires more than technological superiority—it demands solutions to the practical challenges of clinical integration, including workflow compatibility, staff training, and interoperability with existing health IT infrastructure.

Emerging trends in startup financing reflect the sector's maturation. While early-stage funding remains plentiful for promising technologies, later-stage investors increasingly demand clear paths to clinical adoption and reimbursement. Strategic partnerships with pharmaceutical companies and health systems provide startups not just with funding but with access to crucial clinical datasets and validation opportunities. Some of the most forward-thinking startups are positioning themselves as platforms rather than point solutions, developing adaptable AI architectures that can expand across diagnostic specialties and integrate new data modalities as they emerge.

10.2.4 Regulatory Challenges and Compliance Strategies

Navigating regulatory pathways presents one of the most significant challenges for diagnostic AI startups. The regulatory landscape varies substantially by jurisdiction and continues to evolve as authorities adapt to AI's unique characteristics. In the United States, the FDA has established a precertification program for AI-based software as a medical device (SaMD), but most startups still pursue traditional 510(k) or de novo pathways depending on their technology's novelty and risk profile. The European Union's Medical Device Regulation (MDR) imposes rigorous clinical evidence requirements that can be particularly challenging for resource-constrained startups. Many innovative companies adopt a phased regulatory strategy, initially launching less-regulated wellness applications to generate real world data before pursuing full diagnostic claims.

Startups face unique challenges regarding algorithm transparency and explainability—regulators increasingly demand insight into how AI systems reach diagnostic conclusions, which can conflict with proprietary concerns and the inherent complexity of deep learning models. Successful companies develop comprehensive documentation strategies that satisfy regulatory requirements while protecting intellectual property. Post-market surveillance presents another hurdle, as continuous learning algorithms may evolve beyond their initially approved versions—startups must implement rigorous version control and change management protocols to maintain compliance while still improving their products.

Many startups now employ regulatory specialists early in development to design "compliance by design" architectures that streamline approval processes. Some participate in regulatory sandbox programs that allow controlled real-world testing under regulatory supervision. Collaborative approaches, where startups work with regulators to shape evolving AI governance frameworks, are proving particularly effective. The most sophisticated companies view regulatory strategy not as an obstacle but as a competitive advantage, using rigorous validation and compliance measures to differentiate their offerings in an increasingly crowded market.

10.2.5 Clinical Validation and Evidence Generation

Building robust clinical evidence represents both a necessity and a challenge for diagnostic AI startups. Unlike traditional diagnostics validated through controlled trials, AI systems often require ongoing evaluation as they learn from new data. Leading startups employ multi-stage validation frameworks beginning with retrospective studies on archived patient data, progressing to prospective clinical trials, and culminating in real-world effectiveness studies post-deployment. The most sophisticated companies implement continuous validation mechanisms where every diagnostic output contributes to ongoing performance assessment.

Study design presents unique considerations for AI diagnostics. Startups must carefully define the appropriate comparator—whether specialist human interpretation, existing diagnostic standards, or both. Many employ "human-AI team" study arms to evaluate how their technologies augment rather than replace clinician judgment. Endpoint selection requires particular attention, as traditional diagnostic accuracy metrics may not fully capture AI's value in early detection or risk stratification. Increasingly, startups are expected to demonstrate impact on downstream clinical outcomes and healthcare utilization rather than just technical performance. Data quality and diversity present ongoing challenges. Startups must ensure their training and validation datasets represent the full spectrum of patient populations and clinical scenarios their technologies will encounter. Partnerships with academic medical centers and healthcare systems provide access to diverse clinical data but require careful navigation of privacy regulations and data use agreements. Some startups have pioneered federated learning approaches that allow algorithm training across multiple institutions without transferring sensitive patient data—an innovation that simultaneously addresses data needs and privacy concerns.

The most successful startups recognize that evidence generation is not a one-time effort but an ongoing commitment. They invest in robust data infrastructure to support continuous learning and performance monitoring across deployment sites. Many participate in industry-wide efforts to establish standardized evaluation benchmarks for diagnostic AI, understanding that credible, transparent evidence represents their most powerful asset for gaining clinical adoption and securing reimbursement.

10.3LESSONSFROMCOVID-19:AIFORMASSTESTINGANDTRIAGE

The COVID-19 pandemic has provided invaluable lessons on the role of AI in mass testing and triage, revealing both its transformative potential and the challenges that must be addressed. AI-driven innovations have enabled more efficient, scalable, and data-driven approaches to diagnostics, supporting clinicians and public health authorities in managing unprecedented demand. As healthcare systems continue to evolve, the integration of AI into diagnostic workflows will be essential for building resilience, improving equity, and ensuring preparedness for future public health emergencies. The legacy of COVID-19 will be a new era of AI-enabled diagnostics, characterized by agility, inclusivity, and a commitment to safeguarding global health.

The COVID-19 pandemic has accelerated the adoption of AI in diagnostics, demonstrating its potential to transform mass testing, triage, and public health surveillance. The experience has highlighted both the opportunities and challenges of integrating AI into healthcare at scale. As the world moves beyond the acute phase of the pandemic, the lessons learned will inform the development of more robust, equitable, and responsive diagnostic systems. AI will continue to play a central role in pandemic preparedness, early detection, and rapid response, shaping the future of global health security. The ongoing evolution of AI-driven diagnostics promises to enhance the capacity of health systems to protect populations, save lives, and respond effectively to future health crises.

At the onset of the COVID-19 pandemic, the ability to rapidly identify infected individuals was critical for controlling the spread of the virus. Mass testing became a cornerstone of public health strategies, enabling early detection, isolation, and contact tracing. However, the sheer scale of the pandemic quickly overwhelmed traditional laboratory-based testing methods, leading to bottlenecks, delays, and shortages of reagents and personnel. Simultaneously, hospitals faced surges in patient volumes, necessitating efficient triage systems to prioritize care for those most in need. The dual challenges of mass testing and triage highlighted the need for scalable, automated, and data-driven solutions—an area where AI technologies could make a significant impact.

AI played a pivotal role in enhancing the efficiency and accuracy of COVID-19 testing. Machine learning algorithms were developed to optimize the allocation of testing resources, predict testing demand, and identify high-risk populations. AI-powered image analysis tools were used to interpret chest X-rays and CT scans, providing rapid preliminary assessments of lung involvement in suspected COVID-19 cases. These tools helped supplement traditional PCR testing, especially in settings where laboratory capacity was limited. AI also facilitated the development of novel diagnostic assays, such as rapid antigen and antibody tests, by analyzing large datasets to identify optimal biomarkers and assay designs. Furthermore, AI-driven data integration platforms enabled real-time monitoring of testing results, supporting public health authorities in tracking outbreaks and deploying targeted interventions.

The surge in COVID-19 cases placed immense pressure on emergency departments and intensive care units, making effective triage essential for optimizing patient outcomes and resource utilization. AI-powered triage systems were deployed to assess patient risk based on clinical data, symptoms, comorbidities, and imaging findings. These systems could rapidly stratify patients according to the severity of illness, guiding decisions about hospitalization, intensive care admission, and ventilator allocation.

By automating the initial assessment process, AI reduced the burden on frontline healthcare workers and minimized delays in care. In some cases, AI-driven chatbots and virtual assistants were used to screen patients remotely, directing those with mild symptoms to self-care resources while flagging high-risk individuals for further evaluation. These innovations demonstrated the potential of AI to enhance the scalability and responsiveness of healthcare systems during public health emergencies.

A key lesson from the COVID-19 pandemic was the importance of integrating data from diverse sources to inform testing and triage decisions. AI-enabled platforms aggregated data from electronic health records, laboratory systems, imaging devices, and public health databases, creating a comprehensive view of the evolving pandemic. Real-time data integration allowed for dynamic risk assessment, outbreak detection, and resource planning. AI algorithms were used to identify emerging hotspots, predict surges in testing demand, and optimize the distribution of testing supplies and personnel. This data-driven approach enabled more agile and targeted responses, reducing the impact of the pandemic on healthcare systems and communities.

While AI offered significant benefits during the COVID-19 pandemic, several challenges and limitations became apparent. One major challenge was the variability in data quality and availability across different regions and healthcare settings. Inconsistent data standards, incomplete records, and delays in data reporting hindered the performance of AI models and limited their generalizability.

The rapid pace of the pandemic also meant that AI models had to be developed and deployed quickly, sometimes with limited validation or oversight. This raised concerns about the reliability and safety of AI-driven decisions, particularly in high-stakes clinical environments. Additionally, the use of AI in mass testing and triage raised ethical questions about privacy, consent, and the potential for bias in algorithmic decision-making. Addressing these challenges required ongoing collaboration between technologists, clinicians, public health officials, and ethicists.

The pandemic underscored the importance of ensuring equity and access in AI-driven diagnostics. Disparities in healthcare infrastructure, digital literacy, and access to technology meant that some populations were better served by AI innovations than others. For example, rural and underserved communities often faced barriers to accessing AI-powered testing and triage tools, exacerbating existing health inequities. To address these gaps, public health strategies needed to prioritize inclusive design, community engagement, and targeted outreach. AI models also needed to be trained and validated on diverse datasets to ensure fair and accurate performance across different demographic groups. The experience of COVID-19 highlighted the need for ongoing vigilance to prevent the digital divide from widening health disparities.

The lessons learned from the use of AI in mass testing and triage during COVID-19 are informing future pandemic preparedness efforts. AI is now recognized as a critical component of early warning systems, capable of detecting emerging threats, modeling disease spread, and guiding resource allocation. Investments in data infrastructure, interoperability, and real-time analytics are being prioritized to ensure that health systems can rapidly scale testing and triage in response to future outbreaks. AI-driven simulation and scenario planning tools are being developed to support decision-makers in preparing for a range of public health emergencies. The integration of AI into pandemic preparedness plans is expected to enhance the resilience, agility, and effectiveness of global health responses.

The deployment of AI in mass testing and triage raises important ethical and regulatory considerations. Ensuring transparency, accountability, and explainability in AI-driven decisions is essential for maintaining public trust. Regulatory frameworks must balance the need for rapid innovation with the imperative to safeguard patient safety and privacy. Clear guidelines for data sharing, consent, and algorithmic oversight are needed to support the responsible use of AI in public health. Ongoing dialogue between stakeholders, including patients, clinicians, policymakers, and technology developers, is critical for addressing ethical dilemmas and aligning AI innovations with societal values.

10.4 FAILURES AND LESSONS FROM MISDIAGNOSIS OR MODEL DRIFT

The deployment of AI in diagnostics carries significant potential but also introduces new types of risks. Misdiagnosis and model drift are among the most critical challenges that can undermine the safety, reliability, and acceptance of AI diagnostic systems. By examining failures in real-world implementations and drawing lessons from them, healthcare providers, developers, and regulators can build more robust, transparent, and adaptable AI tools.

The future of AI in diagnostics depends not just on technological advancement, but also on the ethical, clinical, and systemic frameworks that support its safe integration into patient care. Learning from past errors and proactively designing systems to anticipate and mitigate them is the path forward to truly transformative and trustworthy AI in healthcare.

Institutions often encounter similar challenges in AI deployment, yet lessons are not always shared. Creating platforms for cross-institutional learning can accelerate improvements and prevent repeated mistakes. Hospitals and research centers should collaborate to document and analyze AI diagnostic failures, identify root causes, and publish findings in shared repositories. These collective insights can inform regulatory guidelines, development standards, and best practices. National health authorities and international bodies can also play a role by creating audit frameworks and encouraging open reporting of adverse AI events, much like the pharmacovigilance systems used for drug safety.

10.4.1 Misdiagnosis in AI Diagnostics

Misdiagnosis refers to the incorrect identification of a disease or condition, which can arise when an AI model interprets data erroneously or fails to detect critical clinical patterns. In many reported cases, AI tools trained on limited or biased datasets have failed to generalize to broader patient populations, leading to inaccurate outcomes. For example, AI algorithms that were trained predominantly on images from specific demographics have underperformed when applied to patients of different ethnicities or age groups. This failure highlights the importance of data diversity during training and the dangers of overfitting models to narrowly defined datasets. Additionally, misdiagnosis can occur when AI systems are treated as black boxes, with clinicians relying on them without questioning or validating the outputs, resulting in blind trust that may overlook contradictory clinical signs.

10.4.2 Phenomenon of Model Drift

Model drift, also known as data drift or concept drift, occurs when the statistical properties of input data change over time, reducing a model's performance. In healthcare, this can be particularly dangerous as diagnostic tools are expected to maintain accuracy over years or even decades. A model trained on historical data may struggle when new diseases emerge, when treatment protocols evolve, or when population health metrics shift. For instance, during the COVID-19 pandemic, many AI models that had been optimized for standard pneumonia detection failed to correctly interpret COVID-19-related lung damage due to the novelty and complexity of the disease presentation. This gap exposed the risk of relying on static models in a dynamic clinical environment. Model drift undermines diagnostic reliability and can go unnoticed if systems lack performance monitoring mechanisms.

10.4.3 Case Studies of AI Failures in Diagnostics

Several documented failures in AI diagnostics offer instructive case studies. One such case involved an AI system used in skin cancer detection. The model was found to rely heavily on visual cues such as the presence of surgical skin markers, inadvertently associating them with malignancy because these markers often appeared in images of confirmed cancer cases. When tested on images without such markers, the model's performance significantly dropped. Another example comes from diabetic retinopathy screening tools, where AI systems misdiagnosed cases due to differences in image quality, lighting, and equipment between training data and real-world settings. These cases reveal the need for contextual awareness, better preprocessing, and careful feature attribution during model development. The lesson is clear: models must be tested rigorously in real-world scenarios before being deployed in high-stakes medical settings.

10.4.4 Ethical Implications of Misdiagnosis and Drift

The ethical implications of misdiagnosis or model drift in AI diagnostics are profound. When an AI tool leads to incorrect diagnoses, the responsibility becomes diffuse. Unlike human error, where a clinician may be held accountable, AI failures often raise questions about who is liable—the developers, the hospital, or the clinical user. This ambiguity creates ethical dilemmas in patient care and legal accountability. Moreover, the psychological impact on patients misdiagnosed by AI systems can be significant, eroding trust in both technology and medical professionals. Ethical AI development thus requires transparency, fairness, and clearly defined responsibilities among all stakeholders. It also necessitates informed consent, where patients understand the role of AI in their diagnosis and are given opportunities to question or seek second opinions.

10.4.5 Importance of Continuous Validation and Recalibration

To mitigate model drift and reduce misdiagnosis, AI systems must undergo continuous validation and recalibration. Hospitals and developers should adopt a lifecycle approach to AI, where models are not simply deployed and forgotten but are regularly updated with new data. This process includes retraining models on recent patient cases, comparing outputs with clinician assessments, and identifying statistical anomalies. The establishment of AI monitoring units within healthcare institutions can help track model performance and trigger alerts when accuracy dips below acceptable thresholds. By embedding feedback loops into the diagnostic process, institutions can ensure that AI systems remain relevant, reliable, and aligned with current clinical standards.

10.4.6 Human-in-the-Loop as a Safety Mechanism

The concept of "human-in-the-loop" is critical in minimizing the risks of AI failure. While AI can analyze vast datasets and recognize complex patterns, it lacks clinical intuition and contextual understanding. Therefore, clinicians must be empowered to interpret AI outputs critically and override them when necessary. In many successful implementations, AI is used as a second opinion or screening tool rather than a definitive source of diagnosis. This collaborative model reduces the risk of overreliance on AI and ensures that final decisions are grounded in comprehensive clinical judgment. Encouraging a culture of skepticism and review among healthcare providers helps safeguard against the propagation of errors.

10.4.7 Training and Education for Clinical Users

A key lesson from AI diagnostic failures is the importance of training for end users. Many errors occur not because the model is inherently flawed, but because clinicians misunderstand the model's capabilities, limitations, or proper usage. Hospitals must invest in training programs that educate healthcare providers about how AI tools work, how to interpret outputs, and how to integrate AI findings with clinical observations. This training should also include ethical considerations and risk mitigation strategies. By building AI literacy among clinicians, institutions can foster more effective and safer adoption of diagnostic tools.

10.4.8 Data Governance and Quality Control

Failures in AI diagnostics often stem from poor data governance. Inaccurate labels, missing values, inconsistent data formats, and unrepresentative samples can all lead to flawed model training. Establishing robust data governance frameworks ensures that data used for AI training and inference is accurate, complete, and representative of the target population. Hospitals should implement quality control checkpoints where datasets are regularly audited, annotated by experts, and tested for bias. Moreover, collaboration between data scientists and clinicians during data preparation can help ensure that the model's learning is clinically meaningful rather than statistically misleading.

10.4.9 Transparency and Model Explainability

One of the major reasons for unrecognized AI failures is the lack of transparency and explainability. Many AI models, especially those based on deep learning, function as black boxes that provide little insight into how decisions are made. When a diagnosis is wrong, it becomes difficult to trace the source of error or understand the model's logic. This opacity hinders both accountability and improvement. Efforts to enhance model explainability—through techniques like saliency maps, attention mechanisms, or rule-based overlays—allow clinicians to inspect and challenge AI recommendations. Increasing transparency not only improves trust but also facilitates early detection of model drift and potential failures.

CHAPTER 11

Appendices

11.1 GLOSSARY OF TERMS

- **Adverse Event:** Any unintended or harmful outcome resulting from a misdiagnosis or incorrect recommendation made by an AI system.
- **Algorithmic Risk:** The likelihood that an AI system will make an incorrect or harmful decision due to flaws in logic, data, or environment.
- **Algorithmic Transparency:** The clarity and openness with which an AI algorithm's logic, assumptions, and functioning can be examined and understood.
- **Annotation Error:** Mistakes made during data labeling, which can mislead AI training and contribute to model inaccuracies.
- **Audit Trail:** A detailed record of the decisions and processes behind an AI prediction, used for accountability and review.
- **Bias:** Systematic error introduced into AI models due to non-representative data, leading to unfair or inaccurate predictions, especially across different demographic groups.
- **Black Box Model:** A term used for complex AI systems whose internal decision-making processes are not easily interpretable by humans.
- **Clinical Bias:** A distortion in AI model outcomes caused by uneven or prejudiced training data related to clinical factors.
- **Clinical Oversight:** Supervision by healthcare professionals to validate AI-generated results before decisions are acted upon in patient care.
- **Clinical Validation:** The process of confirming that an AI tool performs accurately and safely in the intended medical context, with real patient data.
- **Concept Drift:** A specific form of model drift where the statistical relationship between input variables and target outcomes changes over time.

- **Confidence Score:** A numerical value representing the AI model's certainty about a specific prediction, often used to gauge trustworthiness.
- **Continuous Monitoring:** The practice of regularly evaluating the performance of AI models after deployment to detect degradation or model drift.
- **Cross-validation:** A technique used to evaluate model performance by dividing data into subsets and training/testing across multiple iterations.
- **Data Annotation:** The process of labeling data with relevant information (e.g., disease presence) for AI training purposes.
- **Data Drift:** A type of model drift that occurs when the distribution of input data shifts from what the model was trained on, leading to inaccurate outputs.
- **Data Governance:** A set of policies and practices to ensure data used for AI development is accurate, secure, and ethically managed.
- **Data Quality:** A measure of the accuracy, completeness, and consistency of data used to train and test AI systems.
- **Deployment Risk:** The potential negative consequences that arise when AI models are introduced into real-world clinical workflows without sufficient safeguards.
- **Diagnostic Accuracy:** A metric evaluating how correctly an AI system identifies or rules out a condition, often compared with a gold standard
- **Domain Shift:** A change in the environment or context between training and deployment phases, leading to potential degradation in AI performance.
- **Ethical AI:** The practice of designing and using AI in a way that upholds fairness, accountability, transparency, and respect for human rights.
- **Explainability:** The degree to which the internal mechanics of an AI model can be understood by humans, especially clinicians and stakeholders.
- **Fairness:** Ensuring that AI models treat all individuals equitably, avoiding discrimination against any group based on race, gender, or socioeconomic status.
- **False Negative:** A diagnostic error where the AI model fails to detect a condition that is actually present.
- **False Positive:** A diagnostic error where the AI model incorrectly identifies a condition as present when it is not.

- **Feedback Loop:** A system that collects outputs and user responses to refine and improve AI model accuracy over time.
- **Ground Truth:** The actual, confirmed diagnosis or outcome used as a benchmark to evaluate the accuracy of AI predictions.
- **Human-in-the-Loop:** A design principle in which human experts are involved in overseeing, verifying, or correcting the outputs of AI systems to improve safety and reliability.
- **Interpretability:** The extent to which a human can understand the cause of a decision made by an AI model in a given context.
- **Learning Health System:** A healthcare ecosystem that continuously collects and analyzes data, including AI outcomes, to drive improvements and reduce errors.
- **Liability:** Legal responsibility for harm caused by faulty AI predictions or decisions, which may be attributed to developers, vendors, or healthcare providers.
- **Misdiagnosis:** An incorrect or delayed diagnosis of a disease or condition, which may result from errors in data interpretation by AI systems or flawed model outputs.
- **Mitigation Strategy:** Actions or policies designed to reduce the risks and impacts of AI diagnostic failures.
- **Model Drift:** A decline in model performance due to changes in data patterns over time, which can cause AI predictions to become less accurate or relevant.
- **Model Robustness:** The capacity of an AI system to maintain performance under varied or unforeseen conditions.
- **Out-of-Distribution Data:** Data that differs significantly from what the AI model was trained on, which may lead to unreliable predictions.
- **Overfitting:** A modeling error that occurs when an AI system learns the training data too closely, including its noise and outliers, reducing its ability to generalize to new data.
- **Post-deployment Surveillance:** The ongoing process of observing and assessing AI system behavior after it has been deployed in clinical settings.
- **Real-world Testing:** The process of evaluating an AI system in live clinical settings to ensure its effectiveness and safety under practical conditions.

- **Regulatory Oversight:** Supervision by authorities (such as the FDA, EMA, or CDSCO) to ensure the safe and lawful use of AI in medical diagnostics.
- **Retrospective Audit:** A review process where past AI decisions are analyzed for accuracy and consistency with medical records and outcomes.
- **Safety Margin:** A built-in allowance within AI systems to account for uncertainty or risk, reducing the chance of harmful misdiagnoses.
- **Saliency Map:** A visual representation that highlights areas of an input (e.g., a medical image) that most influenced the AI's prediction.
- **Systemic Error:** A consistent, repeatable error embedded within the AI system, often due to flawed assumptions or biased data.
- **Transfer Learning:** A machine learning method where a model developed for one task is reused as the starting point for another, potentially related task.
- **Transferability:** The ability of an AI model to perform well across different clinical sites, populations, or conditions from those in its training data.
- **Transparency:** Openness in how an AI model functions, including clarity about data sources, decision rules, and performance metrics.
- **Underfitting:** A modeling problem where the AI fails to capture the underlying trend in data, resulting in poor performance on both training and unseen datasets.
- **Validation Dataset:** A subset of data used to assess the accuracy and performance of an AI model during development, prior to deployment.

11.2 LIST OF REGULATORY BODIES AND AI GUIDELINES

11.2.1 United States (FDA: Food and Drug Administration)

- **FDA's Digital Health Center of Excellence (DHCoE):** Oversees AI/ML-based medical software, including diagnostic tools.
- **Software as a Medical Device (SaMD) Framework:** Guidelines for AI-driven diagnostic software, including premarket submissions.
- **AI/ML-Based Software as a Medical Device (SaMD) Action Plan:** Outlines regulatory approach for adaptive AI in diagnostics.
- **Pre-Cert Program (Pre-Cert for Software):** Pilot program for streamlined approvals of AI diagnostic tools.

11.2.2 European Union (EMA & EU MDR/IVDR)

- **European Medicines Agency (EMA):** Regulates AI in diagnostics under medical device laws.
- **Medical Device Regulation (MDR) & In Vitro Diagnostic Regulation (IVDR):** Classifies AI diagnostic tools based on risk (Class I-IV).
- **EU AI Act (Proposed):** First comprehensive AI law, categorizing medical AI as high-risk, requiring strict compliance.

11.2.3 World Health Organization (WHO)

- **WHO Guidelines on AI in Health (2021):** Ethical and regulatory principles for AI in diagnostics.
- **AI for Health Framework:** Focuses on safety, efficacy, and equity in AI-driven healthcare.

11.2.4 International Medical Device Regulators Forum (IMDRF)

- **AI as a Medical Device (AIaMD) Working Group:** Harmonizes global regulatory approaches for AI diagnostics.
- **Machine Learning in Medical Devices (MLMD) Guidelines:** Covers adaptive AI models in diagnostics.

11.2.5 United Kingdom (MHRA: Medicines and Healthcare products Regulatory Agency)

- **MHRA Guidance on AI as a Medical Device (2023):** Regulatory expectations for AI diagnostic tools.
- **Software and AI as a Medical Device Change Programme:** Ensures post-market monitoring of AI diagnostics.

11.2.6 Canada (Health Canada)

- **Regulatory Framework for Software as a Medical Device (SaMD):** Includes AI-based diagnostic tools.
- **Guidance on Machine Learning in Medical Devices (2023):** Covers adaptive AI models in diagnostics.

11.2.7 Japan (PMDA: Pharmaceuticals and Medical Devices Agency)

- **AI Medical Device Guidelines (2020):** Regulatory pathway for AI diagnostics.
- **Fast-Track Approval for AI in Healthcare:** Expedited review for AI-based diagnostic innovations.

11.2.8 China (NMPA: National Medical Products Administration)

- **AI Medical Device Classification & Approval Guidelines:** Strict regulations for AI diagnostics.
- **Cybersecurity & Data Compliance for AI in Healthcare:** Ensures patient data protection in AI diagnostics.

11.2.9 Australia (TGA: Therapeutic Goods Administration)

- **Regulatory Framework for Software-Based Medical Devices (2021):** Covers AI diagnostics.
- **AI and Machine Learning in Medical Devices Guidance:** Risk-based approach for adaptive AI models.

11.2.10 India (CDSCO: Central Drugs Standard Control Organization)

- **Draft Guidelines on AI in Medical Devices (2023):** Regulatory framework for AI diagnostics.
- **Digital Health Policy & AI in Healthcare:** Encourages innovation while ensuring safety.

11.2.11 Key AI Guidelines for Diagnostics

- **Transparency & Explainability:** AI must provide interpretable results (e.g., FDA's XAI guidelines).
- **Clinical Validation:** Requires robust testing on diverse datasets (WHO IMDRF).
- **Post-Market Surveillance:** Continuous monitoring of AI performance (EU MDR, FDA).
- **Bias & Fairness:** AI must be tested across demographics (WHO, EU AI Act).
- **Data Privacy & Security:** Compliance with GDPR (EU), HIPAA (US), and local laws.

11.3 OPEN DATASETS FOR DIAGNOSTIC AI

11.3.1 Medical Imaging (Radiology & CT/MRI/X-ray)

Chest X-ray & Pulmonary Datasets

- **CheXpert (Stanford University)** – 224,316 chest radiographs with labels for 14 pathologies.
- **MIMIC-CXR (MIT Lab for Computational Physiology)** – 377,110 chest X-rays with free-text reports.

- **NIH ChestX-ray14** – 112,120 frontal-view X-rays with 14 disease labels.
- **PadChest** – 160,000 chest X-rays with 174 different radiographic findings.

Brain MRI & CT Datasets

- **BraTS (Brain Tumor Segmentation Challenge)** – Multimodal brain tumor MRI scans.
- **OpenNeuro** – Open repository for brain imaging data (fMRI, MRI, EEG).
- **RSNA Intracranial Hemorrhage Detection** – 25,000+ CT scans for hemorrhage detection.

Abdominal & Musculoskeletal Imaging

- **DeepLesion (NIH)** – 32,735 CT lesion annotations across multiple organs.
- **Osteoarthritis Initiative (OAI)** – Knee MRI dataset for osteoarthritis research.

11.3.2 Pathology & Histopathology Datasets

Cancer & Tumor Detection

- **Camelyon16 & Camelyon17** – Whole-slide images for breast cancer metastasis detection.
- **TCGA (The Cancer Genome Atlas)** – Large-scale cancer histopathology images with genomic data.
- **PANDA (Prostate cANcer graDe Assessment Challenge)** – Prostate biopsy images for Gleason grading.

General Histopathology

- **Kather Multiclass Dataset (NCT-CRC-HE-100K)** – 100,000 histopathology patches for colorectal cancer.
- **Lymph Node Metastasis (PatchCamelyon)** – 327,680 histopathology patches for metastasis detection.

11.3.3 Ophthalmology & Retinal Imaging

Diabetic Retinopathy (DR) & Retinal Diseases

- **EyePACS (Kaggle Diabetic Retinopathy Detection)** – 88,702 retinal fundus images.

- **MESSIDOR (Methods to Evaluate Segmentation and Indexing Techniques in Ophthalmology)** – 1,200 retinal images with DR grading.
- **ODIR-2019 (Ocular Disease Intelligent Recognition)** – 8,000 fundus images for multi-disease classification.

Glaucoma & OCT Imaging

- **REFUGE Challenge (Retinal Fundus Glaucoma Challenge)** – 1,200 images for glaucoma detection.
- **Duke OCT Dataset** – Optical coherence tomography (OCT) scans for retinal diseases.

11.3.4 Dermatology & Skin Lesion Datasets

Skin Cancer (Melanoma & Non-Melanoma)

- **ISIC (International Skin Imaging Collaboration) Archive** – Largest public dermatology dataset (25,000+ images).
- **HAM10000 (Human Against Machine)** – 10,015 dermatoscopic images for skin cancer classification.

11.3.5 Cardiology & ECG Datasets

Electrocardiogram (ECG) Datasets

- **PTB-XL (Physikalisch-Technische Bundesanstalt ECG Dataset)** – 21,837 clinical 12-lead ECGs.
- **MIT-BIH Arrhythmia Database** – 48 half-hour ECG recordings for arrhythmia detection.

11.3.6 Miscellaneous Diagnostic AI Datasets

COVID-19 & Infectious Diseases

- **COVID-19 Image Data Collection** – X-ray & CT scans for COVID-19 detection.
- **BIMCV-COVID-19+** – Large-scale COVID-19 imaging dataset (X-ray & CT).

General Medical Datasets

- **PhysioNet** – Open repository for physiological signals (ECG, EEG, PPG, etc.).
- **Open-i (NIH Open Access Biomedical Image Search Engine)** – Diverse medical images with annotations.

11.4AITOOLKITSANDFRAMEWORKS(TENSORFLOW,MONAI,ETC.)

11.4.1 General-Purpose AI Frameworks

TensorFlow & TensorFlow Extended (TFX)

- **Use Case:** End-to-end deep learning for medical imaging (X-rays, MRI, CT scans).
- **Key Features:**
  - High-level APIs (Keras) for rapid prototyping.
  - TensorFlow Lite for edge deployment on medical devices.
  - TFX for MLOps pipelines (data validation, model monitoring).
- **Diagnostic Applications:** Chest X-ray classification, tumor segmentation.

PyTorch & PyTorch Lightning

- **Use Case:** Research-focused AI model development.
- **Key Features:**
  - Dynamic computation graphs for flexible experimentation.
  - PyTorch Lightning for scalable training.
  - TorchIO for medical image augmentation.
- **Diagnostic Applications:** Brain MRI segmentation, histopathology analysis.

JAX (Google Research)

- **Use Case:** High-performance AI research (e.g., Google's DeepMind Health).
- **Key Features:**
  - GPU/TPU-accelerated numerical computing.
  - Autograd and XLA for optimization.
- **Diagnostic Applications:** Large-scale medical imaging analysis.

11.4.2 Specialized Medical AI Frameworks

MONAI (Medical Open Network for AI)

- **Use Case:** Medical imaging AI (radiology, pathology, etc.).
- **Key Features:**
  - Domain-specific layers for 3D medical images (DICOM, NIfTI).
  - Federated learning support for multi-institutional studies.
  - Integration with PyTorch and TensorFlow.
- **Diagnostic Applications:** Tumor segmentation, lung nodule detection.

NVIDIA Clara & Clara Imaging

- **Use Case:** AI-powered medical imaging pipelines.
- **Key Features:**
  - Pretrained models for radiology (CT, MRI, X-ray).
  - Federated learning for privacy-preserving AI.
  - GPU-optimized inference.
- **Diagnostic Applications:** COVID-19 detection, cardiac MRI analysis.

DeepLesion Toolkit (NIH)

- **Use Case:** Lesion detection in CT scans.
- **Key Features:**
  - Preprocessed CT datasets with annotations.
  - Pretrained models for tumor tracking.
- **Diagnostic Applications:** Oncology imaging, metastasis tracking.

11.4.3 AI for Pathology & Digital Histopathology

HistomicsTK

- **Use Case:** Whole-slide image (WSI) analysis.
- **Key Features:**
  - Tools for stain normalization, nuclei segmentation.
  - Integration with TensorFlow/Keras.
- **Diagnostic Applications:** Breast cancer grading, tumor microenvironment analysis.

QuPath

- **Use Case:** Open-source pathology image analysis.
- **Key Features:**
  - Interactive annotation tools.
  - Scriptable in Groovy/Python.
- **Diagnostic Applications:** Prostate cancer detection, immune cell quantification.

PathML (MIT/Harvard)

- **Use Case:** AI-driven computational pathology.
- **Key Features:**
  - End-to-end pipeline for WSI preprocessing and modeling.
  - PyTorch integration.

- **Diagnostic Applications:** Lymph node metastasis prediction.

11.4.4 Ophthalmology & Retinal AI

RetinaNet (FAIR)

- **Use Case:** Diabetic retinopathy (DR) detection.
- **Key Features:**
  - Object detection for retinal lesions.
  - Pretrained on EyePACS dataset.
- **Diagnostic Applications:** DR grading, glaucoma screening.

OphAI (Open-Source Retinal AI)

- **Use Case:** Fundus image analysis.
- **Key Features:**
  - UNet-based segmentation for retinal vessels.
  - Integration with MONAI.
- **Diagnostic Applications:** Macular degeneration detection.

11.4.5 Deployment & MLOps for Diagnostic AI

ONNX Runtime

- **Use Case:** Cross-platform model deployment (DICOM viewers, PACS integration).
- **Key Features:**
  - Optimized inference for CPUs/GPUs.
  - Interoperability (TensorFlow → ONNX → PyTorch).
- **Useful For:** Hospital-grade AI model deployment.

DICOM Standard & pydicom

- **Use Case:** Medical imaging interoperability.
- **Key Features:**
  - Python library for DICOM metadata handling.
  - Essential for PACS integration.

Flyte (Lyft)

- **Use Case:** Scalable AI workflows for diagnostics.
- **Key Features:**
  - Kubernetes-native MLOps.

  - Reproducible pipelines for clinical validation.

11.4.6 Emerging & Niche Toolkits

Framework	Use Case	Key Feature
FastPath (Amazon)	Pathology AI	Serverless inference for WSIs
AI4COVID (UNESCO)	Respiratory diagnostics	Pretrained models for lung ultrasound
Med3D (MICCAI)	3D medical imaging	Multi-organ segmentation

11.5 RECOMMENDED READING AND RESEARCH JOURNALS

11.5.1 Recommended Books

- **"Deep Medicine: How Artificial Intelligence Can Make Healthcare Human Again"** – Eric Topol *(Explores AI's role in diagnostics, personalized medicine, and patient care.)*
- **"Artificial Intelligence in Healthcare: A Practical Guide"** – Anthony C. Chang *(Covers AI applications in imaging, pathology, and decision support.)*
- **"Machine Learning for Healthcare"** – Finale Doshi-Velez et al. (Eds.) *(Technical focus on ML models for diagnostics and treatment.)*
- **"AI in Clinical Medicine: A Practical Guide for Healthcare Professionals"** – Michael F. Byrne et al. *(Case studies on AI in radiology, cardiology, and lab diagnostics.)*

11.5.2 Key Research Journals

High-Impact General Journals

- **Nature Digital Medicine:** Publishes interdisciplinary AI/ML research for diagnostics.
- **The Lancet Digital Health:** Focus on AI in clinical decision-making and validation studies.
- **JAMA Network Open:** Peer-reviewed studies on AI in imaging, pathology, and predictive analytics.

Specialized AI/Medical Imaging Journals

- **Radiology: Artificial Intelligence** (RSNA): Focus on AI in radiology (e.g., CT, MRI, X-ray interpretation).
- **Journal of Pathology Informatics:** AI applications in digital pathology and histopathology.
- **npj Digital Medicine** (Nature Partner Journal): Covers AI-driven

diagnostics and wearable tech.

Technical/AI-Focused Journals

- **IEEE Transactions on Medical Imaging:** Algorithms for medical image analysis.
- **Medical Image Analysis** (Elsevier): Deep learning for diagnostic imaging.
- **Artificial Intelligence in Medicine** (Elsevier): Clinical AI models and ethical considerations.

11.5.3 Key Review Articles & Papers

- **"AI in Medical Imaging: Current Trends and Future Directions"**: Esteva et al. (*Nature Medicine*, 2023).
- **"Guidelines for Clinical Translation of AI in Diagnostics"**: Topol et al. (*The Lancet*, 2021).
- **"Ethics of AI in Healthcare"**: Char et al. (*NEJM*, 2023).
- **"AI for Early Cancer Detection"**: McKinney et al. (*Nature*, 2020 – Google Health's mammography study).

11.5.4 Additional Resources

- **Conferences:**
- **RSNA** (Radiological Society of North America) – AI in imaging.
- **MICCAI** (Medical Image Computing & Computer-Assisted Intervention).
- **Datasets:**
- **MIMIC-CXR** (chest X-rays), **The Cancer Genome Atlas (TCGA)** for pathology AI.

References

AI Algorithms for Medical Image Segmentation: Jorge J. G. Barbosa (2023, CRC Press)

AI and Robotics in Diagnostics: Guang-Zhong Yang, Robin Murphy (2022, CRC Press)

AI for Disease Diagnosis and Prognosis: S. S. Iyengar, R. B. Berlin (2021, Wiley)

AI for Early Disease Detection: Binseng Wang, James Keller (2023, Elsevier)

AI for Genomics: Jürgen Schmidhuber, Pierre Baldi (2021, World Scientific)

AI for Ophthalmology Diagnostics: Pearse Keane, Daniel Shu Wei Ting (2023, Thieme)

AI for Wearable and Mobile Health Tech: Hassan Ghasemzadeh (2023, Springer)

AI Governance in Healthcare: I. Glenn Cohen, Sara Gerke (2022, Cambridge UP)

AI in Cancer Diagnostics: Anant Madabhushi, George Lee (2023, Springer)

AI in Cardiology: Innovations and Applications: Angelo Auricchio, Frits Prinzen (2023, Springer)

AI in Cardiovascular Imaging: Subhi J. Al'Aref, Leon Axel (2021, Elsevier)

AI in Clinical Medicine: A Practical Guide: Michael F. Byrne, Nikhil Gopal, et al. (2023, Wiley)

AI in Diagnostics: Case Studies from Mayo Clinic: Bradley J. Erickson (2023, Springer)

AI in Emergency and Critical Care Diagnostics: Leo Anthony Celi, Alistair Johnson (2021, MIT Press)

AI in Global Health Diagnostics: Joao Carriço, Rumi Chunara (2023, World Scientific)

AI in Healthcare: Legal and Regulatory Challenges: Laura B. Pincus, Jacob T. Brogan (2021, Routledge)

AI in Neuroimaging: Christos Davatzikos (2022, Academic Press)

AI in Neurology and Brain Disease Diagnostics: Vasileios Kokkinos, R. Mark Richardson (2022, Elsevier)

AI in Respiratory Disease Diagnostics: David A. Lynch, Hiroto Hatabu (2020, CRC Press)

AI in Telemedicine and Remote Diagnostics: Sandeep Reddy (2021, CRC Press)

AI Startups in Medical Diagnostics: Arjun K. Manrai, Kun-Hsing Yu (2020 Springer)

Artificial Intelligence in Healthcare: A Practical Guide: Anthony C. Chang (2020 CRC Press)

Artificial Intelligence in Medical Imaging: Erik R. Ranschaert, Sergey Morozov, Paul Algra (2019, Springer)

Artificial Intelligence in Medicine: Technical Basis and Clinical Applications: Lei Xing, Maryellen L. Giger (2020, Academic Press)

Artificial Intelligence in Pathology: Stanley Cohen (2022, Elsevier)

Bias in AI Medical Diagnostics: Ziad Obermeyer, Sendhil Mullainathan (2023, Harvard UP)

Bioinformatics and Machine Learning for Cancer Diagnosis: S. Balaji, M. A. Jabbar (2020, CRC Press)

Clinical Decision Support Systems and AI: Eta S. Berner (2020, Springer)

Computational Pathology and AI in Diagnostic Medicine: David Foran, Tahsin Kurc (2023, Springer)

Deep Learning for Medical Image Analysis: S. Kevin Zhou, Hayit Greenspan, Dinggang Shen (2021, Academic Press)

Deep Learning in Biomedical Diagnostics: S. R. S. Prabhu, S. K. Shukla (2022, Springer)

Deep Medicine: How Artificial Intelligence Can Make Healthcare Human Again: Eric Topol (2019, Basic Books)

Digital Health and AI in Diagnostics: Homero Rivas, Katarzyna Wac (2022, Oxford UP)

Ethics of AI in Biomedical Diagnostics: Effy Vayena, Alessandro Blasimme (2022, MIT Press)

Explainable AI in Medicine: Andreas Holzinger, Randy Goebel (2020, Springer)

Federated Learning for Medical AI: Quoc-Viet Pham, Nguyen Cong Luong (2023, Springer)

Generative AI for Synthetic Medical Data: Alex Zhavoronkov, Evelyne Yehudit (2023, Elsevier)

Google DeepMind's AI in Healthcare: Dominic King, Mustafa Suleyman (2022, Penguin)

Handbook of Medical Image Computing and Computer-Assisted Intervention: S. Kevin Zhou et al. (2020, Academic Press)

IBM Watson Health: AI in Oncology: Tanveer Syeda-Mahmood (2021, IBM Press)

Machine Learning for Healthcare: Finale Doshi-Velez, Jim Fackler, et al. (2019, MIT Press)

Machine Learning for Medical Diagnostics: S. S. Iyengar, Qiang Zhu (2021, Wiley)

Machine Learning in Medical Imaging: Qian Wang, Yinghuan Shi, Heung-Il Suk (2022, Springer)

Natural Language Processing for Clinical Diagnostics: Tristan Naumann, Özlem Uzuner (2021, MIT Press)

Precision Medicine and AI in Cancer: Emmanuel Ifeachor, Mamoon Rashid (2022, Academic Press)

Quantum AI in Medical Diagnostics: Sabrina Maniscalco, Samuel Mugel (2024, Springer)

Radiomics and Radiogenomics in Medical Imaging: Issam El Naqa, Martin J. Murphy (2021, CRC Press)

Reinforcement Learning in Healthcare Diagnostics: Prashant Natarajan, John C. Frenzel (2020, O'Reilly)

Smart Diagnostics with AI and IoT: Parag Kulkarni, Pradeep Churi (2020, Springer)

The Future of AI in Diagnostics: Bertalan Meskó (2024, Webicina)

Index

www.ingramcontent.com/pod-product-compliance
Lightning Source LLC
LaVergne TN
LVHW071245210926
848486LV00008B/353